William Malcolm Hailey (1872–1969) was by common consent the most distinguished member of the Indian Civil Service in the twentieth century, and one of the few raised to the peerage (1936). Going out to India in 1894, he served as the first chief commissioner of Delhi (1912–18), as finance and then home member of the Viceroy's Council (1919–24), and then as governor of the Punjab (1924–28) and the United Provinces (1928–34). As adviser to five viceroys, he was one of the most intelligent developers of the British strategy in response to the challenge of Gandhi and the Indian National Congress. After leaving India he had what amounted to a second career in relation to Africa, during which he directed two editions of the *African Survey* (1938, 1956), wrote two important reports on British colonial administration, and served as an adviser to the Colonial Office.

This is the first book-length study of Hailey's career. Its larger theme, in which the man himself played a truly amazing number of central roles, is the cycle of colonialism–nationalism–decolonization: spanning more than half a century on two continents.

Hailey

Lord Hailey at eighty-two

Hailey

A study in British imperialism, 1872–1969

JOHN W. CELL

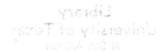
CAMBRIDGE
UNIVERSITY PRESS

Published by the Press Syndicate of the University of Cambridge
The Pitt Building, Trumpington Street, Cambridge CB2 1RP
40 West 20th Street, New York, NY 10011-4211, USA
10 Stamford Road, Oakleigh, Victoria 3166, Australia

First published 1992

Printed in the United States of America

Library of Congress Cataloging-in-Publication Data
Cell, John Whitson.
Hailey : a study in British imperialism, 1872–1969 / John W. Cell.
        p.   cm.
Includes bibliographical references and index.
ISBN 0-521-41107-6
1. Hailey, William Malcolm Hailey, Baron, 1872–1969. 2. Great
Britain – Colonies – Administration – History – 20th century.
3. Colonial administrators – Great Britain – Colonies – Biography.
4. Colonial administrators – Africa – Biography. 5. Colonial
administrators – India – Biography. 6. Imperialism – History – 20th
century. I. Title.
DA17.H3C45   1992
325'.341'092 – dc20
          [B]   91-22678
                                                 CIP

A catalog record for this book is available from the British Library

ISBN 0-521-41107-6 hardback

Photo and map credits

Frontispiece – copy by George Bruce at Rhodes House, Oxford, of an original painting by
James Gunn, 1954, at Chatham House, London, used by permission of the warden of
Rhodes House; pp. 16–17 – Map Collection, Duke University, Durham, N.C.; p. 108 –
photograph at Anarkale's Tomb, the Secretariat, Lahore, Pakistan, used by permission of the
archivist; p. 216 – from the *Cambridge History of Africa*, vol. 7, *From ca. 1905 to ca. 1940*, ed.
A. Roberts (Cambridge: Cambridge University Press, 1985), p. 5; pp. 225–7 – taken during
the tour of 1935–6, from albums of Donald Malcolm, Rhodes House, Oxford, used by
permission of the archivist.

For Gill

Contents

Abbreviations

AICC	All-India [National] Congress Committee
AR	Annual Report
CO	Colonial Office
CWMG	*Collected Works of Mahatma Gandhi*
FO	Foreign Office
HPA	Hailey papers, African. Rhodes House Library, Oxford
HPI	Hailey papers, Indian. India Office Library. MSS EUR E 220
IOL	India Office Library
IOR	India Office Records, India Office Library
MLC	Member of Legislative Council
NAI	National Archives of India, New Delhi
NML	Nehru Memorial Library, New Delhi
NWFP	North-West Frontier Province
PP	Great Britain. Parliamentary Papers
PRO	Public Record Office, London
PSV	Private Secretary to the Viceroy
RH	Rhodes House, Oxford
SS	Secretary of State for India
SWJN	*Selected Works of Jawaharlal Nehru*
VR	Viceroy

Glossary of foreign words

Adi Granth	Sikh holy scripture
badmashes	troublemakers
bania	money lender
dacoity	gang violence
darshan	obeisance
dhoti	loose lower garment, worn by Hindu males
feringhi	Westerners
goonda	criminal element
gurdwara	shrine, especially Sikh
Harijans	children of God; Gandhian term for Untouchables
hartal	general shutdown
jatha	Sikh column of 25 to 100 men
jihad	holy war
kanagu	assistant, e.g., surveying
kharif	autumn
killa	square
kirpan	sword worn by Sikh males
kisan	tenant
kurti	worker
lakh	100,000
lambardar	village headman
mahant	Hindu priest
morcha	demonstration
munshi	clerk
nazrana	entry fee paid by tenants
Panth	Sikh congregation
patwari	record keeper
rabi	spring
Raj	rule, government
ryot	peasant
Sangathan	Hindu strengthening movement
Sarkar	the Government (personified)
satyagraha	struggle for truth; coined by Gandhi

Glossary of foreign words

Shuddhi	Hindu reconversion movement
swadeshi	movement to buy only Indian goods
swaraj	freedom
tahsil	portion of a district
talukdar	big landowner, in Oudh
zail	group of villages
zamindar	landowner

Preface

I first encountered Lord Hailey in his role as director of the *African Survey* (1938), the pivotal project that culminated the discussion of African affairs by Britain's interwar generation, helped set the agenda for the colonial reform movement of the war years, and indirectly pointed toward decolonization in the postwar era. Paradoxically, despite the fact that Hailey served forty years in India and was commonly regarded as the most distinguished member of the Indian Civil Service in the twentieth century, his African phase is better known. When I began research for this book I was already conscious that the imbalance needed to be corrected. More important, I wished to move into what for me was then the virtually unknown field of India. Hailey was my bridge across the Indian Ocean.

His sheer longevity and ubiquity bear stressing.[1] Born in 1872, the year Disraeli at the Crystal Palace gave the speech sometimes regarded as the end of Little Englandism and the beginning of the New Imperialism, Hailey was educated at Merchant Taylors' School and Oxford, joining the Punjab branch of the Indian Civil Service in 1895. After five years in the secretariat, between 1901 and 1906 he was the founding colonization officer for the Lower Jhelum canal colony in the western Punjab, the formative experience of his adult life. In 1907–11 he was secretary in the finance department of the central Government of India. In 1912, at forty, he became chief commissioner of the new Delhi capital enclave, which he ran throughout World War I. In 1919 he wrote the official Punjab government report on martial law in the province, including the infamous massacre by General Dyer at Jallianwala Bagh in Amritsar. From 1919 to 1922, during one of the most turbulent and controversial periods in modern Indian economic history, he served as finance member of the Viceroy's Council and then, in 1922–4, as home member.

Two governorships followed: the climax of his career. In the Punjab, 1924–8, he dealt with the last phase of the Sikhs' agitation for control of their *gurdwaras* (shrines), achieving a compromise that effectively resolved the Sikh question for a generation. Although he perceived as a curse the province's virulent communal conflict between Muslims, Hindus, and Sikhs, he skillfully manipulated it to

1 See Philip Mason's excellent sketch in the 1961–70 Supplement to the *Dictionary of National Biography.*

secure cooperation with the Statutory (Simon) Commission to review the Indian constitution. In 1928, on the death of Sir Alexander Muddiman, Hailey succeeded as governor of the United Provinces, the senior position in the Indian Civil Service. In UP the highlights were the simultaneous occurrence of the world economic depression, an acute agrarian crisis, and the Congress's civil-disobedience campaigns of 1930–1 and 1932–4. Although Hailey realized that Indian nationalism must ultimately triumph, he threw himself into building a conservative party as a bulwark against Congress. By the time he retired from India in December 1934, however, he knew he had failed.

Then came Africa. Having agreed in 1933 to direct the *African Survey*, at sixty-three he started to retool himself. After touring the continent in 1935–6, he intended to write a brief, readable report, painfully discovered that he was constitutionally incapable of doing so, shifted to a longer, more exhaustive format, found himself unable to complete that either, and suffered a nervous breakdown that almost killed him. Although this fact was partially covered up, he therefore played a comparatively small role in writing and editing the *Survey*. Between 1939 and 1943 he occupied a position of great influence: spokesman for the colonial reform movement, leader of a mission to the Belgian Congo, author of an important report in 1941 on African colonial governance, propagandist to America, and adviser to the Colonial Office. With the accession of the Conservative Oliver Stanley as colonial secretary in 1943, however, Hailey became increasingly peripheral. After the war he toured Africa again, revised his 1941 report, presided over the second edition of the *African Survey* (1957), and continued to speak and write on African and Commonwealth affairs for some twenty years. He died in 1969, aged ninety-seven. He had served the British Empire on two continents – from high noon to sunset.

I have called this book a "study." Although it follows a chronological format, it is primarily an exploration of a public career, an analysis of the relationship between an individual and the evolving political context in which he was so centrally involved, rather than a close, intimate portrait of a personality. It is more "times" than "life."

There are two reasons for this. First, although Lord Hailey's care, thoughtfulness, and scrupulous honesty in preparing his papers for deposit in archives where they could be consulted by scholars demonstrate the man's profound sense of the obligation of important public figures to the integrity of the historical record, the few surviving members of his family have withheld cooperation. The result is that there are elementary pieces of information – how he met his wife, the precise nature of his illness in 1931, how he reacted to the death of his son – that I have simply been unable to find out. Second, and more significant, at least by the time Hailey reached middle age and the materials become really abundant, the private man had been almost entirely subsumed in the public persona.

Although more can and will be inferred throughout the book, the astonishingly small amount of hard information available about Lord Hailey's

Preface

family life can be sketched very briefly. In 1896, at what for Indian civil servants was the unusually early age of twenty-four, he married Andreina (anglicized to Alexandra) Balzani, the daughter of a Roman count. They had two children: a son, Alan B. (1900), called Billy, and a daughter, Gemma (1906). Although Billy took a long time to find a niche, he eventually qualified as a barrister and died on active service with the RAF in 1943. Gemma died as a teenager from a burst appendix in 1922. As I explain in more detail at the appropriate point, Lady Hailey never really recovered from this crisis; she became increasingly eccentric and alcoholic, and her behavior was commonly thought to have prevented her husband from being appointed viceroy of India. She died in 1939. After all three deaths Hailey's response was the same. He threw himself still more intensely into his work and provided not a single written word to indicate his feelings. Partly in response to private unhappiness, which in turn contributed to the problems of those who were near him, he built a wall around himself. Probably only two people – his wife, and that for only part of their marriage, and Sir Geoffrey de Montmorency, his number two in Delhi and the Punjab and his successor as governor of the latter – ever got close to him. I seriously doubt whether Hailey and Sir Geoffrey ever called each other by their first names.

What you saw was what you got. At an inch or two above six feet, as tall as the Muslim males of the western Punjab with whom he identified so closely, with a hawk's nose that made his face hard and austere, and a deep, commanding voice, Hailey looked and sounded the part. An Indian who as a boy saw him riding in the park in Lahore remarked that this was a man born to rule. An Indian journalist in the late 1920s, in one of the most perceptive portraits of Hailey ever written, described him as a cross between a Machiavellian and a demagogue. Socially adept, witty, with a wealth of funny stories, Hailey was no recluse. Indeed, as governor he toured as though campaigning for office. He could be bold and decisive, patient and cautious, capable of either the rapid thrust or the long end-game. He could be passionate or, as in his report on Amritsar in 1919, detached to the point of bloodlessness. Beneath the unflappable exterior he suffered from the recurrent and extreme pain of kidney stones and was subject to periods of deep depression.

Malcolm Hailey was what psychologists term an obsessive–compulsive personality – a man driven to master, dominate, and control.[2] He was the embodiment of the so-called Protestant work ethic. Brilliant, quick, with a mind able to go to the heart of complex problems while keeping in touch with massive amounts of detail, as a worker he was phenomenal. A member of a service that expected and demanded it, he always worked hard. As he grew older, however,

2 This is the so-called anal syndrome made famous by Freud. Psychologists now agree, however, that although the personality ordinarily appears first in conflicts with parents, it has very little to do with toilet training. See particularly Jerrold Pollak, "Obsessive-Compulsive Personality: A Review," *Psychological Bulletin, 86* (1979), 225–41, and Gail Sheehy, *Passages: Predictable Crises of Adult Life* (New York: Dutton, 1974).

the need to work, the dread of being idle even for a minute, became truly obsessive, as though he feared that if the machine ever stopped it would fall apart completely. Philip Mason wrote that he could find no fault in the character, and though the result might be dullness a man had no obligation to develop flaws for the benefit of his biographer.[3] As administrator, investigator, and statesman, Lord Hailey had many admirable qualities. But it would not have been easy to be his wife or child.

∞∞∞∞∞∞

I have to acknowledge the extremely generous support of the following foundations: the Social Science Research Council; the Indo-European Sub-Commission of the Council for the Exchange of Scholars, which financed a trip to India; the John S. Guggenheim Foundation for research in England; the American Institute of Pakistan Studies for work in Pakistan; the National Endowment for the Humanities; and the National Humanities Center, an ideal setting where I finished writing the manuscript. Duke University provided me with a sabbatical leave, and the university's research council gave me a substantial award during a year when I was on half pay.

   I am most grateful to the following people, who read substantial portions or all of the manuscript: Janet Ewald, Kelli Kobor, Evan Nelson, Kenneth Robinson, John Salmond, Anne Scott, Richard Soloway, B. R. Tomlinson, and Joselyn Zivin. The readers who vetted the work for Cambridge University Press gave valuable and constructive criticism, as did Frank Smith, the excellent history editor for the Press's New York branch. Tony Kirk-Greene arranged a fellowship for me at St. Antony's College, Oxford; Aditya and Mridula Mukherjee aided my faltering attempts to come to terms with Indian historiography; Mueen Afzal was especially helpful to me in Lahore. I want to thank several retired colleagues – Taylor Cole, Arthur Ferguson, Harold Parker, Richard Preston, and Richard Watson – for their long-term friendship and encouragement. Philip Mason generously shared with me his knowledge of Hailey, India, and how to write books; he turned out to be one of my most helpful critics.

   My children – Tom, Kate, and John – have lived with this book as teenagers

---

3 Philip Mason [Woodruff], *The Men Who Ruled India*, 2 vols. (London: Cape, 1953–4), 2:288–91. After reading my manuscript, Mason said he had rethought his earlier estimate, which might have been a bit too uncritical. Hailey "was an eagle who very seldom became airborne!" he put it. "He was a superb thinking machine and I have never met anyone who was his equal in memory and reasoning power. But I cannot feel that he was quite a great man, certainly not in the top class of great men." Perhaps surprisingly, the man Mason compared him with was Lord Wavell: great because he was capable of detachment, drawing historical parallels, not losing the ability to laugh at himself, determined to take his own line irrespective of his personal position. Although I myself suggest that detachment, historical perspective, and sense of humor were some of the man's finest qualities, in Mason's view "Hailey had not got that degree of detachment nor that depth of historical comparison." And he could never quite relax. Letter of 31 October 1990.

xiv

Preface

and young adults. Though it must at times have seemed that I was more concerned with it than with them, I thank them for their tolerance and understanding. I am dedicating this book to my wife, Gillian. She has encouraged and supported me for many years. I am profoundly conscious of how much I have taken her for granted. I love her more than I can adequately say.

~~~~~~

Early life

William Malcolm Hailey was born in 1872 at Newport Pagnell, a small town in north Buckinghamshire, the third son of Hammett Hailey, a country doctor who died when Malcolm was nine. His mother, Maria Coelia Clode, was from a family long established in the City of London, where her brother, John, had served as president of the Merchant Taylors' Company. All three Hailey brothers attended the Merchant Taylors' School. The eldest, Hammett (b. 1869), who was called by his initials, H.R.C., preceded Malcolm to Oxford and into the Indian Civil Service (ICS), serving in the land and revenue departments of the United Provinces (UP), where his more distinguished younger brother would one day retire as governor. Hammett's son, Peter, also joined the ICS. Malcolm's second brother, Rupert (b. 1870), was sent down after only four years at school and eventually became manager of a gold field in the northern Celebes. A younger sister, Violet, was the only one of Malcolm's siblings who survived him. Although they were late arrivals compared with the Stracheys or the Butlers, for instance, the Haileys were becoming an established Anglo-Indian family. Even the black sheep went overseas.[1]

Merchant Taylors', which Malcolm attended from 1883 to 1890, had been founded by the company of the same name in 1561 as a quasi-charitable institution. By the nineteenth century, however, the company had become vestigial and the school was supported by the Corporation of the City of London. It occupied a site recently vacated by the more prestigious Charterhouse across from the Smithfield meat market near Ludgate Circus at the foot of Fleet Street. Although it possessed an old closed-scholarship link with St. John's College, Oxford, and a reputation for the quality of its education, it was and remains one of England's lesser public schools. As Hailey explained at a reunion in the 1950s, boys went there because their parents could not afford Eton or Harrow.[2] Because most students, like Malcolm himself, were day pupils on

---

[1] Biographical information drawn from Philip Mason's essay in the 1961–70 Supplement to the *Dictionary of National Biography; Who Was Who* (1961–70); GEC, *Complete Peerage*, 13:569; Frederic Boase, *Modern British Biography*. A sketch of Newport Pagnell is in the *Victoria County History, Buckinghamshire* (London, 1927), 4:409–22.

[2] Transcript of speech, 11 December 1957, HPA/343. *Merchant Taylors' School: Its Origin, History and Present Surroundings* (Oxford: Blackwell, 1929); E. P. Hart, *Merchant Taylors' School Register, 1561–1934*, 2 vols. (London: Merchant Taylors' School, 1936).

at least partial scholarship, the school was comparatively slow in building a corporate identity. Cricket and rugby teams, as well as the alumni magazine, *The Taylorian*, were established only in the 1870s. Although the curriculum was changing gradually – by the time Malcolm arrived French was required and German could be substituted for Greek – it was still predominantly classical, with mathematics but, of course, no natural science.

Hailey therefore received a standard Victorian classical education. It was supposed to shape both mind and character. As a Merchant Taylors' headmaster put it later, Latin especially provided not only mental but moral discipline through the immersion of young minds in the exemplary literature of a great imperial race.[3] Associated with educators like Thomas Arnold at Rugby, Mark Pattison at Oxford, and John Seely at Cambridge, the training was intended not for technical specialists in business or industry but for administrators – that is, for precisely the sort of man Malcolm Hailey would become.[4] He excelled in it, taking top prize for his English essay, being recognized in the Tercentenary Scholarship competition, and winning an open scholarship to Corpus Christi College, Oxford. He succeeded at university too, taking a first-class degree in classics in 1894. That year, apparently without the common recourse to a crammer, he came third in the Indian Civil Service examinations.[5]

Apart from his obvious brightness only a few facts are available about the kind of boy Malcolm was. He belonged to the Church of England and, he testified late in life, had once been deeply religious. *The Taylorian* mentioned him for theatricals and debates – a successful portrayal of Dr. Pangloss in scenes from George Colman's popular play *Heir-at-Law*, a spirited but unsuccessful argument for a resolution in support of the Irish Home Rule leader Charles S. Parnell – but not for organized sports. Apart from tennis, which he joked that he kept to a minimum out of regard for the feelings of his partners, his main recreations were fishing and hiking: both solo. Among his siblings he corresponded only with H.R.C., and there the linkage was largely professional. Even by Victorian standards the Hailey household may have been unusually cold and reserved. The death of the father deprived the sons of a male role model and the natural focus of formative adolescent conflicts, which would necessarily have been transferred to the mother. The obsessive-compulsive personality of the adult man – the fixation on work, the acute need to prove himself long after by all objective criteria he had accomplished every conceiv-

[3] J. Arbuthnot Nairn, *Latin Prose Competition* (Cambridge: Cambridge University Press, 1928), p. viii.

[4] There is a huge literature on Victorian education. See particularly J. R. de S. Honey, *Tom Brown's Universe: The Development of the English Public School in the Nineteenth Century* (New York: Quadrangle, 1977); John Sparrow, *Mark Pattison and the Idea of a University* (Cambridge: Cambridge University Press, 1967); and Sheldon Rothblatt, *The Revolution of the Dons: Cambridge and Society in Victorian England* (New York: Basic Books, 1968).

[5] *Oxford University Calendar.* See also the standard history of the college by its president, Thomas Fowler, *Corpus Christi* (London: Robinson, 1898), although it has very little information on the modern period.

able objective – may well point to a mother the boy never felt able to satisfy, but that is pure speculation, and, of course, the three sons all turned out very differently.

Malcolm Hailey was precisely the sort of model recruit the Indian Civil Service strove to attract.[6] His social origins reflected a common process in nineteenth-century Britain, the gentrification of the middle class. As a physician his father was a member of one of the first occupations to secure its professional status; although not gentry his mother's family was notable. He went to a good if not elite public school and he had a first-class Oxford degree. Entering the law or medicine would have required financial backing that his fatherless family did not possess. Both his class and education therefore pointed toward an administrative career, and although it posed risks to health, the ICS promised a high living standard, financial security, social respectability, and responsibility at an early age. A young man with his credentials could have gone into the home civil service. Like his brother, however, Malcolm chose India. Arriving in December 1894, he spent the first few months in the secretariat at Calcutta. He was then assigned to the Punjab, again to the secretariat.

Half a century later Lord Hailey tried to recall the frame of mind in which he had first gone out to India. After his retirement a few years earlier, he told a student group in 1939, unpacking books he had bought as a schoolboy had brought back his affection for Kipling and other writers on what had been called the imperial mission.[7] In another talk to schoolboys at the end of the war he returned to the theme. In the 1890s, he reflected, Britons had been imperially minded only to a degree. What were later called the dominions were regarded with affection but not yet as a source of strength. India was therefore central and special. Although his young audience no doubt regarded Kipling as obsolete, he observed, the writer had fired the imagination; the belief in the white man's burden had been genuine. The Victorians might have been arrogant and ethnocentric, but their sense of duty and honor had been remarkable.[8]

If imperialism in Kipling's sense – mission, duty, honor – sums up the general attitude the young Malcolm Hailey carried to India in 1895, he was soon being indoctrinated into a more specific ideology, that of the Punjab tradition.[9] Its origins were in the early 1850s, when a small group of men had come over to take charge of the territory just conquered from the Sikhs, containing some of India's best farmland, driest deserts, and bravest soldiers. Led by the Lawrence brothers – Henry a martyr of the Great Mutiny of 1857–8 and John a hero – their efforts to form a government over the vast territory, which included what later became the North-West Frontier Province, were rough and

6 See Bradford Spangenberg, *British Bureaucracy in India: Status, Policy, and the I.C.S. in the Late 19th Century* (Columbia, Mo.: South Asia Books, 1976).
7 7 January 1939, Hailey Collection, HPA/334.
8 "The Empire," Abbotsholme School, 16 June 1945, HPA/336.
9 P.H.M. Van den Dungen, *The Punjab Tradition: Influence and Authority in Nineteenth-Century India* (London: Allen & Unwin, 1972).

makeshift. Like Sir Frederick Lugard and the indirect rulers in Northern Nigeria, however, the Punjab school made a virtue of their shortcomings.

With an enthusiasm that sometimes made it seem as though they might have invented the concepts, the Punjab school stressed authoritarianism and paternalism. Combining judicial, revenue, and administrative powers often separated in more established regimes, Punjab officials were instructed to act firmly at the first sign of trouble lest their notoriously turbulent peoples should explode in violence. Their decisions were supposed to be simple and direct, rough justice, consistent with the spirit of the law if not necessarily its letter. The ideal officer was not a desk man. He spent his days on horseback, at polo or pigsticking when not touring, carefully investigating complaints and making quick, commonsense decisions under a tree. In a province where agriculture was virtually the sole industry he was to gain and keep the loyalty of the landowning and peasant classes. The personal bond between the man on the spot and *his* people could not be overstressed. These, the millions of ordinary villagers, unlettered and unsophisticated, not the small minority of educated townspeople of Lahore, Amritsar, or Delhi, were the "real India." Identifying themselves rather arrogantly as the authentic spokesmen of the agrarian masses, British officials called themselves Punjabis.

Mediating among the three main religious communities – Muslim, Hindu, Sikh – civil servants must act impartially. For the province was a tinderbox where religious sparks might set off a raging conflagration at any time. The regime depended on the direct, personal influence of its officers. In the words of a John Lawrence biographer, "a unique truthfulness, simplicity, and singleness of purpose" characterized them. Doing their simple duty, seeking no favor, fearing no blame, "they loved the people . . . , put themselves in the people's place and made the interests of the people their own." The language of the Punjab school was unapologetically paternalist. As Lawrence's famous Hoshiarpur proclamation put it: "What is your injury I consider mine; what is gain to you I consider my gain; return to me, as children who have committed a fault return to the fathers, and their faults will be forgiven them."[10]

During 1857–8 the Punjab had played a crucial role. In Delhi, in the southeast corner of the province, most of the British were killed and the Mughal emperor was restored. In the western portion, however, support for the new masters held firm. As nationalist leaders would later pointedly remind them, it was the Punjab's so-called martial races who had enabled Britain to reconquer central and northern India. After the Great Rebellion the British had shifted their recruiting grounds from UP (then western Bengal) to the Punjab and Bombay presidency, adding further to the prestige of the Lawrence regime. By the 1860s the Punjab school was no longer merely a makeshift framework for the governance of a huge, backward, potentially troublesome province. Like Sir Frederick Lugard's later scheme of indirect rule in Northern Nigeria – with

10 Charles Aitchison, *Lord Lawrence* (Oxford: Clarendon Press, 1892), pp. 59, 69.

which, although it was certainly not indirect, the Punjab tradition had much in common – it had become an ideology.

In 1961, reflecting on his governorship of the Punjab in the 1920s, Lord Hailey wrote that as a junior official he had been secretary and disciple of the financial commissioner, S. S. Thorburn. No one could make sense of that period, he stressed, without first understanding the origins of the Punjab Land Alienation Act of 1900.[11] This valuable clue needs to be followed up in detail.

During the last three decades of the nineteenth century and, as Hailey indicated, far beyond, one problem became the central preoccupation of Punjabi civil servants. It was peasant indebtedness. During the 1860s officers making revenue-settlement reports had noticed that large quantities of land seemed to be passing from their hereditary owners, mainly from the Rajput or Jat castes (or tribes) of all three religions, to Hindu moneylending castes. The complex problem appeared to be new and it seemed to be getting worse. Within the Punjab branch of the ICS, as well as among the provincial government, the central Government of India, and the India Office in London, the debate on the issue was long and intense. Was it after all any of the government's business?

According to the orthodox political economy of the period, which was especially favored in Calcutta or London although it also had exponents in Lahore, however unpleasant the effects might seem in the short run, natural economic processes should be left alone. From the free-trade perspective movement in the land market was not only inevitable but a sign of progress, reflecting the flow of badly needed capital into agriculture, consolidating holdings, increasing prosperity and security. If market forces were left alone then productivity would rise and profits would improve, attracting still more capital and replacing inefficient landowners. Developing the country was Britain's sacred duty. And that, the orthodox maintained, was precisely what was happening.

Gradually Punjab civil servants became converted to the opposite view. As Hailey noted the principal advocate of the interventionist doctrine was his mentor, Thorburn, the author of a sensationally written book, *Musalmans and Money-Lenders in the Punjab* (1886). "The Punjab is an agricultural province," the opening sentence asserted, "a land of peasant proprietors, a large and annually increasing portion of whom are sinking into the position of serfs to the money-lenders."[12] Because especially in the western part of the territory these peasant landowners were almost entirely Muslim, whereas the moneylending castes were Hindu, the problem was politically dangerous. Moreover, Thorburn charged, by creating a right in land that could be sold, and that could therefore be borrowed against, the British were responsible.

[11] Hailey to D. A. Low, 10 January 1961, HPI/51.
[12] Septimus S. Thorburn, *Musalmans and Money-Lenders in the Punjab* (Edinburgh: Blackwood, 1886), p. 1.

Before the British, Thorburn argued, the Punjab's agrarian economy had been conducted virtually without cash. Even the land revenue had ordinarily been paid in kind. Moneylenders had occupied relatively humble positions, making advances for seed or livestock for which they were paid in grain – but only if the harvest had been a good one. In this primitive economy the burden of indebtedness had been low. Moneylenders were unwilling to make large advances, even supposing they had been able, because above a relatively low level borrowers would be incapable of repaying them. Although Indian regimes might have seized a larger share of the crop, the consequence had not been rising indebtedness. Moreover, because the balance between peasants and moneylenders had been relatively even, religious conflict had remained minimal. Even in the mid-1880s, Thorburn testified, Muslim, Sikh, and Hindu landlords and peasants lived side by side "in happy indifference to the petty jealousies which superior knowledge stirs up in the hearts of their Hindu and Musalman brethren in the towns."[13]

"The Bunniahs," Thorburn sneered at Hindu moneylenders, "are men of miserable physique and no manliness of character," much like Jews in Europe. Yet "Shylock was a gentleman by the side of Nand Lall Bunniah – as Shylock, though he spoiled the Gentiles, was yet a man of honor. Nand Lall has none, commercially speaking."[14] Greedy, shrewd, and ruthless, moneylenders hustled ignorant, thoughtless peasants into taking out mortgages to pay for weddings or funerals, subtracted discounts as high as 50 percent in advance, and then charged interest of 36 percent or so on the whole principal. Whereas earlier moneylenders had suffered along with their debtors, now they simply foreclosed. Borne down by debts they could never hope to repay, peasant and landlord families sank deep into peonage enduring unto the third and fourth generation.

Although the court system was one of the supposed benefits of British rule, Thorburn charged, it had tipped the balance decisively in favor of the moneylenders. Traditionally they had been constrained by the village community, in which they were essentially aliens. If they went beyond proper and reasonable bounds, their clients refused to pay or killed them. British law had taken off the brakes. Its most basic element was the contract, which presumed that creditor and debtor had entered freely into an equitable and binding agreement. In the circumstances of the Punjab, however, that was a ludicrous and tragic fiction. Hindu moneylenders had superior education, the shrewd business sense of their caste, larger financial resources, and the services of the largely Hindu bar. The legal profession was, of course, also available to peasants, who were urged forward in reckless suits foredoomed to fail – and the lawyers took their cut too. The odds might be better at Monte Carlo.

This was no simple matter of leaving economic laws to run their course, Thorburn pleaded. British rule having upset the fragile equilibrium of agrarian

---

[13] Ibid., p. 14.   [14] Ibid., p. 37.

society, it was up to the government to restore it. He called for legislation to prevent land passing from hereditary agricultural castes – in the Punjab they were usually called tribes – into the hands of nonagriculturist moneylenders. To be sure, peasants were also at fault. Although outsiders might call such intervention paternalist, however, "ignorant natives must be protected against the consequences of their own ignorance." Otherwise the largely Muslim peasantry of the western Punjab, from which so large a portion of the Indian army came, would be ruined and antagonized. A prudent government that also claimed to be moral must guard the people's welfare. And the Indian people, Thorburn concluded, in language characteristic of the Punjab school, "are the dumb toiling millions of peasants inhabiting the villages, hamlets, and scattered homesteads of the land. The town-bred exotics who are annually forced through in our educational hot-houses" had less claim to pose as "representatives of that people . . . than the puny operatives of our [English] manufacturing towns have of being typical specimens of John Bull."[15]

The Punjab doctrine was appropriate, if at all, for a backward society, not for sophisticated presidency capitals like Calcutta or Bombay. By the 1890s, indeed, it no longer fitted the Punjab. In the province's principal towns – Delhi, Lahore, Amritsar – students most of whom were Hindu were entering mission schools and universities. Already the government was carefully monitoring a lively English-language and vernacular press. An important Hindu reform movement with a sharp political edge, the Arya Samaj, was well under way.[16] Urban Hindus perceived the Land Alienation bill as part of a discriminatory package that included quotas for each community for appointments to government jobs. The British, they concluded, were threatening their very economic and political survival. Government officials responded that they were simply being evenhanded, attempting to correct a dangerous imbalance. By the first decade of the twentieth century the lines of communal conflict that would ultimately lead to the tragedy of partition in 1947 were already being drawn.

The Punjab Land Alienation Act of 1900 designated agricultural and non-agricultural tribes, prohibiting the latter from acquiring agricultural land in satisfaction of unpaid debt. Although the Punjab government overrode the strenuous and to some extent well-founded Hindu and official opposition, the law had several defects. First, as even the *Punjab Settlement Manual* admitted, the list of approved tribes was really not all that practical, for many people whose caste names were not on the approved list were in fact hereditary agriculturists.[17] Second, if mortgages on land could not be foreclosed, then either the debt would be moved over to crops, livestock, or farm implements, or capital would dry up. Third, the act did not prohibit land from being alienated to agricultural capitalists, mainly Rajputs, who were not hereditary moneylenders.

---

15 Ibid., p. 54.
16 See Kenneth W. Jones, *Arya Dharm: Hindu Consciousness in 19th-Century Punjab* (Berkeley: University of California Press, 1976).
17 James M. Douie, *Punjab Settlement Manual*, 5th ed. (Lahore: Government Printer, 1961), p. 199.

As Malcolm Darling explained in his classic study, if there was one thing worse than caste moneylenders, it was the new agricultural-capitalist class created by the act of 1900.[18]

The Punjab school was far from monolithic. Like any successful ideology it provided room for maneuver and disagreement. It contained men like Sir Denzil Ibbetson, who as lieutenant governor presided over the government's panicked response to the canal-colony tax revolt of 1907, and Sir Michael O'Dwyer, the authoritarian, heavyhanded ruler who imposed martial law in 1919. But it also included Malcolm Darling, whose travel journals reveal profound sympathy and insight into the lives of ordinary peasants; F. L. Brayne, the champion of village uplift; and Herbert Emerson, who was so strikingly successful in negotiating with Gandhi in 1931. Although it was of course politically biased, helping the government combat the claims of nationalist leaders to represent all of India, the strong identification of Punjab officials with the interests of rural people was not entirely hypocritical. Moreover, with rather more to show for their efforts than Joseph Chamberlain's contemporary doctrine of undeveloped estates in tropical Africa, the members of the Punjab school were pioneers in the evolution of a powerful imperial ideology: colonial development.

Although it is doubtful whether Malcolm Hailey ever went in for pigsticking, in most respects he was an authentic and wholehearted member of the Punjab school. On leave in London in 1912, for instance, he spoke at a meeting of old Punjaubis, as he spelled it. He told his retired colleagues how much had changed: the canal colonies had opened up thriving new agricultural areas; towns were growing in sophistication and political consciousness; the recent selection of Delhi as the new capital of the Government of India would add to the province's importance. Perhaps the Punjab might gain Karachi in compensation, he suggested, as though he were speaking of a sovereign state. The idea appealed "to the imagination: the Punjaub stretching from the Himalayas to the sea, mistress of her own port, and controlling the whole line of the Indus with all its vast possibilities for irrigation."

The speaker turned to what was called the peasant's Magna Carta, Thorburn's brainchild, the Land Alienation Act. Although it had its critics, Hailey conceded, it had been "a great moral gain. The member of an agricultural tribe has now an increased interest in thrift, and his character has gained from the improvement and stability of his position." He extolled the Punjab peasant: keen, industrious, firmly attached to the land, and driven to get his share of it. "We all know what he has done in the Army," he concluded; "we know the character which he has earned throughout the East wherever his enterprising disposition has carried him."[19] The self-proclaimed disciple of S. S. Thorburn had learned his lesson well. Half a century later, during World War II, Lord Hailey would be a leading spokesman for the colonial reform movement, which

18 Malcolm Darling, *The Punjab Peasant in Prosperity and Debt* (1925; New Delhi: Manohar, 1977), pp. 197–9.
19 Transcript in HPA/338.

in many ways was a natural extension of the Punjab tradition.[20] More specifically, as chairman of a Colonial Office committee on land tenure, he would attempt to export into Africa his mentor's doctrine on peasant indebtedness.

∞∞∞∞∞∞

In 1896, at twenty-four, which was young for Indian Civil Servants, Hailey had married Andreina (Alexandra) Balzani, the daughter of a Roman count. Disappointingly little information is available, even including how they met. Evidently a woman of spirit and independence, she was described as slim and beautiful, athletic and musical, with glorious hair.[21] But she was both a foreigner and a Catholic, and it was therefore she who had to make most of the adjustments. In 1900 she bore their first child, a son named Alan Balzani, whom they called Billy.

At the turn of the new century Malcolm Hailey was twenty-eight. At over six feet he was as tall as most Punjab soldiers, his large hawk's nose made him stern and still more commanding, and his hair was already receding. His formal education and his apprenticeship were behind him. He had come from the middle-class background typical of the Indian Civil Service. The classical studies in which he had distinguished himself at Oxford were precisely the generalist education the service's recruiters believed most appropriate. During his first years in India he had learned his languages. He and Alexandra Hailey had acclimatized themselves to the Punjab: the cool and pleasant winters, the notorious hot weather that only the secretariat was fortunate enough to leave behind in the annual trek to the summer capital at Simla, the wet season that brought diseases as well as relief from the heat. He had already contracted malaria, from which he would suffer periodically the rest of his life. He had done his work with enough competence and flair to catch the eye of his superiors. He had been indoctrinated generally into the creed of the British imperial mission and specifically into the Punjab tradition.

The truly formative period lay just ahead. In November 1901 Hailey was appointed the first colonization officer of the Lower Jhelum Canal Colony, where he would serve through 1906. In the interim, which was so brief that it was not even recorded in the *India Office Lists*, he went on special assignment to the western Punjab district of Dera Ismail Khan. I might have overlooked it too, except that some sixty years later when he was arranging his papers for deposit in the India Office Library he asked a former client to retrieve from a district record office in Pakistan what might seem to be an obscure document. It is a settlement (revenue-assessment) report on the district's Thal tract. As Lord Hailey himself obviously realized, it provides a valuable insight into his mind and personality on the eve of his first important assignment.

---

20 I have benefited from a conversation with D. Anthony Low on this point.
21 Letter in the *Times*, 2 February 1939, after her death.

9

Although he wrote sympathetically and even powerfully, the form of the report was of course prescribed. The detailed studies of Indian districts – local history, anthropology, demography, analysis of agriculture, and so on – embodied in settlement reports and gazetteers are among the ICS's most valuable and enduring contributions. Comparable to lawyers' briefs or scholars' monographs, they were professionally significant, being published by government printers and carefully reviewed by revenue commissioners as a basis for promotion. Some reports – for example, Denzil Ibbetson's of Karnal, or James Wilson's of Shahpur, both in the Punjab – became classics. Possessing a jargon and a specified format they were also a sort of cult, part of the ICS lore.

Yet the subject of the settlement reports was intensely serious. Although the government levied income, sales, and customs duties, as well as the salt tax that Gandhi would select as his symbolic target in 1930, the land revenue was the primary direct levy on the mass of India's people, in many cases one of the state's few significant intrusions into their daily lives. The settlement report was also a record of rights, sorting out landlord–tenant relations tract by tract. It was an article of faith that the land revenue was a stimulus to thrift and industry rather than a cause of poverty. If an assessment were too high, however, it could create hardship, famine, and unrest; if too low, the public would be robbed of important state services. An admittedly sloppy settlement in the Bardoli district of Bombay presidency would provide an opening for an important tax strike in the late 1920s. The settlement officer's investigations put his finger on the pulse of village India.

It would be hard to imagine an area more desolate than the Thal, Hailey reported, "barren and lifeless, devoid not only of bird and animal life, but almost of vegetation." In the north scanty rainfall provided scanty pasturage for Pathan herders. In the south, where a few Hindu-dominated villages struggled to live from cultivation, well water was so salty that it was often undrinkable. Even the best land needed manuring. Because cow dung was often the only available source of fuel, however, it was at a premium, often being bartered for well privileges that were even more precious. Water levels were sixty feet or more beneath the surface. Well digging was therefore a highly respected art and complex rules governed access: "The maintenance of a Thal well involves as much labour and nicety as its construction."

The chief characteristic of this intricate, fragile ecology of desert and semi-desert zones was poverty, "a poverty not only of resources but also of enterprise and intelligence. A continual struggle with Nature in her most niggard and capricious mood leaves them too exhausted for any other effort." Unlike other hard-pressed Punjab peasants, men from the Thal did not join the army, which would have brought them income. Aptly they described themselves as camel-hearted, "for they have to undertake an immense amount of the dullest kind of labour on the poorest of diets, and for the meanest of rewards." Comparatively energetic and farsighted, the well owner stood at the apex of society, parceling out the scarce water according to complex rules. Even he had little grain, surviving most of the year on turnips, melons, and wild fruit. Although pastoralists ate less grain, they did get a good deal of meat, "for besides the food afforded by an institution resembling a mutton club, they never hesitate to use the knife on an animal dying of disease, be it bullock, goat, or . . . camel." There were some compensations. Spared the fevers of moister regions the people were comparatively healthy, "and the age of their men and the strength of their women are a bye word in the district. Indeed, it is the poverty of poor living only, for there is never any actual famine, and in the worst of times temporary migration is no hardship to a half nomadic people." They grew them tough in the Thal: "How arduous the lives of these people must be, only those who have experience of the scorching sun and devastating sand storms . . . can realize."[22]

The standard form for such reports called for a historical section. Unfortunately, however, not much was known. According to local tradition the first occupiers had been a half-mythical people, the Belemas, whose huge bones and clay pots were still said to be found beneath the sand. The great invading tribes – Jats, Rajputs – had passed through, and the remains of a sizable ancient town had been found. All these invaders had moved on to better agricultural regions, leaving the Thal to pastoralists and struggling cultivators. Although the Mughals had declared their sovereignty over the area, it had little to attract them; apart from a few irregularly collected taxes in kind they had largely left it alone. The Mughals might have been right, the young settlement officer may have reflected. Like the Roman empire, however, the Government of India had decreed that all its subjects must be taxed. A light assessment would accustom the people to authority, Hailey concluded. It might even help to cure their camel-hearted stoicism.

Arriving at a practical and defensible tax was difficult. Laboriously Hailey compiled price tables, the trouble being that fluctuations resulting from capricious rain and undependable wells were so wide that averages were meaningless. The fact that there were virtually no rents ruled out the common method of claiming a percentage for the state, turning landlords into tax collectors. Water was the only commodity for which payments were made regularly either in cash or in kind, so Hailey proposed a tax on well owners' collections. But even that was complicated, for wells fluctuated almost as widely as crops: a well that seemed inexhaustible one year might fail completely the next. Someone would therefore have to go round frequently to check water flows. Hailey also recommended a light fluctuating assessment on agricultural and grazing land, to be collected in cash from the users. Because the standard work, Douie's *Settlement Manual* (1899), declared that assessments should ordinarily stand for twenty to thirty years – the debate between the advocates of fixed and periodically adjusted evaluations went back at least to Cornwallis's permanent set-

---

22 "Assessment Report of the Thal Tract of the Dera Ismail Khan District," submitted September 1902, HPI/52B.

tlement of the 1790s in Bengal – Hailey had to defend his proposal. Only a heartless and unintelligent government would insist on an inflexible rate, he argued, when all else in the Thal was so completely at the mercy of a harsh and capricious nature. It would cause more trouble for the deputy commissioner (as district officers were called in the Punjab). But a light, flexible tax seemed the only way.

The report earned high marks. Its proposals were "characterized by good sense and intelligent sympathy for the people in the hard life they lead," wrote the settlement commissioner, James Wilson. The financial commissioner, Sir Lewis Tupper, thought the "description of the vegetation of the Thal, its physical characteristics, the conditions of life there, and the systems of agriculture and grazing ranks with the best descriptions of the kind . . . in Punjab Settlement literature."[23]

If Malcolm Hailey had not been a high flyer, if he had spent his career as an ordinary Punjab district officer, he would have written many other reports like the one on the Thal. Because he spent most of his career in high administrative positions, however, he would do little sustained analytical inquiry. Indeed, the next time he would set out to do a comparable research project would be in 1936. Then the scale would be not part of a district but most of a continent: the *African Survey.*

[23] Comments on settlement report, ibid.

2

Colonization officer, 1901–1906

Although his years in the Punjab secretariat had placed Malcolm Hailey near the seats of power in Lahore and Simla, he must have found the apprenticeship frustrating. It was as though his very talent had trapped him. Men with lesser credentials had become assistant district officers at once. Their rugged outdoor lives, exercise of personal authority, and direct service to the "real people" of India all fit the Punjab tradition in which he too had been indoctrinated. The desk man must take care. Too long a stretch in the secretariat, especially if the work were done too well, and people would assume one belonged there. In the Indian Civil Service as in the army the lack of field experience would eventually tell. In short, Hailey needed to run his own show. At twenty-nine he was too young to be a deputy commissioner (district officer), but putting him in at the bottom where he might have gone in 1895 would also have been unjust. The opening of a new canal provided a way out. Although the Lower Jhelum colony in the Jhech Doab tract of the western Punjab's Shahpur district, lying between the Jhelum and Chenab rivers, commonly called the Bar, was smaller than an ordinary district, there would be plenty of responsibility. The next few years were to have an enormous impact in shaping Hailey's adult personality: his basic attitudes, identifications, habits, and instincts. He was to be the first colonization officer. He was to found a new society.

Irrigation was among Britain's most spectacular works in India. Quoting biblical prophecies about new lands springing forth in deserts, propagandists made the most of it. Already the richest grain-producing region in India, with peasants renowned for their hard work, the Punjab had enormous potential for expansion – if only there were water. But annual flooding brought moisture and silt only to tracts directly adjacent to one of the five rivers. Elsewhere irrigation was essential. Some areas had wells operated by Persian wheels or bullocks, but in other tracts water levels remain seventy feet or more below the surface. Much of the region has average rainfall of fifteen inches, some parts less than ten. And the rain is highly concentrated, failures of the main July–August monsoon being not infrequent and the winter rains quite capricious. Utilizing the vast storage area of the Himalayan glaciers, canal colonies could relieve congestion in overcrowded districts, feed less fortunate parts of the country,

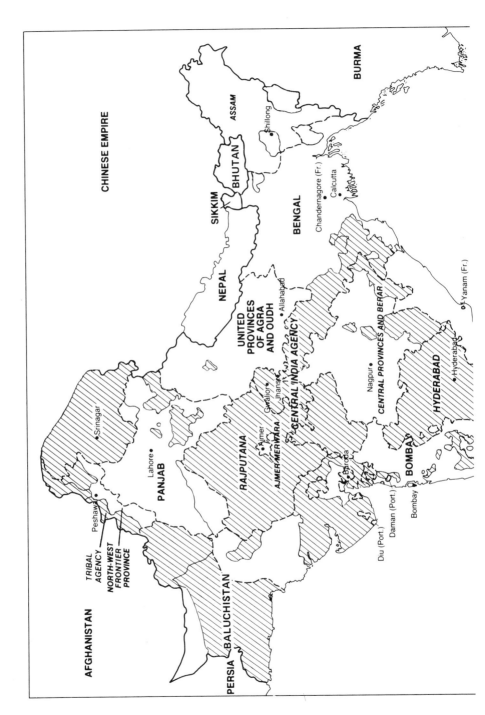

CHINESE EMPIRE

BURMA

ASSAM

•Shillong

SIKKIM

BHUTAN

NEPAL

BENGAL

Chandernagore (Fr.)•

•Calcutta

UNITED
PROVINCES
OF AGRA
AND OUDH

•Allahabad

AFGHANISTAN

•Srinagar

Peshawar•

Lahore•

PANJAB

TRIBAL
AGENCY

NORTH-WEST
FRONTIER
PROVINCE

RAJPUTANA

•Ajmer

AJMER-MERWARA

Gwalior•

•Jhansi

CENTRAL INDIA AGENCY

Nagpur•

CENTRAL PROVINCES AND BERAR

HYDERABAD

•Hyderabad

•Yanam (Fr.)

•Baroda

BOMBAY

Bombay▾

Daman (Port.)

Diu (Port.)

PERSIA   BALUCHISTAN

14

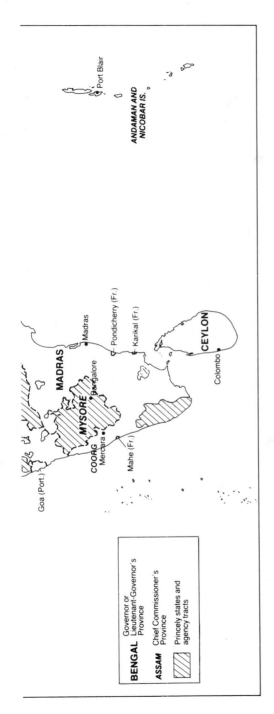

India ca. 1939

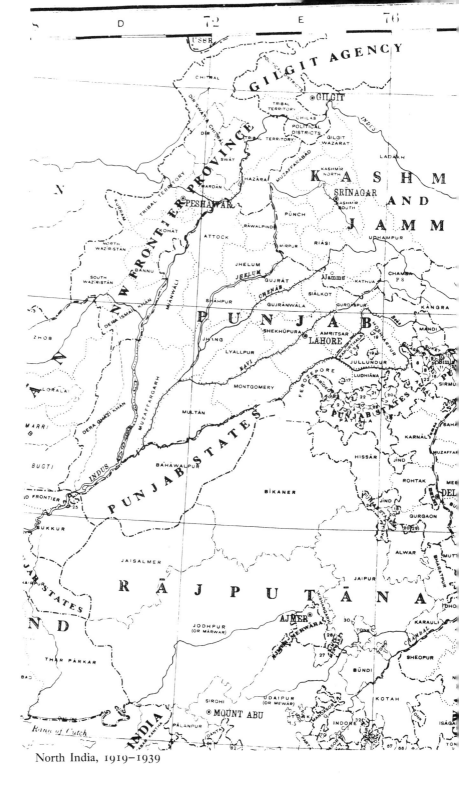

North India, 1919–1939

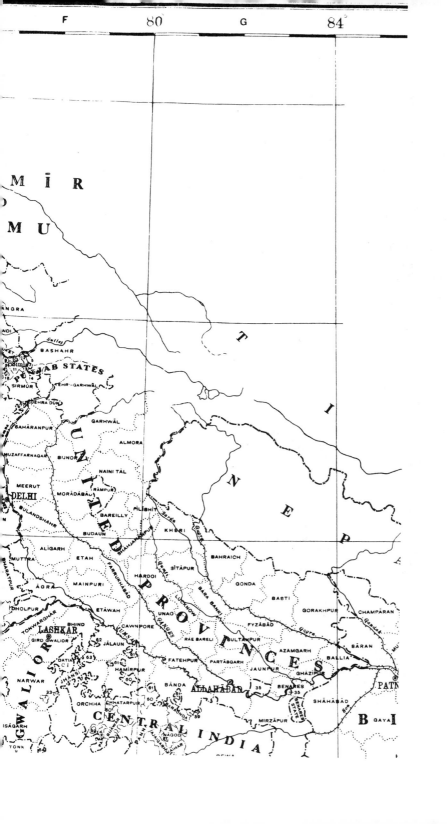

earn foreign exchange by increasing exports to Europe, augment the state's revenue, and ensure the loyalty of a prosperous, contented peasantry.[1]

Shortly after taking over the province, following earlier precedents under the Mughal and Sikh regimes, the British had built the Bari Doab canal. Encouraged by its modest success, they stepped up the pace, completing in 1887 the huge Chenab project that watered more than 2 million acres. By 1900 it was already financially successful, by 1918 it was averaging a return of 40 percent of the cost per year, and by 1946 it had repaid the original capital investment by more than 1,100 percent. Yet the government's targets were limited. The Chenab was meant to make the predominantly agrarian economy larger and more efficient in degree, but not different in kind. Revenue was not used as capital; projects for secondary industrialization were few, late, and poorly funded. The Punjab canal colonies, their historian concludes, aimed at expansion but not true development.[2]

The Chenab was a prototype of social engineering. A classic document of canal-colony literature described how prospective colonists were chosen. When he walked along the row, a colonization officer explained, unsuitable applicants were easily spotted: the opium addict by his color, the fop by smooth hands that had never worked behind a plow. Men like those would never make it in the Bar. Accompanied by *patwari* (record keeper), *munshi* (clerk), and *lambardar* (village headman), he went down the line, determining whose holdings were already sufficient or whose mortgages were too high, and "these too were weeded out. The residue would be put down for a square each."[3]

This superficially amusing but disturbing passage – the colonization officer playing God, making snap decisions in the context of a Darwinian struggle for survival – is misleading not in its portrayal of the rapidity of judgments but in its suggestion that the rural poor were ever considered at all. For although one of the official objectives was to relieve congestion, another was to settle prosperous "yeomen" who would be self-cultivating farmers, the backbone of "healthy agricultural communities of the best Punjab type."[4] As a press communiqué of 1914 put it, selecting colonists from the landless would lower the quantity and raise the price of agricultural labor, it being obviously inappropriate for the government to "upset the existing social and economic order."[5] The Chenab colony reflected the Punjab tradition, which it was intended to reinforce. Most

[1] Report of the Indian Irrigation Commission, 1901–3, PP, 1904 [Cd. 1851–4], 56.
[2] Imran Ali, *The Punjab Under Imperialism, 1885–1947* (Princeton, N.J.: Princeton University Press, 1988). See also Ian Stone, *Canal Irrigation in British India: Perspectives on Technological Change in a Peasant Economy* (Cambridge: Cambridge University Press, 1984), which concerns the United Provinces.
[3] Quoted in Malcolm Darling, *The Punjab Peasant in Prosperity and Debt* (1925; New Delhi: Manohar, 1977), pp. 115–16.
[4] *Chenab Colony Gazetteer* (1904), p. 29, quoted by Imran Ali, *Punjab Under Imperialism*, p. 13. In addition to comparatively accessible materials at the India Office Library and the Punjab Secretariat, Imran Ali used exhaustively the voluminous and uncatalogued collection of the Punjab Board of Revenue. I thank him for his exceptional help while I was in Lahore in 1987.
[5] Punjab press communiqué, 8 December 1914, quoted ibid., p. 157.

colonists came from the central Punjab, half the land going to Muslims, the rest to Hindus and Sikhs. On the assumption that colonists would fare better if they settled in primary groups, the government tried to aggregate people from different religions and castes. The Chenab therefore became more segregated than the colonists' original homes.

By January 1899, when the engineers started the Lower Jhelum canal, the job had become routine. Costing Rs. 1.15 crores (£ 1.5 million), financed by bonds on the London money market, the canal would serve some half a million acres. As modern technology blended with labor patterns that had built the pyramids – lines of women snaking back and forth, gracefully balancing on their heads pots of earth and cement requiring two men to lift – the work went ahead quickly.[6] In October construction began on the headworks. By May the head regulator, undersluices, and a fourth of the weir were done. Although work virtually stopped during the summer floods, a year later the entire weir was finished. Hailey's appointment took effect in November. The next month the river was diverted over the weir. Irrigation and colonization could begin.

In its plans for the new colony the Punjab government departed from the Chenab model the better to achieve the same objectives: (1) creating prosperous model villages of self-cultivating peasant proprietors, seasoned with retired soldiers and government servants, (2) increasing revenue and exports, and (3) building support for the government. Yeomen, defined as men able to bring followers, were to receive two to three squares, a stipulation that reinforced the bias in favor of the well-to-do. Primogeniture would be imposed on all grantees. And grants would be given only to colonists from western districts where Muslims were a huge majority.

The last two changes were the most significant. Primogeniture was proposed by S. S. Thorburn, Hailey's mentor, in the hope of avoiding congestion later on.[7] Such a rule would contradict the customary subdivision of land among the sons, causing endless conflict, objected Lewis Tupper, Thorburn's successor; an eldest son who drove his brothers off the land after their father's death would be considered hard and grasping.[8] Instead of creating centers of loyalty, Tupper insisted, primogeniture would create tension and unrest. Within a few years Hailey would come to agree with him. Meanwhile, the settlement commissioner, James Wilson, sided with Thorburn, maintaining that in making grants of its wastelands the state should impose any conditions it thought best.[9] And so it was decided.

The preference for Muslims was also Thorburn's idea. The grounds were admittedly not economic, for Hindu and Sikh Jats were the province's best

---

6 This description is in fact drawn from a scene I witnessed in 1966 near Baroda, the site of the construction of an atomic reactor.
7 Finance Commissioner (S.S. Thorburn) to Revenue & Financial Secretary, 15 September 1899, Punj. Sec., Rev/Ag (Irrig), January 1900, File No. 1.
8 Fin. Commr. to Rev. & Fin. Sec., 29 March 1901, Punj. Sec., Rev/Ag (Irrig), May 1901, No. 14.
9 Wilson letter to Fin. Commr., 28 May 1900, ibid.

farmers, and its eastern and central districts where they predominated were the most crowded. Punjab Muslims, he argued, were "strong, manly, and hitherto dominant tribes and families," and they provided many soldiers. The sad truth, however, was that Hindus were outhustling them. For their resulting backwardness Muslims were blaming the government, which could not afford to disregard them. Thorburn also linked colonization policy to the culmination of his life's work, the pending Land Alienation Act. "Further persistence in the principles of free trade in land and the survival of the intellectually fittest," he insisted, would be extremely dangerous.[10]

The Punjab government submitted its colonization scheme in May 1901, only to have it replaced by a different plan based on a proposal from the Government of India's Horse and Mule-Breeding Commission that the Jhelum become a horse-breeding colony, saving foreign exchange and making the army self-sufficient.[11] Punjab officials were skeptical. Ordinary peasants were not experienced breeders, district officers reported, while concentrating ten thousand brood mares on the Jhelum would strip the region of good horses. Capital would be required, which would drastically reduce the number of potential colonists. Grants would have to be larger than those on the Chenab, and primogeniture would be essential to prevent them from being broken up. Whereas the Chenab would have prosperous, self-cultivating peasants, Wilson foresaw, on the Jhelum primogeniture would prevent subdivision, creating a subtenant class and ultimately even rack-renting. Yet the Indian army's need seemed to be compelling. Perhaps the Jhelum's "squireens" would prove more progressive than the Chenab's "dead level of prosperity."[12] Where the interests of province and empire conflicted, the Punjab government concluded, the former must give way gracefully.[13] In July 1901 Hailey had expected to proceed on the lines of the Chenab model. By the time he took charge in November it was already clear that the scheme would be entirely different.

While his superiors were preparing the horse-breeding plan Hailey and his staff of two dozen *kanagus* (surveying assistants) began their work of transforming a desert. During the 1890s Wilson, who was then the deputy commissioner of Shahpur district, had published a revised settlement report, a compilation of customary law, and a new edition of the gazetteer. Containing nearly five thousand square miles, the district was split in half by the Jhelum River, the western part being called Khushab tahsil (or portion), the eastern being further subdivided into the Bhera (southern) and Shahpur (northern) tahsils. Like the Thal, where Hailey had made his revenue settlement just before taking up his new assignment, the area is one of the subcontinent's hot spots. Although the

---

[10] Fin. Commr. to Rev. & Fin. Sec., 15 September 1899, Punj. Sec., Rev/Ag (Irrig), January 1900, No. 1.

[11] Rev. & Fin. Sec. to Govt. of India, Rev. & Agric. Dept, 11 May 1901, Punj. Sec., Rev/Ag (Irrig), May 1901, No. 48; Report of Horse and Mule-Breeding Commission, cited by Imran Ali, *Punjab Under Imperialism*, p. 24.

[12] Wilson note, 23 March 1902, Punj. Sec., Rev/Ag (Irrig), October 1902, Nos. 1–25.

[13] Tupper note, n.d. [May 1902], Punj. Sec., Rev/Ag (Irrig), October 1902, No. 1–25.

temperature sometimes topped 115 degrees Fahrenheit in May and June, Wilson assured readers that during the monsoon it rarely went over 105, and average rainfall was below fifteen inches.[14] Shahpur stood ninth in area among the Punjab's thirty-one districts but twenty-fourth in population. Ninety percent of the district's half a million people were classed as rural, living in villages under 5,000, and only the town of Bhera was over 10,000. The district was 85 percent Muslim, 13 percent Hindu, and 2 percent Sikh.[15]

The population was more or less clearly divided into tribes, Wilson reported, and these were further subdivided into clans that were much like family clusters in Europe. Just as a man would be known as Donald Campbell in London, but the son of Duncan in the Campbell village in Scotland, in Shahpur, "Jehana, the son of Bakshu of the Tatri clan, is among Tatris known as 'Jehana Bakshu da,' but to other people as 'Jehana Tatri.'"[16] The most politically powerful groups were Muslim Rajput landowners, the Tiwanas and Awans; trade was dominated by Hindu moneylenders, the Khatris and Aroras. Since the 1850s, Wilson concluded in 1894, cultivation of cotton, oil seeds, and especially of wheat and other cereals had nearly doubled. Meanwhile, however, driven by the rising value of land, the tendency of landowners to live beyond their means, and the rigidity of British law in enforcing contracts, agrarian indebtedness was serious and accelerating.[17] Knowing as he did of the impending transformation, Wilson described a region on the verge of economic miracle. Although most of the soil was loam, superior to the sandy soil of the Chenab colony, water levels were fifty to eighty feet below the surface and wells were few and far between. Apart from some precarious cultivation most of the Bar remained scrubland.[18] All it needed was water.

In November 1901, when Hailey took charge, the engineers had only to turn a few wheels to fill the main canal and the rows of crisscrossing ditches. The young man worked methodically, tract by tract, preparing the land to receive a batch of immigrants, then repeating the cycle. In ordinary settlement work the land was measured into squares with basic surveying equipment: level, protractor, telescope, and chain. But a square was roughly twenty-eight acres, which is a very large farm in India, and it might contain considerable variations in soils, drainage, and hence in yields. The squares were therefore subdivided into twenty-five smaller units, 220 feet to a side, called *killas*, and the process of cutting up a tract was called *killabandi*. Once killas were laid out and marked with pegs, villagers supervised by patwaris connected the pegs with ropes and dug trenches that later became semipermanent embankments. Two or three decades later the next settlement officer would merely have to record changes

---

[14] James Wilson, *Final Report on the Revision of Settlement of the Shahpur District in the Punjab. 1887–94* (Lahore: Civil and Military Gazette Press, 1894), p. 2.

[15] James Wilson, *Gazetteer of Shahpur District* (1897).

[16] James Wilson, *General Code of Tribal Custom in the Shahpur District of the Punjab* (Lahore: Civil and Military Gazette Press, 1896).

[17] *Shahpur Gaz.* (1897), pp. 144–5.   [18] *Shahpur Settlement Report* (1894), p. 2.

in ownership, improvements, and average yields and prices. A killabandied tract would resemble a vast chessboard, here and there interrupted by a rock out-cropping or perhaps a phallic monument, square after square of waving grain as far as the eye could see.[19]

A canal colony had to be killabandied too. When Hailey arrived, however, the engineers had already surveyed, laying down baselines on either side of the canals and cross lines at thousand-foot intervals, while the irrigation ditches had cut the tract into squares. The trouble was that although it was quite sufficient for the canal officers' purposes, the standard of surveying was far below that of the usual revenue settlement, so that as distance from the canal increased the squares became more irregular. Although colonists and future settlement officers might complain, however, Hailey chose efficiency over tidiness. The canal squares were already there, he reasoned, and having two sets on the same land would be confusing. The sooner colonists could begin clearing, cultivating, and paying land and water rates the better.

The original inhabitants, who were called Janglis, posed a second problem. The Bar territory having been largely scrubland used for occasional pasturage, the government had declared it wasteland. Herdsmen could be allotted some squares in the hope that they would abandon pastoralism for what, in the classic British view, was the higher calling of sedentary agriculture. But there were also scattered villages eking out a precarious existence from cultivation. Because they would want water, for which they could be charged, their land also had to be killabandied. A few pastoralists might be no problem. Villages of farmers who had preexisting rights, and who would no doubt have access to a lawyer, had to be taken more seriously. Yet the colonization officer had the upper hand. No farmer would refuse water, the government did not have to provide it, and theoretically could charge as much as it liked, including fines for those who refused killabandi. Thus, Hailey reported brightly, "after a good deal of pres-sure the majority of villagers have begun to comply."[20]

First the land, then the people. During the colonization of the Chenab deputy commissioners from the sending districts had taken the lead, choosing applicants from the most congested areas, checking off caste names against the list of approved agriculturist tribes, making sure they had demonstrated success as farmers. Ordinarily, although he had the right to make objections for cause, the colonization officer's role was subordinate.[21] The horse-breeding scheme on the Jhelum reversed the precedence. Although approved agriculturists were still preferred, the most essential condition was now the possession of a mare the army's veterinarians had approved for the breeding of good-quality cavalry

[19] See Douie, *Punjab Settlement Manual*, app. XIV; Hailey note on killabandi, 28 February 1904, IOR V/24/2486.

[20] Jhelum Colony AR (1902–3), ibid.

[21] Hailey's distinctly subordinate role was explained in Fin. Comm. to Rev. & Fin. Sec., 27 September 1901, Punj. Sec., Rev/Ag (Irrig), October 1901, No. 11.

horses, which were called remounts. Central control having superseded local knowledge, the primary role belonged to Hailey.

Leaving his assistant to continue with the surveying Hailey and a veterinarian toured the western Punjab. "While the Veterinary Officer judges the mare," he explained, "I examine the man. If he has too much land already – or is a Lambardar or is not a self-cultivating zamindar [landowner] – or is likely to be the heir to a good deal of land – I reject him whether his mare passes or no. He will never become a self-cultivating resident tenant, whatever his qualifications as a horse-breeder." He tried not to miss much: "The appearance of the man, the number of his brothers and his sons, the state of his village, are all important factors in deciding on the fitness of the applicant, and I generally leave a note on the back of each . . . giving details of this nature." If man and mare both qualified a positive decision was made at once.[22] To Wilson's surprise Hailey obtained a thousand colonists with approved mares from his first tour, which covered only half the districts in the region, so a target of three thousand did not seem unreasonable. It would be achieved, however, only by sweeping the country of first-class mares. At least for the time being their numbers would not increase. They would merely be concentrated.[23]

The price of mares was rising sharply, Hailey reported. The riskiest part of the Jhelum experiment was the stipulation that ordinary peasants would breed the horses, one mare per allotment. But horse breeding required capital, organization, and thus a large scale. The case for big grants and reduced occupancy fees for proven breeders was therefore strong.[24] Moreover, sooner or later the original mares would have to be replaced, and at inflated prices. There was also some question about the standard, for the army wanted only mares capable of producing good cavalry horses, whereas some mares who had been approved by civilian veterinarians might be qualified only to produce mules. One might imagine the colonist's bewilderment and feeling of betrayal, Hailey warned, if after buying a mare bearing the *Sarkar*'s (government's) stamp he was told she would not do.

The authorities should be content with humble beginnings, Hailey advised, gradually breeding up in the hope of meeting the higher standard in twenty years or so.[25] Standing by the original recommendation of the Horse and Mule-Breeding Commission, however, the army decided otherwise. For ordinary peasant grants the standard would be at least that of good-quality Indian cavalry, while for larger allotments it would be that of British cavalry remounts.[26] The consequences were obvious. The higher the standard the fewer the mares, the higher their price, and the fewer the prospective colonists.

---

22 Hailey note, n. d. [May 1902], Punj. Sec., Rev/Ag (Irrig), October 1902, No. 1–25.
23 Wilson note, 30 May 1902, ibid.
24 Hailey to Settlement Commissioner, 27 July 1902, Rev/Ag (Irrig), November 1902, No. 1–25.
25 Hailey note, 14 August 1902, Punj. Sec., Rev/Ag (Gen), November 1902, No. 25.
26 Director Army Remount Dept., Calcutta to Col. Officer, Jhelum, 24 August 1902, ibid., No. 29–30.

The stark realities of that formula, especially the rising price of mares, which by 1903 had risen from an average of Rs. 250 to as high as Rs. 600, continued to determine the evolving colonization policy of the Jhelum. Was the horse-breeding experiment, after all, going to be compatible with the ideal of a colony of self-cultivating peasants? Hailey strove to achieve both. Genuine breeders were scarce, he warned, and the government had not yet reached the point of giving out land to speculators "who would produce mares (much as they would produce unicorns)."[27] If not then the capital requirements had to be kept within reach of prosperous peasants. But the sums would just not work out. Occupancy fees had to be kept far below the government's expectations and the grants had to be enlarged from one and a half to two squares per mare.[28] Not until the end of his tenure did Hailey complete the colonization process. Moreover, compared with the Chenab, the Jhelum would never be truly successful financially.[29]

Choosing the site for the colony's headquarters turned out to be difficult and controversial. The soil had to be at least good enough for gardens; a water-logged area would be malarious, so drainage must be satisfactory; much of the region's water was salty or brackish, so tests had to be run. The location must be near the projected line of rail and within reach of existing or practicable metaled roads. The canal engineer's first choice lay within the boundaries of Mithalak village. But settling the villagers' claims would be prohibitive, Hailey objected, while a new town there would have trouble competing with existing markets. His own choice was Sargoda (the spelling was later changed to Sargodha). The dispute with the engineers continued – "I am quite prepared to put my house and garden on the very worst soil that Mr. Laurie can point out," Hailey declared – and when the settlement commissioner, James Wilson, visited in February 1902 he won his point.[30]

A few months later an interesting discrepancy in dates was discovered. Several weeks before the colonization officer had received approval, auctions had been announced for lots in the new capital of Sargodha; sales had been spirited, he reported blandly, and the prices good.[31] "Mr. Hailey would have been more in order if he had waited for the final sanction of the Financial Commissioner to the site and plan of the town," Wilson commented dryly. Although he "ought to have taken orders before finally committing us to the site," the financial commissioner Sir Lewis Tupper agreed, the auctions could not be canceled now.[32]

---

[27] Hailey note, n. d. [May 1902], Punj. Bd. of Revenue, Rev/Ag (Irrig), October 1902, No. 23.
[28] Hailey note, n.d. [March 1903], Punj. Bd. of Revenue, Rev/Ag (Irrig), June 1903, No. 28.
[29] Imran Ali, *Punjab Under Imperialism,* pp. 166–7.
[30] Hailey note, 16 February 1902, Punj. Sec., Rev/Ag (Gen), May 1902, No. 63. It is unlikely that Hailey's house, now the district commissioner's residence, was in fact built on the worst soil that could be found by a soil specialist, because the garden today is certainly a thing of beauty. Rev. & Fin. Sec. to Fin. Comm., 9 May 1902, ibid.
[31] Hailey to Sett. Comm., 15 January 1903, Punj. Sec., Rev/Ag (Irrig), September 1903, No. 41.
[32] Sett. Comm. to Fin. Comm., 16 February 1903, ibid., No. 40. Fin. Comm. to Rev. & Fin. Sec., 20 June 1903, ibid., No. 41.

Tired of waiting for red tape to wind back and forth, with so many things to do, anxious to move ahead, and confident of the eventual decision, the young man had gone ahead. Moreover, Wilson and Tupper having given him the lightest of wrist slaps, he had gotten away with it. Having made him colonization officer they expected him to take charge, and he had done so. They had already marked him out as a man who would rise in the world. Chaps like that would have to cut a corner or two.

In November 1901 the Bar tract of half a million acres had been dry scrubland crisscrossed by newly cut irrigation ditches. Gradually colonists had come, put up houses, planted crops, grazed cattle and mares. The surveying was done and some thirty thousand people had arrived, but colonization was only half complete. Sargodha was chosen but not yet built. By the end of 1903 Hailey's colony had made a good beginning. The future looked promising. Then came the plague.

∞∞∞∞∞∞

"Macies et nova febrium terris incubit cohors" ("Wasting diseases, fresh cohorts of fevers, fell on land and sea"). In writing his annual report for 1903–4, like the Victorian public school product he was, Malcolm Hailey reached for his Horace. Then followed what must be one of the more severe understatements in the history of the Indian Civil Service. The year had been "somewhat unfortunate." First had come a severe type of malaria, which slowed cultivation and effectively closed government offices for nearly two months. Then in the spring bubonic plague had struck Bhera tahsil in the north, killing some twenty-one thousand in that section alone, though it was milder in Shahpur tahsil. But that figure did not include those who had fled to their former homes and might have died there. Nor was it a complete record of mortality in the villages, for headmen and record keepers were often victims too. The full extent of the calamity could therefore only be guessed at, although many villages had 50 percent mortality and some as high as 70 percent.[33] Left unwatered the *rabi* (spring) crop failed almost entirely, and where it ripened it remained unharvested. Since the coming *kharif* (autumn) harvest would also be reduced, the fall in revenue would be substantial. By the autumn of 1904, however, the first shock had passed and most of the survivors had gradually returned.

By then the colonization officer was back too. Early in June Hailey had caught plague, which nearly killed him, and he spent two months in the hills recovering. His assistant, Lala Paira Ram, was not so fortunate. An assistant colonization officer from the Chenab colony came over, helped Alexandra Hailey nurse her husband, and kept the Jhelum from folding completely. He became

---

[33] AR (1903–4), IOR V/24/2478. The quotation is from *Odes*, bk. 1, Ode 3, lines 30–1. I thank Mary Boatwright for her help in identifying this passage.

Hailey's closest and most enduring friend, his number two and alter ego in Delhi and later in the Punjab, where with Hailey's influence behind him he would one day succeed as governor. He was Geoffrey de Montmorency.

In 1904–5 plague recurred and Sargodha was immediately deserted. This time the epidemic was comparatively mild, the people soon returned, and no harvests were lost. Next year the attack was also light. In February 1907, however, just before Hailey's transfer, it reappeared in force in surrounding villages, though not in Sargodha itself, which drew refugees from as far away as Lahore. Although it is now clear that recurrence within an infected region is quite unpredictable, the men in charge naturally credited their own measures, congratulating the townspeople for their cooperation in trapping rats, disinfecting houses, and reporting suspicious cases. Even though the total mortality in the colony was higher than in 1904, Hailey's replacement reported, many villages having lost one-third or more within a few weeks, the panic had been much less severe.[34] By 1907, then, the peasants of the Punjab had learned to bear yet another heavy burden. During the first half of the twentieth century plague would kill more than 13 million Indians. Although its toll and horror persisted, however, the scourge had been routinized.[35]

Hailey's colony had been struck during a transitional period in the medical history of this dread disease. By the time the fourth – some say the third – and still current pandemic of bubonic plague reached Bombay from China in 1896, Pasteur's disciple Alexandre Yersin had already isolated the parasite, which he called *Bacterium pestis*. (Since the 1960s it has been known as *Yersinia pestis*.) But the discovery could fit into either of the two historic theories of Western medicine: contagion, the direct transmission from person to person, and miasma, infection from agents in air, soil, or water. At first most authorities, including the Indian Plague Commission, favored the miasmic explanation that plague was a filth disease – which, of course, it is, though not for the reason they thought. By 1903, when plague reached the Punjab, the weight of medical opinion had fixed on the rat. In 1907 the Plague Research Commission, an entirely different body, identified the flea as the most likely vector, although the extremely complex process of transmission from rat to flea to human was verified only in 1914.[36]

Driven in part by their own folk memory of the Black Death, the British had reacted quickly to the outbreak in Bombay. Identifying cases, segregating pa-

[34] AR (1906–7), IOR V/24/2479.

[35] Prakash Tandon, *Punjabi Century* (Berkeley: University of California Press, 1961), p. 113.

[36] The standard medical textbook is Thomas Butler, *Plague and Other Yersinia Infections* (New York: Plenum, 1983), while the most current guide to public health policy is M. Bahmanyar and D. C. Cavanaugh, *Plague Manual* (Geneva: World Health Organization, 1976). William H. McNeill, *Plagues and Peoples* (Garden City, N.Y.: Anchor, 1976), is a superb account of epidemiology in world history, being especially good on the changing ecological balance among humans, animals, insects, and bacterial–viral parasites. See also Ira Klein, "Urban Development and Death: Bombay City, 1870–1914," *Modern Asian Studies*, 20 (1986), 725–54, and my own article, "Anglo-Indian Medical Theory and the Origins of Segregation in West Africa," *American Historical Review*, 92 (April 1986), 307–35.

tients in well-lighted rooms or removing them to hospital, restricting travel, evacuating infected houses, removing roofs to let in light and air, using tons of chloride, sulfur, carbolic acid, and whitewash, they tried to cover all the angles. All these measures involved substantial invasions of privacy, however, including violation of purdah; they were imposed by an alien government; and they were obviously unsuccessful. Bombay had serious riots, and the extremist B. G. Tilak made the plague measures a major item in his attack on British rule. The blunt truth, the Indian Plague Commission admitted in 1901, was that the government and medical science alike were impotent. Although the Bombay measures could all be justified according to one theory or another, coercing the people into complying with antiplague regulations was simply unproductive.[37]

By 1903, when the disease began to spread through the Punjab, the local health authorities suspected a combination of contagion and miasma and urged rat destruction, segregation, disinfection, and especially evacuation. Unlike Bombay presidency, in the Punjab villages and small towns were hit hardest. The concentration in rural areas, where the Sarkar's paternal authority ought to have been most effective, was an affront to the Punjab school. Although the peasants had shown sturdy independence in face of the calamity, the lieutenant governor reported, their calmness and stolidity were based on a sense of fatalism that amounted to evasion. Perhaps the government had been over-cautious, he admitted. The only reason for the absence of unrest had been the lack of compulsion.[38]

Apart from plague the colony faced other problems, the most serious being the requirement of primogeniture, which contradicted custom and altered the relationship between colonists and British authority. Unlike Chenab grantees, Hailey pointed out, Jhelum colonists had undertaken to maintain a mare and the state was therefore bound to provide land and water. "We enter into a contract," he argued, "and our relations with the Colonist are no longer on the same footing."[39] The rising price of mares made horse breeding difficult, expensive, and hard to administer, while the mere fact that enough colonists had come forward did not mean they understood what they were letting themselves in for. In any future horse-breeding scheme, he advised, it would be far simpler if the army chose the mares itself and leased them to colonists. Meanwhile he suggested a cooperative fund to help when mares needed replacing.[40]

Primogeniture and other regulations were exacerbating the natural demor-

---

37 Indian Plague Commission, PP, 1902 [Cd. 141], 72.
38 *Report on Plague and Inoculation in the Punjab, 1902–3* (Lahore: Government Printer, 1904). The point must be stressed that there was literally nothing the authorities could do. Even the commonsense strategy of rat killing is counterproductive except in very small areas such as airports, where according to WHO guidelines it is essential to destroy the fleas first, since fleas prefer rats to humans. Not until after World War II would antibiotics, insecticides, and especially the breeding of resistance in rats halt the plague in India, although it has recurred in Southeast Asia and continues in Africa.
39 AR (1904–5), IOR V/24/2479.
40 Hailey to Settlement Comm., 13 July 1906, Punj. Bd. of Rev., Rev/Ag (Irrig), March 1907, No. 20. Same to same, 11 December 1904, ibid., April 1905, No. 21.

alization of grantees who were dependent on the state, Hailey warned.[41] "The fact that hard cases occur is not in itself a reason for amending the rules," the settlement commissioner James Douie demurred; "in an eastern country . . . the Deputy Commissioner will be in a very invidious position who is asked to assist in . . . supplanting Esau by Jacob, or Leah's child by Rachel's child."[42] The army's requirements being primary, Lieutenant Governor Sir Charles Rivaz concluded, "the mere executive difficulty" that some people might be unhappy did not need to be considered.[43] Investigation after the canal-colony tax revolt of 1907 would show that Hailey's criticisms had been absolutely right.

The Jhelum colony provided a new focus for the western Punjab, quickening the pace of life, linking the territory to the wider economic and political networks of region, empire, and world. A new thing had indeed sprung forth in the desert. Yet the colony reinforced the demography of the area. Although they were lightly seasoned with Hindus and Sikhs, the colonists were predominantly Muslim. In the first decade of the twentieth century, however, the division into cohesive, bitterly antagonistic communities was still in the future. These colonists, Hailey observed, tended to group themselves along territorial rather than tribal or religious lines: "Sikhs from Khushab have petitioned to be settled with [Muslim] Tiwanas from their own tahsil rather than with Hindu Jats from Wasirabad."[44]

Although he received little encouragement from his superiors, Hailey worked at improving methods and crop yields. Near Sargodha he founded a twenty-acre farm where selected seed could be grown and better techniques demonstrated.[45] His hobby did not amount to much until after World War I, when a special officer was appointed to take charge of it. "It is an expert's business," Hailey pointed out, "and it will require something more than a knowledge derived from the Cawnpore Hand-books and an imperfect recollection of the Georgics [Vergil]."[46] Yet his enthusiasm may have been more infectious than he realized. According to oral tradition locals called him the Arain (a noted market-gardening caste) of England.

To the Indian army and the Punjab government the priorities on the Jhelum were military and political: breeding good horses and paying off supporters. Naturally the colonization officer's main concern was economic. "It is not perhaps too much to venture a hope," Hailey wrote sarcastically, "that Government will some day be able to devise a more appropriate method of rewarding the retired Meteorological Observer, the superannuated ticket collector, or the blameless but very unagricultural individual whose life has been passed in the

[41] AR (1904–5), IOR V/24/2479.
[42] Douie to Hailey, 9 January 1905, Punj. Bd. of Rev., Rev/Ag (Irrig), April 1905, No. 5.
[43] Rivaz comment on AR (1904–5), IOR V/24/2479.
[44] AR (1901–2), IOR V/24/2478.
[45] See speech in reply to address from Shahpur District Agricultural Association, Sargodha, 13 December 1926, HPI/44.
[46] AR (1903–4), IOR V/24/2478.

cloistered retreats of the Accountant-General's Office." Even though their names might be on the approved list of agricultural tribes, such folk made poor colonists. "One by one they appear, full of forlorn memories of Anarkali or the Chadni Chauk," the famous bazaars of Lahore and Delhi, "and beg plaintively for land near a Railway Station," the best land being "that from which they can get away soonest."[47] The young colonization officer's concern was getting the best colonists. In the 1920s, however, when he was governor of the Punjab, Hailey would insist on maintaining what he called the East's settled habit of rewarding one's friends.[48]

By the time Hailey left the Jhelum in March 1907 the nucleus of Sargodha had been built according to the segregated pattern typical of British India: the civil station with offices, treasury, courthouse and jail; the civil lines, including houses for the colonization officer and other officials, a tennis club for Europeans, and a church; the Indian quarter, with less stringent sanitary requirements, a market, vernacular school, and mosque. The railroad had reached the town in 1903 and a hospital was planned.[49] Prakash Tandon described Sargodha, where his family moved from Gujrat district just after the Great War: "planned, well laid out . . . plenty of light and air. Its streets and lanes were wide and straight. Somehow the clean, hygienic, impersonal layout seemed to mould the population into the pattern that the settlement officer of the late Victorian period [*sic*] must have had in mind." Dancing-girl establishments were moved farther out of town; the municipal authorities even tried to ban fireworks. Yet "Sargodha was drab and had none of the colour of Gujrat, neither the city nor its people."[50] Apparently only one thing was wrong with Hailey's model town. It wasn't Indian!

When he was made colonization officer in 1901 Malcolm Hailey had been twenty-nine. When he departed in March 1907 he had just turned thirty-five. Although Oxford was called a university for imperialism, it was on the Jhelum that he underwent his truly formative period, developing attitudes and patterns of behavior that remained with him all his life. Far from higher authority, in a new society to which he was literally giving birth, he was on his own. All his assistants were Indian, and he became accustomed to conducting all his business in Punjabi or Urdu, speaking English only with his wife. Even his son's playmate was Indian, a boy the Haileys virtually adopted named Ahmed Shah. Hailey would pay his school fees and use his influence to get jobs, first for Ahmed Shah and then for his son, in the provincial civil service. Apparently the last letter he ever wrote was a request to have the close, long-term relationship between the two families placed on record.[51]

---

[47] Ibid.
[48] See Hailey note on colonization of Nili Bar, 15 January 1928, Punjab Bd. of Revenue, 304/14/00/21.
[49] AR (1905–6), IOR V/24/2479.
[50] Prakash Tandon, *Punjabi Century*, p. 161.
[51] S. Mohammad Shah to Librarian, IOL, 17 December 1966, HPI/60.

There was nothing unusual in young men being thrust into positions of great responsibility. With its 1,250 members spread out thinly across a vast subcontinent of 250 million inhabitants the Indian Civil Service had no alternative. Hailey's formal education had been deliberately shaped to prepare him to exercise authority. But for the fact that his intellectual credentials had impressed his superiors, he might well have been given lonely administrative responsibility even sooner. Clearly he was not in awe of the job. But we may be.

As Philip Mason pointed out it would have been virtually impossible for any young man from such a background and with such an education not to develop in India an authoritarian personality, an "expectation that anyone would do whatever you told him." What Mason called the henchman motif permeated Indian society; "it was impossible not to be affected by this network of hereditary authority, just as it was impossible not to be affected by the idea of caste." Young Englishmen found themselves "superimposed on top of this system, like an additional caste, as patrons or protectors above the whole network." The machine worked automatically: "You would find that a junior official had mysteriously attached himself to you and become your henchman because you had given him a word of praise or encouragement; not only that, but everywhere, anywhere, at a word or a gesture, you could summon temporary henchmen who would do anything you told them."[52] The Punjab ideology, into which Hailey had been indoctrinated by men like Thorburn, made a virtue of paternalism. It was on the Jhelum, however, that the young officer became accustomed to giving orders and to being obeyed. It was this experience that made Malcolm Hailey into an imperial ruler.

Because the irrigation canals had such high propaganda value the Jhelum became a routine stop on the Indian grand tour. A. C. Macleod Wilson, James Wilson's wife, described the tents where the colonization officer's family lived while Sargodha was being built; at night, under the stars, Alexandra Hailey would get out her guitar and sing.[53] And Sidney Low, in a volume commemorating a tour by the Prince of Wales, described Hailey as "a man with . . . force of character, clearness of insight, relentless industry, and restrained enthusiasm." The Jhelum got a whole chapter called "The Blossoming of the Desert." It was a plantation in the eighteenth-century sense and the colonization officer had a blank sheet: "He is the mandatory of a despotic Government, intended to act the part of a beneficent autocrat himself." Here villages of Muslims, Hindus, and Sikhs were being molded into a society: "And here the structure stands today, in its outlines and relative proportions, pretty much as it may be found a century or two hence, save for some cataclysm of Nature or politics: a complete little province, a miniature state, thriving and self-sustaining."

Not suspecting how prophetic the phrase "political cataclysm" would sound half a century later, the writer returned to the founders: "The men at the head

---

[52] Philip Mason, *A Shaft of Sunlight: Memories of a Varied Life* (London: Andre Deutsch, 1978), p. 97.
[53] A. C. Mcleod Wilson, *Letters from India* (Edinburgh: Blackwood, 1911), pp. 252–66.

of these irrigation colonies must know the natives thoroughly, and they should love them – wisely, but perhaps not too well. They must have that combination of deep sympathy and equable justice wherein lay the strength of the great Anglo-Indian administrators in the past." Gradually one began "to understand something of the meaning of paternal government. He is judge, governor, supreme adviser, tax-collector, chief magistrate, agricultural expert, and general admonisher, of his subjects." As he made his rounds on horseback voluble crowds gathered. Lordly and aloof "he lets them chatter."[54] In the common phrase he was "Something in India." Beneath the heavy cant and succession of clichés there was just enough truth in all that to help explain why the colonization officer would one day ask to be called Lord Hailey of Shahpur.

---

[54] Sidney Low, *A Vision of India* (London: Smith, Elder, 1906), pp. 183–92. Although I have reproduced Low's portrait, Hailey would not have been aloof toward "his" Indians.

3

~~~~~~

From Sargodha to Delhi, 1907–1912

After leaving his canal colony Hailey became chief secretary to the Punjab government. The following summer he joined the Government of India's finance department, and in 1911 he was appointed to a committee to prepare for the Delhi Durbar during the coronation visit of the king-emperor George V. Although enteric (typhoid) fever forced him to miss the ceremony, the durbar assignment brought him into close contact with the viceroy, Lord Hardinge, who was sufficiently impressed to make him the first chief commissioner of the new Delhi capital enclave. Delhi put him in line for further assignments in the central government – finance member and then home member of the Viceroy's Council – and finally for the job he wanted most, the governorship of the Punjab.

Even though he was being promoted, with a good increase in salary, Hailey must have left Sargodha with mixed feelings. On the Jhelum he had been a petty despot with direct authority over thousands of people. In Lahore or Calcutta he would be just another paper-pushing bureaucrat. The biographer must also regret the move, the effect of which is to reduce the amount of available evidence very severely. Whereas the colonization officer submitted his own reports, the chief secretary of the Punjab or deputy secretary in the finance department wrote only notes. And these, on the apparent assumption that the internal working of administrative offices could be of no conceivable interest, the indefatigable record-weeders at the National Archives of India have destroyed almost entirely. Only when he became chief commissioner of Delhi in 1912 did Hailey have a staff under him and begin to save his papers systematically. The canal-colony phase of his life is comparatively well documented. In the period covered by this chapter it is as though the man had gone underground.

The year 1907, when Hailey was chief secretary in the Punjab, was a pivotal one in modern Indian political history. There were two primary foci. In Calcutta, where Surendranath Banerjea had founded the British India Association in 1881, a well-organized boycott of British goods called the Swadeshi movement was at its height, directed against Lord Curzon's partition of Bengal. The other focus was in the west, in the financial center of Bombay and in Poona, formerly the capital of the Maratha empire, where the Indian National Congress had been founded in 1885. In 1907 the extremist leader B. G. Tilak, whose militant program had split the Congress, was being tried for sedition and his explosive courtroom speeches were filling newspapers all across India. Although the Punjab still lagged behind the presidencies – as the provinces of Bengal, Madras, and Bombay were called – by the late 1880s, when the young Rudyard Kipling was a Lahore newspaperman, it was no longer the backwater the Lawrences had taken over in the early 1850s. It had an English-educated middle class, a lively press, and active branches of what the government would regard as the spearhead of the Punjab disturbances of 1907, the Arya Samaj.

As though it were deliberately setting the stage for the half-century celebration of the Great Mutiny of 1857, the Punjab government was energetically creating local issues. Early in the year the lieutenant governor's council passed a Colonisation of Government Lands Act, which clarified the status of colonists as tenants at will, enlarged the already substantial powers of colonization officers, and specified that their decisions could not be challenged in court. Many of the act's provisions were retroactive, so the Government of India's lawyers had been dubious. Moreover, although in the case of the Jhelum the bill largely codified existing practice, in the older Chenab colony the tenants' anger at the erosion of their customary rights was not hard to foresee. It was also easy to predict that outrage would spread through the central Punjab villages and, because many colonists were military pensioners, to the army. Simultaneously water rates were being increased. The tenants owed their prosperity and status entirely to the beneficence of the government, the Punjab authorities concluded, and they could therefore have no justifiable complaint. Naturally the canal colonists saw matters rather differently.

If provoking confrontations with peasants and soldiers was somewhat unusual behavior for the government, rows with the Lahore intelligentsia were more routine. The dispute in 1907 involved a European's murdering an Indian servant, being found guilty of a minor charge by a jury of his countrymen, a reasonably accurate if somewhat inflammatory statement of the facts by a local opposition newspaper, the *Punjabee,* and the prosecution of its proprietor and editor for promoting enmity between the races of His Majesty's subjects. It happened, however, that the demi-official *Civil and Military Gazette* was just then printing a series of viciously racist letters from Europeans, which were indeed calculated to promote interracial bitterness. Bearing in mind the extreme difficulty of persuading a European jury to vote for a conviction, however, the government had decided not to prosecute. It was all rather messy. As Lieutenant Governor Sir Denzil Ibbetson later admitted "we did not come into court with clean hands."[1]

---

[1] Sir Denzil Ibbetson, minute of 30 April 1907, in Danda Singh, ed., *History of the Freedom Movement in the Punjab,* Vol. 4: *Deportation of Lala Lajpat Rai and Sardar Ajit Singh* (Patiala: Punjab University Press, 1978), pp. 3–13. The best accounts of the 1907 disturbances are Imran Ali, *The Punjab Under Imperialism,* and Gerald Barrier, "Punjab Politics and the Disturbances of 1907" (unpublished Ph.D. dissertation, Duke University, 1966). There is also a useful collection of documents edited by Sri Ram, *Punjab in Ferment* (New Delhi: Chand, 1971).

These issues drove the Punjab disturbances of 1907. First in Lahore and Amritsar, then in Lyallpur and other canal-colony towns, finally throughout the center of the province from whence the colonists had come, protest meetings were held, attended by soldiers of all three religions. According to police reports speeches were colorful and seditious. In strikingly similar language petitions demanded that the government withdraw the colonization acts, return water rates to their previous level, and abandon the *Punjabee* prosecution. Otherwise rents and water rates – the major sources of the government's revenue – would be withheld. As Ibbetson advised the viceroy, once a no-rent campaign gathered steam it was hard to see exactly what the government could do about it.

Facing what was an apparently concerted effort to arouse the province's notoriously excitable peasants, the local government asked for emergency powers including authority to deport the two men it regarded as the ringleaders: Lajpat Raj and Ajit Singh. Late in May, the Viceroy's Council and India Office having objected to its retroactive clauses, the colonization act was disallowed. At the same time the local government announced the postponement of the water-rate increase pending further study.[2] When Punjab officials pleaded that they would lose face if they had to back down, the commander in chief, Lord Kitchener, retorted that the colonists' holdings were being "turned into English model farms and model villages against their will, by faddists who have evidently little consideration for the feelings, religion and contentment of these poor cultivators of the soil who have thus come under their grandmotherly legislation."[3] Poor cultivators indeed! The Punjab government was being upbraided in the language of the Punjab school.

Also at issue were the deportations of Lajpat Rai and Ajit Singh. Although conspiracies were difficult to prove, Ibbetson acknowledged, there was really no doubt about this one. In May the Government of India approved. Lajpat Rai was arrested at once, but Ajit Singh remained free until early in June, by which time the agitation had long since passed its peak. In the autumn the secretary of state, Lord Morley, ordered the two men released. Although they returned in triumph, however, the province remained quiet.[4]

That in outline is the Punjab disturbances of 1907. The most interesting and controversial question has always been the government's conspiracy thesis, which centered on the Lahore branch of the Arya Samaj. The Aryas were a reform movement founded by the guru Dayanand in the 1870s. They were monotheists and accepted only the Vedas as sacred texts, eliminating later works including even the *Bhagavad Gita*. They attacked caste, favored the emancipation of women, encouraged education, and generally aimed to transform Hinduism into a religion fit for a modern, progressive society. Supposedly such objectives were not entirely incompatible with British values. Ever since the

---

[2] Sri Ram, *Punjab in Ferment,* pp. 416–18 and passim.
[3] Kitchener note, 20 May 1907, ibid., pp. 411–13.
[4] Danda Singh, *Deportation,* pp. 267–8 and passim.

Mutiny of 1857–8, however, the Government of India had actively discouraged the sort of reformist intervention that had helped to provoke it, and any group attempting to force the pace of social change aroused the authorities' suspicion. Certainly many Aryas were highly political people. Was the Arya Samaj an essentially religious organization with political overtones? Or was it the other way around?[5]

The allegation that agitators led by Ajit Singh, a former tutor of Persian in Lahore, were circulating through the canal colonies is not in dispute. According to police reports the government was said to be deliberately spreading plague. If the urine of the Indian people could be collected in one tank, one speaker was quoted, the feringhi (Westerners) would all be drowned in it.[6] In a symbolic anniversary year such language naturally alarmed the authorities. Was all this furor simply the result of an error in choosing to prosecute the *Punjabee* for promoting racial antagonism rather than for simple sedition? The product of bad timing and worse publicity in the case of the colonization act and the water rates? The work of a few unknown agitators?[7] The government was faced, Ibbetson concluded in April 1907, with a fanatical conspiracy, organized and financed by an Arya Samaj faction led by Lajpat Rai, a Hindu lawyer who had converted from Islam. Although the evidence was admittedly circumstantial, Ibbetson was confident: Remove the central directors from the scene and the agitation would collapse. Since the canal-colony revolt did wind down after the deportations, the conspiracy theory became self-fulfilling.[8]

The conspiracy allegation remained controversial. The *Times* correspondent Valentine Chirol devoted a chapter of his influential book, *Indian Unrest*, to the Arya Samaj, agreeing with the Punjab government that it was a politically subversive organization masquerading as a religious movement.[9] The Sedition (Rowlatt) Committee of 1918 wrote as though the hypothesis had never been in doubt.[10] Census reports from the rival United Provinces were scornful, however, and by 1921 even the Punjab census conceded that the hypothesis remained unproven.[11] The historians of the event agree that in the spring of 1907

---

5 The standard work on the Arya Samaj is Kenneth W. Jones, *Arya Dharm: Hindu Consciousness in 19th-Century Punjab*. See also Lajpat Rai, *A History of the Arya Samaj*, ed. Sri Ram Sharma (Calcutta: Orient Longman, 1967), and Kripal C. Yadav, *Arya Samaj and the Freedom Movement* (New Delhi: Manohar, 1988).

6 Reports of speeches in Danda Singh, *Deportation*, appendixes, pp. 14 ff.

7 The word "agitator" is, of course, loaded with value judgments. Like other authorities, the British used it to cast doubt on the motives and legitimacy of those who were leading popular resistance against them. It seems unnecessarily pedantic to put the word in quotation marks every time it appears. Anyway, men like Gandhi or Nehru would have agreed that that was precisely what they were doing.

8 Ibbetson note, Danda Singh, *Deportation*, pp. 3–13. See Lajpat Rai, *Writings and Speeches*, ed. Vijaya C. Joshi, 2 vols. (Delhi: University Publishers, 1966), and *Autobiographical Writings*, ed. V. C. Joshi (Delhi: University Publishers, 1965).

9 Valentine Chirol, *Indian Unrest* (London: Macmillan, 1910), pp. 106–17.

10 *Report of the Sedition (Rowlatt) Committee* (1918; reprinted, Calcutta: New Age, 1973), pp. 141 ff.

11 E.A.H. Blunt, *United Provinces Census Report* (1911), pp. 132–40.

the Punjab government panicked. Assuming that peasants were incapable of mounting a concerted protest themselves, unwilling to accept that the true leaders were nobodies with no previous records as agitators, the authorities manufactured a conspiracy thesis, then gathered and cooked the evidence to support it. The two alleged comrades in arms, Lajpat Rai and Ajit Singh, turn out to have been enemies. Although the government perceived close coordination, the rural and urban protests remained largely autonomous and distinct. And the canal-colony unrest died down in June, not because the accused ringleaders had been deported, but because the government had removed the colonists' specific and quite limited grievances.[12]

Because no internal office papers survive from this period, there is nothing to indicate any role the chief secretary of the Punjab government may have played in this incident or precisely how he reacted to it at the time. Hailey may have drawn some quiet satisfaction from the canal-colony revolt, which demonstrated that his warnings about the unpopularity of primogeniture and other regulations had been extremely well founded.[13] Despite the absence of contemporary documentation, however, it is clear he embraced the conspiracy thesis, which he would cite repeatedly during later confrontations with the Congress. There is also no doubt that the canal-colony revolt impressed him profoundly. Like Sir Denzil Ibbetson he realized that, although they might be slow to move, the Indian peasantry represented a powerful and virtually irresistible force, a fertile field for nationalist politicians and therefore a priority for the government. For Hailey 1907 strongly reinforced the doctrine of the Punjab school. It was the benchmark political experience of his life.

∞∞∞∞∞∞

When Hailey transferred from the Punjab secretariat to the finance department of the Government of India in July 1908 – the summer headquarters of both governments were in Simla – he shifted from one emergency to another: one of the most severe financial storms in modern Indian history. In the autumn of 1907 it had become apparent that widespread monsoon failures would cause poor harvests. Because trade and railways depended on agriculture, a commercial depression and sharp fall in government revenue were also taking place. Simultaneously an American bank crisis was sending shock waves through the world economy, creating an insatiable demand for precious metals and putting

---

[12] Barrier, "Punjab Politics," and Imran Ali, *Punjab Under Imperialism*, differ slightly in degree, Imran being still more emphatic in arguing for the autonomy of the rural agitation. At the time, the interest of the alleged conspirators was to prove their innocence. After 1947, however, the objective of Lajpat Rai's supporters was to find as much evidence of revolutionary activity as possible. Despite several collections of primary documents that have been compiled on this celebrated event, however, no evidence supporting the conspiracy thesis has come to light.

[13] Jhelum AR, IOR V/24/2479. Hailey's testimony before the investigating committee is not available.

gold-exchange currencies such as the rupee under extreme pressure. Thus, witnesses before the Royal Commission of 1913 agreed, the country was exposed to two of the three possible sources of squeeze: internal depression and international financial chaos. Fortunately, 1907–8 having been years of peace, the third factor did not come into play.[14]

During the summer of 1908, when the gold reserve in London was falling at the dizzy rate of up to a million pounds a week, the crisis was at its height. The new deputy secretary would have been exposed to much heated debate. Too much control and day-to-day decision making were centered in London, Indian critics protested angrily; home charges (the secretary of state's expenses for pensions, the cost of the Indian Office in London, interest payments, purchases of military or railway equipment) were outrageously high; India's stolen gold was supposedly being used to stabilize interest rates in the City of London. The general effect of the financial system imposed on India, argued members of what was called the Bombay school, was to keep its economy poor, short of investment capital, dependent, and underdeveloped. All very valuable reading for a future finance member. But the important policy decisions were being made above and beyond him. Hailey's own concerns were getting and spending: that is, the details of the Indian budget.

The finance department had two divisions, the military and ordinary branches, the latter being Hailey's. The climax of the budget process came each March when the finance member delivered the annual budget speech to the Governor-General's Council. If the sequence could be said to have a beginning, it was November, when prospects for the winter crop could be forecast. By early January, having thrashed out questions about whether an expected surplus should be used to reduce taxation or to modernize the army, pay off railway loans, and so on, a draft budget was sent to London, where the secretary of state had power either to veto or to require adjustments. Meanwhile the department prepared a program of capital expenditure, some of which was covered by taxation, the rest by borrowing. Again the secretary of state, who was responsible for protecting India's credit standing in the London money market, had to approve.

Still in early January the department received draft budgets from the provincial governments, and these had to be checked against district crop estimates. The main items of imperial expenditure also had to be examined closely. The commander in chief could be expected to paint a dark picture of Russian designs on Afghanistan and the army's desperate need for manpower and equipment. The obvious response was that G. K. Gokhale, the leader of the Council's unofficial members, would be presenting an equally grim vision of an Indian peasantry groaning under a heavy burden of taxation that had been levied for British not Indian purposes. Customs and railway revenue, which

---

[14] Royal Commission on Indian Finance and Currency, PP, 1914 [Cd. 7069], *19–20*. The classic account is John Maynard Keynes, *Indian Currency and Finance*, volume 1 of his *Collected Writings* (London: Macmillan, 1971).

depended on agricultural prospects, were hard to predict. Complicating matters still further was opium, which had long been a windfall monopoly for Indian financiers but which was now subject to international negotiations. Depending on how the talks went, opium might boom or bust.

About the middle of January the India Office's estimates were received, covering home charges, interest payments, and the like, after which revised estimates went back to London. Once more the finance department went through district forecasts of the crop and revenue situation, as well as the military, railway, and other demands, and made one last guess on opium. By the middle of February the draft financial statement had been prepared. On budget day the viceroy gave a general report on the state of the Indian empire, it being customary for unofficial members to offer criticisms.

After 1909, when the Morley–Minto reform scheme (named, respectively, for the secretary of state and the viceroy) increased the unofficial membership of the Council and extended its powers of debate and legislation, resolutions could be proposed on any item, and although the government did not have to accept these it was ordinarily considered good form to offer a reasoned reply. The department therefore went through the estimates one last time, perhaps conceding a point or two and making last-minute adjustments in ways and means according to the latest forecasts. Late in March the budget went to the Council, which could still debate although it could propose no changes. By that time the summer crop was already in the ground. If the monsoon should fail, however, the land revenue would have to be reduced in districts where famine was declared, and both railway and customs proceeds would dry up. Indian finance was complex, mysterious, and controversial. And it was all, as Finance Member Sir Guy Fleetwood Wilson put it, a gamble in rain.[15]

In 1919–22 Hailey would be presented with one of the most difficult crises ever to confront a finance member of the Government of India. He had received a generalist's education, reading classics at Oxford, and his formative adult experience had been on the Jhelum. As deputy secretary of the ordinary branch he was at the heart of the budget-making process. He mastered the jargon and the routine – complex, Byzantine, in many ways unique – of Indian finance. In England, however, Treasury officials or the India Office's financial experts were typically professionals with long experience in the City or, like John Maynard Keynes, they had held academic positions in economics. Increasingly finance members of the Government of India were also becoming specialists. His on-the-job training as deputy secretary in 1908–11 was the only preparation Hailey ever received.

In January 1911 Hailey was named treasurer of the preparation committee for the Coronation Durbar of the king-emperor George V, which would be held

---

15 Evidence of Bhupendra Nath Mitra, Royal Commission on Indian Finance, PP, 1914 [Cd. 7069], 19, 710–12. Mitra was assistant secretary and budget officer in the finance department, Government of India. During the summer, people in Calcutta gambled on the day the water in a certain cistern would reach a particular level.

in Delhi at the end of the year. Although notable state occasions had been held there before – the Prince of Wales's visit in 1876, Lytton's Durbar in 1877, when Victoria had been crowned Empress of India in absentia, Curzon's in 1903, another for the Prince of Wales (now George V) in 1905 – this would be the first visit by a reigning British monarch and the Raj meant to make the most of it. Prosaic, phlegmatic Europeans could hardly imagine the symbolic importance the East attached to royalty, the official account explained; at least for the time being unrest would be subsumed in an atmosphere of joy that would leave none of the king-emperor's Indian subjects untouched.[16] Besides, a cynic might have observed, His Majesty's British subjects rather liked a good show themselves.

Under the chairmanship of Sir John Hewett, the durbar committee had a budget of over half a million pounds, which was Hailey's direct responsibility. The task was formidable. The former Mughal capital of Delhi was now a city of a quarter of a million, but it had no paved footpaths, perhaps a dozen motorcars, and fewer than thirty telephone subscribers. Its water and sanitation services were primitive. It would have to be cleaned up and some of the streets would need widening. Because the official durbar participants would temporarily double its population the city would obviously be unable to absorb them. So, in the traditional Indian manner, they would camp. But the site of Curzon's show in 1903 would have been too small. The new tract consisted of forty-five square miles. The part of it that lay along the Jumna River would need draining, and villagers who were moved would have to be compensated. Virtually everything had to be laid on: water and sanitation facilities, flower gardens, roads, temporary rail lines, telegraph and electricity, food for people and animals, thousands of tents. Unofficial Indian visitors, of whom estimates would range as high as a million – holy men, merchants and craftsmen, flag-waving schoolchildren – were expected to look after themselves. Security arrangements had to be tight, some three hundred local badmashes (troublemakers) being locked up for the occasion.[17]

The array of detailed decisions and paperwork can be imagined. So can the scene, as thousands of workmen and their families toiled through one of the hottest summers on record. The durbar is remembered for the king-emperor's surprise announcement that the capital would be moved from Calcutta to Delhi and that Lord Curzon's controversial partition of Bengal, which had been a target of fierce agitation for half a dozen years, would be reversed. Hailey's financial management drew praise and he received his first Honour, the CIE (Commander of the Indian Empire). But he did not attend the durbar, having been stricken in November 1911 with enteric (typhoid) fever.

Because Alexandra Hailey happened to be in England the illness can be documented in some detail. According to letters to her from Sir Guy Fleetwood

---

16 *The Historical Record of the Imperial Visit to India, 1911* (London: J. Murray, 1914).
17 Charles Hardinge, *My Indian Years, 1910–1916* (London: J. Murray, 1948), pp. 47–8.

Wilson, the finance member, it was serious enough that a house in Delhi had to be rented for the patient, and only his older brother, H.R.C., of the UP revenue department, was allowed to see him. After the critical twenty-first day Hailey began to recover, and although a relapse followed, by the end of January he was well enough to go on leave: his first trip home since coming out to India seventeen years before and his last until 1922. The attack had been the last in "a succession of bad blows, the plague, stone, Delhi sores," Sir Guy wrote, "and it is most important that his whole system should get a thorough change."[18]

"It does not require much in the way of prophetic power," the retiring lieutenant governor of the Punjab had written to Hailey in 1908, "to see that you will in time rise to the highest distinction that is open to men of our service."[19] It turned out that the durbar committee was Hailey's big break, for it brought him into daily contact with the viceroy, Lord Hardinge. In December 1911 Hailey's superiors in the finance department nominated him for the chief commissionership of the just-established Delhi capital enclave. Although it could not be made official so far in advance, by the time Hailey sailed late in January he had been told the offer was probably safe. "Better times will come," his division chief, Sir James Meston, wrote; "H[is] E[xcellency] and Sir Guy [Fleetwood Wilson] between them are determined to put the future of Delhi in your hands & nobody else's as soon as you are physically fit for the burden. So give yourself up to the quest of health, & let everything else slide."[20]

When Hailey returned from England late in the summer of 1912, Hardinge put the nomination before his executive council. Hailey was "very clever," protested Sir Harcourt Butler, the education member and former lieutenant governor of the United Provinces, "but he has only 17 years service, has not been a District Officer, or, at any rate, has had little or no district experience, is intensely disliked by Natives, and has an impossible wife." The prestige of the new capital would be lowered in the eyes of Indians by the choice of "a man of Hailey's position, who in his own province would be a Deputy Commissioner."[21] The home member Sir Reginald Craddock also protested, if less spitefully.[22]

In 1912, at the age of forty, Malcolm Hailey was indeed still nominally ranked in the third of four grades of Punjab settlement commissioners. Ever since 1901

[18] Fleetwood Wilson to Alexandra Hailey, 14 December 1911.
[19] Sir Thomas Gordon Walker to Hailey, 26 May 1908, HPI/1A.
[20] Meston to Hailey, 28 January 1912, HPI/1A.
[21] Butler to Hardinge, 20 August 1912, Hardinge Papers, vol. 84. These statements are hard to evaluate. Some Indian witnesses before the Hunter Commission would criticize Hailey's administration of Delhi, but that hardly indicates how they might have felt about a deputy secretary in the finance department in 1912. Alexandra Hailey would indeed one day become "impossible." But the decisive turning point in her life would be the tragic death of her daughter, Gemma, in 1922. Before then, the most that can be said is that she may have been somewhat eccentric – and she was not English. Using a wife's alleged deficiencies against her husband is after all a common if despicable tactic, and Butler's main point was seniority.
[22] Craddock to Hardinge, 25 July 1912, ibid.

his appointments had vaulted him over numerous men with more seniority. Now he was to be placed on the same level with the administrators of Assam or Central Provinces, so opposition was natural enough. But Hardinge was adamant and the decision stood. A disappointed competitor told Hailey that he had just read his own obituary notice, except that burial was being postponed so he would go on being a deputy commissioner for another twenty years. "I want you to realise the intense bitterness of my own disappointment," he wrote, "in order that you may appreciate the fact that my heartfelt congratulations mean more than do those of the many who will salute your rising star." At the top of the letter Hailey commented: "I am proud of having received it & admire the man who wrote it."[23]

[23] F. Popham Young to Hailey, 20 September 1912, HPI/1A.

4

~~~~~~

Chief commissioner of Delhi, 1912–1918

In December 1912, Delhi was again the scene of a celebration, this time the state entry of the viceroy Viscount Hardinge into the new capital of the Indian empire. Once more "the whole of Delhi was radiant" and expectant.[1] From the railway station the procession passed through the Lahore gate of the Mughals' Red Fort and on through the city. Just before noon, however, as the viceregal elephant reached the Punjab National Bank in Chadni Chowk bazaar, there was an explosion. "I suddenly felt an upheaval and was thrown forward," Lady Hardinge recalled. With icy calm the viceroy said: "I am afraid that was a bomb."[2]

A police inspector thought he heard shouts from the rooftop of the bank building. Turning his horse he saw yellow fumes coming from the back of the viceroy's howdah; one attendant was killed instantly and another was maimed. Although Hardinge ordered the procession to go ahead, after a few yards he lost consciousness and was taken by car to Viceregal Lodge. The parade then continued on to the reviewing stand, where Finance Member Sir Guy Fleetwood Wilson read the viceroy's speech. Lady Hardinge was unhurt. But shrapnel had struck the back of her husband's right shoulder and torn through the body, missing the lungs but exposing bone and muscle; nails had caused minor injuries to the neck and right hip. Next day the doctor reported that barring complications the fortunate viceroy should be able to work in a month.[3] The bomber or bombers had escaped.

The individual directly responsible for security was the newly appointed first chief commissioner of Delhi. On Christmas Day Malcolm Hailey therefore appeared before the viceroy's executive council, which was sitting as a board of inquiry. Why had special arrangements not been put into effect? Had ordinary precautions been observed? What could be learned about the presumed con-

---

[1] Sir Guy Fleetwood Wilson to Lord Stamfordham (private secretary to the king), 26 December 1912, Fleetwood Wilson Papers, IOL, MSS Eur E 224/2B.

[2] Quoted by Donald W. Ferrell, "Delhi, 1911–1922: Society and Politics in the New Imperial Capital of India" (unpublished Ph.D. dissertation, Australian National University, 1969), pp. 201–2.

[3] Statement by P. Bramley, Deputy Inspector-General of Police, United Provinces, 24 December 1912, IOR L/P&J/6/1216; medical report by Lt. Col. T. R. Roberts, Surgeon to Viceroy, 23 December 1912, NAI, HomPol 96–112/1913.

spiracy? How had the police and other officials behaved? How had the bomber or bombers escaped? Was any punitive action against the neighborhood warranted? Hailey had of course relied on the Criminal Investigation Department (CID), whose director explained that Hardinge himself had insisted on minimal precautions. More elaborate measures would require some twenty-five hundred soldiers, show distrust of local police and people, and make viceregal touring virtually impossible. Besides there had been no reason for apprehension.[4]

In 1911, when the Royal Durbar was being planned, the agitation against the partition of Bengal had already passed its peak. According to the CID's graphs the incidence of violence had been in inverse proportion to the success of organized protest. By 1911, however, violence had receded too; although the authorities had put emergency powers into effect the durbar had passed without incident. Had the Morley–Minto reforms of 1909 improved the atmosphere, the authorities speculated? Perhaps the reversal of the partition of Bengal? As for Delhi itself, Hailey reported that there had been no hint of any trouble, for the city had shown scant interest in politics and had a remarkably low crime rate. Given the same information, David Petrie of the CID testified, he would make the same decision again.[5] According to current regulations, what were classed as ordinary precautions required examination of premises along the route, surveillance of suspects, and personal attendance by the CID. In retrospect it was regrettable – and to modern readers astonishing – that no police had been stationed on rooftops, but that was in the special category. In fact, as the Indian Office noted later, the viceroy's insistence on minimal precautions had obviously been the controlling factor.[6]

Admittedly after the bomb went off there was some confusion. The two Indian CID men kept their heads, moving to secure the building instead of jumping to attend the wounded. It would have been better if one of them had been a European, investigators concluded, not because the Indians were incompetent but because in that case the lieutenant governor of the Punjab, Sir Louis Dane, might have been less likely to order them peremptorily to leave their posts and clear away debris so the procession could continue. Not until perhaps fifteen minutes after the explosion, when a police superintendent took charge from the excitable Sir Louis, did anything useful start to happen, and by that time the criminal or criminals had fled. Because the bank was actually a compound of houses surrounding a courtyard it would have been hard to find and block all exits.

As the investigation dragged on Hailey felt compelled to ask his superiors for an expression of confidence. In the end the responsibility was not fixed for what was agreed to have been a general lapse in judgment. All the available evidence, especially fragments indicating that the bomb was of a type used earlier at

---

[4] Sir Charles Cleveland report, 31 December 1912, Papers re Enquiry into Delhi Bomb Outrage, Fleetwood Wilson Papers, IOL, MSS Eur E 224/20.

[5] Hailey report, 30 December 1912, David Petrie statement, 24 December 1912, ibid.

[6] Seton note, 17 March 1913, IOR, L/P&J/6/1216.

Calcutta and Midnapur, pointed toward Bengal. But investigation of Bengali suspects in Delhi had turned up nothing. Having established that the bomb had come from the bank, Petrie and the local police had obtained a photograph taken by a spectator, from which they hoped to identify faces. All those leads had come within the first week. Since then, virtually nothing. Everything remained as mysterious as it had been half an hour after the bombing.[7]

In fact the CID needed two full years to bring its investigation to a conclusion. According to Petrie's final report in November 1914 the complex, far-flung conspiracy had indeed originated in the Bengal revolutionary movement.[8] By then all but one of the principal suspects had been convicted in a related case, including Basant Kumas Biswas (the actual bomber), Abad Bihari, and a longtime master at Delhi's St. Stephen's College named Amir Chand, all of whom were hanged in 1915. But the mastermind, Rash Bihari Bose, had escaped to Japan and there was no hope of extradition.[9]

Just after the attack an Indian revolutionary in exile in San Francisco hailed "one of the sweetest and loveliest" bombs for many a day. Who could do justice to its moral power? Although true patriots had hoped for a fitting climax at the Royal Durbar of 1911, now at last the lull was over: "May durbars and bombs go together till there are no more durbars on the face of the earth."[10] The Delhi outrage "changes the whole aspect from which we must regard the question of safeguarding State processions," Hailey observed.[11] Security arrangements were indeed tightened. Then the excitement died down and things returned to normal. Whether in colonial regimes or self-governing democracies, if public figures are to have any exposure their safety can never be absolutely guaranteed. Like their Indian successors British officials would continue to run risks. There would be further attacks. Sometimes they would succeed.

∞∞∞∞∞∞∞

[7] Hailey note, 30 December 1912, Fleetwood Wilson to Lord Stamfordham, 15 January 1913, Stamfordham to Fleetwood Wilson, 19 February 1913, Fleetwood Wilson Papers, MSS Eur E 224/20.

[8] See David M. Laushey, *Bengali Terrorism and the Marxist Left: Aspects of Regional Nationalism in India, 1905–1942* (Calcutta: Mukhopadhyay, 1975), and Shaileshwar Nath, *Terrorism in India* (New Delhi: National Publishing House, 1980). See also the Rowlatt report (Government of India, *Report of the Sedition Committee, 1918*), which in Laushey's view probably overrated the organization of the Bengal terrorists, as well as the extent of their activities.

[9] Petrie report, 8 November 1914, NAI, HomPol 11/1914. The fullest account of the investigation is Sangat Singh, *Freedom Movement in Delhi, 1858–1919* (New Delhi: Associated Publishing House, 1972), although he disparages Petrie, who appears to have been extremely competent. See also James C. Ker, *Political Trouble in India: 1907–1917* (1917; Delhi: Oriental Publishers, 1973), pp. 354–9, and the biography of Rash Bihari Bose by Dharmavira, *I Threw the Bomb* (New Delhi: Orient, 1979).

[10] Text of Har Dayal, *Yugantur Circular*, January 1913, in Dharmavira, *Lala Har Dayal and Revolutionary Movements of His Times* (New Delhi: Indian Book Company, 1970), pp. 173–8.

[11] Fleetwood Wilson to Hailey, 24 and 28 December 1912; Hailey to Fleetwood Wilson, 24 December; all in Fleetwood Wilson Collection, IOL, MSS Eur 224/20.

"Delhi is still a name to conjure with," Lord Hardinge wrote in July 1911 when he recommended the transfer of the capital. The ancient seat of Hindu and Mughal dynasties, agreed the secretary of state, enshrined an imperial tradition comparable to Constantinople's or Rome's.[12] To Sir Herbert Baker, one of the architects, the new capital should symbolize the unity and good government that British rule had brought to India by blending the best architecture of East and West.[13] The Delhi Town Planning Committee also wished to pay homage to the peace and dignity of the British Raj.[14] If a new capital were built at all, Sir Harcourt Butler thought, it "should be done on a big scale; something which will impress the Indians with our determination to stay here."[15] The grandiose project would be a millstone round the Indian taxpayer's neck, charged the former viceroy Lord Curzon, who was a strong defender of Calcutta, for once agreeing with Indian politicians like G. K. Gokhale.[16] The controversy would continue until the dedication in February 1931 and even beyond.

In the late nineteenth century, when town planning in India had sometimes resembled a form of warfare, the British had constructed great public buildings in often magnificent Gothic. By the early twentieth century, however, Gothic was no longer fashionable in Britain, and at least some deference needed to be given to Indian taxpayers' reluctance to pay for a capital if it bore no relation to their tradition. But there was more than one Indian tradition, and Indian architecture had decayed under the suffocating weight of cultural imperialism. The absence of world-class Indian architects made it easier to justify the selection of British ones. Fortunately there were plenty of good Indian craftsmen, Hailey told the press, and local marble and sandstone would be employed.

Although lip service would be paid to the Mughal legacy, the classical motif that loomed so large in the imperial mind would be the stronger theme in a blend intended to represent a rapidly changing empire. In 1912 the name was Imperial Delhi, symbolizing symmetry and order imposed on a turbulent subcontinent by British rule, reflecting a state of mind that has been called an illusion of permanence.[17] Fifteen years later "Imperial" was dropped in favor of

---

12 Quoted by Robert G. Irving, *Indian Summer: Lutyens, Baker, and Imperial Delhi* (Delhi: Oxford University Press, 1981), p. 29.

13 Quoted by Thomas R. Metcalf, "Architecture and Empire: Sir Herbert Baker and the Building of New Delhi," in R. E. Frykenberg, ed., *Delhi Through the Ages: Essays in Urban History, Culture and Society* (Delhi: Oxford University Press, 1986), p. 396.

14 Delhi Town Planning Committee, Final Report, PP, 1913, [Cd. 689], 20.

15 Quoted by Narayani Gupta, *Delhi Between Two Empires, 1830–1931: Society, Government and Urban Growth* (Delhi: Oxford University Press, 1981), p. 179.

16 In 1912 Hardinge estimated the new capital could be built in four years at £4 million. Curzon's unfriendly projection of ten years and £11 million was closer to the mark. In 1914, after receiving the report of the Imperial Delhi Planning Committee, Hardinge's budget rose to £6 million. World War I and the postwar financial crisis delayed and almost killed the project. In 1922, when Hailey himself chaired a committee of inquiry, only the fact that so much had already been spent safeguarded its completion, the final cost being more than £10 million. See Report of the New Capital Enquiry Committee, 1922, IOR V/26/780/5.

17 See Francis Hutchins, *The Illusion of Permanence: British Imperialism in India* (Princeton, N.J.: Princeton University Press, 1967).

"New." In 1931 the dedication ceremony would stress the intermeshing of East and West in an era of partnership.[18]

Hailey's role in this undertaking was to coordinate, and in April 1913 he became president of the Imperial Delhi Committee.[19] Its secretary was Geoffrey de Montmorency, Hailey's close friend from their canal-colony days, who also became his assistant commissioner and alter ego.[20] Already de Montmorency had been secretary to the Delhi Town Planning Committee. Waging what Fleetwood Wilson called the battle of the sites – three in all – it had weighed a multitude of factors.[21] The new capital ought to be close, but not too close, to the present city and military cantonments. Some ancient monuments would enhance the image; too many would impede construction and make geometrical designs impossible. The cost of buying out landowners, the quality of soil and water, and shelter from dust storms all had to be taken into account. The northern site along the ridge was rejected on health grounds. A few years earlier its marshiness would have been considered a source of malaria-causing vapors. Now, a decade after Sir Ronald Ross's discoveries, entomologists counted anopheles mosquitoes.[22]

In November 1912, Hardinge recalled in his memoirs, he and Hailey rode to the top of Raisina Hill, which provided a grand view of Old Delhi and the surrounding monuments, with the Jumna River winding like a silver streak in the distance. This was where Government House must be.[23] The site was not man-worn, the town planning committee concurred. Although remains of older Delhis added majesty, they were far enough away so the ground would not be cluttered with tombs and monuments. Room for expansion was practically unlimited and though the new capital would be separate from Old Delhi, it was close enough that communications would be no problem. The cantonment too would be "near but not too near."[24]

Hailey's most difficult problem was the prolonged dispute between the two

18 Irving, *Indian Summer*, pp. 101–11 and passim. See also Thomas Metcalf, *An Imperial Vision: Indian Architecture and Britain's Raj* (Berkeley: University of California Press, 1989).

19 Hailey memorandum, 9 November 1912; resolution of Govt. of India (Home), 25 March 1913: Delhi Archives, Home, A29/1913.

20 Recommending De Montmorency for Commander of the Indian Empire, Hailey explained that his role as secretary had been crucial. Without his efficiency and tact, the Town Planning Committee would not have been able to agree on reports, which De Montmorency himself had written. Hailey to J. H. DuBoulay (private secretary to VR), 12 September 1913, Hardinge Papers, vol. 86.

21 Fleetwood Wilson to private secretary, SS for India, 24 February 1913, Fleetwood Wilson Papers, MSS Eur 224/20.

22 Delhi Town Planning Committee report. Anopheles are one of the varieties of mosquitoes most likely to serve as a vector for malaria.

23 Charles Hardinge, *My Indian Years, 1910–1916*, p. 72. In fact, Hardinge considerably telescoped the decision, which was still being hotly disputed in the winter of 1913. Moreover, Hailey himself was not completely sold on the southern site that was eventually adopted for he argued before the committee on behalf of the northern. DuBoulay to Hailey, 21 February 1913, HPI/1A.

24 Delhi Town Planning Committee report.

architects, Sir Edwin Lutyens (Government House) and Sir Herbert Baker (the Secretariat), which centered on the gradient to be left after the top of Raisina Hill was cut away. Whereas Lutyens wanted his building to command the whole, Baker wanted the Secretariat on an equal plane. In 1913 Lutyens hastily agreed to a scheme incorporating Baker's design. Later, riding up Kingsway (now Raj Path), he discovered that Government House would be hidden from processions and demanded that the whole plan be revised. At one point it seemed that a professional arbitrator might be necessary.[25] When Hardinge sided with Baker on financial grounds Lutyens appealed to the royal family. Although Baker won in the end, the architects' Gilbertian duel endured even beyond the completion of their capital. Although Hardinge spent all he could in an effort to commit his successor, after 1915 the project halted for the rest of the war.[26] Meanwhile the Government of India spent the cold-weather months in Temporary Delhi in the north of the city. During Hailey's period, then, the new capital amounted to plans of the feuding architects, holes in the ground, foundations, and piled-up building materials.

∞∞∞∞∞∞

The old Delhi district in the Punjab had contained three tahsils, or subdivisions: Delhi, Stonepat, and Ballabgarh. Citing Canberra and Washington, D.C., as examples – the latter had originally been only ten square miles — the province's lieutenant governor, Sir Louis Dane, urged that the enclave be restricted to little more than the space required for government buildings. Under Dane's proposal even Old Delhi would remain in the Punjab. Fortunately, for though they have very different characters Old and New Delhi now merge with no real break, the decision went against him.[27] The new capital enclave contained Delhi tahsil and part of Ballabgarh, along with a few square miles taken from Meerut district in the United Provinces – all told nearly six hundred square miles, with a population of some 400,000, of whom about a quarter of a million lived inside the municipal limits of Delhi city.[28]

The Delhi enclave also had three parts: the cantonment, Delhi Municipality, and the Notified Area consisting of the Civil Lines and temporary capital in the north. Although the home member of the Viceroy's Council urged that the whole enclave should be placed under cantonment (military) law, that would have robbed Delhi of even a pretense of self-government and raised a storm of protest. Instead, when Hailey took office each area had its own administrative

---

[25] Hailey to DuBoulay, 3 March 1916; Hardinge to Hailey, 13 March; Hardinge note, 21 March, HPI/1C.

[26] Hardinge to Hailey, 26 June 1915, HPI/1A.

[27] Punjab Govt. to Govt. of India (Home), 20 June 1912; Govt. of India to Punjab, 13 July 1912; Delhi Proceedings, IOR, P8949.

[28] *Census of India* (1921), *15, Punjab and Delhi;* the *Times,* 1 October 1912.

committee. But Delhi's citizens objected so strongly to paying for the Notified Area that a unified Imperial Delhi Committee was constituted. Hailey was on a seesaw with the municipal committee on one end and the Government of India on the other. Divided financial responsibility continued to cause problems, and in 1917 the Imperial Delhi Committee was abolished, its functions being vested directly in the commissioner.[29]

Running the Delhi enclave was much like governing a full-sized province. The land revenue had to be collected, the jail inspected, police corruption kept within tolerable limits, the so-called criminal tribes reported on. After all, however, it was a small-scale operation and analyzing its administration at length would be unnecessarily tedious.[30] Nevertheless, two of Hailey's miscellaneous reports deserve comment.

The first concerned the use of civil courts to realize usurious debts, and though it was a routine inquiry it struck a nerve in a man of the Punjab school. Delhi's courts were indeed enforcing unconscionable contracts, Hailey reported, for unless coercion could be proved they had no choice. Pathan moneylenders were charging menial servants 150–225 percent, while higher-caste *banias*, or moneylenders, typically got 2–3 percent a month from agriculturists. Numerous nefarious schemes – the Persian wheel, the Hundi system – made interest exorbitant if a single payment were missed. The consensus in favor of reform was almost unanimous, the sole exception being moneylenders themselves and the Delhi Bar Association. Among the Indian people at large, he asserted, what mattered were not the political themes favored by "publicists" but more basic issues like the revenue system, police corruption, and the attitude of courts on inheritance or mortgages. British law having taken the brakes off the moneylenders, "it is our administration which has to bear the entire odium." The best corrective was the Punjab Land Alienation Act, Hailey concluded, the work of his mentor, S. S. Thorburn, which had overridden prevailing economic theory and the opposition of powerful interests to win the goodwill of the peasantry.[31]

The second memorandum, a proposal to have a projected Oriental Institute placed in Delhi, is noteworthy only because more than thirty years later its writer would direct the *African Survey*. In view of its long history as a cultural center, Hailey argued – the city where Akbar had encouraged Hindu pandits, where Urdu had developed as a military language, where the Kutb ruins preserved Hindu sculpture, where Raja Jai Singh had built his observatory – Delhi's credentials were far superior to those of the upstart port of Calcutta,

[29] See Scheme for the Administration of the Province of Delhi, 24 September 1912, Delhi Admin. Archives, Home, A29/1913; Proceedings, Chief Commissioner Delhi, 30 September 1913, IOR P9214; report by Deputy Commissioner Delhi on finances of Municipal Committee, 23 October 1913, IOR P9464; Government of India (Public Works) to Chief Commissioner Delhi, 5 February 1917, IOR P10179.

[30] Besides, Gupta, *Delhi Between Two Empires*, is excellent.

[31] Hailey to Govt. of India (Home), 5 October 1914, Delhi Administrative Archives, Home B 305/1914.

which the British themselves had founded less than two centuries before. The president of the British Anthropological Association, James G. Frazier, author of the classic *Golden Bough*, wanted to have an anthropology section. Anthropology in India had been mainly ethnological, Hailey commented, "accounting for types, classifying the elements to which they owe their origin and thus establishing their connection with one of the great families of man," all of which seemed quite irrelevant for an institute that was intended to study the cultural foundations of a great civilization. Anthropology was a general science like medicine, he concluded, "and it would be as little logical to insist on having a special anthropological section as to . . . have a medical section . . . merely because India gives wide opportunities for investigating . . . malaria, kala azar, bubonic plague, cholera and cataract."[32]

In his settlement report of 1901 on the Thal Hailey had demonstrated a lively interest in how people live and do things, how they form and maintain social institutions. By 1913, when he wrote his memorandum, social anthropology was still in its very early stages. In the 1930s, when he was retooling himself to be an Africanist, Hailey would read the work of Bronislaw Malinowski and other social anthropologists. Still later he would chair the International African Institute and serve on the board of the School of Oriental and African Studies. He would become a good deal more respectful of anthropologists. Yet there is something to be said for his brusque statement of 1913. Would anybody have thought of placing an anthropological section in an English institute?

∞∞∞∞∞∞

During the inquiry into the bombing of 1912 Hailey called Delhi apathetic, while police investigators found witnesses hostile and mistrustful. The city had not always been backward. Apart from the distinguished history he cited when he was seeking the Oriental Institute, Delhi had experienced an early-nineteenth-century renaissance.[33] During and after the Great Mutiny of 1857–8, however, the city had suffered an assault from which it required at least a generation to recover. First the mutineers, coming over from Meerut to restore the Mughal emperor, had attacked centers of what was called the New Learning. The British reign of terror had followed: Thousands were hanged or shot, for nearly two years Muslims were excluded, and the question of razing the city was seriously discussed.

Instead it was remade. To the north of the walled Old City, which they allowed to deteriorate, the British built a new town — for their own purposes and in their own image. "Where is Delhi?" gasped an Indian poet. "By God, it

---

32 Hailey to Govt. of India (Education), 26 July 1913, Delhi Proceedings, IOR P9214.
33 The standard work is Thomas Percival Spear, *Twilight of the Mughals* (Cambridge: Cambridge University Press, 1951). See also Gail Minault, "Sayyid Ahmad Dehlavi and the 'Delhi Renaissance,'" in Frykenberg, ed., *Delhi Through the Ages*, pp. 287–98.

is not a city now. It is a camp." Late-nineteenth-century Delhi, wrote its historian, had become "a vast cantonment and an undeveloped civil lines, with the indigenous inhabitants huddled into two-thirds of the walled city and into the ragged western suburbs."[34] Gradually Delhi became one of northern India's leading rail and commercial centers, and durbars were held there. But the enduring legacy of 1857 was reflected in the apathy and sullen hostility the police and Hailey himself had encountered.

Like other parts of the Punjab, Delhi experienced agitation in 1907. By 1912, however, extremism comparable to that of Calcutta or Poona seemed a long way off. What *had* developed was communalism, organized on religious lines although it was not fundamentally religious, a form of ethnicity that like tribalism in modern Africa was both a precondition and an obstacle to nationalism. The Hindu spearhead was the Arya Samaj. Delhi was also a center of the pan-Islamic movement, and by 1909 it had a branch of the Muslim League.[35] Communal rivalry was intense but sporadic, a serious riot in 1886 being the most violent episode. Modern political consciousness in Delhi, then, dates essentially from the period of Hailey's commissionership.

In August 1914 the king-emperor declared the British Empire including India at war. Fortunately for Alexandra Hailey, who took a leading part in organizing the local Red Cross, although her native Italy had been a member of the Triple Alliance it chose to remain neutral, entering the war on the Anglo-French side in 1917. During the Great War India fully justified the jewel-in-the-crown cliché with sacrifices in blood and treasure, sending more than a million soldiers to the Middle East and France and contributing some £130 million in gifts and war loans. Although the subcontinent itself was never threatened directly, with so much of the army away a local rebellion would be serious. The Defence of India Act of 1915 therefore gave local governments sweeping powers, including internment without trial. Although he often acted under orders from the Government of India, Hailey showed no compunctions about employing those provisions. In time the transfer of the capital to Delhi was bound to accelerate its politicization. But it was wartime and he meant to keep the city quiet.

Hailey's fortnightly reports paid close attention to sources of local tension.[36] Because Hindu merchants feared that withdrawals of British troops might

---

34 Gupta, *Delhi Between Two Empires*, p. 30. See also Veena T. Oldenburg, *The Making of Colonial Lucknow* (Princeton, N.J.: Princeton University Press, 1984), which is extremely suggestive on the intense and continuing relationship between imperialism and town planning in northern Indian cities.

35 See Minault, "Sayyid Ahmad Dehlavi"; Barbara D. Metcalf, "Hakim Admal Khan: Rais of Delhi and Muslim Leader," and Kenneth W. Jones, "Organized Hinduism in Delhi and New Delhi," all in Frykenberg, *Delhi Through the Ages*, pp. 287–98, 299–315, 332–50.

36 These fortnightly reports are all in the Deposit class of the Home Political records in the National Archives of India. They are the basic source for two detailed studies: Donald W. Ferrell, "Delhi, 1911–1922," the unpublished dissertation already cited, and Sangat Singh, *Freedom Movement in Delhi, 1858–1919*.

invite attacks from Afghanistan, he tried to reassure them with lantern (slide) lectures and fact sheets. He monitored savings accounts, the panicked exchanges of rupees for silver bullion, the price inflation that was outstripping wages and pressing against fixed incomes. Periodically he intervened, selling grain at fixed prices. He watched falls in exports resulting from the loss of most of the central and eastern European markets. He recorded when the rains came and when they failed. Aware of how religious sentiment might explode – a riot in Cawnpore in 1913 resulting from the government's stubborn destruction of a mosque was a recent reminder – he made lists of sacred sites, graded them carefully, and consulted appropriate religious authorities before acting.[37] Throughout the war, but especially during 1918 when the German offensive nearly succeeded, he reported on subscriptions to war loans. Like the nearby Punjab, the rural part of the Delhi enclave was prime ground for the army. Virtually nothing could stand in the way of recruiting.

The political history of wartime Delhi falls into three phases: first a period of activity centering on the pan-Islamic movement led by the brothers Mohammad and Shaukut Ali; then a two-year lull after the brothers' internment in May 1915; finally, beginning in the summer of 1917, sustained agitation featuring the home rule leagues, the Rowlatt Satyagraha, and Gandhi's noncooperation movement.[38] Although the climax of unrest came after Hailey's transfer in November 1918, it was during his commissionership that Delhi shook off its lethargy and began to become a true capital of India. The growing Indian nationalist movement found him a formidable antagonist.

The agitation led by the Ali brothers centered on the fact that the British Empire, including His Majesty's Muslim subjects, was now at war with the sultan of Turkey, who in his role as caliph was widely regarded as the political head of world Islam.[39] Articles in Mohammad Ali's newspaper, *Comrade*, were clearly intended to damage the war effort, Hailey advised. Since most of them consisted of verbatim extracts of speeches in the British Parliament lifted from the London *Times*, however, it was hard to make out a case against him. In May 1915, the Defence of India Act having removed the inconvenience of having to go to court, he interned the Ali brothers in nearby villages. A few token protests, he reported, but no more.

---

[37] See, for example, Hailey's report to the governing committee of the Jaama Masjid, 31 October 1912, on the proposed surrender and restoration of the Sonhari Mosque. After investigating carefully he concluded that this particular mosque was not needed, that it would block needed roads, that the committee lacked the funds to maintain it, and that local Muslims did not really care about it anyway. Hailey to Government of India (Home), 31 October 1912, Delhi Proceedings, IOR P9203. In 1913–4 there was a dispute concerning the demolition of a wall surrounding the Rakabgunj Gurdwara at Raisina, near the site for the future secretariat building. Sikhs elsewhere in the Punjab became agitated, but Hailey maintained close contact with local Sikhs, who remained calm. See Ferrell, "Delhi, 1911–1922," pp. 178–82.

[38] Ferrell, "Delhi, 1911–1922."

[39] See Gail Minault, *The Khilafat Movement: Religious Symbolism and Political Mobilization in India* (New York: Columbia University Press, 1982).

For nearly two years Hailey's fortnightly bulletins had little to report. Executions in the conspiracy case relating to the assassination attempt against Lord Hardinge; the deaths of many thousands of Indian soldiers in Mesopotamia, where rumors of gross mismanagement turned out to be quite true; the Ghadr revolutionary conspiracy led by Sikhs returning from overseas to the nearby Punjab; inflation, grain shortages, even a declaration of *jihad* (holy war) by the caliph of Turkey against the Christian infidel: any of these might have caused trouble but none did. Delhi's commissioner kept close watch. In July 1916, for instance, he interned Hakim Mohammad Ahmad, a distinguished physician of the city, merely because he suspected that an intended trip to the frontier might have a political object. "It is possible that his actions were harmless," Hailey conceded, admitting that he possessed no evidence at all, "but the air of mystery which surrounds his escapade quite warrants his movements being restricted."[40]

In 1917 Annie Besant in Madras and B. G. Tilak organized home rule leagues patterned after the Irish model. Hailey responded by sealing Delhi off. In February, when the CID informed him that Tilak and Bepin Chandra Pal were planning a lecture tour, he consulted with the lieutenant governor of the Punjab, Sir Michael O'Dwyer, and then prohibited them from entering Delhi at all. Leonora Gmeiner, whom Hailey described as "a school mistress of Theosophical tendencies," founded a local home rule branch. Though its membership remained small and though she appealed to "your real sympathy for the Indian people," he abruptly withdrew the government's grant to her school.[41] The affair had become "complicated by a very serious rumour affecting the morality of the girls" at her school, he advised in studied passive voice, neglecting to mention that newspapers were charging the government with pressing parents to withdraw their daughters.[42]

As the home rule movement gained strength Hailey prohibited meetings outright. In that summer of disasters in France and Mesopotamia, he told the organizers, the reason was "simply that it is undesirable that we should in the Punjab and Delhi, where we are making efforts to secure military assistance from every branch of the population, have meetings the purport of which the general population can only interpret as evidence that the present form of administration is condemned and is shortly to be replaced by purely Indian government." Home rule was "a very attractive cry," he explained, "which naturally appeals to some extent to every Indian, and owes a great deal of its attractiveness to its vagueness." If only the government would put forward a specific program the discussion would become more practical, "and minorities would be in a position to consider how far their interests were likely to be

---

[40] Report for 1st half August 1916.
[41] Quoted by Gupta, *Delhi Between Two Empires*, p. 203.
[42] Report for 2nd half June 1917. On the Gmeiner affair, see Sangat Singh, *Freedom Movement in Delhi*, pp. 241–2.

safeguarded. This is, for the greater part of Muhammadans and Sikhs, the really vital question, and they are unlikely to have any sympathy with a scheme of self-government which left any doubt on the subject."[43] In short: propose reform, the better to divide and rule.

As Hailey knew very well, discussions were going on in Simla and London that would result in the declaration of August 1917 by the secretary of state, Edwin Montagu, promising that India would move progressively toward responsible government and eventual dominion status. Hailey's immediate priority was recruiting. Village headmen, he advised, in a description reminiscent of British navy press gangs in the eighteenth century, were facing "a serious difficulty in the opposition of women. So many of the men have gone that the women are being sent into the fields, and quite apart from any marital or maternal feelings, they resent the enforced labour." Recruiting parties fared better than local officials: "They take their recruits and escape; the village officer has to face the women."[44]

After the Montagu declaration a bit more latitude was allowed for constitutional agitation. Annie Besant and Tilak were released from internment. The local home rule branch, which was now under the leadership of the respected Dr. M. A. Ansari, drew respectable crowds. Nationalist leaders came and went routinely, although Hailey quipped that their speeches were sometimes too moderate for those "who have looked for something even more potent than the stuff served out to them by local fire-eaters."[45] In October 1917 a fracas occurred when Hindu and Muslim processions were kept apart during religious festivals: essential to prevent communal violence, declared the Delhi administration; high-handed interference with the assertion of Indian national fraternity, protested Hindu organizers, who urged Muslim shop owners to join in a hartal (general closing). Hailey was relieved to report that the latter's attitude was "correct."[46] On through the desperate, climactic year of 1918 the home rule agitation continued to build. But the war loan subscriptions and the recruits kept coming.

Neither the fortnightly reports nor the actions of Delhi's chief commissioner, then, displayed any great sympathy toward Indian nationalism during the period when it was beginning to transform itself into an organized popular movement. Hailey censored newspapers, interned leaders, sealed the city off from outside agitators, and harassed the local home rule league. According to his own testimony the recruiting campaign was intense and high-handed. In the aftermath of the Rowlatt Satyagraha of 1919, when police firing in the city killed five and injured many others, some witnesses cited the oppressive wartime regime as a cause. Although that indictment is not very persuasive – there were grievances everywhere in India; sometimes there was violence, sometimes not; the decisive

---

[43] Report for 1st half July 1917. [44] Report for 2nd half July 1917.
[45] Report for 2nd half March 1918. [46] Report for 2nd half October 1917.

factor was how local authorities responded to the immediate situation – Hailey did indeed run a tight ship.[47] He was, however, carrying out the policy of the Government of India and His Majesty's Government. When their policy shifted in 1917, permitting more latitude, his did too.

Hailey's own explanation stressed the circumstances. It was wartime, an extreme emergency. Millions of young men including Indians were fighting and dying. His job was to keep his city quiet and maintain the level of recruitment. He did that with a minimum of outright conflict and apparently without a single death from police firing on crowds. With the empire's fate in the balance, in his view, temporary curtailments of political freedom and civil rights were fully justified.

Fortnightly bulletins or actions taken during an emergency do not necessarily reflect deeper attitudes toward Indian nationalism. Hailey did however write two extended statements on the subject. The first was in 1915, when it was already apparent that some changes would be necessary but before the home rule leagues had begun to build up pressure. The second, a note on Lionel Curtis, was actually written forty years later. More than a mere recollection it was an attempt to understand this pivotal period in the historical perspective of two world wars and of what by then was Hailey's own experience of having lived through two nearly complete cycles of nationalism and recolonization, Indian and African.

Hailey wrote the first statement in response to a circular from Lord Hardinge. Indian publicists were calling for advances earned by their country's sacrifices, the viceroy pointed out, adding as Macaulay might have put it that the agitation proved the success of British rule. Some changes might be in order: commissions for Indian officers, removal of the cotton excise, limited extension of the Morley–Minto reforms, more Indian civil servants, and so on. Indians were not hard to govern, Hardinge concluded, provided they felt that Britain sympathized with their legitimate aspirations – though why he thought such relatively minor adjustments would make any appreciable difference was not entirely clear.[48]

Boons capturing the imagination of the masses and concessions to the politically conscious would both be necessary, Hailey responded. But it was "no longer possible to represent the 'intelligenzia' as a class which represents no body but itself and voices no views but its own." The political ferment now involved classes formerly apathetic. No longer merely a negative response to British rule, it was part of "a growing belief in the possibility of a social, moral and political 'resorgimento' of the East." The revolt of Asia was already a

---

[47] See P. G. Robb, *The Government of India and Reform: Policies Towards Politics and the Constitution, 1916–1921* (Oxford: Oxford University Press, 1976), pp. 172–3. The fullest account of the events in Delhi is by Donald W. Ferrell, "The Rowlatt Satyagraha in Delhi," in Ravinder Kumar, ed., *Essays on Gandhian Politics: The Rowlatt Satyagraha of 1919* (Oxford: Clarendon Press, 1971), pp. 189–235.

[48] Hardinge circular (draft), 30 August 1915, HPI/1B.

fundamental force of the twentieth century, and "it appears to be sound states-manship to take every reasonable opportunity to meet this growing feeling of responsibility and independence." Not only Britain's own idealistic principles but ordinary prudence suggested that this feeling should not be allowed "to degenerate into one of hopeless and incurable race antagonism." Some observers feared that concessions would be dangerous. The real danger, he insisted, was not making concessions but delaying them unreasonably.

Although ordinary people had made no definite demands, Hailey continued, their contentment was crucial. Reasonable nationalist aspirations should be no threat, "but until we can be certain that the ordinary man in India is strongly with us, extremist agitators will always be an anxiety. They cease to be, as soon as we have secured the active instead of the passive good will" of the masses. In fact, he judged, reflecting the lull of late 1915, extremism seemed to be waning, the government had "held on for a year of anxious war without showing any signs of 'nerves,'" and Hindus had "come, as a body to learn the value of our protection." When it came to specifics Hailey was no bolder than the viceroy: certainly commissions for Indian officers, perhaps longer land leases?[49]

It is important to remember that this note was written in 1915 rather than two years later, when, as Hardinge's successor Lord Chelmsford put it, what was radical six months before had become hopelessly reactionary.[50] Yet Hailey's appraisal was profoundly ambivalent. Some of it – the recognition that India's political development was part of an Asian awakening, the acknowledgment that educated leaders could not be dismissed as exotics with no local following, the argument that although concessions might invite pressure for further ones it was still more dangerous to delay them – was progressive. But the assumption that if only the government looked after the real India it had nothing to fear from extremists reflected his Punjabi roots. As he fully recognized at least by the early 1930s, Indian politicians possessed a degree of influence over their countrymen no alien government could hope to match.

Although the note of 1958 on Lionel Curtis might be one of the most valuable personal memoirs in existence on the evolution of the Commonwealth, it belongs rather to a life of Curtis than of Hailey.[51] In a score of dense, single-spaced pages, which demonstrate the memory and powers of concentration he retained at eighty-six, Hailey traced in detail his friend's earlier career in South Africa, his involvement with India in 1915–19, the context of British and Indian attitudes of that period, and the evolution and working of the much maligned transitional system known as dyarchy.

In 1909, it seemed, during a trip to Canada, Sir William Marris (later a lieutenant governor of UP) had persuaded Curtis that, however distant, self-government was the only intelligible objective of British policy in India. Al-

---

[49] Hailey response to Hardinge circular, September 1915, ibid.
[50] Robb, *Government of India and Reform*, p. 72, quoting Chelmsford to Chamberlain, May 1917. See also Sir Algernon Rumbold, *Watershed in India: 1914–1922* (London: Athlone Press, 1979).
[51] Deborah Lavin's biography of Curtis is being published by the Clarendon Press.

though such a vision could be traced back to Macaulay and beyond, it had remained just that – visionary. Nor had Indian politicians appeared to be thinking all that hard about the subject either. Not until the Lucknow Pact of 1916, when Congress and the Muslim League reached agreement on proportional representation for the minority community, did the two organizations put forward a united demand for home rule. Seeking a logical basis for India's continuing role in a projected Commonwealth of fully autonomous nations, Curtis injected a fresh perspective. He also changed the plane of discussion, shaping the language of the debate at least until Motilal Nehru's independence constitution of 1928. It was Curtis, Hailey thought, who influenced Indian nationalists to concentrate their demands on dominion status.

Dyarchy, under which some departments in provincial administrations were transferred to Indian ministers responsible to legislatures while reserved departments remained in the hands of officials, emerged as a transitional device enabling a dependency to make some progress, but neither too much nor too fast. On the whole, Hailey thought, although by definition any transitional system must possess severe defects, at the provincial level dyarchy had actually worked rather well.

That was not the point. In retrospect, Hailey reflected, the British failure to understand psychology was striking. Indian home rulers had no wish to be told about the long apprenticeship they would need in order to become a dominion. Neither visitors like Curtis nor officials like himself seemed to realize that they were dealing not with some sort of static "Indian problem" but with the dynamic, ultimately irresistible force of nationalism. Above all, Hailey stressed, and a lifetime of experience lay behind the observation, there had been so remarkably little understanding of the profound impact a world war could have on the lives and consciousness of ordinary people. Accelerating old currents, developing new ones in unforeseeable ways, war changed things for good. Just as the full effects of World War I had been revealed in India only in the early 1920s, so in Africa the results of World War II had become apparent only several years after its conclusion.

The true significance of Lionel Curtis, Hailey considered, concerned neither dominion status nor dyarchy. It was his encouragement to moderate Indians. Often mistakenly regarded as reactionaries, Indian Liberals had been inspired by the constitutional gradualism of the Morley–Minto reforms. During the crucial war and postwar period their courageous cooperation had helped fill the void between the more militant agitators and British conservatives. Congress's successful campaign for independence, he concluded, made it easy to overlook the debt both the British government and in his view the people of India owed to them.[52]

That was probably as close as Hailey ever came to a definitive answer to a question Indian journalists sometimes asked: Given that he had to carry out the

[52] Hailey note on Lionel Curtis, April 1958, HPA/343.

policies of his superiors, what were his own principles? His sympathies lay with the Liberals, men like the Allahabad lawyer Sir Tej Bahadur Sapru. Yet the retrospective note of 1958 must be used cautiously. By 1915, although Hailey recognized that Indian intellectuals were an integral part of an Asian revolution, he had not yet acknowledged that Indian nationalism would ultimately prove to be irresistible. No one could have known then how rapidly and decisively a world war can change pace and direction, making what was once unthinkable seem normal and inevitable. By 1918 he had certainly moved some distance. Yet his identification with the Liberals solidified only during 1919–24 when he sat on the government bench in the Indian assembly. And even then the conversion was only partial. His mind might belong to the Liberals. His heart remained in Shahpur.

∞∞∞∞∞∞∞

In August 1918 Hailey took a three-month leave and went alone to Japan. During his later African travels he kept diaries; this time he wrote a circular letter for friends. He was struck by the cleanliness, by the similarity between the attitudes and social conditions of industrializing Japan and what he knew of Britain's in the 1840s, by the use of every square foot of land and, albeit vicariously, by Yokohama's red-light district. Because it needed to import coal, oil, and above all steel, he predicted unoriginally, Japan would clearly be a storm center. Repeatedly he returned to the contrast with India. The Japanese were materialistic, he observed, aggressive and secretive. But they were efficient, economical, and clean, not handicapped by caste or divided by religion. Although there might be higher virtues, he concluded, it would be well if the same could be said of India.

After a little fishing Hailey returned through Korea and northern China. The latter reminded him of the Punjab: millet instead of rice, much pasture, and lots of dust. Observing the effects of informal empire, and apparently quite unconscious of the irony, this imperialist felt sympathetic toward the Chinese who, despite their long history of independence and self-sufficiency, were now being carved up into spheres of influence. Returning by way of Singapore, where he was feted by the sizable Punjabi contingent, he arrived back in Delhi in the middle of October.[53]

He found "Delhi in the throes of a horrible attack of influenza – very fatal when neglected. Yesterday's deaths amounted to 264. Nearly everyone is down with it."[54] It was in fact one of the most catastrophic pandemics in world history, killing off in just two months an estimated 12 to 13 million in India alone. In late October and early November, the sanitary commissioner of the adjacent Punjab reported,

---

[53] Journal of journey to China and Japan, 1918, HPI/1C.
[54] Hailey to Chelmsford, 19 October 1918, Chelmsford Collection, IOL, MSS Eur E 264/18.

the state of the Province was such as to render adequate description impossible. The hospitals were choked so that it was impossible to remove the dead quickly enough to make room for the dying; the streets and lanes of the cities were littered with dead and dying people; the postal and telegraph services were completely disorganised; the train service continued, but at all the principal stations dead and dying people were being removed from the trains; the burning ghats and burial grounds were literally swamped with corpses, whilst an even greater number awaited removal; the depleted medical service, itself sorely stricken by the epidemic, was incapable of dealing with more than a minute fraction of the sickness requiring attention; nearly every household was lamenting a death, and everywhere terror and confusion reigned.[55]

The death toll in the Delhi enclave was estimated at 23,000, and in the Punjab the rural death rate was computed at 51 per thousand, compared with 36 in urban areas. Given the almost total breakdown in services, however, including the deaths of many village record keepers, all these figures were only educated guesses.

Inevitably, and in this instance with some justice, such acts of God tended to be blamed on the alien government. As had been the case with plague, once the epidemic struck there was little the medical service could do about it, for though nursing could make a difference in 1918 doctors were beside the point. There was rather more in the clear correlation which the census later revealed between mortality and class: 5 percent in cases involving Europeans, 6 percent among educated Indians, "and anything over 50 percent amongst the Indians of the countryside."[56] Although that appalling figure owed much to ignorance and primitive communications, which prevented the medical service from distributing instructions about care, it also reflected inflation, poor monsoons, and huge grain shipments to Europe, which had continued throughout the war despite shortages in India. "There is no doubt," Hailey stated tersely, "that many deaths have been caused by malnutrition, and those who have carried out house to house visits in distributing medical aid report numerous cases of great distress."[57]

The flu epidemic had already passed its peak by 6 November 1918, a few days before the armistice, when Hailey handed over to the next commissioner of Delhi. During the past few months he had apparently been undergoing a period of some difficulty. Having served without interruption since 1912, he was a very tired man. The fact that he went on leave in August 1918, at the very climax of the critical summer during which Germany nearly won the war, suggests he may also have been a sick one, very possibly suffering from acute depression, rather like the breakdown that would be ascribed to "overwork" in

55 "A Brief Note on the Influenza Epidemic of 1918," Punjab State Archives, Lahore, Home, February 1919.
56 Delhi Admin. Report (1918–19), IOR, V/10/365; *Census of India* (1921), *15*, 60–2. There is astonishingly little information on this disaster, and certainly nothing comparable to Alfred W. Crosby, *Epidemic and Peace, 1918* (Westport, Conn.: Greenwood, 1976), which concentrates on the United States.
57 Fortnightly Report, 2nd half October 1918.

1937 when he was trying to write the *African Survey*.[58] Moreover, he was seriously considering early retirement. Undoubtedly he was disappointed not to be chosen to succeed Sir Michael O'Dwyer as lieutenant governor of the Punjab, a post that went instead to Sir Edward Maclagan. When Lord Chelmsford offered him Maclagan's job as education member, Hailey took nearly two weeks to decide to accept, his hesitation being "due to the fact that if I took the post, it would compel me to stay on in India instead of leaving the country on the termination of my service for pension, as I had for some time intended to do." As commissioner, he added, he had grown accustomed to independence and had "no great liking for Secretariat work, with its very limited opportunities for expressing one's private views or carrying them into execution."[59]

At the end of 1918, both his doubts about his career and his possibly intense personal crisis apparently resolved, the retiring commissioner looked back at Delhi. "I shall leave my work here with very deep regret," he told the viceroy's private secretary, "how deep, it is not possible for me to express here; whether my work has been of value or not, I am not the best judge, but for six years I have lived for nothing else."[60]

---

58 This whole house of cards would collapse if some sort of secret mission had been involved, but though I looked hard for it I found nothing either in the Hailey collection or in the official records.

59 Hailey to Maffey, PSV, 2 December 1918, Chelmsford Collection, MSS Eur E 164/18. Hailey had told Hardinge that he had planned to seek employment in England, presumably in the City of London, for which his experience in the finance department would have prepared him and where he had good family connections. Hailey to Hardinge, 13 June 1918, Hardinge Papers, Cambridge University Library, vol. 38. Hardinge had raised the question of the Punjab: "I see that O'Dwyer is leaving the Punjab soon. I wonder if there is any chance of your being his successor? I wish it could be so as nobody would do it better. O'Dwyer has been the best Lieut. Governor that I have known of any province." Hardinge to Hailey, 21 October 1917, HPI/1C. Although there is no evidence from this period, I also suspect problems with the marriage.

60 Hailey to Maffey, 2 December 1918, Chelmsford Collection, MSS Eur E 164/18.

∽∽

5

A report on the Punjab

Shortly after Hailey accepted the post of education member of the Governor-General's Council the Montagu–Chelmsford (Montford) report was published, provoking a storm of protest from advanced Indians who saw it as a sellout. Progress toward responsible government and dominion status would be very gradual indeed, it now appeared, Parliament would control the pace entirely, and dyarchy would be installed only at the provincial level. The viceroy, Lord Chelmsford, tried to sweeten the pill by enlarging the Indian membership of his council. The education membership therefore went to an Indian and Hailey had to wait for a vacancy.

Meanwhile he was given special duty, charged with implementing the recommendations of the Islington Commission on reorganization of the public services. Having been appointed in 1912 as part of the Morley–Minto reform package, the commission had submitted its report in 1915, when it had been shelved till the end of the war. The central question was Indianization: how many, how fast, how high up? And the proposed solution was decentralization. Many positions in the central departments would be transferred to greatly enlarged provincial services, whose members would be recruited locally whenever possible. For the more senior positions in the Indian Civil Service and the police, examinations would be held simultaneously in England and India, and though color was not supposed to be a factor three-fourths of the appointees were to come from the former.[1] Implementing the report required a systematic survey of all the services, position by position: which jobs should be transferred, how many still needed to be recruited in Britain, the pay, and so on. Because a fundamental redistribution of revenue between the center and the provinces was also involved, complex and protracted negotiations were going on.

It all sounds like precisely the kind of grinding secretariat work that had made Hailey think about leaving India in the first place. Moreover he must have sensed that he was marking time. Years later he reflected that much more rapid Indianization might have made a difference. If the British had "given intellectual India a far larger share in our administration," he suggested, then "we

---

[1] Report of the Royal Commission on the Public Services in India, PP, 1916 [Cd. 8382], 7. The proportion was later altered to half and half.

might perhaps have developed a constitution on the lines of an Indianised autocracy" instead of what he considered the ill-suited model of British parliamentary democracy.[2] Africanization of the public services, he would advise the Colonial Office in 1941, was the only way to prevent deep and permanent alienation of educated Africans. But timing was crucial. The program needed to be well under way before what he called the agitator succeeded in making nationalism synonymous with extremism.[3] If the Islington Commission's recommendations had been put into effect in 1912, he believed – better yet, well before 1907 – they might have had a chance. By 1919 the critical point had already passed. The war, the home rule leagues, the responsible-government declaration of 1917, the Montford report: By 1919 the Islington Commission was already badly out of date.

By 1919 the agitators had come into their own too. By then, it seems clear in retrospect, compared with any tropical African colony to which Britain transferred power so comparatively quickly after World War II, India already possessed a high degree of readiness for self-government: judges learned in the law, well-trained civil servants and army officers, a sophisticated press, a relatively mature form of nationalism. As Hailey soon perceived, if indeed he did not know it already, he was involved in a struggle in which the winner was predetermined. The most imperialists could hope for was to delay the inevitable outcome behind reasonably well-fortified redoubts.

The origins of Indian nationalism are commonly traced to the emergence of an articulate, educated middle class, roughly in the 1880s, the usual landmark being the foundation of the Indian National Congress in 1885. Yet complex historical forces like nationalism do not really have beginnings. To Jawaharlal Nehru the ultimate origins of the Indian nation were coterminous with those of Indian civilization itself, and after placing his reader in his World War II jail cell he began his story in the ruins of Harappa and Mohenjo-Daro in the Indus valley.[4] For nationalists Indian history was a quarry to be mined and a process of which the freedom struggle was the logical conclusion. It was also an obstacle. Like China, India was both a culture and a civilization. Unlike China, however, although successive indigenous and invading dynasties had sometimes controlled large parts of the subcontinent, not until the British was it a unified empire. The British provided the framework within which Indians necessarily worked to make a nation from a civilization. Yet the framework was not a neutral container. It was itself a determinative force, setting short-term limits, making some alternatives more favorable than others, shaping alliances and enmities. The British provided other crucial preconditions. In view of the subconti-

---

[2] Speech at Raleigh Club, Oxford, 6 May 1933, HPI/49.

[3] The word "agitator" was of course loaded, enabling the British to convey the presumption that their nationalist opponents had no real following among the masses nor any right to speak for them – in precisely the way that white Americans have used the term for black civil rights leaders. Although Hailey knew better, he used the word frequently and, largely because a superb copyeditor once taught me to regard unnecessary quotation marks with distaste, so shall I.

[4] Jawaharlal Nehru, *The Discovery of India* (New York: John Day, 1946).

nent's many languages political leaders usually corresponded with each other in English, although they were often fluent in several Indian languages as well. They used the railways and the postal service. Communicating with their rulers required knowledge of British history, constitutional and economic theory, and political idiom. So as best they could, and it was sometimes very good indeed, they got that too. Educated publicists were often dismissed as imitative, with no links to the real people of India, and though the charge was partly true – Gandhi said much the same thing – it was beside the point. In the nature of things building political consciousness in a largely illiterate people must be undertaken by a cosmopolitan, imitative elite. After all the British themselves were still self-consciously emulating their former colonial rulers, the Romans – after some fifteen hundred years of home rule.

When Hailey first came to India in the mid-1890s nationalism was in an early phase. From the perspective of the 1920s he characterized this first generation as having had a flair for politics, and though he said that in order to disparage Gandhi's noncooperation campaign, he had a point.[5] Few in numbers, lacking widespread support, the early nationalists convinced their rulers that channels would be needed to contain agitation, the result being the Morley–Minto reform scheme of 1909. Reinforcing their arguments with British precedents and political ideas, they fought to set limits on the exercise of arbitrary bureaucratic power. Although these boundaries had to be defended continually, they provided the legal space within which a freedom movement could develop and operate. The first generation also evolved a critique of colonialism, of the relationship between the British imperial and the local economy, of the means by which an alien bureaucracy turned Indians into instruments of their rule. Developing a vocabulary of key words – drain, exploitation, deindustrialization – they contributed to what is now called dependency theory.[6] At least by 1915 Hailey was ready to concede that the intelligentsia were authentic spokesmen for an insurgent force that was sweeping the Eastern world from Egypt to Japan. It would not go away.

Precisely what "it" was – that is, the nature and dynamics of the Indian freedom movement – is a matter of intense debate. A heroic school stresses the charisma of Gandhi and other leaders in galvanizing the masses. The so-called Cambridge school starts from an assumption common to contemporary administrators that the political system of British India was composed, as it is now, of local and interest-group power brokers for whose loyalty government and freedom fighters were competing; Congress won because in the long run it had more to offer; ultimately the British ran out of collaborators.[7] The Subaltern

---

5 "India," *Round Table, 12* (September 1922), 844–55.
6 See Bipan Chandra, *The Rise and Growth of Economic Nationalism in India: Economic Policies of Indian National Leadership, 1880–1905.* (New Delhi: People's Publishing House, 1966).
7 See particularly Anil Seal, *The Emergence of Indian Nationalism: Competition and Collaboration in the Later Nineteenth Century* (Cambridge: Cambridge University Press, 1968); Judith M. Brown's two monographs, *Gandhi's Rise to Power, Indian Politics 1915–1922* (Cambridge: Cambridge

school stresses the variety, continuity, and autonomy of popular resistance; Congress won because it capitalized on energy manufactured from below.[8] Communist historians have interpreted Congress as the class instrument of the bourgeoisie.[9] There is a Hindu nationalist or communal school that equates the freedom movement with the surge of Hinduism as a political force.[10] Finally, what may be called the Congress school understands the Indian freedom struggle as a national liberation movement, driven not by self- or class-interest but by nationalist ideology, evolving strategy and tactics which experience found most appropriate for a unique situation.[11]

All schools agree that Gandhi made a difference. Whether because he was charismatic, because he best represented the bourgeois interest of Congress, or – what seems most persuasive – because his program appealed to large numbers of Indians and because his nonviolent strategy best fit the particular circumstances of British India, in 1919 he took charge. Having made his reputation by leading the Indian community in South Africa, he was fifty, three years older than Hailey.[12] After his return in 1915 he had engaged in a series of satyagrahas (struggles for truth) to redress local grievances. Hoping to gain full Muslim participation in the nationalist cause, he supported the Khilafat movement on behalf of the caliph of Turkey, the leader of international Islam, whose fate would be decided at the peace conference. As late as 1918, however, when he was recruiting for the army, Gandhi remained loyal to the crown and in a sense even imperialist, still believing that a reformed British Empire-Commonwealth and Indian nationalism would ultimately be compatible, "that India can deliver her mission to the world better through England."[13]

In January 1919 the Rowlatt Acts, which perpetuated many of the wartime restrictions under the Defence of India Act, provided the issue that within one short year confirmed Gandhi's leadership of Congress and transformed him into an irreconcilable opponent of British rule. Late in February, responding to

University Press, 1972) and *Gandhi and Civil Disobedience: The Mahatma in Indian Politics, 1928–1934* (Cambridge: Cambridge University Press, 1977), and her biography, *Gandhi: Prisoner of Hope* (New Haven, Conn.: Yale University Press, 1989); John Gallagher, *The Decline, Revival, and Fall of the British Empire* (Cambridge: Cambridge University Press, 1982); and Ronald Robinson, "Non-European Foundations: Sketch for a Theory of Collaboration," in Roger Owen and Bob Sutcliffe, eds., *Studies in the Theory of Imperialism* (London: Longman, 1972).

8 See Ranajit Guha, ed., *Writings on South Asian History and Society* (Delhi: Oxford University Press, 1982–).

9 The classic work from the left is R. Palme Dutt, *India To-day,* 2nd ed. (Bombay: People's Publishing House, 1949).

10 See Ramesh C. Majumdar, *History of the Freedom Movement in India,* 2nd ed. (Calcutta: Mukhopadhayay, 1971–).

11 See Bipan Chandra et al., *India's Struggle for Independence, 1857–1947* (New Delhi: Vikas, 1988), and Chandra, *Indian National Movement: The Long-Term Dynamics* (New Delhi: Vikas, 1988).

12 See Maureen Swan, *Gandhi, the South African Experience* (Johannesburg: Ravan, 1985); Robert Huttenback, *Gandhi in South Africa: British Imperialism and the Indian Question, 1860–1914* (Ithaca, N.Y.: Cornell University Press, 1971), and William Keith Hancock, *Smuts,* 2 vols. (Cambridge: Cambridge University Press, 1962–8), vol. 1.

13 Gandhi to Herbert S. Jevons, 11 August 1918, CWMG 15:15–16.

what he called an inner voice, he declared that he would lead nonviolent resistance. The pattern of the Rowlatt satyagraha of early April was mixed, depending on its local leadership and particularly on the reaction of the British authorities on the spot.[14] The Punjab government went mad, as Gandhi put it, preventing him from going to Delhi and arresting two leaders in Amritsar. On 10 April a serious confrontation occurred in Lahore and a violent anti-European riot took place in Amritsar. Three days later, at the enclosed space in Amritsar called Jallianwala Bagh, General Reginald E. Dyer fired on a crowd for between ten and fifteen minutes, killing at least four hundred. Only afterward did Lieutenant Governor Sir Michael O'Dwyer receive approval for martial law, which went on through the summer. As Hailey reflected later, that afternoon changed the course of history.

In 1956, when Lord Hailey deposited his Indian papers in the India Office Library, he noted on his copy of the official Punjab Disturbances report that he had written it while on special assignment relating to the Islington Commission report. In 1965 he added two notes explaining his role in the affair. In mid-April 1919, he recalled, he spoke with the viceroy, Lord Chelmsford, persuading him that a factual statement was needed to counter Congress accounts of the Jallianwala Bagh massacre that were already filling the local press. At Lahore he discovered that no one was doing the job and pitched in. Perhaps his earlier claim to authorship had been exaggerated, he qualified, though parts of it did seem familiar, but because he had also carried on the Islington work he must have had some help.[15]

Not surprisingly – the note was written forty-six years after the event – the old man's memory was a little shaky on detail. First, although the Indian press was attacking martial law in the Punjab, General Dyer and Jallianwala Bagh became household names only gradually.[16] Second, the Punjab government having requested his services during the emergency, Hailey spent the summer in charge of press censorship and propaganda, which included the preparation of an official account.[17] The report was therefore his job.

Section IV of the account was published separately as a command paper and used by both sides in the British parliamentary debates of July 1920. Its tone cool and detached, it turned on several crucial points. First, although a serious confrontation had taken place in Delhi, Hailey conceded that the hartal, or

---

14 Ravinder Kumar, ed., *Essays on Gandhian Politics*.
15 HPI/57.
16 P. G. Robb, *The Government of India and Reform*, pp. 201–3, and Sir Algernon Rumbold, *Watershed in India, 1914–1922*, p. 174.
17 Punjab (O'Dwyer) to GofI, 17 April 1919, NAI, HomEstab, 167–8, Pt. B/May 1919. See J. P. Thompson to G. A. Cocks, 23 April 1919: "His Honour would be glad if you would send all the daily draft communiqués to Mr. Hailey to be passed before they are issued. He is generally in his office by 8:45 in the morning and you should arrange to let him see the draft for tomorrow the first thing in the morning. He will also pass other items which the newspapers propose to publish." Punjab Secretariat, HomMil, 1920 B 252.

shutdown, at Amritsar had been both orderly and successful. Second, Sir Michael O'Dwyer had nevertheless ordered the arrests of the two Congress leaders, Drs. Kitchlew and Satyapal, while prohibiting Gandhi from entering the province: actions that were said to be provocative. The atmosphere had been tense, Hailey explained, and further agitation "was likely to have very undesirable consequences – given the character of the people in the Central Punjab – on the rural areas." In short it had seemed like a replay of the canal-colony revolt of 1907, "and a fair estimate of its probabilities seems to indicate that their [the doctors'] removal was far more likely to disorganize an agitation rapidly growing dangerous, than to lead to open disorder. The case was almost exactly parallel with that of Lajpat Rai and Ajit Singh," he concluded – and the reasoning remained just as circular.[18]

Hailey now came to 10 April, when four Europeans were killed, banks and churches destroyed, and a female European missionary assaulted. That evening Amritsar was handed over to military authority. Next day General Dyer took charge, the railway was disrupted and the telegraph cut. Learning that a prohibited meeting would take place, Dyer took to Jallianwala Bagh fifty riflemen reinforced by forty soldiers armed with long knives. The paragraph describing the firing was terse and factual:

He had with him two armoured cars in reserve, but the lane through which he entered was too narrow to admit them and they were left in the street outside; he took no machine gun with him. When he arrived, at about 5 o'clock, he found that the crowd had swollen to several thousands. . . . His troops deployed on either side of the entrance, the ground on which they stood being some feet higher than the general level of the enclosure. He did not order the crowd to disperse, but proceeded to take action to disperse it at once by fire. 1,650 rounds were fired, fire being directed on crowds not on individuals, and redirected from time to time where the crowds were thickest. . . . On the conclusion of the firing the troops retired; the number of casualties were not counted.

As if deliberately, the report raised obvious questions only to leave them unanswered. Why had no warning been given? Why had the firing continued so long and with so many casualties? Why had the wounded not been cared for or the dead not counted? Instead the report went directly to what it concluded were the effects. Right across the Punjab agitation had ceased abruptly. The authorities agreed emphatically that this admittedly drastic action had averted a serious uprising.[19]

In the first three sections of the report, which were presented to the committee of inquiry chaired by Lord Hunter but not published, Hailey analyzed the

---

[18] Hailey report on 1919 Disturbances, HPI/57.

[19] Although the notorious "crawling order," public whippings, and police extortion could not be condoned, Hailey reported, O'Dwyer had suspended the first, very few had been whipped (mostly juveniles), and opportunities for extortion were a principal cause for bringing cases quickly before the military courts.

broader causes of disorder – price inflation, the rising level of political activity and expectations during the war, the new income tax, poor monsoons, the influenza epidemic of 1918, the Rowlatt agitation – all of which had no doubt played some role, though none was unique to the Punjab. The Ghadr conspiracy of 1915, which had been fomented by Sikhs after their return from North America, was peculiar to the Punjab, but it seemed to have had little lasting impact; during the last two years of the war the province had actually been unusually quiet. As Hailey's own fortnightly reports had described, the military recruiting drive had been strenuous; yet recruiting had centered in the rural areas and agitation had been largely confined to the towns. It was alleged that the Punjab government was peculiarly hostile to advanced politicians. Even if that were true, it might explain why leaders became involved in the Rowlatt agitation but not why the agitation became violent. For, Hailey insisted, there was absolutely no evidence of revolutionary conspiracy. "The object of those responsible for the agitation," he concluded, "was not primarily to produce disorder." Consciously or unconsciously, however, as Annie Besant and at times even Gandhi himself had realized, their words had made it inevitable.

The explanation of why the Punjab had become so peculiarly violent, Hailey reasoned, must therefore be sought in local causes. Had the government acted provocatively by arresting the local leaders, Drs. Kitchlew and Satyapal, or by preventing Gandhi from entering the province on what the Mahatma had called his mission of peace? Again Hailey cited the precedent of 1907 and the tinderbox nature of the rural areas. What the Rowlatt Committee of 1918 had said of Sikhs was true of Punjabis in general: "The interval between thought and action is short. If captured by inflammatory appeals, they are prone to act with all possible celerity, and in a fashion dangerous to the whole fabric of order and constitutional rule." Gandhi's intentions were no doubt sincere. Because he spoke no Punjab language, however, few people would have understood him: "Men committed arson and assaulted women with the name of the apostle of passive resistance on their lips." The case for excluding Gandhi had therefore seemed persuasive.

Had the imposition of martial law been justified? Hailey set the scene as it must have appeared to the government on 13 April 1919: The atmosphere in Amritsar and Lahore tense and hostile, communications cut, an unauthorized meeting having just been fired on with hundreds of deaths, numerous demobilized soldiers who might become involved, an apprehended war with Afghanistan on the frontier, rumors circulating that the government had been overthrown and the bazaars would be looted. If the fire spread to the rural Punjab it was hard to see how it could be put out. Both in law and fact, Hailey concluded, the appropriate word was therefore "rebellion."

There was no doubt that civil authorities were legally justified in calling on the military to restore order, Hailey continued, the only condition under the Civil Procedure Code being that officers should "use as little force, and do as little injury to person and property, as may be consistent with dispersing the assembly and arresting and detaining" those involved in it.[20] "Minimum force" was in question only twice: air bombardment at Gujranwala and the firing at Jallianwala Bagh. In the former instance bombing had been much the quickest and most certain way to aid local officials whose communications had been cut. In the latter "a military officer, charged by civil authority to prevent assemblies among a town population which had for some days been in open rebellion . . . found a large crowd" defying authority. Although the question of minimum force would be settled by inquiry, Hailey's report concluded, two points were not in doubt: "It was his duty to disperse the assembly by any means in his power; and the effect of the action . . . was definitely to settle the attitude of the inhabitants of the central Punjab."[21]

The definitive account of Jallianwala Bagh and its impact on India's drive for independence, Lord Hailey wrote near the end of his life, remained to be written. The best attempt so far has condemned Hailey's report for having relied on the findings of the martial-law commissions, which the Hunter Committee later rejected, and generally for confirming "the suspicion that the men who ruled the Province were political dinosaurs in their concept of how to govern and ostriches when it came to recognizing legitimate political demands."[22] The document was after all written by an officer of the Punjab government whose job was to explain and as far as possible justify its actions. Not to have accepted the findings of martial-law commissions would have condemned them in advance and, although the Hunter Committee could make a decision of that kind, Hailey obviously could not. In retrospect, his report undoubtedly underestimated severely the degree to which nationalism had penetrated the consciousness of ordinary Indians. Its most questionable judgment, however, was its repeated use of the precedent of the deportations of Lajpat Rai and Ajit Singh in 1907.

The most interesting aspect of Hailey's report, however, is what it did not say. Sir Michael O'Dwyer was firmly convinced that the disorders had resulted from a deeply laid conspiracy among hard, unscrupulous men who had made Gandhi their pawn. In his perception the agitation against the Rowlatt Acts, attacks against rail and telegraph communications, and the Afghan invasion were all supposed to be linked, timed to take place simultaneously in the middle of May when most British troops would have gone to the hills for their health during the hot weather. For the conspirators, he concluded, the outbreaks in Amritsar and Lahore were therefore premature, and only firm and timely force prevented a recurrence of 1857.[23] During the summer and autumn of 1919 the

---

[20] The press had suggested that troops should have fired blanks or into the air, but Hailey argued that nothing could be worse; a mob must understand that if the authorities were forced to fire, they would shoot to kill.

[21] Ibid.

[22] Alfred Draper, *Amritsar: The Massacre that Ended the Raj* (London: Cassell, 1981), pp. 162–5.

[23] See O'Dwyer's testimony before the Hunter Committee, vol. 6, IOR, V/26/262/8, and his autobiography, *India as I Knew It* (London: Constable, 1925), pp. 263–317.

Punjab secretariat was preparing memoranda to support this hypothesis, including one on the supposed controlling influence of agitators from Delhi. Shortly before O'Dwyer left India, however, Hailey told him that although no doubt some Congress members had hoped for violent confrontation, he had been unable to discover any evidence of conspiracy.[24] The Punjab government submitted its documents and its ex-lieutenant governor presented his conspiracy hypothesis to the Hunter Committee. But that government's official report was strangely silent.

Still more curious is the Hailey report's reticence on the issue of General Dyer and Jallianwala Bagh. Although Hailey's own papers are virtually blank for this period, other sources fill the gap. The diary of Sir John Thompson, the Punjab's chief secretary, recorded on 14 April that two hundred people had been killed: "Seems to have been a bloody business."[25] Dyer's initial statement stressed military necessity:

Deputy Commissioner had warned inhabitants not to hold meetings. I had further proclamation made by beat of drum on morning of 13th that meetings would be fired on. I was informed that a meeting was going to be held at Jalhen Walian [sic] Bagh at 4:30 PM, but I did not think this would take place. At 4 PM I received a report that a gathering was beginning. I at once sent picquets to hold gates of City and with [50 riflemen] and 2 armoured motor cars I entered the city. On entering I saw a dense crowd estimated at about 5,000. I realised that the situation might invite attack on my small forces so I immediately opened fire. I estimate that between two and three hundred of the crowd were killed.[26]

In his note of 1965 Hailey recalled talking with Dyer in April 1919 at Amritsar, where the general stressed his preoccupation with standing orders on the necessity of protecting troops from being overwhelmed by hostile crowds. Many of the later problems might have been avoided, he added, if Dyer had stuck to that line.[27]

Why then did Dyer change his defense? Why, as General Sir Charles Monro is supposed to have put it, did the general destroy himself "by failing to keep his mouth shut"?[28] After Dyer's return to England he suffered several strokes, and these have been cited to suggest mental incapacity during the firing: a rush of blood to the head.[29] Megalomania seems more persuasive: The Anglo-Indian press called him the savior of India so often that he came to believe it. Another hypothesis is that clever Indian lawyers on the Hunter Committee offended the "plain soldier," who lost his head. Indians have advanced yet another conspiracy

[24] Hailey note of 1965, HPI/57.
[25] Sir John Thompson Collection, MSS Eur F 137/13.
[26] Précis quoted by telegram, GOC Lahore Division to War Section, AHQ, Simla, 15 April 1919, Punjab Sec, HomMil 1920 B 250.
[27] Hailey note of 1965, HPI/57.
[28] Arthur Swinson, *Six Minutes to Sunset: The Story of General Dyer and the Amritsar Affair* (London: Peter Davies, 1964), p. 203. In 1965 Hailey had recently listened to a radio dramatization based on Swinson's book.
[29] Rupert Furneaux, *Massacre at Amritsar* (London: Allen & Unwin, 1963).

theory, which centers on a meeting of O'Dwyer and his chief subordinates on 8 April in Lahore. Having been informed that the mob was in control of Amritsar, the lieutenant governor allegedly decided to bring the issue to a head, provoked a confrontation by arresting Kitchlew and Satyapal, and sent Dyer with instructions to make an example. As the general's admiring biographer explained, Dyer had worried about whether his forces would be able to cope in the narrow, winding streets of a traditional Indian city. Finding his opponents gathered in the open had therefore seemed like a heaven-sent opportunity.[30]

How much did Hailey know of the change in Dyer's line of defense and when did he know it? Whatever may have been in the general's mind that fateful afternoon of 13 April he began to stray from the strictly military terms of his first report very quickly. In a conversation he happened to overhear in May, Jawaharlal Nehru recalled, Dyer said he had been tempted to reduce Amritsar to ashes.[31] On 8 August Thompson recorded that he and Hailey had gone by car to Lahore, where Dyer "said he felt he knew what we were up ag[ain]st"; but the general "insisted on view that whole series of events be regarded as one trans[actio]n." Once he entered,

his mind was made up in 3 seconds that it was his business to suppress the insurrection then & there. That was why he went on shooting. His evidence of between 200–300 killed was based on experience in France which pointed to 1 in 6 killed on the spot as result of rifle fire – 1650 rounds fired. The men sometimes collected in knots instead of bolting and he thought they meditated attack. Did not attend to wounded [because] his ammunition was nearly exhausted, & his men cd. not have defended selves if attacked. He seems to regard it as his mission, his religious duty, to kill the rebellion.[32]

At least by early August, it seems, although he continued to justify his action on military grounds, Dyer regarded himself as God's chosen instrument to save India.

In September 1919, before the Hunter Committee, Dyer completed the transition, abandoning the narrow military defense and stressing political motives. The crowd might well have scattered without firing, he admitted; indeed it had begun to flee at once: "I thought it my duty to go on firing until it dispersed. If I fired a little, the effect would not be sufficient. If I had fired a little I should be wrong in firing at all." Mr. Justice Rankin: "Excuse my putting it this way, General, but was it not a resort to what has been called 'frightfulness' for the benefit of the Punjab Districts as a whole?" Dyer: "No. I don't

30 Ian Colvin, *The Life of General Dyer* (Edinburgh: Blackwood, 1929), pp. 170–2. On the conspiracy thesis see Raja Ram, *The Jallianwala Bagh Massacre: A Premeditated Plan* (Chandigarh: Punjab University Press, 1978), and V. N. Datta, *Jallianwala Bagh* (Ludhiana: Bhopal-Chandigard-Kurukshetra, 1969). Draper, *Amritsar*, pp. 84, 124–44, suspects there may be something to the hypothesis that a suspected CID agent, Hans Raj, helped arrange the meeting; his exceptionally detailed testimony before the martial-law commission suggests he had been carefully coached. Unfortunately the cover-up continues. In both India and Pakistan, independent countries since 1947, the Special Branch records for this period remain firmly closed!
31 Jawaharlal Nehru, *An Autobiography* (1936; London: Oxford University Press, 1980), pp. 43–4.
32 Thompson Collection, IOL, MSS Eur F 137/13.

think so. I think it was a horrible duty for me to perform. It was a merciful act that I had given them a chance to disperse. . . . I had decided if I fired one round I must shoot a lot of rounds or I must not shoot at all." Sir C. H. Setalvad: "Supposing the passage was sufficient to allow the armoured cars to go in would you have opened fire with the machine guns?" Dyer: "I think probably yes." Setalvad: "You thought that by striking terror in that manner you would save the British Raj?" Dyer: "No, the British Raj is a mighty thing." Setalvad: "Did it ever occur to you that by adopting this method of 'frightfulness' – excuse the term – you were really doing a great disservice to the British Raj by driving discontent deep?" Dyer: "I thought it would be doing a jolly lot of good."[33]

More than General Dyer's actions, Hailey reflected later, it was his words that sealed his fate. By January 1920 both His Majesty's Government and the Government of India, of which Hailey was by then a member, had concluded that the general's actions and his justification amounted to frightfulness, or state-sponsored terrorism, and the Army Council decided that he would not be offered another command. Heated debates occurred in both houses of Parliament, the Lords passed a resolution deploring his treatment, and the *Morning Post* organized a subscription campaign. It was also Dyer's words that Secretary of State Edwin Montagu had in mind when he said he had learned the details only from the newspapers. Why had they not been quoted in Hailey's report?[34]

Although Hailey officially submitted his report in October 1919, it had evidently been written in stages over the summer and it was completed no later than the first week in September. He could therefore not have included Dyer's self-incriminating testimony before the Hunter Committee. Yet the general's statement of 25 August, which was not wrung from him by clever lawyers, had said precisely the same thing:

I fired and continued to fire . . . and I consider this as the least amount of firing which would produce the necessary moral and widespread effect. . . . If more troops had been at hand the casualties would have been greater in proportion. It was no longer a question of merely dispersing the crowd; but one of producing a sufficient moral effect . . . not only on those who were present but more specially through the Punjab. There could be no question of undue severity.[35]

Hailey therefore had ample opportunity to read Dyer's August statement. Moreover, according to the general's uncorroborated testimony to a family member, he suggested only that the word "rebels" should not be used. "But if they were not rebels whom General Dyer shot," his biographer charged, "there was the less need to create 'a moral effect throughout the Punjab'; and Mr. Hailey, as a member of the Government of India, afterwards condemned General Dyer for this 'mistaken conception of his duty.' Singular procedure, to

[33] Hunter Committee, vol. 3, IOR, V/26/262/5.
[34] See exchange of telegrams, IOR, L/P&J/6/1583.
[35] Dyer statement of 25 August 1919, Punjab Sec., Home Military, B 250.

suggest the weakening of the defence before condemning the defendant!"[36] This allegation – not only Indian lawyers but equally clever politicians like Churchill and bureaucrats like Hailey had conspired to trap the plain-speaking soldier – is quite improbable. Although the judgment was questionable, Hailey's report did use the word "rebellion" both for the general situation in the Punjab and specifically for the crowd at Jallianwala Bagh.

Probably by 8 August, and certainly when he read Dyer's statement of the twenty-fifth, Hailey ought to have realized that trouble lay ahead. Not including all he knew in his report meant that, once the general's testimony before the Hunter Committee was published, his superiors would be in for a nasty shock. Presumably he could have warned Dyer to keep his mouth shut – but apparently he did not do that either. The most probable explanation is that, having already written his account of Amritsar, Hailey looked over the 25 August statement perfunctorily, not reflecting sufficiently on the profound impression it would make.[37]

Could Dyer, if only he had kept quiet, really have gotten away with it? Even on the narrow military grounds of his first statement of April, to which he returned once he received legal advice in England, the suggestion still seems preposterous. Although some of the crowd that afternoon undoubtedly possessed lathis (long sticks tipped with iron), although the scene was perhaps not quite the prayer meeting portrayed in Richard Attenborough's film *Gandhi*, it was essentially unarmed. Even though assemblies had been prohibited the normal procedure would have been to warn before firing. Eyewitnesses, including Dyer himself, agreed that the crowd did not move toward the troops.[38] Even if what lawyers call the reasonable person might have supposed that the situation had been threatening, there could have been no convincing military justification for firing that lasted from ten to fifteen minutes, on a crowd that was attempting to escape, until his ammunition was exhausted. Even if the general himself had not explained that his intent was to make as large a psychological impression as possible, that would have been the only logical inference from the facts.

Only with extreme reluctance, however, would the British authorities have refused to support an officer who claimed to have thought his troops were in danger of being overwhelmed. If officers became too timid to order their men to fire on mobs, or if soldiers or policemen refused to carry out such orders, then the implications could be extremely dangerous. As would be demonstrated during Hailey's governorship of the United Provinces in the savage communal

---

[36] Colvin, *Dyer*, p. 331.

[37] In September 1919, during an Assembly debate on the Indemnity Bill, Hailey like other speakers held that Dyer's actions were sub judice and therefore not discussable, and he may have framed his report on that assumption. It is also possible that Home Member Sir William Vincent and other members of the Government of India had already decided to distance themselves as far from Dyer as possible.

[38] See Indian National Congress, *The Congress Punjab Inquiry, 1919–1920* (Lahore, 1920).

riot at Cawnpore in 1931 – indeed as Nehru himself would learn in the Punjab in 1947 – unless the force behind it is credible the rule of law fails. The Punjab doctrine contained two points crucial to the case: the need to bring overwhelming force to bear in the initial phase, before a situation got out of hand; and the equally important obligation of superiors to back their subordinates. Despite his realization that Jallianwala Bagh went beyond the minimum-force criterion, Hailey's carefully worded report prepared the ground for the general's only possible defense. Spurning the opportunity, Dyer gave an explanation that made a caricature of the Punjab school. In the end it was therefore what he said, more than what he did, that tipped the balance against him.

The central importance of Jallianwala Bagh in what he quaintly called Congress's disruptive movement against the Government of India could not be doubted, Lord Hailey reflected in 1965. Until 1919 even radical Congressmen had been demanding responsible government and dominion status; the claim for independence could be traced to Jallianwala Bagh. Historians would have to try to understand the psychology of the situation, he stressed, especially the impact of the vitriolic Anglo-Indian press and the debate of the House of Lords, which made it hard for Indians to trust even progressive Englishmen.[39] Ultimately the British Raj rested on force. But more than military power explained the ability of a few thousand Europeans to govern 250 million people, to a large degree through Indians. In a quarter of an hour General Dyer had gone a long way toward destroying Britain's moral authority.

---

[39] Hailey note of 1965, HPI/57.

6

~~~~~~

Finance member, 1919–1922

When Hailey joined the Viceroy's Council without portfolio in September 1919 it was supposed he was being groomed to succeed Sir William Vincent as home member. In November, however, came an announcement that, failing eyesight having forced the early retirement of Finance Member Sir James Meston, Hailey would replace him instead. The press reaction was mixed: Some Indian papers remarked that firmness was already overrepresented in the Government of India; a prominent London banker criticized the appointee's lack of experience.[1] Indeed the only preparation had been four years as deputy secretary in the finance department, and even that had ended as long ago as 1911. Nevertheless Hailey occupied what a colleague called the seat of the scornful. He would remain there for three years, through one of the most tempestuous periods in modern Indian financial history.

Late in 1919 it was still unclear whether Gandhi would lead Congress along constitutional or unconstitutional lines, or even whether he would lead it at all. The previous April, a week after Jallianwala Bagh, declaring himself still more horrified by mob violence on the part of Indians in Bombay, Ahmedabad, and Delhi than by government repression in the Punjab, he had abruptly suspended civil disobedience. In June he threatened to resume it but then backed off, devoting himself instead to Congress's exposé of General Dyer and martial law in the Punjab. In December he cautiously welcomed the Montagu reforms. Although they were not enough, he asserted, patriotic Indians should refrain from hair-splitting criticism and work to make them succeed.[2] Meanwhile, however, asserting that such an opportunity to cement Hindu–Muslim unity might not recur for a century, he remained involved in the Khilafat agitation against the threatened dismemberment of the Ottoman empire at the Paris Peace Conference. In January 1920 he and the Ali brothers discussed the problem with the viceroy, whom they found courteous but noncommittal. By March Gandhi had begun to talk of a campaign not merely of civil disobedience but of total noncooperation against a government guilty of a moral wrong.[3]

---

[1] Letter of George H. Sutherland, the *Times*, 11 November 1919.
[2] CWMG, *16*, 360–1.
[3] Ibid., *17*, 1–2, 73–5. Lloyd George and British cabinet having decided to drive the Turks out of Europe, Chelmsford had no option. See Gail Minault, *The Khilafat Movement*.

When the Government of India responded in May 1920 to the Hunter Committee report, it called General Dyer's firing at Jallianwala Bagh "excessive" but refused either to censure Sir Michael O'Dwyer and other Punjab government officials or to admit that martial law had been unjustified. The Punjab became Gandhi's second issue. His third plank was the swadeshi movement, which had been a feature of the earlier agitation against the partition of Bengal. This time, he declared, the boycott of foreign goods would not be negative. The goal was not the ruin of British industry but the regeneration of the traditional cotton-handicraft economy of village India.

Would constitutional agitation ever force the British to make meaningful concessions, Gandhi asked rhetorically? Throughout the nineteenth century the Irish had tried that tactic repeatedly, with no results. After the South African War, however, as he himself had observed first-hand, General Louis Botha had led the Afrikaner people in boycott, swiftly winning responsible government and then dominion status. If Indians could but withdraw their implicit acquiescence, he reasoned, there would be no alternative "but despotic rule pure and simple," and world opinion had advanced to the point that Britain could not conduct a military dictatorship with impunity. Noncooperation would therefore "constitute the peacefullest revolution the world has ever seen." If participation were wide and staunch enough, he declared, *swaraj* (freedom) might come remarkably quickly, even within one year.[4]

The strategy of the Government of India under Chelmsford and Lord Reading, who became viceroy in March 1921, was very different from the panicked response to the Rowlatt satyagraha of 1919. Hailey called it the long game. It was based on an analysis of Indian politics that was cool and rational, fixed on the hard rock of interest. Beneath the moral facade of national liberation, intelligence experts concluded, a rather ordinary contest was going on for place, patronage, and party leadership. Congress in their view was only one of several parties, Gandhi an outsider possessing no regional power base of his own. For the time being more orthodox politicians were tolerating him because his mass following strengthened them in their bargaining with the British. Both his methods and his dictatorial habits were threatening, however, and they would welcome the chance to be rid of him. It was in an attempt to bolster his own position against Congress bosses that Gandhi was courting Muslims. Yet the more extreme the Khilafat movement became the more it would alienate Hindus. On the other hand, was it likely that Muslims, whose religion enjoined jihad, or holy war, would long follow a Hindu apostle of nonviolence? If these contradictions were given time and room to develop, the experts reasoned, Gandhi's noncooperation campaign would surely destroy itself.[5]

---

4 CWMG, *18*, 55–7, 68–70, 245–55, 576–8. The comparison with the concept of "hegemony" of the contemporary Italian communist Antonio Gramsci is brought out by Bipan Chandra, *Indian National Movement*.

5 See D. Anthony Low, "The Government of India and the First Non-Co-Operation Movement, 1920–1922," in Ravinder Kumar, ed., *Essays on Gandhian Politics: The Rowlatt Satyagraha,*

The government intended to allow it to do just that. The movement would therefore be allowed to develop. Gandhi would be given plenty of rope. His proposals that lawyers boycott courts and students leave government schools would alienate middle-class opinion. The longer the campaign lasted without achieving its goals the more desperate it would become. The more extreme it grew the more it would antagonize people. The government's coercive power would be employed selectively to assist fragmentation rather than retard it. A good deal of clearly seditious propaganda would be tolerated. If the chances of conviction seemed favorable there might be prosecutions – but only as a means of fanning resentment. Gradually Gandhi's prominent opponents, his Muslim allies, and his own henchmen would be jailed. The longer he himself remained free the more he would be isolated and distrusted. "Gandhi would, I think, give his boots, only he does not wear boots, to be prosecuted," Hailey put it in November 1920. "Such influence as I have has always been thrown on the side of leaving [him] alone. If you hang a patriot he is a martyr; if he hangs himself, he is a mere corpse."[6]

The second part of the government's strategy was the Montagu–Chelmsford reform package, which aimed to strengthen moderates. "The whole future administration of the country seems to me to depend on the gradual growth of a strong moderate party," Hailey put it. "We cannot create this ourselves," he explained, yet despite the Punjab controversy, "I think the extremists are doing the work for us." Although the men who dominated the new central and provincial legislatures would not be old-style loyalists, it might be hoped that their opposition would flow through constitutional channels. The primary danger, he thought, was that "we may have driven the extremists into such a hole that they will now attempt something rash," which would force the government in turn to act prematurely and drive moderates underground.[7]

It was to the reform scheme that Hailey's position as finance member related most directly. If moderates were to have a chance at viability they must be given something substantive. They needed to be able to argue persuasively that they had made a difference. Under the reforms, it was true, the government would retain undiminished control over finance, foreign relations, the army, and internal security, as well as the power to restore taxes it regarded as essential if the legislature rejected them. Theoretically it could do as it pleased. In practice, however, if the strategy of dividing moderates from extremists were to succeed, some concessions would have to be made. This political reality would strengthen Hailey's hand. Like other finance ministers of the 1920s he would be pressing for economy, retrenchment, and balanced budgets. Although he would be required to support the program of the Government of India, important aspects of which were dictated from London, he would use the Legislative

---

pp. 298–323. Apart from his belief in the imperative need to pare expenditure in order to strengthen the moderates, the Hailey Collection contains disappointingly little information on what precisely may have been his influence on the determination of this policy.
Hailey to Sir Edward Hilton Young, 19 November 1920, HPI/2C.   [7] Ibid.

Assembly as a lever with which to pry reductions out of his colleagues. Sometimes he would even overstate the strength of Indian opposition.

Indian finance was largely determined by two factors over which Hailey could exercise very little influence: military expenditure and currency-exchange policy. In both areas not only ultimate control but much of the routine decision-making centered in London. Nor did the chain of command necessarily stop conveniently in the India Office. Military matters had to be negotiated with the War Office and the Imperial General Staff, who often acted on their own.[8] On currency issues the secretary of state's financial advisory committee, which included prominent men from the City of London, the British Treasury, and the Bank of England, had a say.

At the time Hailey took office both of these areas happened to be undergoing major reviews. The monetary question was being examined by the Babington Smith Committee, whose report favoring a high two-shilling rupee was published in February 1920 and accepted at once by the India Office.[9] "We have of course accepted the proposed announcement of the Secretary of State," Hailey explained, making clear that consultation with Delhi had been perfunctory, "as it was obviously no use cavilling against it."[10] Meanwhile a committee of the Imperial General Staff under Viscount Esher was reviewing military policy. Its report of November 1920 would recommend a larger, more modern, and far more expensive Indian army.[11] Even before the Esher Committee report, however, the military-spending problem was already serious. After the brief Afghan invasion in the summer of 1919 the Indian army had pursued the amir's forces into Waziristan, it was planning to stay there, the bills were mounting up alarmingly, and the end was nowhere in sight. "It is always difficult to calculate the odds on a horse," Hailey alerted Chelmsford, "but it would baffle the most brilliant tipster to fix the odds on a hypothetical horse in a problematical race."[12]

Undoubtedly reflecting the views of his military colleagues rather than his own, the draft budget Hailey presented to the Viceroy's Council in mid-February 1920 was grounded in the threatening circumstances of the postwar world. Indeed it was strikingly like the language of the later Esher report that Indian politicians and Hailey himself would find so objectionable. With the defeat of Germany in the West, the draft declared, "the centre of gravity of danger to the Empire has shifted to the East." As in 1914, when the British had sent their army to fight in Belgium and France, India would need to be capable of sending expeditionary forces overseas – the obvious question being why

8 "We are being continually urged from Home to undertake fresh Military expenditure," Hailey told a colleague; "hardly a day passes in which we do not see fresh orders increasing the pay of the British portion of the services." Hailey to Gubbay, 29 January 1920, HPI/2A.
9 Report of the Committee to Enquire into Indian Exchange and Currency, PP, 1920 [Cmd. 527–30], *14*.
10 Hailey to Gubbay, 29 January 1920, HPI/2A.
11 Committee re administration and organization of the army in India, PP, 1920 [Cmd. 943], *14*.
12 Hailey to Chelmsford, 19 December 1919, HPI/2A.

India, as distinguished from its British rulers, would want to do that. Because new situations required new measures, the draft argued, comparisons between military needs of 1914 and 1920 were quite irrelevant; both the size and cost of forces would have to rise substantially.[13] Just two weeks later Hailey actually presented to the last unreformed Legislative Council a radically different document, that is, the tight budget he had clearly favored all along.

The reason for the change was that meanwhile the second major determinant, monetary policy, had come powerfully into play. Earlier that month the Babington Smith Committee had published its report on Indian currency, recommending an official exchange rate for the rupee of two shillings gold.[14] At this point, in order to understand the intensely controversial atmosphere in which Hailey would be operating, a little background on the history of Indian monetary policy is essential.

Ever since the 1880s, when Dadabhai Naoroji and other spokesmen of the so-called Bombay school had developed their critique of British rule, no subject had been closer to the nerve ends than the management of Indian finance.[15] The metallic composition of the currency, exchange value, flow of bullion, location of reserves, mechanisms of remission: no aspect was spared. Because a cheap rupee would favor Indian exports, whereas a dear one would encourage imports including British manufactures, exchange was closely related to fiscal policy. It was also linked to the home charges: army and civil-service pensions, interest on railway and other debts, costs of the India Office, purchases of arms and equipment in England, and so on.

Far from ending, economic nationalists charged, the drain of the East India Company era had actually increased. Looting had merely become more systematic. The government claimed that the gold reserves were kept in the vaults of the Bank of England in order to be used if India's financial solvency were threatened. On the contrary, critics contended, supposing any gold were there at all – had any Indian ever seen it? – it was providing a base of stability for the City of London's prosperity. Indian finance, they claimed, amounted to one vast network of mechanisms, operating more or less independently of the individual Englishmen who had charge of them for the time being, the purpose of which was to manipulate India's potentially wealthy economy on behalf of British interests. This was no mere matter of economic theory to be countered with rational argument, Hailey asserted. It amounted to an article of religious faith.

The problems were structural, economic nationalists maintained, and so must be the remedies. On one issue in particular a growing number of British

---

[13] Draft of budget statement, 16 February 1920, HPI/2A.

[14] Government of India announcement, 2 February 1920, HPI/2B. The situation was extremely confusing. Soldiers and civil servants were being paid at what was supposed to be the current rate of 1s. 10d. sterling; in fact the exchange was 1s. 6d. and falling. But the India Office insisted on retaining the old standard of 1s. 4d. sterling as the basis for budget calculations. Although Hailey had counted on a gain from exchange, he wound up with a loss.

[15] See Bipan Chandra, *The Rise and Growth of Economic Nationalism in India: Economic Policies of Indian National Leadership, 1880–1905.*

businessmen in India agreed with them. Not only routine decision-making but as far as possible the control of Indian finance should be moved from London to Delhi. Unless those who managed the country's finances were answerable to public opinion the Montagu–Chelmsford reforms would remain a sham. "The goal of any exchange and currency policy for India," urged the editor of Bombay's *Times of India*, Sir Stanley Reed, should be "a free, open and automatic system, conducted with the widest possible measure of publicity. In the East," he observed, as though the truism were confined to Orientals, "finance and currency cannot be divorced from politics." As long as India remained in a state of dependency, "it is inevitable that the acts of the administration should be looked upon with suspicion and distrust."[16]

The year 1919 was not the most auspicious one in which to reorganize Indian finance. With the possible exception of 1907 the immediate postwar period was the most unstable era since the silver crisis of the 1890s, when both the Herschell Committee (1893) and the Fowler Commission (1898) had recommended placing India on the gold standard (including gold coinage), closing the silver mints, and setting official exchange at 1s. 4d. sterling.[17] In fact – because of Indian hoarding, said the government; because the government had not minted enough gold sovereigns, critics replied – the gold standard had never come into effect. Instead, John Maynard Keynes wrote in 1913, without anyone's ever planning it India had evolved something called the gold-exchange standard, possessing many features economists ever since Ricardo had regarded as ideal. The basic unit, the rupee, was a token of little intrinsic value that theoretically could be exchanged for gold. In reality, however, gold had been removed from the system entirely, being kept in London solely in order that it could be used immediately and decisively in emergencies.

Moreover, Keynes observed admiringly, the mechanisms were largely automatic. During harvest seasons, when demand in India was high, the secretary of state's council bills, sold once a week by competitive tender in London, enabled capital to be transferred quickly and cheaply there by telegraph. Other bills called reverse councils, which were sold in India, allowed it to flow equally smoothly to Britain – and all without any gold ever leaving the vaults.[18] Persuaded by Keynes, who was then at the Treasury, and Sir Lionel Abrahams of the India Office, the Chamberlain Commission had agreed in 1914 that the gold-exchange standard was there to stay. If to Keynes, however, India's financial system looked like an economist's dream, to Indian economic nationalists it looked like a managed currency, an ideal arrangement for manipulation by the people who were directing it – and they all happened to be British.

In May 1919, when the Babington Smith Committee began hearings, it had

---

16 Appendix 22 to Babington Smith report, PP, 1920 [Cmd. 527–30], *14*.
17 See the reprinted *Reports of Currency Committees* (New Delhi: Agricole, 1982). The best overall survey of currency policy is B. R. Tomlinson, *The Political Economy of the Raj, 1914–1947: The Economics of Decolonization in India* (London: Macmillan, 1979).
18 John Maynard Keynes, *Indian Finance* (1911), vol. 1 of Keynes, *Collected Writings*.

seemed as though the wartime boom that had lifted India's agricultural-export economy to new heights might continue indefinitely. Despite wide fluctuations the rupee remained strong, reaching as high as 2s. 4d. sterling late in December, reflecting the pound's weakness against the American dollar. The Government of India wanted a high rupee, which would reduce the real cost of home charges, help balance the budget, and counter the price inflation that had fueled unrest in the Punjab and elsewhere. Was it conceivable, Indian witnesses retorted passionately, that an agricultural country free to make its own decisions would deliberately make its exports uncompetitive by raising its currency? Arguing the need to encourage exports and develop local manufacturing, they favored reverting to the gold standard at 1s. 4d.

The government also planted its defense of the two-shilling rupee in the high ground of morality. The interests of consumers were cited, especially those of the lowly, inarticulate ryot (peasant), it being alleged by official spokesmen that "those who were engaged in marketing his produce and skimming off the cream" were perhaps not his fittest advocates. Fortunately the ryot had a champion, for it turned out that "the Government's interest was practically identical" with his.[19] As Hailey put it privately, although undoubtedly a cheap rupee would raise agricultural prices, it would benefit the cultivator little and create "widespread economic distress among all the classes on whose good will the political atmosphere depends. I have spent the greater part of my life among agriculturists," he concluded, "and believe I have their interests at heart." In this case, however, "I think we have to consider the interests not merely of the agriculturists but of the whole body politic."[20]

Among all the unpredictable factors in the postwar situation the Babington Smith Committee had counted on a continuing high price of silver, and thus a strong dollar and weak pound. If silver had remained dear, then the 2s. gold rate might have borne some relation to reality. In fact the appearance of the report coincided with a sharp decline. The pound–dollar exchange, called the American cross rate, rose to $3.65. Because that was also the figure at which the government was selling reverse-council bills, exporters hurried to exchange banks, raising the rupee by 4d. in a single day and to 2s. 10½d. by 11 February. Then came chaos. Although the cross rate and the rupee both declined sharply, the latter fell further, leaving a substantial gap between market and reverse-council rates. Speculators, whom the Indian press identified as overwhelmingly European, bought as much as £5 million of reverse councils in one week and £11 million during the month of February.[21]

It could not be more ironic, commented the *Times of India* – a committee assigned to put the system on a sound footing had created the most confused

[19] The quotations are actually taken from questions posed to M. M. Gubbay, Q. 399–403, Babington Smith Committee.
[20] Hailey to Reed, 19 January 1920, HPI/2A.
[21] The best detailed account is in H. Stanley Jevons, *Money, Banking and Exchange in India* (Simla: Government Press, 1922).

situation in the history of Indian exchange – advising that the flight of capital be stopped by halting reverse-council sales at once.[22] In prewar days, charged S. R. Bomanji of the Indian Merchants' Chamber and Bureau of Bombay, Britain had conducted its drain of India under a veil. Now, its debt to America having created difficulties, it was carrying out a policy amounting to organized loot and daylight robbery without even attempting to hide the fact.[23] "One set of people clamour to us for a definite policy of a million Reverse Councils in a day," Hailey put it, while "a second bombard us with accusations of deliberately helping British capital out of the country. Everybody anyhow is excited."[24]

It was in this heated climate that on 1 March 1920 Hailey presented his financial statement. Evidently the chaos in the money market had strengthened his hand. The grand imperial-defense language of the draft budget just two weeks earlier, emphasizing the eastward shift in the world's political gravity and the need for a large force capable of intervention east of Suez, had gone entirely. Although an army adequate to defend the country's own frontiers would no doubt cost more in future, Hailey advised, at present the ordinary military expenditure would be 60 crores of rupees or £40 million, down from slightly over £41 million in the previous budget, still more than half the total central government expenditure, but well below the £57 million or so the Afghan war had actually cost.[25] Taxes, which had increased markedly during wartime, would rise only slightly. It might have been a good deal worse, Indian legislators realized. Although his inexperience had created skepticism about his appointment, the *Leader* of Allahabad commented, Hailey had shown himself "a man of no mean financial ability . . . with the gift of lucid exposition of intricate questions."[26]

The real debate came a week later. Did anyone seriously suppose that his predecessors, men like Sir Guy Fleetwood Wilson or Lord Meston, had been conspiring to rob India, Hailey responded heatedly? Nevertheless, he conceded, the ordinary man must be puzzled. The usual indicators – an excellent autumn harvest, promising winter rains, a favorable if declining trade balance – all seemed to be positive. Yet the government was selling sterling remittances at 3d. above the market rate. It was not unnatural to view these remittances either as a bonus from Indian taxpayers to the few who were fortunate enough to obtain reverse-council allotments or as an invitation to transfer capital to Britain. Such a removal was indeed taking place, and "we are receiving in India only about Rs. 725 for £100 in London, though this £100 cost us originally about Rs. 1,500 to deposit there."

Or so the ordinary man might think. In fact, Hailey tried to persuade his audience, the behavior of reverse-council bills was more effect than cause.

---

[22] Quoted in VR to SS, 25 February 1920, IOR, L/F/7/235. See also Indian Merchants' Chamber and Bureau to Government of India Finance Department, 27 February 1920, IOR, L/F/7/606.
[23] *Bombay Chronicle*, 3 March 1920.   [24] Hailey to Gubbay, 21 February 1920, HPI/2A.
[25] Legislative Council Debates, *58* (1919–20).   [26] *Leader*, 3 March 1920.

British capital having piled up in India during the war, "the loss is there all the time potentially, and sooner or later it becomes a reality." The real question was therefore not reverse councils but the exchange rate. Although the Government of India fully supported high exchange, he declared, going at least to the brink of what it was permissible to disclose about negotiations that were going on between Delhi and London, he hoped the India Office would agree to recently submitted proposals aimed at reducing the 3d. gap between market and reverse-council rates.[27]

The ordinary man had more than held his own, Indians commented ironically. Especially when he had been defending the high level of military spending, the finance member had evidently been unconvinced by his own arguments. His indignant defense of his predecessors had been pure camouflage, they added. The problem was not personal dishonesty, but structural: the Government of India was only a post office transmitting the India Office's orders.[28] It was the old game, Hailey observed, of trying to drive a wedge between Delhi and London.[29]

The game worked best if the wedge was there already. As the currency agitation persisted, as sterling reserves shrank in weekly reverse-council sales, as Hailey and his colleagues tried to defend the policy in Calcutta and Bombay, as the beginning of Gandhi's noncooperation campaign drew nearer, relations between the two centers of Indian governance grew testier. The India Office had no doubt that Delhi would "take every possible opportunity of bringing home to people of India weighty arguments . . . for adhering to essentials of existing currency scheme."[30] Speculative remittances were dissipating reserves to a degree that could not have been foreseen, the Government of India replied.[31] The India Office seemed to think "our troubles can be countered by economic articles pure and simple," Hailey observed. However sound the high-rupee policy might appear on rational grounds, however, "it is in the present condition and temper of India difficult to maintain it if it affords a loophole for the political agitator to raise a really good cry against us." Nothing would persuade the ordinary man that the secretary of state was not restricting gold imports "purely in the interests of his presumed friends in London."[32] The India Office, reported a colleague who was on leave, was "floundering about in search of a piece of friendly driftwood."[33]

In London they were saying much the same thing. First, to the dismay of sober financiers, the Government of India had recklessly sold off £5 million in reverse councils in a single week. Then, although selling bills in large lots at

---

[27] Legislative Council Debates, *58* (1919–20). The Government of India had proposed that sales be conducted by competitive tender, which would remove the basis of the charge that large and mainly British remitters were getting favored treatment. VR to SS, 13 March 1920, IOR, L/F/7/235.

[28] Report of S. R. Bomanji speech, 20 March 1920, IOR L/F/6/606.

[29] Hailey to Seton, 27 March 1920, HPI/2B.

[30] SS to VR, 17 March 1920, IOR L/F/7/235.   [31] VR to SS, 9 April 1920, ibid.

[32] Hailey to Seton, 27 March 1920, HPI/2B.   [33] Cook to Hailey, 19 May 1920, ibid.

fixed rates seemed the only way to force the rupee up, it had proposed to sell small quotas competitively. Scarcely had the telegraph stopped clicking before Delhi proposed to end sales altogether. Indian opinion was fluctuating even more wildly. The *Times of India* kept calling on the authorities to do something – but never the same thing two weeks running, and often reversing positions entirely. The Government of India itself had advocated a high rupee, and no one who had read the Hunter report on the unrest of 1919 could doubt the importance of holding down inflation. Especially in comparison with Europe, the India Office maintained, the Indian economy was basically sound. A little calm firmness now might achieve a stable currency that would enable trade to flourish for decades. The only alternative was to drift along with no policy at all.[34]

The India Office and Government of India differed not on the merits of the high rupee, but on the wisdom of maintaining it in the political circumstances of 1920. Although Gandhi had not yet officially launched the noncooperation campaign, the currency agitation was bringing him large contributions from business interests in Bombay, Karachi, and elsewhere. Should not the controversial policy be jettisoned before it created an enduring alliance between Gandhian extremism and the Indian capitalist class? Although the India Office was the more stubborn, as the reserves continued to dwindle it too recognized that the rot could not go on indefinitely. Late in August Hailey tried one last time to persuade the Legislative Council of the virtues of the two-shilling rupee. Early in September, however, he had to disclose that £41 million had been lost on reverse councils since February.[35] Two weeks later, as the stampede showed no signs of abating, the India Office recommended that sales be suspended indefinitely. Although the situation should be watched for another chance to try to raise exchange, it directed, for the time being the rupee would be left to float, pegged neither to gold nor to sterling.[36]

The reason for the retreat was obvious. India's sterling reserves of £55 million, which had built up as a result of its wartime balance of trade with Britain, had vanished into thin air. Couched in language that made it hard to tell the difference between economic theory and religious dogma, the currency agitation would remain intense through the Hilton Young Commission of 1925 and beyond.[37] Hailey's ordinary man, as well as generations of Indian economic historians, would never be persuaded that London's financiers had not contrived to manipulate the currency in order to rob a colonial economy of precious

---

[34] India Office note enclosed in Montagu to Chelmsford, pvt. letter, 15 April 1920, L/F/7/235. See also notes by H. F. Howard, 29 April 1920, and C. H. Kisch, 8 May 1920, HPI/2B.

[35] 31 August 1920, India, Legislative Council Debates, *59*, 1906 ff.

[36] Kisch minute, 5 October 1920, IOR L/F/235.

[37] "While we are still far from making the 2s. gold rupee effective," wrote Kisch of the India Office's financial division in February 1921, "it would be regrettable to suggest by our actions that we do not hope one day to do so." Indeed, in view of rising administrative costs, the Babington Smith Committee's arguments seemed to him even stronger than when they had originally been presented. Note of 24 February 1921, IOR L/F/6/1054.

capital. If only India had been free like the United States, the debt would have been paid in full and in gold.

On 1 August 1920 Gandhi officially launched the noncooperation campaign. As if deliberately to give him a send-off the House of Lords stirred the embers of Jallianwala Bagh with a vitriolic, racialist debate. On the justice of the case "I have never had the slightest doubt," Hailey confided. "I myself was clear on the point . . . when I visited the scene . . . and heard an account of what had happened from the lips of [General] D[yer] himself." Because the campaign itself seemed to focus entirely on Gandhi's personality, he doubted that it could succeed. It was hard to believe, he concluded, "that we can for many years to come have to face a real Sinn Fein party in India and it is only a party of such determination and with so strong a national backing that can hope to carry out a true policy of non-cooperation."[38]

Hailey was less troubled by Gandhi than by military expenditure. "I wish I could describe the anxiety and bother," he wrote. "The worst legacy of the war has been the belief that you *must* give soldiers everything they ask for; and their training in France has not led them into paths of reason."[39] The War Office had ordered large pay raises for British troops and the Indian army remained in Waziristan. In November 1920 came the Esher report. Reflecting the early years of the war, he judged, its authors had not grasped the fact that Britain simply could not afford a big world army. Indian troops were admittedly badly paid, housed, and equipped. "My blood curdles," he wrote, in a statement that would have astonished the late moderate G. K. Gokhale, for instance, "when I think of the way . . . we utilized our large [prewar] surpluses [for] huge subventions for education and the like."[40]

The previous March, Hailey explained, he had managed to get a military bill of 60 crores (£41 million) through the council fairly easily, but only because he had imposed no fresh taxation. All through the summer he had been chairing a committee charged with reducing the size of the army while improving its equipment. The army had appeared to cooperate, but "alas they were deceiving us." Military strength was actually increasing, investigation had persuaded him that Indian politicians' charges about wastage were completely justified, and the army was still lodged firmly in the money trap called Waziristan.

Any rise in military expenditure would require tax increases. These would have to be proposed in the midst of a serious commercial depression and the political unrest of the noncooperation campaign to a new, suspicious Assembly. "I believe that this will go far to kill the growing moderate party on whose strength the future of the reformed constitution depends," Hailey warned. The Assembly would be bound to reject taxation, the viceroy equally bound to restore it, fusing extremists and moderates into a strong nationalist party. Earlier Hailey had been confident that Congress could not match the achievement

[38] Hailey to Hilton Young, 25 September 1920, HPI/2C.
[39] Hailey to Howard, 24 November 1920, ibid.
[40] Hailey to Hilton Young, 19 November 1920, ibid.

of the Sinn Feiners in Ireland and make noncooperation a reality. Now he was not so sure.[41]

The perspective of the commander in chief, Lord Rawlinson of Trent, who took office in November 1920, was naturally different. The Indian army's campaign in Mesopotamia in the Great War had been a fiasco, exposing severe weaknesses in training and logistics. His task was to reequip, overhaul, and prepare it to fight a modern war. In this effort, as the collapse of Singapore in 1942 would reveal so starkly, Rawlinson and his British military colleagues east of Suez would fail. "It is no exaggeration," a standard work concludes, "to say that the financial aspect dominated the discussion . . . throughout the inter-war period."[42] Neither British chancellors of the exchequer nor Indian finance members like Hailey were willing or able to commit the necessary resources.

Although his own job was hard enough, Rawlinson noted in his diary, Hailey's was even tougher. The budget would not balance, the exchange situation was worsening, and "he has to fight to save every rupee."[43] To carry out desperately needed improvements on the frontier and make a decent start toward meeting the Esher Committee's recommendations would require an annual military budget of 75 crores, Rawlinson estimated, compared with 29.5 crores in 1913–14. Because the main problem was the rising cost of British troops, he agreed with Hailey that the only way to cut spending substantially was to reduce their number. Where the two men differed was on timing. Rawlinson stressed the turbulent northwestern frontier, the long-term threat from Soviet Russia, and the danger of severe internal disorder. "If we cannot hold down the rioter and the revolutionary with Indian troops," Hailey put it shortly, "we cannot hold India at all."[44]

The showdown came in January 1921. Rawlinson brought his figure down to 65 crores; the Viceroy's Council told him to cut it to 60. Since that would mean sending home two cavalry regiments, an artillery brigade, and five infantry battalions, he threatened to resign. In London the secretary of state, Edwin Montagu, under pressure from the War Office, objected that such deep slashes in the military budget would undermine the confidence of investors in the government's ability to maintain order and make it practically impossible to float a railway loan in the City. Unfortunately, Hailey noted, someone in the War Office apparently leaked information about the proposed cutbacks to the press. If the viceroy were now to restore taxation after the Assembly had voted it

---

41 Hailey to Sir William Duke, 1 December 1920, ibid. According to the recent Brussels conference, noted H. F. Howard of the India Office's finance department, 35.7% of India's national expenditure was devoted to the military, exceeded only by that of Japan (47.9%) and Greece (37%), compared with that of Britain itself (16.8%) and Canada (0.6%). Note of 3 December 1920, IOR L/F/1073.

42 Brian Bond, *British Military Policy Between the two World Wars* (Oxford: Clarendon Press, 1980), p. 125. See also Keith Jeffery, *The British Army and the Crisis of Empire, 1918–22* (Manchester: Manchester University Press, 1984), ch. 6.

43 Entries of 18 and 30 December 1920, Frederick Maurice, *The Life of General Lord Rawlinson of Trent* (London: Cassell, 1928), pp. 283–4, 287–8.

44 Hailey to Howard, 30 March 1921, HPI/4A.

down, he would obviously have done so on orders from home. No doubt the Assembly would walk out, "and we shall have non-cooperation in a new and unpleasant form."[45]

In the Viceroy's Council, Hailey's majority held firm. The top priorities, declared the official telegram to London, must be to make the Montagu–Chelmsford reform scheme work, deny martyrdom to extremists, and help the moderates.[46] Montagu referred the troop question for arbitration to the Committee of Imperial Defence. That "will cut no ice here," Hailey warned; if the India Office forced the Government of India's hand, it would be "impossible to prevent it being known that we have been compelled" to raise taxation. If the levy were refused would the viceroy restore it? "I should certainly not attempt to support him in doing so."[47] Ultimately, both Rawlinson and Hailey having threatened to go public, they compromised on 62.2 crores, which would be presented to the new Legislative Assembly as the minimum beneath which the united Government of India would not go.

On 9 February 1921 the uncle of George V and only living son of Victoria, the duke of Connaught, opened the first reformed legislature in the still un-completed capital of New Delhi. He read a telegram from the king-emperor: "To-day you have beginnings of Swaraj within my Empire, and widest scope and ample opportunity for progress to the liberty which other Dominions enjoy." On the people's representatives lay responsibility for convincing the world that this unparalleled step had been wise. Freedom had often been won by violent revolution; rarely had it been a "free gift of one people to another." With obvious reference to General Dyer and the Punjab the statement repudiated "the idea that the administration of India has ever been or ever can be based on principles of force or terrorism." And then the duke made a personal plea. Ever since he had arrived in Bombay he had felt "bitterness and estrangement. . . . The shadow of Amritsar has lengthened over the fair face of India."[48] Let the dead past bury its dead, the old man appealed.

It was perhaps as sincere a gesture as could be imagined, Hailey reflected later. But the time had not been right, Swarajists had scoffed, and the plea had fallen flat.[49] And so the two sides returned to what from the British perspective was a mundane process of political bargaining, and to what in the Indian view was a freedom struggle that must endure until swaraj arrived indeed.

On 1 March 1921 Hailey presented his second budget. A year ago, he noted, the uncertain currency situation notwithstanding, the outlook had seemed reasonably hopeful. The position now was grim: severe trade depression, a poor monsoon, a fall in the rupee from a high of 2s. 7d. sterling to its present low of 1s. 4d. Although many people blamed the government's currency policy instead of the decline in purchasing power of India's customers in Europe and Japan,

---

[45] Hailey to Cook, 23 January 1921, ibid.   [46] VR to SS, 30 January 1921, IOR L/F/6/1018.
[47] Hailey to PSV, 26 February 1921, HPI/4A.
[48] Legislative Assembly (LA) Debates, *1* (1921).   [49] Hailey to Irwin, 23 May 1930, HPI/18A.

the fact was that the Babington Smith Committee's two-shilling rupee had never really come into effect. He did not deny that the effort to support exchange had severely harmed India's sterling resources or that selling reverse councils in large lots at fixed prices rather than by competitive tender had encouraged speculation. Beyond the obvious fact that the government was not infallible, however, what were its intentions? Was it waiting quietly for a chance to put exchange back up to two shillings? Would a new committee be appointed? "Have we, in short, any policy at all?" The short answer was no: "no practical step which Government can take at present" could conceivably correct the situation. All that could be done was wait for world demand for India's exports to resume, while candidly confessing impotence.[50]

Projecting some 111 crores of revenue against total expenditure of 129, of which an irreducible minimum of 62.2 would be military, Hailey brought in a deficit budget of 18 crores, which would have to be covered by new taxation: 16 from increased customs and excise, including British cotton manufactures, the remaining 2 to come from higher income and supertaxes on company profits. The only alternative would be to raise the salt tax paid by even the poorest Indian. The Assembly and press alike called it a bankruptcy budget. Of India's total public expenditure, central and provincial, declared the *Leader* (Allahabad), more than a third went to the military, 4 percent for education, and less than 1 percent for sanitation: No wonder "ignorance and illiteracy are the badge of the tribe!"[51] Why had the finance member been unable to explain the reverse-council muddle? Was it because he would "once more expose the fact that the Lombard Street clique is at the bottom of all this and really pulls the wires of . . . the India Office?"[52]

In the end, although one member said the finance member reminded him of a schoolmaster about to use the birch, the Assembly backed away from confrontation. "If we have managed to get through," Hailey warned, "it is . . . rather by reason of the defects of the Assembly than by our own virtues." Provincial and communal jealousies along with parliamentary inexperience had enabled the government to pull through. But "the lesson . . . is that we shall never do so again." Next time, unless civil and military budgets were both cut substantially, "we shall be up against a brick wall."[53]

In April 1921, as Lord Reading succeeded Lord Chelmsford as viceroy, Hailey judged the prospects reasonably hopeful. The new legislatures had managed to function; even on the currency question a sort of undeclared truce seemed to have emerged. People were tiring of noncooperation, he felt. If only a treaty more favorable to Turkey could be secured, Muslims would be placated

50 LA Debates, *1*, 434 ff.
51 *Leader,* 11 March 1921. When the Manchester cotton lobby protested Montagu responded firmly that the convention that India now enjoyed fiscal autonomy would be respected.
52 8 March 1921, LA Debates, *1*, 720 ff.
53 Hailey to Howard, 24 March 1921, HPI/4A. See also Hailey to Hilton Young, 28 March 1921, ibid.

and "a split would soon develop within the ranks of the extremists themselves." The real danger, he thought, came not from extremist politicians but from the alienation their propaganda was creating among supposedly nonpolitical people, such as striking workers in Bombay or Ahmedabad or peasants who were conducting a no-rent campaign in the United Provinces. Although "Gandhi and his friends have succeeded in stirring up agrarian and labour trouble to an extent that we could not have anticipated a few years ago," Hailey still stressed that it was "largely a one-man show and cannot last for ever."[54] The long game still seemed best.

To be sure the India Office soon handed its critics more ammunition by floating a loan in the City of London at 7 percent, a full point above the going rate in Bombay.[55] The government's financial situation remained severe, and only marked improvement in the export trade along with very substantial retrenchment, especially in military outlay, could possibly restore it. Not only was the army still in Waziristan, however; not only was the commander in chief reluctant to send British troops home during such a tense time. Hailey himself had given a hostage to fortune. In order to reduce the demand for new taxation as far as possible he had budgeted for a 1s. 8d. rupee. At the end of April, however, it remained disconcertingly at 1s. 4d. Translated into pounds – and salaries of soldiers and officials as well as the home charges all had to be converted – the difference for his total budget of 118 crores worked out to £20 million.

Military expenses, Hailey pointed out in a long memorandum, had reached a crippling 59 percent of the central government's budget. Before the war, apart from temporary fluctuations caused by famines, the silver crisis of 1907, or the end of the opium windfall in 1911, and even including the cost of Lord Kitchener's army reorganization scheme of 1904–5, revenue had risen somewhat faster than expenditure. After 1915–16 the graph was entirely different: large increases in taxation chasing exponential rises in spending. Deficits were of course expected during wartime and their true extent had been hidden by the blockage of equipment orders and retrenchment in civil departments. Since the armistice, however, a rush of orders had come for British machinery, along with claims for salary increases, the army's expenses in Afghanistan, and finally the Esher Committee's recommendations. The result had been four deficit budgets in a row. The government's critics were quite right, Hailey concluded. The situation was utterly out of control.

In 1914 the Indian army had consisted of 233,000 men – 80,000 British and 153,000 native troops – costing 30 crores of rupees. Although the postwar army was slightly smaller, its cost was more than double. The reason was obvious:

---

[54] Hailey to Sir William Meyer, 25 April 1921, ibid.

[55] Although Hailey offered ironic congratulations to a former colleague for "getting a share of our very profitable loan," making clear that he had nothing to do with the terms, the India Office's finance committee had feared failure. Hailey to Gubbay, 23 May 1921, ibid.; note of meeting at Barclays Bank, 16 April 1921, IOR L/F/7/783.

Costing more to pay, feed, house, and transport, British soldiers were roughly four times as expensive as Indian. Compounding the problem was the recent division between central and provincial revenues, the so-called Meston award, which had caught the reform program in a squeeze. Insisting on larger contributions to the central government would wreck the scheme at the provincial level; not doing so would place the Government of India's solvency in jeopardy. The long-awaited equilibrium between revenue and expenditure had proved to be a mirage. The government's field for taxation was extremely limited. Income and supertaxes were already high. And an increase in the salt tax, Hailey noted presciently, "would be so unpopular in the Assembly and in the country at large that it would be most impolitic to attempt it."[56]

There was apparently only one way out. Although some would think it mad to cut British troops in present circumstances, a beginning must be made. Hailey could not "envisage a future in which India has Dominion status but is to be told that . . . we must keep up a large and expensive body of British troops in order to maintain internal peace."[57] There were either too many soldiers or too few.

Ordinarily a commander in chief makes a case for the largest army conceivable. In principle, however, Rawlinson and Hailey were surprisingly close. In the context of the reform program, the general noted in his diary, an army of occupation could no longer be justified. Although his projection of two or three generations sounded ludicrously slow to Indian ears, he did begin planning Indianization, including an Indian Woolwich and Sandhurst to train officers. Indians must either be trusted or not, he reasoned. Either there must be clear progress toward dominion status or a "return to the old method of ruling India with the sword. There is no half-way house."[58]

The political situation had deteriorated over the summer, Hailey judged in August 1921. Astutely Lord Reading had held an interview with Gandhi, the apparent effect of which had been to raise suspicions among fellow extremists. Nevertheless Gandhi had managed to raise a crore of rupees, and Hailey conceded that the campaign had "made far greater progress than we thought possible." The noncooperators "raise strikes without reason; they make the position of the district officer almost impossible by a species of boycott; they make it exceedingly difficult for any enterprise run by British capital to get its labour." In short it had come down to "a kind of race [as to] whether political concessions and the atmosphere introduced by them downwards can restore our position among the people at large, before the nationalists get such a complete hold" that the reforms became meaningless.[59]

---

[56] Hailey note on general financial position of India and its bearing on military budget, 12 July 1921, IOR L/F/6/1018.
[57] Hailey to Hilton Young, 1 August 1921, HPI/4B.
[58] Rawlinson journal entry and letter to unidentified military friend in UK, n.d. [summer 1922], Maurice, *Rawlinson*, pp. 295–6, 306–7.
[59] Hailey to Hilton Young, 1 August 1921, HPI/4B.

From the late summer of 1921 until well into 1922 there is a gap in the Hailey Collection. Although the Reading administration continued to play the long game it stepped up the pace, arresting the Ali brothers in September on charges of sedition and promoting disaffection among Indian troops. When Gandhi read out their statements verbatim, declaring that "sedition has become the creed of the Congress," he was left untouched. In November a boycott of the visit of the Prince of Wales led to serious riots in Bombay. Calling off mass civil disobedience in atonement, Gandhi fasted. More arrests followed. Lord Reading offered a round-table conference, but only on condition that the non-cooperation campaign ended. It was for the government to indicate a change of heart by redressing its wrongs, Gandhi replied firmly. When the new year passed without swaraj moderates taunted him. All he had said, he replied, was that India could be free if only noncooperation were carried out faithfully and universally. Late in January 1922, in the single tahsil of Bardoli in Bombay presidency, he prepared to mount the final stage of the campaign: a rent and tax strike.

Once again violence intervened. This time, at a place called Chauri Chaura in the United Provinces, two dozen Indian policemen were burned alive. A warning from God had saved him from another Himalayan blunder, declared Gandhi, who suspended civil disobedience. But the halt was still temporary. By early March rumors were widespread that, as the Mahatma put it, the end of his leave was long overdue.[60] Throughout this period the Hailey Papers consist of little more than a round of congratulations in January 1922 on his appointment as Knight Commander of the Order of the Star of India. A month shy of fifty, he was Sir Malcolm at last.

As budget day approached Hailey again fought to reduce military spending. This time, Rawlinson having agreed to reach a figure of 60 crores by cutting British troop strength, the roadblock was in London.[61] "Indications are that the extremists are about to stake their last card," Delhi advised, referring to Gandhi's intended no-rent campaign. If taxes were raised the Assembly would surely refuse them, "involving serious risks of complete breakdown of the Reforms Scheme, and rendering administration of this country most difficult."[62] The India Office should understand, Hailey warned the viceroy's private secretary, that the Assembly had to be persuaded of "the honesty of our own convictions . . . when not only do such convictions not exist but the fact . . . is well known in advance to the legislature."[63] Reading had already warned the secretary of state that he expected "serious difficulty with Hailey."[64] In the end, however, the British cabinet held firm: the Committee of Imperial

---

60 CWMG, *12*, 221–3, 415–21; *13*, 20–1. The most detailed account is Judith Brown, *Gandhi's Rise to Power*, pp. 309 ff.
61 See scheme for Indianization of Indian army, 24 January 1922, Cab 24/133, CP 3709 (1922).
62 VR (Army) to SS, 6 February 1922, Cab 24/133, CP 3711 (1922).
63 Hailey to PSV, 15 February 1922, HPI/5A.
64 VR to SS (Pvt.), 6 February 1922, Cab 24/133, CP 2712 (1922).

Defence's consideration of Indianization would not be hurried; the military figure would be 62.5 not 60 crores; and no commitment to reduce British troops would be made lest it be interpreted as weakness in the face of agitation.

In the interval since his last budget, Hailey told the Assembly on 1 March 1922, just about everything imaginable had gone wrong: deepening trade repression, heavy imports of wheat and coal forced by strikes and poor monsoons. The financial results had been disastrous. Revenue had been 20 crores less than projected, while owing largely to military overspending in Waziristan and the serious Moplah rebellion among Muslims in south India, expenditure was up by 14 crores. It was the fourth deficit in a row, adding up to a cumulative figure of 90 crores since 1918–19. With the country's very solvency at stake, budgeting a large deficit was unthinkable. As usual the military budget was irreducible. Taxes and services of all kinds – fares, postal and telegraph charges, tariffs, the excise duty on cotton, income and supertaxes – would have to go up. Despite his own prediction the previous summer of the grave political consequences, the salt duty would be doubled. Surely, Hailey rationalized, although Gandhi's dramatic march to the sea in 1930 would focus on that issue, it could not be held that 3 annas per head "will be felt appreciably by even the poorest classes."[65]

This time, as Hailey had warned, the Assembly was better organized. At least this bankruptcy budget clarified matters, speaker after speaker asserted. The simple truth was that India could afford neither its alien government nor the bloated army which that government thought essential. Only the government could reduce military costs; the Assembly could do no more than withhold its approval from new taxes. "Have we now come to the parting of the ways?" Hailey asked. His Indian colleagues should remember that Parliament had laid down a road to constitutional advance; "unless you desire to attempt it by the force of arms," progress could be gained in no other way.[66] Although these remarks were widely regarded as a threat, the Assembly had in fact been the finance member's strongest allies on the military-spending issue. He might even have been a little disappointed if he, and therefore the India Office, had been let off scot-free. After all, he reasoned, the Assembly could neither touch the army nor force the executive to resign. What else could it do but be obstructive? "I really cannot believe," he concluded, "that the present state of things can continue for the ten years provided by the Government of India Act. We have given them either too much or too little."[67]

On 11 March, concluding that Gandhi had effectively isolated himself, the government arrested him. When Congress volunteers had been rounded up on the theory that a little firmness would rally the moderates, Rawlinson mused, the action had made things worse; "now we have arrested Gandhi and looked for no end of trouble, and lo! the arrest has caused no trouble at all." A week

---

[65] LA Debates, 2 (1922), 2653–76. [66] 7 March 1922, ibid., 2, 2754–1812.
[67] Hailey to Howard, 4 February 1922, HPI/5A.

later, after explaining eloquently why he was indeed guilty of sedition as charged, the Mahatma received a six-year jail term. Meanwhile the Assembly hacked away, item by item, cutting the salt tax, reducing departmental allocations 10 percent across the board, playing out the constitutional crisis – but all in remarkably good humor. Hailey grew jocular and Rawlinson noted privately that the Assembly had behaved quite responsibly.[68] In the end the budget passed with a deficit of 9 crores (£6 million) which would have to be covered by borrowing, but obviating the need for the viceroy to restore taxation and thus avoiding a deadlock.

In April 1922, as Sir Malcolm and Lady Hailey prepared to go to England on leave, he may already have known that his occupancy of the seat of the scornful was almost over. If so, Philip Mason's judgment that he gave up the office entirely without regret seems eminently reasonable.[69] Hailey had not been an experienced financier. Moreover, since 1919 the record showed an exchange fiasco, severe depression, spiraling taxes, rampant military spending, and four deficits in a row – not exactly an unqualified success story. Although these failures would be cited against him repeatedly, however, the indictment was usually qualified. Everyone knew that the crucial decisions had been made in London, that after all he had been a messenger. What he called the old game of trying to split the Government of India from the India Office helped save his reputation. Although his successor Sir Basil Blackett, ironically the man Edwin Montagu had wanted to appoint in the first place, would not be announced until the autumn, Sir Malcolm Hailey had survived his last budget. Whether India would do so remained to be seen.

---

68 Rawlinson journal entries, March 1922, Maurice, *Rawlinson,* pp. 303–4. Simultaneous with the arrest, but unconnected to it, Secretary of State Edwin Montagu was forced to resign from the Lloyd George coalition cabinet over a press leak, his replacement being a Conservative, Lord Peel.

69 *Dictionary of National Biography* (1961–70 Supplement). Although I have found no contemporary evidence to confirm this judgment, I can think of no reason why Hailey would not have been glad to escape.

7

<hr>

Home member, 1922–1924

At the end of May 1922 Sir Malcolm and Alexandra Hailey arrived in London for a three-month leave, his first trip home since before the war. Apart from visiting family and fishing he had interviews with the king, the Prince of Wales, and the prime minister, David Lloyd George.[1] He also wrote an article on Indian affairs, published anonymously in *Round Table*.

Since 1895, his first year in India, Hailey began the article, there had been four intense political spasms: the first, centered in the Deccan, ending in the conviction of B. G. Tilak for sedition in 1897; the second, also focused in the west, with a secondary wave in the Punjab, terminating in Tilak's second imprisonment in 1907; third, the long conflict over the partition of Bengal; and last, Gandhi's recently concluded noncooperation campaign. Each convulsion had similar features: "its intensity, its revolutionary, not to say its anarchical character; the suddenness with which it has subsided – at all events temporarily – as soon as the principal protagonist or protagonists were deprived of the power to lead the agitation; and the almost baffling apathy of the reaction period."

Thus did Indian political history repeat itself. Readers would find it hard to identify the country of the summer of 1922 with the scene even as recently as the previous February. At that point strikes, peasant revolts, and the Akali movement among Sikhs in the Punjab had all been threatening to explode, while Gandhi's words of peace had evoked acts of violence and coercion in his followers, so that the country had seemed in "a state of suspended revolution." Overnight all that had changed. A favorable monsoon, a good harvest and, at last, an upturn in the export market had begun to relieve the long commercial depression. Hartals were now unheard of. Civil disobedience was regarded as impractical. The Akali movement seemed to be on the wane, and a new tenancy act in the UP had apparently removed the peasants' grievances: both judgments, as Hailey's later governorships would demonstrate, being strikingly premature. Over most of India, he concluded, there was "something very near the political peace of stagnation."

<hr>

[1] The *Times*, 10 June 1922; Hailey note for Lloyd George, June 1922, and notes of discussion at India Office, 6 July 1922, HPI/5A.

Although English readers might understandably have grown exasperated, the author conceded, the Government of India had played the long game astutely. Waiting patiently until the dynamics of the movement had isolated the leader and deprived him of his power, at just the right psychological moment the state had struck and struck hard. The result was "a paralysis so dramatic that those unacquainted with the history of Indian politics cannot understand it."[2]

Even so, the article recognized, Congress remained by far the best-organized party in Indian politics. As its leaders came out of jail they would survey the wreckage and conclude that Gandhi's greatest blunder had been the boycott of councils. For the elections had been held on schedule. Legislatures dominated by liberals and moderates had managed to function. Congress, in short, had failed to occupy the available constitutional space. The next elections would therefore see extremist politicians participating all across India. Judging from their rhetoric Congress representatives would be uncompromisingly obstructionist, a wrecking crew built on Irish lines. But the country's mood had changed. It was tired of nihilism. Although civil disobedience might reappear, the writer concluded, the contest between the government and the extremists would move into the legislatures. Such a change in focus would put the next home member squarely in the center. And that, as the anonymous author probably knew already, would be Sir Malcolm Hailey.

∞∞∞∞∞∞

In October 1922, shortly after their return from England, the Haileys' talented, attractive, and popular teenage daughter, Gemma, died suddenly from a burst appendix. Although Sir Malcolm left no written evidence of his reaction it is not hard to imagine how he dealt with his grief. His natural inclination would have been to throw himself still more intensely into his work.[3] Undoubtedly that was the best possible therapy for him. But it was not so for his wife. As Philip Mason stated in his sensitive biographical sketch of her husband, this was the truly traumatic experience of Alexandra Hailey's life. It was one from which she never fully recovered.[4]

This judgment, which Mason said he made on the basis of common knowledge at the time, was confirmed for me in a moving interview with Mrs. Iqbal Jehan Afzal in Lahore in 1987. In 1922, about a month after Gemma's death,

[2] "India," *Round Table, 12* (September 1922), 844–55. Commissioned in John Dove, editor of *Round Table*, to Hailey, 14 May 1922, HPI/5A. Apart from Lionel Curtis, who would be instrumental in his selection to direct the *African Survey*, Hailey did not have a close relationship with the *Round Table* group, the former acolytes of Lord Milner in South Africa who played such a crucial role in the evolution of the Commonwealth. Even Curtis was not a regular correspondent during Hailey's Indian career.

[3] Chirol to Hailey, 11 March 1924, HPI/6A. The Hailey Collection contains some two hundred letters of condolence, including many from Indians.

[4] *Dictionary of National Biography*, Supplement (1961–70).

when she herself was a girl of fourteen, she was taken by her mother to see Lady Hailey, who had worked with her father in the Red Cross in Delhi during the war. The families were close, Afzal recalled, and Sir Malcolm knew the children's names – or at least the boys'. Since Afzal's mother observed purdah, Sir Malcolm appeared only briefly, thanked them for coming, then tactfully withdrew. Throughout the visit Lady Hailey cried uncontrollably. Her intense grief impressed the girl so profoundly that six decades later she still remembered it vividly.[5]

In her youth, it will be recalled, Alexandra Hailey was beautiful, athletic, and musically talented. But she was also foreign and Catholic, with a tendency toward eccentricity that Sir Harcourt Butler had used in 1912 in his attempt to block her husband's appointment to the commissionership of Delhi. Especially after they left the Jhelum canal colony it seems likely that she never really fit in. In many ways service wives led hard lives: continual demands for so-called volunteer work but no possibility of a career; prevented by convention from much genuine contact with Indians; often blamed rather unfairly for race prejudice and exclusiveness; a constant struggle against boredom and apathy. For a married woman Lady Hailey was perhaps unusually independent; at least she organized hunting trips to Kashmir without her husband.[6] In 1918, it will be recalled, at the climax of the war, in what seems likely to have been a state of acute depression, he had gone alone to Japan. There are therefore hints that the relationship may have become strained during or even before the war.

Hailey's attitude toward his work may well have been a source of tension. The Indian Civil Service gave demanding, responsible positions to extremely young men, and he had always worked hard. At some point, though it is not clear when, the trait became rather more than that. At least by the early 1930s he had become the classic workaholic. Although it was not in fact true, for he was an avid hiker and fisherman (both solo occupations), he often described himself as having no hobbies or diversions, as a man who lived through and for work. He dreaded retirement. His relief when he was offered the directorship of the *African Survey* in 1933, or when Malcolm Macdonald asked him in 1939 to go to Africa, would be obvious. The mountain of African material in the Public Record Office and at Rhodes House is among other things testimony to what had become an obsessive fear of being unoccupied even for a minute: writing away on Christmas morning in Uganda, or compiling a survey of native administration in the Congo for no other reason than that time was on his hands.

Grief at the death of a child will subject even the strongest marriage to intense strain. Whether Hailey's withdrawal into his work was cause or effect of his wife's deterioration is unclear; most likely it was both. What is apparent is

---

5 Interview with Afzal, Lahore, 4 March 1987.
6 See the amusing correspondence of October 1916 concerning disputes that had taken place among "beaters" of Mrs. Hailey, Gladys Barlow, and Motilal Nehru over possession of a hunting field in Kashmir. HPI/1C.

that in this severe personal tragedy he did not or could not provide the support she needed so desperately. Perhaps a lesser man might have been a more successful husband. But, one reflects, perhaps not.

The husband workaholic, the wife alcoholic. During the 1920s Lady Hailey struggled to regain her composure and control. Confronting her grief directly and publicly, she presided in Simla at annual assemblies of the Gemma Hailey Girl Guides. She put up a bold front. When the first airplane flew direct from England to India in 1927, she went up as a passenger, crashed at the local airfield, and walked away saying she could hardly wait to go up again.[7] When the editor of *Muslim Outlook* took exception to a resolution which her European–Indian woman's club had passed, deploring the disappearance of Jawaharlal Nehru's moustache – because the eyes of proper women were cast down they shouldn't notice – she wrote with spirit: so silly that people could get so excited about a harmless joke.[8]

It was a losing fight. By the early 1930s, when her husband was governor of the United Provinces, the senior and by common agreement the most distinguished member of his service, Lady Hailey suffered from acute and sometimes suicidal depression. Only her behavior, it was said, prevented Sir Malcolm from becoming viceroy. Stories circulated, as they did even half a century later. The thoughtless or spiteful gossipers would have better have reflected on how deeply a mother can feel the death of her child.

It might have been different if the Haileys had had a different, closer relationship with their son, Billy. Here again there are only a few scraps of evidence. Although he graduated from his father's Oxford college, Corpus Christi, he evidently had a troubled boyhood and very likely a delayed adolescent rebellion. Throughout the 1920s and early 1930s he moved back and forth between England and India, unable to hold a job or find a niche. Among the sparse documents is an extremely revealing letter the young man wrote to his father from England in 1927 after a solo expedition in a lifeboat in the North Sea, enclosing newspaper clippings about how the sailor had been rescued after a close call in a storm.[9] Not close at all, he wrote with deliberate understatement. The obvious pride at being recognized publicly, at having achieved something his famous, masterful father had never done, is touching. It could not have been easy to have been Malcolm Hailey's son – or his wife.

∞∞∞∞∞∞∞

---

[7] After the crash, she told a reporter, "some Tommys came with stretchers," but she said, "Wait a bit lads, I can manage, don't pull; I'll ask for a hand when I want it." After crawling out she saw "the poor broken machine, such a jolly little aeroplane," the aide-de-camp, chauffeur, etc., all "pretty green, I can tell you. They had all the horror of it, and I had all the fun." See press clippings and correspondence of April 1927, HPI/10A.

[8] Clippings from September–October 1925 in HPI/8B.

[9] A. B. Hailey to his father, 29 September 1927, HPI/11A.

In November 1922 it was announced that Sir Basil Blackett would become finance member and that Hailey would succeed Sir William Vincent in the home membership. Once again the press reaction was mixed. The *Leader* (Allahabad) remarked that there was no reason to think Sir Malcolm had changed his unprogressive political views; where Vincent had been tactful Hailey was likely to be abrasive. Even the *Statesman*, a Calcutta Anglo-Indian paper, questioned whether he was quite "the guide, philosopher and friend of whom the Assembly stands in need at the present critical juncture." Fate would have been fairer, the writer added acidly, if the retiring finance member had been given the job of removing the deficit his three years in office had left behind.[10]

Just as Hailey's *Round Table* article had predicted, the dominant issue was whether Congress would enter the councils. During the summer, after interviewing witnesses across the country, a Congress committee had concluded that the essential preconditions for a renewal of mass civil disobedience laid down at Bardoli in February – especially intercommunal unity, unswerving commitment to nonviolence, and removal of discrimination against untouchables – remained unfulfilled. After that the committee split. Arguing that different times required new tactics, half the members recommended that Congress candidates should enter central and provincial legislatures: this would become the platform of the Swarajist party in 1923. The other members, who were called No-Changers, favored continuing Gandhi's program intact, including the boycott of councils.[11]

All these developments were, of course, well known to the home department's political division.[12] By design – Gandhi said the practice made Indians more courageous – Congress was an open organization conducting the vast majority of its business in broad daylight. Although its bank accounts were sometimes hidden, only meetings of the all-India and provincial working committees were closed, and even those were ordinarily reported by informers within a few days. Knowing that the postal service routinely intercepted their mail, politicians calculated that the government knew nearly as much about their activities as they did. The home political division therefore knew in advance the outline of the Congress committee's report as well as the positions its members would take. The appraisal it sent to London in November was virtually a restatement of Hailey's *Round Table* article.[13]

[10] *Leader*, 4 November 1922, *Statesman*, 2 November 1922.
[11] See report of Congress Civil Disobedience Enquiry Committee, October 1922, in Motilal Nehru, *Selected Works*, ed. Ravinder Kumar and D. N. Panigrahi (New Delhi: Vikas, 1982–), vol. 3, and Lal Bahadur, *Indian Freedom Movement and Thought: Politics of "Pro-Change" versus "No-Change," 1919–1922* (New Delhi: Sterling, 1983).
[12] The home department had two branches. The establishment division handled personnel matters in the all-India public services. The home political division had been formed in 1907, the year of Tilak's second conviction and the canal-colony revolt in the Punjab, in recognition of the fact that extremism had become a permanent force in Indian political life.
[13] Intelligence reports of 23 August and 16 October 1922, NAI, HomPol 900/III/1922 and 900/IV/1922; VR to SS, 9 November 1922, ibid.

As Hailey told the Legislative Assembly, the noncooperation campaign had made people in Britain fear that India was succumbing to an anarchy "very akin to that which destroyed Russia."[14] People were "fed up with India," Secretary of State Edwin Montagu had written to Lord Reading.[15] In March, at the time of Gandhi's arrest, Montagu had been forced to resign from Lloyd George's coalition cabinet because of a press leak, and his successor, Lord Peel, was known to be much less favorable to reform. Once, wrote Sir Tej Bahadur Sapru, the distinguished Allahabad Liberal who was serving as law member, "we looked up to Whitehall against the Government of India."[16] It was "always best for India," Hailey observed, meaning of course the Government of India, "when the English public forgets its existence."[17]

To the new home member neither rapid constitutional advance nor unduly severe repression seemed appropriate. Only a few months ago the country had seemed on the brink of revolution, and though some extremist leaders now recognized that noncooperation had become farcical, Congress had still not officially abandoned civil disobedience. There were of course demands for Gandhi's early release. Such a gesture might improve the atmosphere, Hailey thought, but only if it were well timed; otherwise it would fall flat or even rejuvenate the agitation. Provincial governments might discreetly comb through their still-numerous prisoners, he suggested, but there should be no general amnesty.[18]

On the other hand the riot squads should not be called out every time somebody unfurled a swaraj flag. People at the India Office sometimes forgot their Bacon: "Neither doth it follow that because these fames are a sign of troubles, that the suppressing of them with too much severity should be a remedy of troubles. For the despising of them many times checks them best; and the going about to stop them doth but make a wonder long lived."[19] The English now rued the day they had banned the wearing of the green in Ireland, and the Bande Mataram might never have become a national freedom song if the government had not prosecuted Indian boys for singing it. By the early 1930s Hailey would come to believe that the Reading administration had allowed the noncooperation campaign too much time and space in the early stages. As home member after 1922, however, he continued to favor the long game.

Hailey's term coincided with a lull in Congress activity that would last until the appointment of the all-white Simon Commission in 1927. Although the home political papers at the Indian National Archives are comparatively well

14 8 September 1922, LA Debates, 3.
15 Quoted by Aruna Sinha, *Lord Reading: Viceroy of India* (New Delhi: Sterling, 1985), p. 57.
16 Sir Tej Bahadur Sapru, "The Problem of India's Aspirations," *Contemporary Review, 124* (1923), 578.
17 Hailey note, 9 April 1923, NAI, HomPol 198/1923.
18 Hailey note, 23 February 1923, NAI, HomPol 56/1923.
19 Hailey note, 9 April 1923, NAI, HomPol 198/1923.

preserved, far surpassing those of the finance department, for example, they are still insufficient for a detailed examination of how the department worked administratively. The treatment must therefore by topical.

The most difficult issue before the home department was the effort by Sikhs in the Punjab to take control of their gurdwaras, or shrines, a campaign that has sometimes been called the Third Sikh War. When Hailey took office the agitation was at its height. In 1921 several hundred Sikh demonstrators were enticed by the mahant (priest) into a gurdwara at Nankana. There they were set upon by thugs, cut to pieces, doused with petrol and burned, while many of them were still alive. In the autumn of 1922 marchers at Guru-ka-Bagh, a shrine near Amritsar, were routinely being beaten senseless. It was like witnessing the martyrdom of hundreds of Christs, testified Gandhi's friend the English clergyman C. F. Andrews. Meanwhile in the central Punjab the Criminal Investigation Department was engaged in a massive operation to suppress the revolutionary terrorists known as the Babbar Akalis.

In 1924, as governor of the Punjab, Hailey would confront the Sikh agitation directly. The following year he would resolve it, in what is commonly regarded as one of the most spectacularly successful political maneuvers in the history of British India. Although as home member he gave much time to the issue, the subject will therefore be reserved for the next chapter. A second major item on the home department's agenda was the strenuous effort to check the spread of Indian communism. Especially after 1920, when Lenin declared the whole colonial world a battleground against capitalism, it seemed clear that the British Empire had become a principal Bolshevik target, with India the most vulnerable point.[20]

The main figure in the early phase of Indian communism was Narendranath Bhattacharya, better known as M. N. Roy. A product of the Bengal revolutionary movement, Bhattacharya went in 1915 to Batavia, where he failed to persuade the Germans to ship arms to India. From there he moved on to San Francisco, where he changed his name and married an American radical (Evelyn Trent), eventually reaching Moscow via Mexico. At the Communist International in 1920 he supposedly impressed Lenin by the quality of his arguments against some aspects of the latter's colonial theses. Creating a newspaper, the *Vanguard*, a military school at Tashkent, and a thin but extended network of agents, Roy pressed the Indian National Congress to adopt a radical program aimed at workers and peasants. In December 1922, however, partly because many mainstream leaders were bourgeois lawyers, partly because their movement had gained substantial backing from the Indian capitalist class, partly because they feared being labeled the tool of a foreign power, Congress repudiated Roy's proposals.[21]

[20] David Petrie, *Communism in India, 1924–1927* (1927; reprinted Calcutta: Editions Indian, 1972), p. 2.
[21] Lenin regarded formal or informal colonies such as India, China, or Turkey as so economically backward that a Marxist working class would be premature, so that Communist parties must support and largely merge into bourgeois-nationalist movements such as the Indian National

That same month British intelligence reported that the Communist International had committed £15,000 to Roy's campaign. Meanwhile seven young men who had studied in Moscow were arrested in Peshawar after crossing the Afghan border. Although they were not Roy's agents the commissioner of the North-West Frontier Province, Sir John Maffey, advised that he could secure conspiracy convictions, thus presenting the first opportunity to strike a blow at communism. The home department's chief secretary, S. P. O'Donnell, was inclined not to accept it. The difficulties confronting communists in India were immense, he thought, and £15,000 would not go far.[22]

Hailey took the situation more seriously. Although recent reports about bombs and pistols being smuggled into India might not be accurate, he noted, conditions favored a resurgence of violence. "When a big popular movement is on foot with a large organisation for agitation," he observed, in a perceptive though not entirely original comment on the anatomy of revolution, "the extreme wing will sink itself in the movement of the general body; but as soon as agitation, pure and simple, seems to have failed in effect and has begun to lose its hold on the general population, the extreme wing will again begin to think of secret conspiracy and anarchical action." An inverse relationship between large-scale agitation and revolutionary violence was "a well recognised principle in the pathology of popular movement." The noncooperation campaign having wound down, "in the immediate future our difficulties are likely to arise from secret combinations of the old Bengal type supported by a certain body of extreme opinion based on preachings of communist agents." The £15,000 contribution might not do much to influence public opinion, he agreed. Invested in arming anarchical cells, however, even so small a sum could cause considerable trouble.[23]

Hailey was more skeptical about whether to prosecute the Peshawar Seven. The young men were not really revolutionaries, he reasoned, and putting them in the dock would force real agents underground. Moreover, if Sir John Maffey thought he could "get a conviction . . . against men in regard to whom his only evidence is that they have been educated to teach Communist principles," then the courts in the North-West Frontier must be singularly complaisant. Once he was informed that those courts were precisely that, however, he readily concurred.[24] In May 1923 the men were convicted and given two years' rigorous imprisonment.

Congress or Chiang Kai-shek's Kuomintang. Roy held that India's industrialization had proceeded very rapidly, especially during the war, providing a base for a quasi-autonomous movement of workers and peasants. The best book on Roy is John P. Haithcox, *Communism and Nationalism in India: M. N. Roy and Comintern Policy, 1920–1939* (Princeton, N.J.: Princeton University Press, 1971). The standard biography is V. B. Karnik, *M. N. Roy: Political Biography* (Bombay: Nav Jagriti Samaj, 1978). Two contemporary studies by officials in the Criminal Investigation Department are valuable and largely factual: Cecil Kaye, *Communism in India*, ed. Subodh Roy (1925; Calcutta: Editions Indian, 1971), which contains other material from the National Archives of India, and Petrie, *Communism in India*.

[22] O'Donnell note, 18 December 1922, quoted in Kaye, *Communism in India*, pp. 199–200.
[23] Hailey note, 17 December 1922, NAI HomPol 103/III/1923.
[24] Hailey notes of 7 January and 9 February 1923, NAI HomPol 103/I/1923.

The Peshawar case was a prelude to the more important Cawnpore trial of 1924, which did involve Roy's agents, four of whom were found guilty of conspiracy to deprive the king-emperor of the sovereignty of British India. Although Roy himself remained at large until his return to Bombay in 1929 after his break with Stalin, the home department had achieved its main objective of proving him to be a paid foreign agent.[25] Hailey took a hard if not hysterical line toward communism. Although the Indian Communist Party would make considerable headway among factory workers in Bombay and elsewhere, as well as among agricultural laborers in Bengal, it was during his home membership that the Government of India delivered a blow from which the movement never fully snapped back.

In the Peshawar case Hailey's initial scruples were based not on any very deep concern about civil liberties but on his doubt that prosecution would succeed. More broadly, his identification with the Punjab school, his record as wartime commissioner of Delhi, and his association with Sir Michael O'Dwyer had all marked him out as a strong law-and-order man. This reputation his later governorships of Punjab and UP would do nothing to dispel. As home member, however, he presided over a thorough recasting of the Indian criminal code, removing racial distinctions favoring Europeans and severely reducing the substantial battery of repressive legislation.

The racial-distinction issue recalled the vehement and effective Anglo-Indian protest against the Ripon reforms of the early 1880s, especially a proposal that would have permitted Indian judges in what was called the Mofussil (i.e., outside the three presidencies of Madras, Bengal, and Bombay) to hear cases involving Europeans. In the early 1920s Europeans accused of serious offenses could still insist on being tried by juries at least half of whom were composed of their peers, making any but the lightest sentences virtually impossible to secure, mocking the claim that courts were dispensing true justice. The revision was directed by the law member, Sir Tej Bahadur Sapru. Most of the work having been done before Hailey became home member, his role was merely to guide the legislation through the Assembly. Years later, when he wrote the Law and Justice chapter for the *African Survey*, he would proudly highlight the contrast between India's almost entirely color-blind statute books and those of South Africa, which were permeated by racial discrimination. Before 1923 the difference had been one of degree.[26]

Repressive legislation reflected a succession of crises over a century and a half of British rule. Some acts, such as Bengal Regulation III (1818), which permitted the state to detain and deport without formal charges persons it believed likely to endanger the peace, dated from the early nineteenth century. Others had been added during the Great Mutiny of the 1850s, still others

---

25 Hailey to Vincent, 31 May 1923, HPI/5D.
26 The main dispute concerned the secretary of state's insistence that British soldiers retain the right to be tried in England, despite the Indian rejoinder that they were the worst offenders.

during the agitation against the partition of Bengal. Most recent were the notorious but never used Rowlatt Acts, against which Gandhi had led the satyagraha of 1919. As long as this imposing array of extralegal powers persisted it was hard to answer the charge that the British Raj amounted to a vast police state.

Naturally the home department denied the allegation, maintaining that the acts had been designed not "to repress but to guide firmly, not to destroy legitimate aspirations but to maintain law and order, so that legitimate aspirations may develop in kindly soil."[27] In the end, however, it agreed to retain only two: Part II of the Criminal Law Amendment Act (1909), which empowered the state to declare unlawful any organization that in its view was aiming to disrupt law and order, and the Seditious Meetings Act (1911), which authorized provincial governments to require permission to hold meetings in proclaimed areas.[28]

Hailey strongly supported maintaining both these acts. The seditious meetings measure was absolutely indispensable for dealing with agitation such as that of the Sikhs, he declared. "Give such a population a little time to sit down and think, without having its feelings unduly harassed, and commonsense will prevail," but only if meetings could be prevented from stirring up "a quick and virile but ignorant and unthinking people." Still persuaded that Regulation III had enabled the state to defuse the Punjab agitation of 1907 by removing the chief agitators Lajpat Rai and Ajit Singh, he had wanted to retain that too. In the end Lord Reading himself, who had been Lord Chief Justice in England, sided with Sapru against Hailey and removed it.[29] After all, the viceroy observed, if powers beyond those contained in the ordinary law were needed they could always be enacted by special ordinance.

Besides being responsible for law and order the home member was the leader of the government bench in the Legislative Assembly. During Hailey's years as finance member even his critics had usually called his speeches lucid, capable of being understood by people who were not financial experts. As home member he became known as a brilliant debater. He treated the Assembly with respect, often demolishing his opponents but not talking down to his audience. His wit was quick and he possessed a large store of literary and historical allusions, which his Indian opponents appreciated, for many of them were fluent in British literature and history. He made good use of journalists' caricatures, quoting with relish when they called him a robber chief, a bullet-headed bureaucrat, or an enemy of mankind. He could be scornful and vehement, philosophical and passionate, and not only moderates but Swarajists like Motilal Nehru evidently enjoyed matching wits with him. Like other legislatures the Assembly was a kind of club, whose members took pride in its

27 C. W. Gwynne note, 26 January 1921, NAI HomPol 29/1921.
28 It is relevant to point out that a good deal of repressive legislation remained on the books after 1947.
29 Hailey note, 3 July 1921, NAI HomPol 29/1922 Pt. II.

standards of debate. Before 1922 Hailey had been well regarded within the Indian Civil Service. It was as home member that he began to become truly eminent.

In his *Round Table* article of 1922 Hailey had predicted that many extremists, recognizing Gandhi's boycott as an error, would take the first opportunity to enter the councils. In 1922–3, however, the Assembly was still dominated by moderates and Liberals, who saw themselves as Indian patriots differing with noncooperationists only on methods. But the Swarajists were coming and the session therefore had an unreal air. On budget day Hailey heard his successor, Sir Basil Blackett, explain that although the economic situation had improved, the military-expenditure problem remained as difficult as ever. A rise in the salt tax seemed to be the only remedy. The preceding year, during the closing phase of noncooperation, the Assembly had refused Hailey's bid for such an increase. This time, despite threats of renewed civil disobedience and cries from moderates that they had been betrayed, Lord Reading stood firm. He had taken no more disagreeable step as viceroy, he wrote; not only was he overruling the Assembly, but the effects of the salt tax "will be felt by everybody in the land and notably by the poor."[30]

"We were threatened with an All-India agitation of the Rowlatt type, but did not believe in its possibility," Hailey explained, adding that a flare-up of kidney stone at the end of the session had made him extremely short-tempered. In fact, he thought, the certification of the salt tax "has not sunk deep and in itself is not likely to lead to serious trouble." Instead "we now have an agitation of a constitutional nature on a constitutional point . . . – not a bad thing in itself." He noted a resurgence of Hindu–Muslim conflict: "Even in the extremist camp there has been a complete split and the non-cooperators are frightened out of their wits at this sign of a break-up." The reappearance of communalism was "a healthy sign for it shows that feeling has swung away from attacks on Government to the really permanent issue which interests India."[31]

In 1923 C. R. Das, Motilal Nehru, and V. J. Patel led in forming the Swaraj Party, which split with the No-Changers over the issue of council entry. In May the two factions announced a compromise, though it amounted to no more than an agreement that Swarajist candidates would not be actively opposed. Whereas 15 to 20 former noncooperators had been expected in the Assembly, the Home Department predicted that the number would probably go as high as 40 (out of a total unofficial membership of 105). Because an increase in their numbers would hold out the possibility of forming a coalition with moderates and controlling the Assembly, Hailey speculated, the Swarajists' radicalism might actually be diluted. But what would happen when their demands were finally rejected? Although they might threaten to "abstain and leave us to carry on a bureaucratic Government," that strategy would not work "unless they can raise

30 Reading to Peel, 16 March 1923, quoted by Sinha, *Lord Reading*, pp. 115–16.
31 Hailey to Vincent, 26 April 1923, HPI/5D.

the country against us and create a condition of things such as that in Ireland or Egypt."[32] After the collapse of Gandhi's noncooperation campaign, that seemed to him no more probable than it had in 1920.

In October 1923 the Swarajists published a manifesto demanding immediate dominion status with full responsible government; if the claim were rejected, noncooperation would continue. In the elections the new party did even better than expected. Once the Assembly met, as Hailey had foreseen, Motilal Nehru toned down his line sufficiently to form a nationalist coalition with Independents. Early in 1924 change took place in Britain too, bringing Labour into office, though since it was a minority government not truly into power. On 4 February Reading released Gandhi for an appendix operation. A few days later came a showdown in the Assembly on a resolution calling for steps, including a royal commission if necessary, to "secure for India full self-governing Dominion status within the British Empire and Provincial Autonomy." There could be no middle course, said the mover, T. Rangachariar (Independent, Madras): "From representative institutions you have to spring to responsible government."

No one must be left in doubt about the government's stand on the proposition that India was ready for full dominion status and must have it at once, Hailey agreed. Even as it stood, however, deliberately weakened though it had been to facilitate the Swarajist–Independent coalition, the resolution was incompatible with the Montagu declaration of 1917, which had spoken of "gradual development of self-governing institutions with a view to the progressive realisation of responsible government." First – and here Hailey put forward an interpretation that would occupy constitutional lawyers for years – responsible government and dominion status were not the same. The former was a term of precision, making the executive responsible to India's legislature rather than to the British Parliament. Dominion status was broader, for "the Legislature will in itself have the full powers . . . typical of the modern Dominion." Responsible government was "not necessarily incompatible with a Legislature with limited or restricted powers." Full dominion status might be "the logical outcome of responsible government, nay, it may be the inevitable and historical development . . . but it is a further and a final step."[33]

Second, although both the 1917 declaration and the Government of India Act specified that progress must be achieved by stages, the resolution rejected that completely. Hailey ticked off a list of problems, notably the minority issue and insufficient social development, which needed to be substantially resolved before the Government of India could recommend a new constitution. Otherwise, no matter which party happened to be in power for the time being, the British Parliament would certainly reject it.

Motilal Nehru offered an amendment: Instead of a royal commission a

[32] Hailey to Vincent, 31 May 1923, ibid.
[33] Debate on self-government, 4 February 1924, LA Debates, 4, 384 ff.

round-table conference of representative Indian leaders, chosen with due regard to minority interests, would frame a constitution, which would be submitted to a new legislature and then to Parliament. Swarajists were not demanding everything at once, he insisted, responsible government and dominion status all in a bundle. But the end of the negotiations, fulfilling the "desire that proceeds from the natural cravings of the human heart for freedom," must be agreed in advance. The Swarajists had come to the Assembly, he pleaded, not as wreckers but in the hope that the government would cooperate with them. Otherwise, it was obvious that things must go on as they were.

As the debate proceeded Hailey grew more aggressive, hoping to split the nationalist coalition by pinning the Swarajists to their original manifesto, which had indeed demanded everything all at once in a bundle, and goad them into threatening renewed civil disobedience. "I was in some difficulty because up to the last I was not certain whether the Home [Labour] Government might not really veer round to a statutory Commission" to review the constitution, he confided, "and since I had very little to offer in reply, the best line on the whole seemed to be to attack."[34]

The atmosphere grew less clublike: "The Home Member is perfectly capable of protecting himself from ordinary interruptions," the speaker complained at one point, "but not against these organised volleys." The round-table proposal was fundamentally unsound, Hailey insisted; "at the last stage the Government will be brought in" to mediate disputes. Indian factions might achieve "unity against Government, but that unity breaks down when any attempt is made to proceed to constructive decisions."[35] The Government of India itself would conduct an inquiry into the working of the reforms, especially at the provincial level. But that was as far as he would go. The amended resolution passed by 76 to 48. It was not of course binding on the government.

Late in February 1924, disabusing Indians of any hope that Labour would change course decisively, Secretary of State Lord Olivier backed Hailey's insistence that after only three years' experience wholesale constitutional change would be dangerous.[36] "I think it is certain that the Swarajist Party and most of the Nationalists will now join in definite opposition to the Budget," Hailey predicted early in March.[37] A few days later, quoting a standard English constitutional-history text on the hallowed principle that redress of grievances must come before the legislature voted supplies, Motilal Nehru moved that the budget item for the Customs department be omitted. For many years the Labour Party had been avowing its friendship for India, he declared angrily; it was time they delivered the goods.[38]

---

[34] Hailey to Sir Malcolm Seton, 28 February 1924, ibid.
[35] LA Debates, 4, 752 ff.
[36] 26 February 1924, 5 Hansard (Lords), 56, 320 ff.
[37] Hailey to Sir Surendra Nath, 4 March 1924, HPI/5D.
[38] 10 March 1924, LA Debates, 4, 1379 ff. On the Labour Party and India, see Partha S. Gupta, *Imperialism and the British Labour Movement, 1914–1964* (London: Macmillan, 1975), and Mes-

His opponent's constitutional history was sound enough, Hailey acknowledged; a legislature did have the right to refuse supplies. But the government retained the power to certify the budget, and Nehru obviously counted on that authority's being exercised, so the action was irresponsible. (Nehru rejoined that he had not written the Government of India Act.) Would throwing out the budget be practical politics? How would Parliament and the British public view the action? Would they agree that His Majesty's Government and the Government of India had been so obviously and obstinately reactionary that no other course was open? If not, what would the Swarajists do then? Try to raise the country once more in civil disobedience? Perhaps even a no-tax campaign? Could the leaders control the agitation any more successfully this time? Had they not read the Congress committee's own report of 1922? The long-term impact of repeated agitation on the Indian political mentality had to be considered. Although this generation might feel the wind, its successors would reap the whirlwind.[39] Having made their point, and fearful that the coalition would indeed split, the Swarajists backed off. The budget would of course be certified anyway.

This encounter with Motilal Nehru was Hailey's last major debate as a member of the Government of India. Since August 1923 he had known that he would be the next governor of the Punjab. When Reading weighed the candidates to succeed Sir Edward Maclagan "one man stands out pre-eminently." Hailey was "a Punjab man in the Service, knows the Province well and is far and away, both in intellect and character, the person most suited to the position. I cannot think of any one who could stand even in the same class with him at however great a distance." Although Maclagan should not be judged too harshly, Reading thought, for he had had to follow Sir Michael O'Dwyer's unpopular regime and contend with the challenge from the Sikhs, "I think the situation will call for a Governor of a somewhat different stamp, and he is to be found in Hailey."[40]

The secretary of state, Lord Peel, agreed, asking only whether the appointee could not be persuaded to take six to eight months' leave. "Whilst it is true that he has not had long leave for considerable time," Reading replied after consulting Hailey, "there are private reasons which do not incline him to leave-taking at present and into which I need not enter."[41] Gemma Hailey had been dead less than a year. The last thing her father wanted was a long period of inactivity.

In 1918 Hailey had been passed over. Saying that he had grown accustomed to running his own show and that the prospect of another stint as a bureaucrat repelled him, he had seriously considered taking early retirement. The reform

bahuddin Ahmed, *The British Labour Party and the Indian Independence Movement, 1917–1939* (New York: Envoy Press, 1987).
[39] LA Debates, *4*, 1386 ff.
[40] Reading to Peel, 28 June 1923, IOR, L/PO/8/17 (iii).
[41] Telegrams, Peel to Reading, 4 August, and Reading to Peel, 15 August 1923, ibid.

scheme having greatly increased the responsibility and public exposure of members of the viceroy's council, his jobs as finance and home member had been more demanding and interesting than he had expected. As Reading realized, however, a Punjab man would want to go out governing his own province. It would be a fitting climax to Sir Malcolm Hailey's already distinguished career.

At the end of March 1924 the customary round of banquets honored the retiring home member. At one, which was given by the European members of the Assembly, Hailey defended the reform scheme. The Montagu declaration of 1917 had been both right and inevitable, he maintained, reminding him of the colonel who was ordered to advance, objected that he was more comfortable where he was, and finally agreed – but said war was a damned nuisance. Gandhi's noncooperation movement had been "a definite game for ousting entirely Western influence from this country," he charged. Yet moderates and Liberals, at great personal sacrifice, had come into the councils. At length the agitation had ended, its leaders had acknowledged their failure, and Swarajists had entered the legislatures, signaling that the struggle was entering a constitutional phase. Not unexpectedly their arrival had not been smooth: "What we have seen in the last few months is a pathological and not a physiological symptom."

It was the sort of after-dinner speech for which Sir Malcolm Hailey was already renowned. For Indian Liberals who were present he predicted a resurgence. He urged European members to be courageous, true "to the innate principles of British liberty," refusing to allow India to return to disorder but also recognizing the need to advance when it was earned. The Assembly had seen remarkably little racial bitterness – well, perhaps a bit in the past few months, but passing and trivial. His successor, Sir Alexander Muddiman, a man learned in the law, would be better qualified to face the Assembly's formidable legal talent. He himself was "going where Patels do cease to trouble and where Pundits are at rest."[42]

---

[42] *Times of India*, 23 March 1924.

8

Governor of the Punjab:
the Sikhs, 1924–1925

"There must be something wrong," the former viceroy Lord Curzon observed in the House of Lords in February 1924, in a situation permitting "a movement . . . religious and Puritan in origin . . . to develop into a political agitation associated with dacoity [gang violence], accompanied by violence and wrapped up in crime." Not for the first time or the last the Punjab was out of hand. Fortunately its recently appointed governor was "a strong and fearless man, and I trust that under his administration an end may be put to these troubles."[1] About the same time General Sir Claud Jacob was touring Sikh villages, where he found a cocky mentality. The younger generation and, what was especially ominous, women seemed to be convinced that their community was invincible. Jacob thought the situation explosive "not in a Western sense but in an Eastern one with the possibility of bloodshed even before the rain." Like Curzon he saw one bright spot. Ordinary Sikhs and even their leaders seemed anxious about the coming of Sir Malcolm Hailey.[2]

Was it really conceivable that after four long years of militant agitation and suffering the mere reputation of a governor for firmness would persuade the Sikhs to stop the confrontation? Despite the cautious optimism of his article two years earlier, he himself entertained no such illusions. The situation for a settlement would not be ripe, he wrote to his predecessor, Sir Edward Maclagan, "until we have hit the present leaders of the movement much harder than we have done so far; in fact until they themselves feel that the game is up."[3]

Historically the line between Sikhism and Hinduism – which the census with studied vagueness defined as the religion of any native of India who was neither Muslim nor Christian – had been indistinct. In some Hindu families one son commonly became a Sikh, while scriptures, gurdwaras (shrines), and mahants (priests) were often shared. Since their founding in the sixteenth century the Sikhs' fortunes had ebbed and flowed. In the early nineteenth century, inspired by the fifth Guru, Govind Singh, and led by their great soldier, Ranjit Singh,

---

[1] 26 February 1924, Great Britain, *Parliamentary Debates* 5 (Lords), *56*, 320 ff.
[2] Report by General Sir Claud Jacob, n.d. [but February or March 1924], in M. L. Ahluwalia, ed., *Gurdwara Reform Movement, 1919–1925: An Era of Congress–Akali Collaboration* (New Delhi: Ashoka, 1985), pp. 159–65.
[3] Hailey to Maclagan, 3 March 1924, HPI/6A.

Governor of the Punjab

they established their rule over most of eastern and central Punjab. After their defeat by the British in the early 1850s, however, they fell on hard times. Squeezed like other peasants in the region by the capitalization of agriculture and the rise of rural indebtedness, deprived of political power and sovereignty, they also faced competition from other religions, especially the Hindu reform movement known as the Arya Samaj.[4]

[4] The best general study is Khushwant Singh, *A History of the Sikhs*, 2 vols. (Princeton, N.J.: Princeton University Press, 1963–6). There are three good detailed studies of the Akali agitation of the early 1920s: Mohinder Singh, *The Akali Movement* (Delhi: Macmillan, 1978); Richard Fox, *Lions of the Punjab: Culture in the Making* (Berkeley: University of California Press, 1985); and Rajiv A. Kapur, *Sikh Separatism: The Politics of Faith* (London: Allen & Unwin, 1986).

In their struggle for survival the Sikhs followed several strategies. Migrating across northern India and overseas, they supported their kinsfolk with remittances. Joining the army in disproportionate numbers, they earned a reputation as one of the premier martial races. They formed an organization of their own, the Singh Sabha, composed of orthodox, Amritdhari Sikhs, who took the name Singh (Lion) in place of Hindu caste designations. Yet censuses showed that they were still declining, apparently facing eventual extinction and reabsorption into Hinduism.

This threat to their survival as a religion was the driving force behind their agitation of the early 1920s, which is known as the Akali movement. Although the struggle also had political aims, its primary focus was religious reform, centering on the control of gurdwaras that Sikhs claimed as their own. As early as 1905 complaints appeared that some mahants were not Sikhs at all but Hindus, while some shrines contained idols and even temple prostitutes. The reform movement proper began in 1920 with the formation of the Shiromani Gurdwara Prabandhak Committee (SGPC) and the quasi-autonomous Akali Dal (army of immortals). The crusade aimed to end specific abuses and bring all shrines under the control of the Panth (Sikh congregation), remove corrupt mahants, take over land and funds belonging to the shrines, and generally to "practise the Sikh religion according to the teachings of the Sikh Gurus as preserved in the Adi Granth [holy scripture]."[5]

Mobilizing the Sikh peasantry in a campaign of direct action the Akalis rapidly became an explosive force. Jathas (columns of twenty-five to a hundred men) would proceed to gurdwaras, where they would conduct morchas (demonstrations) to persuade their mahants to hand control over to the SGPC. The jathas were sworn to nonviolence. Although these quasi-military formations, marching kirpans (swords) in hand, were inherently threatening, on the whole they were victims rather than perpetrators, notably in the tragic incidents at Nankana in 1921 and Guru-ka-Bagh in 1922, both of which were mentioned in Chapter 7. Simultaneously the revolutionary-terrorist faction known as the Babbar Akalis, who were the direct descendants of the wartime Ghadr conspirators, had assassinated numerous collaborators and suspected collaborators, generally intimidating the Doaba region of the central Punjab before they were smashed by a massive CID operation. (Of course, one person's terrorist is another's freedom fighter.)

The relationship between Sikhs and British authority determined that the Akali agitation would evolve into a confrontation with the government. Largely in the hope of stabilizing a community whose participation in the army meant so much to them, the British had become intimately involved in the institutions of the Sikh religion. The Khalsa College in Amritsar, it was charged, had in effect passed under government control. The British registered mahants or appointed them outright, including the sycophant who presided over Amritsar's Golden

[5] Mohinder Singh, *Akali Movement*, p. 18.

Temple, where General Dyer himself was made an honorary Sikh in 1919. Yet the mahants had rights in law. And, even though it might be an ass, the law had to be upheld.

Under Sir Edward Maclagan, a man known for his liberal views, the Punjab government's policy veered between general amnesties and wholesale repression. During the autumn of 1922, for instance, instructions on whether demonstrators at the shrine of Guru-ka-Bagh were to be beaten changed three times within two months. Hailey, who had served as home member after November 1922, had possessed no magic formula either. Yet the obvious remedy was suggested as early as 1920 by Maharaja Bhupinder Singh of the native state of Patiala. It was gurdwara legislation that would split the movement by satisfying moderates and the less militant Akalis.[6] The gurdwara bill that Sir Fazli Husain, the minister for education and a Muslim, introduced in the provincial legislative council in 1921, however, would have included Muslims and Hindus on the managing board. Sikh members boycotted and the measure was dropped.

Going to Lahore himself, Hailey urged that a gurdwara law be passed – if possible with Sikh support, if not then without it. Again a bill was introduced; again Sikh members boycotted. This time it was enacted but, since Sikhs denounced it as illegitimate, never put into effect. Above all, Hailey advised, the government should keep calm. Compared with the canal-colony revolt of 1907 or the Rowlatt satyagraha of 1919, he reflected, the situation did not seem all that dangerous.[7] Although the movement appeared to have passed its peak, however, the jathas kept coming. In February 1924, just before he went on leave, police fired on demonstrators at Jaito in the princely state of Nabha, resulting in several deaths.

In the national Legislative Assembly Hailey defended the firing on the ground that, unlike General Dyer's troops at Jallianwala Bagh, the police had been in real physical danger. He was convinced, he wrote privately, "that we took the right line at Jaito and that an affair of this kind was inevitable." The Punjab government had "prosecuted until they are tired; it has tried again and again to create a better atmosphere by releasing prisoners; it has got nothing from it." Although he believed the great mass of Sikhs were still loyal, "they are in the hands of a band of about 3 or 4 hundred very determined agitators who have no definite programme but are determined not to accept any solution from Government." If he "could get real terms of peace with such guarantees as would secure quiet for the next four or five years," he continued, "I would be perfectly willing to stop prosecutions and release prisoners but I would not concede a single point merely in the vain hope of creating an atmosphere, for it is a mere waste of effort."[8]

---

6 See Barbara N. Ramusack, "Maharajas and Gurdwaras: Patiala and the Sikh Community," in Robin Jeffrey, *People, Princes and Paramount Power: Society and Politics in the Indian Princely States* (Delhi: Oxford University Press, 1978), pp. 184–5.

7 Notes of discussion, Viceroy's Council, 8 November 1922, NAI, HomPol 914/1922.

8 Hailey to Seton, 28 February 1924, HPI/5D.

By June 1924, when Hailey took over the Punjab, events had confirmed his assessment that an early solution was unlikely. In March a force far more potent than a governor's reputation had pushed the Sikhs toward negotiation. A month after his release, still recuperating from an appendectomy, Gandhi was having grave doubts about Congress's support for the Akalis. As usual it is hard to untangle his motives. Some of his qualms were moral. He raised the conundrum – the same one his critics continually posed to him – of how much psychological coercion could be employed before a supposedly nonviolent movement became violent. The sheer size of the five-hundred-man jatha at Jaito had been intimidating, he argued. If the object were simply to go, perform a religious ceremony, and be arrested, would not a much smaller number have served the purpose? The marchers had worn long kirpans and some of the crowd had carried lathis. The police firing and the nine deaths were of course deeply regrettable. But it might have been another Chauri Chaura.[9]

Meanwhile Professor A. T. Gidwani, the agent who had been assigned to work with the Akalis at what he called the Congress embassy in Amritsar, was having trouble with both the provincial Congress committee and the SGPC. Sikhs were cynical about the degree of support they could expect from Congress, and blaming Hindus for not aiding them in a recent communal clash with Muslims. Hindu–Sikh rivalry, wrote Jawaharlal Nehru, secretary of the All-India Congress Committee, had "deprived us of much of the good of the Akali civil disobedience movement." If the rift were not smoothed over the national cause would be severely harmed.[10]

Early in March Gandhi sought to impose conditions on the SGPC. Since "non-violence includes truth, and truth admits of no expedients," he insisted, minimum demands must be stated – and the minimum must be the maximum. The goals of the movement must be entirely religious and they must not be anti-Hindu. The reformers must list precisely which shrines they claimed, authenticate them, and agree to have disputes arbitrated. In particular the program must not include agitation for the restoration of the Maharaja of Nabha, whom the British had removed from office in 1923 on grounds of chronic maladministration.[11] Having also concluded that the Punjab was out of hand, Gandhi was trying to take charge. Shortly after his apparent threat to isolate the Akalis he overrode the local Congress committee and sent to Amritsar his own man, K. M. Panikkar, a young south Indian Hindu then at the beginning of a distinguished career as journalist, diplomat, and author. At their first interview, Panikkar recalled, Gandhi asked for a report on the Nabha

---

9 As pointed out in Chapter 6, Chauri Chaura in the eastern UP was the scene of a mob attack on police, resulting in some two dozen deaths by burning, which had prompted Gandhi to suspend civil disobedience in January 1922.

10 Gidwani to Nehru, 23 January 1924, Nehru Memorial Library, AICC 4 (i)/1924; Nehru to Gidwani, 10 February 1924, ibid.

11 Gandhi open letter to Akali leaders, 4 March 1924, CWMG, *23*, 218–20. See Barbara N. Ramusack, "Incident at Nabha: Interaction Between Indian States and British Indian Politics," *Journal of Asian Studies*, 28 (1969), 563–77.

question, the morality of which troubled him deeply.[12] Like his predecessor Panikkar had trouble working with the SGPC, many of whom resented Gandhi's interference and regarded his agent as a sort of spy – which in point of fact is what he was.[13]

Panikkar's report fully confirmed Gandhi's suspicions. Moreover when home department officials, and at some point presumably Hailey, read the intercepted copy they must have been amused to find how closely it agreed with their own assessments. Panikkar sketched the religious question: the origins of the reform movement of orthodox, Amritdhari Sikhs, their differences with other sects, who were often indistinguishable from Hindus, and what he thought were often their dubious claims to disputed shrines. Under Gandhi's influence, he hoped, the campaign had begun to regain a proper religious focus. Moreover the Sikhs were well organized and their commitment to nonviolence had been tested. The trouble was "that no one knows what they want. They have no definite objective."

Gandhi had pressed for a clear statement of the minimum claims. The Akali movement, Panikkar concurred with Hailey, was open-ended. Indeed it all seemed to him rather frightening. The Akali Dal could call upon some eighty thousand men armed with swords, organized vertically from village to zail (group of villages) to tahsil (subdivision) to district. Sikhs had tried to reassure him that this quasi-military system existed only on paper. For that very reason, however, it could not be disbanded. What would happen if the government decided on full-scale repression? The ablest leaders were already in jail. If their successors were also incarcerated the Akalis might lose their self-discipline and become violent. Congress, he recommended, with an impressive lack of sensitivity as to how Sikhs might react, should form a committee. In the event of emergency it could "come and take direction . . . (of course by way of advice)."[14]

The SGPC did not answer Gandhi until 20 April. Updating his letters by a month in order to hide the delay, they said that if only the Mahatma would take the trouble to read their publications he would find his questions already answered.[15] By that time, although they did not tell Gandhi this, the leaders

---

12 K. M. Panikkar, *An Autobiography* (Madras: Oxford University Press, 1977), p. 40. Gidwani had been arrested in February at Jaito. The Punjab committee had provisionally appointed Karam Chand Shukla and asked the AICC to confirm him; he would not have taken the job, the Punjab secretary wrote with obvious irritation, if he had known it would be temporary. See NML, AICC 4(i)/1924.

13 "The people in jail are evidently wild with Bapu for what they consider his interference in this matter." Intercepted letter from Panikkar to C. F. Andrews, n.d. [April 1924], National Archives of India, HomPol 297/1924.

14 Report of 31 March 1924, NML, AICC 4(i)/1924; copy in NAI HomPol 297/1924.

15 SPGC to Gandhi, 20 April 1924, Ganda Singh, ed., *Some Confidential Papers of the Akali Movement* (Amritsar: SPGC, 1965), pp. 59–69. This interpretation is in agreement with Mohinder Singh, *Akali Movement*, pp. 75–7, and Fox, *Lions of the Punjab*, who follows Mohinder Singh. Many writers, for example, S. L. Malhotra, *Gandhi and the Punjab* (Chandigarh: Panjab University, 1970), stress Congress–Sikh cooperation during this period. Although the contemporary political motive for such an interpretation may be laudable, the evidence is not per-

were already negotiating with the government. Late in March, with Hailey's concurrence, the viceroy, Lord Reading, had asked General Sir William Birdwood (who had commanded several Sikh regiments during his career) to try and break the deadlock. To the bright but inexperienced Panikkar, who talked with Hailey as well as with Gandhi and Motilal Nehru, the problem seemed absurdly simple. Congress would support the SGPC's claim to control Sikh gurdwaras, the government would agree, and the SGPC in turn would drop its agitation on behalf of the Maharaja of Nabha.[16] Because Hailey and his colleagues had been trying to arrive at precisely that formula for some time, they must have found Panikkar's proposal amusing – for of course they were reading his mail.

Throughout the negotiations Birdwood tried to separate the religious and political issues. Contrary to their statement to Gandhi, however, the first proposal by the SGPC included not only Nabha and a demand for the release of prisoners but a bid for an increase in Sikh representation in the Legislative Council to 25 percent of the membership.[17] As the negotiations proceeded they omitted the last and agreed to drop Nabha temporarily, but refused to budge on the prisoner issue.[18] On 31 May, Maclagan having formally handed over to him, Hailey left Bombay for the Punjab summer capital at Simla. That same day Birdwood informed Lord Reading that the negotiations had failed. The viceroy had hoped to improve the atmosphere. Instead recriminations were flying back and forth, with each side accusing the other of bad faith.[19]

In reality both sides had been ambivalent. The Sikhs were continually raising fresh points, the government's negotiator reported. By entering the negotiations at all, the SGPC charged, the government had legitimized the prisoner issue only to retract it later on. Although releases might be considered, Hailey was quoted, concessions should not be made piecemeal but only as part of a final settlement. If the talks failed as expected, Home Member Sir Alexander Muddiman judged, then they would have served their purpose by putting government in a strong position. But what if they succeeded? The Akalis would then boast of their triumph, the government would lose face, and "it is Sir Malcolm Hailey who will have to stand the racket."[20] When Hailey himself was consulted

---

suasive. Congress in the 1920s never really came close to integrating the Sikhs into the national movement.

16 Panikkar, *Autobiography*, pp. 42–3. Panikkar recollected that later on, when he put the question squarely to Mangal Singh of how "the future of the Sikh community had become involved with the Maharajah of Nabha, the answer was startling. Certain prominent Sikh leaders were in the Maharajah's pay and were quite prepared to let the gurdwara problem hang fire to serve the Maharajah's ends."

17 SGPC notes handed to General Birdwood, 16 April 1924, *Akali Papers*, pp. 70–1.

18 The copious documents are in ibid., pp. 71–99.

19 Ibid., 100–5; William Birdwood, *Khaki and Gown: An Autobiography* (London: Ward, Lock, 1941), pp. 371–2. Panikkar analyzed the negotiations as a three-way affair between the SGPC, the Government of India, and the Punjab government, each of whom was playing a dishonest game. Panikkar to Gandhi, 9 May 1924, intercepted copy in NAI HomPol 297/1924.

20 Minutes in NAI HomPol 297/1924.

in London he felt apprehensive about whether it was yet possible to reach a "settlement to which [the] Akalis would logically adhere."[21]

Hailey was therefore partly responsible for the breakdown of the negotiations. He was probably right, however, in doubting that the Akalis were ready for a compromise. There was something after all in Maclagan's discovery, after he had looked "at one or two works on the Covenanters" of the early seventeenth century, that he had acquired a surprising empathy for Charles I. "Though I was brought up in an atmosphere of great sympathy to the Covenanters," he explained, "I find it difficult to put myself in their place."[22] Hailey was relieved the talks had failed. "All we can do," he wrote, was "impress on people the fact that negotiations have broken down, and that no attempt will be made by us to renew them. If anything is to be done, the offer must come very openly and clearly from the other side." And that, for the foreseeable future, seemed quite unlikely.[23]

For the first two weeks after he reached Simla Hailey quietly consulted army and district officers, listened to his Indian visitors, reviewed the documents from the Birdwood negotiations, and read the Akali press. Then he wrote a long note systematically analyzing the situation, evaluating the options, and outlining what he intended to do. The Akalis, he observed with cool detachment, had a new battle cry: "From what they know (or assume) of my own character . . . the Sikhs must now prepare for a new era of tyranny." The gurdwara agitation would resume, and tempers would be further inflamed by a recent government decision to raise water rates in the canal colonies. If either conciliation or repression were chosen then the Akalis might as well know it. But "it is inadvisable that any action of ours should be construed as the initial step of a new reign of terror, or as the sign of a spirit of concession, unless we deliberately intend this result."[24]

Although the Sikhs were by no means homogeneous, Hailey continued, the large majority were supporting the Akali movement and the SGPC. By occupying gurdwaras the extremists had seized the initiative and a series of dramatic confrontations had appeared to validate their contention that their religion was under wholesale assault. Yet there seemed to be surprisingly little personal antagonism, and the Akalis' enthusiasm had apparently waned. Some of the leaders obviously wanted compromise; recruiters were reportedly having trouble filling up the jathas. Most significant, here and there "loyalist" Sikhs had begun to organize anti-Akali associations. It was far too early to say the agitation had been scotched. For some time, however, the Sikh extremist had been unable "to claim a 'success'; nor is he able to claim that with all his efforts he has been able to wring from Government a sign that it is seriously disturbed by his activities. It is these things which count."

[21] SS to VR, tel., 14 May 1924, ibid.
[22] SS to VR, tel., 14 May 1924, ibid.; Maclagan to Hailey, 13 August 1924, HPI/6B.
[23] Hailey to Sir William Duke, 12 June 1924, ibid.   [24] Hailey note, 20 June 1924, ibid.

The government must try to focus on the religious questions, Hailey stressed, for only those could be resolved quickly. Patience was essential. It was often assumed, for instance, that passing a gurdwara bill would produce a favorable atmosphere in which other problems could be tackled. But that was to confuse cause and effect. A bill acceptable to other communities and the state could probably not be passed until the Sikhs' cockiness and paranoia had both been curbed, until they accepted the facts that they could not defeat the state and that the state was not bent on destroying them. How then to secure that change in attitude?

Hailey went through the options. The first was concession. According to his reading of the Birdwood documents, however, the time was not ripe. Just when agreement had seemed close the extremists had raised again the question of the Maharaja of Nabha, apparently in a deliberate effort to prolong the confrontation. It therefore seemed likely that no offer would "satisfy the Sikhs till they are convinced by the attitude of Government that the concession constitutes the maximum which they are likely to obtain." In May he had doubted whether an agreement could be secured "to which the Sikhs would logically adhere." As long as the present mentality persisted – and as Maclagan had observed there was nothing uniquely Sikh about it – concessions would be interpreted as weakness, inviting fresh claims.

Wholesale repression was also possible. Special ordinances could be enacted under which funds would be sequestered, newspapers suppressed, and leaders interned. But the effects were easy to foresee. Enthusiasm would revive and, just when moderates were beginning to raise their heads, they would be driven underground again. If repression were tough enough and went on long enough, "we could perhaps bring the community to its knees." But, apart from the doubt about whether a British government responsible to a democratically elected parliament could pursue such a program to its logical conclusion, what would it achieve? A lasting solution "must be obtained by some measure of consent," Hailey concluded, "and this is admittedly difficult to attain by repression."

Since neither outright conciliation nor repression seemed practical the two must be combined in some way. It had been suggested that religious and political issues might be separated by making the widest possible concessions on the first while striking hard at the second. Small groups of pilgrims might be allowed to go to Jaito and perform any ceremony they wished, for instance, whereas if jathas marched in military formation they would be stopped and prosecuted. Although this approach had tactical merit, Hailey judged, it was not new. Moreover disagreements would arise about which issues were religious, creating fresh incidents, leading to increased enthusiasm – that is, the same vicious circle.

At the moment, Hailey continued, two confrontations were taking place. From the Akali perspective neither seemed to be going very well. The SGPC had apparently all but lost interest in Guru-ka-Bagh, near Amritsar, where the communal-kitchen agitation described in the preceding chapter had degenerated into a stalemate. At Jaito, however, the SGPC was apparently still intent on restoring the Maharaja of Nabha, and in a princely state demonstrators could be jailed without specific charges. Although the British administrator wanted jathas stopped before they reached Nabha, it therefore seemed advantageous to let them proceed. The Akalis could not afford to lose face. At Jaito, a district officer observed, the extremists had "caught hold of a tiger by the tail." They should not be allowed to let go.[25]

The key word was consistency, Hailey stressed. Although the plan was not dramatic, neither was it inactive. He would press on with trials of SGPC leaders. If new men of the same type arose he would prosecute them too. He would block attempts to seize gurdwaras by force. At least for the present he would release no prisoners. He would employ his patronage power, making no secret of the policy of refusing civil or military employment to anyone whose family was "disloyal." In short he would "continue the policy of pressure by all ordinary legal means, only avoiding, if possible, any step which may once more help to bring the extremist section forward as the champion of Sikh interests."[26]

Hailey's note of June 1924 on the Akali agitation was written at the height of his intellectual power. During the next year, ending with the passage of the Gurdwara Bill in July 1925, events would corroborate his analysis with almost uncanny precision. He would enjoy very significant advantages. The Sikhs had already spent a great deal of energy, Gandhi and the Congress largely withdrew their support for the Akalis, the Birdwood negotiations had discredited the policy of concession. And, unlike Maclagan, Hailey would not be second-guessed from above.

One leading authority has also claimed that Hailey's policy was new.[27] Yet all of the individual elements – not resorting to full-blown repression through ordinances but using the ordinary law to the utmost, encouraging moderate Sikh associations, releasing no prisoners in advance, holding out a gurdwara bill to those who were concerned with purely religious issues – had already been employed. Moreover, as home member in 1922–4, Hailey had played an un-usually prominent role in shaping the Punjab government's strategy, so that he had been partly responsible for the vacillation and the fiasco. The most remark-able feature of his approach was not its innovativeness but its analytical rigor. Success would depend not on its brilliance but on the consistency of its applica-tion. Sir Malcolm himself made no claims for originality. "It is of course impossible to lay down any permanent policy," he told General Birdwood, "as things change rapidly, and at any moment we may get an incident which may

---

[25] Perhaps the issue could be quietly defused by installing the minor son as Maharaja, he suggested. Ramusack, "Incident at Nabha," concludes that although the Maharaja was indeed pressed to abdicate, he did so rather than face a general inquiry into his administration. In addition, of course, the Maharaja was unwise enough to back the Akalis against the government and his old enemy the Maharaja of Patiala. He chose the wrong horse.

[26] Hailey note, 20 June 1924, HPI/6A.

[27] Mohinder Singh, *Akali Movement*, p. 77.

force on us action of a totally different character." The Akalis were "not in a mood to come to a settlement now, and no settlement would be of value unless it had something like a reality behind it."[28] Trench warfare "may be a long game," he concluded, but it seemed to be the only one with the hope of success.[29]

Cool and methodical, Hailey set out to implement his plan. Drawing on a fund created by ex-Punjabi officials, district officers nurtured anti-Akali organizations. By early October, Amritsar's moderate faction claimed ten thousand members, Jullundur's seven thousand. Large or small, Hailey remarked, "it all counts."[30] Sure enough there were hints that negotiations might be reopened. But the SGPC still demanded the right to draw up a gurdwara bill unilaterally, the restoration of Nabha, and the release of prisoners without conditions.[31] Besides, as of course Hailey knew from reading their mail, the Akalis were still negotiating with Congress.[32] Ever since the collapse of the Muslims' Khilafat movement, he reasoned, and knowing as they did "the weak material on which they have had to rely," Congress had "been looking for support from more determined people, if not actually from a physical force party." No doubt Gandhi would like "to confront Swarajists with the serried ranks of the Akalis."[33]

The time was not ripe. He would always be glad to hear from his friends in the SGPC, Sir Malcolm replied pleasantly. But the religious issue must be negotiated entirely separately. And it must be settled with all Sikhs.[34] Deliberately raising the stakes he threatened a civil suit that would return one disputed gurdwara to its original mahant and placed another in the hands of a receiver. The Akalis could not ignore these challenges, he calculated, and the ground was favorable, for obviously any government must enforce the civil decrees of its courts. Those courts, he asked General Birdwood to explain to the army, were open to all citizens, including mahants. The obvious remedy was for Sikhs to cooperate in framing a bill they liked better.[35]

Hailey's remaining weapon was himself. Late in July he came down from Simla to tour Sikh districts. In Amritsar, he noted, the Akalis had already "crowded up the Golden Temple with vast numbers of Akalis in preparation for my arrival," placing "an enormous drum on its topmost terrace, in order to call the faithful when the attack is made. It all has an element of the farcical, and

28 Hailey to Birdwood, 27 June 1924, HPI/6A.
29 Hailey to Sir Valentine Chirol, 2 July 1924, ibid.
30 Hailey to Hari Kishan Kaul, Comm. Rawalpindi Division, 15 July 1924, HPI/6A.
31 Hailey to de Montmorency, 20 August 1924, HPI/6B, enclosing Raja Singh to Jogendra Singh, n.d.
32 See several documents in Ganda Singh, *Akali Papers*, especially Panikkar to Mangal Singh, 18 August 1924, pp. 122–3.
33 Hailey to Seton, 17 July 1924, HPI/6A; Hailey to de Montmorency, 21 July 1924, ibid. See SGPC report of negotiations with Maharaja of Nabha, 25 and 27 July 1924, *Akali Papers*, pp. 105–17.
34 Reported in Hailey to de Montmorency, 20 August 1924, HPI/6B.
35 Hailey to Birdwood, 26 August 1924, ibid.

presents a situation full of quiet humour." The local Congress was also preparing to welcome him. Carefully he drew the line – processions would be permitted past the circuit house but not at the railway crossing or in the civil station. But he did not provide a target by announcing the decision. Nor, lest rumors be fed, did he bring in additional troops.[36]

The first stop was Jullundur, once a Babbar Akali stronghold. If government were to make life and property secure, he urged, then ordinary citizens must cooperate. He therefore welcomed the recently formed Sewak committee whose members, in the true interest of Sikhdom, were pursuing religious reform calmly and quietly.[37] At Amritsar, where his visit went off without serious incident, he teased that his audience had "not perhaps seen that vast concentration of troops nor observed that collection of machine guns, bombs, [and] aeroplanes" which supposedly were being massed to destroy the Golden Temple. According to rumors "Government is making an attack on the Sikh religion. Their gurdwaras are in danger; their most sacred possession – their religious life – is in deadly peril." How absurd! "The one essential," he concluded, "is a recognition of the supremacy of the State over all communalistic and sectional claims."[38]

"India is a queer place," Hailey observed, "where the inevitable never occurs and only the unexpected happens."[39] He pressed on with the "loyalist" committees, the gurdwara challenges, and a few prosecutions of Akali newspapers. He was, and was seen to be, unflappable. The problem, he maintained publicly, was after all not very serious. The state would do its duty and uphold the law. If people wanted the law changed all they had to do was cooperate in framing a more satisfactory one. A fresh incident such as the Jaito firing might of course raise the temperature at any time. Nevertheless, he thought, the situation might be turning in his favor.

More than blind faith lay behind Hailey's guarded optimism. Moderate Sikhs were routinely urging that negotiations should take place. Moreover, as the governor knew from intercepted correspondence, Panikkar's efforts were continuing. Like Sir Malcolm himself the young Indian may have been a fisherman, for he had put out several lines. He was trying to persuade the Swarajist leaders to have their party conference support the SGPC but not the Maharaja of Nabha, whose agents were also at work. At least indirectly, however, Panikkar was also involved in a maneuver to have Motilal Nehru or Pandit Madan Mohan Malaviya introduce a gurdwara bill into the central Legislative Assembly. "We may not succeed," wrote Mangal Singh, Panikkar's close associate,

---

36 Hailey to H. F. Howard, 15 July 1924, ibid.
37 Speech of 1 August, *Tribune*, 4 August 1924. See the report of the trip in Hailey to de Montmorency, 5 August 1924, HPI/6A.
38 Speech of 30 July 1924, HPI/41.
39 Hailey to Langon, 29 September 1924, HPI/6B.

"but we will get on all-India status and Sir Malcolm Hailey will simply be confused."[40]

In September 1924 Panikkar resigned his position as Congress agent at Amritsar to become editor of a new newspaper, the *Hindustan Times*, to be published in Delhi under the control of a syndicate composed mainly of Sikhs led by Mangal Singh. Early in October the paper published an article on "The Sikh Situation" by "M. S." (presumably Mangal Singh), charging Hailey not only with "every conceivable form of repression" but with "objectionable methods of 'perjured publicity' and Machiavellian tactics of creating factions amongst the ranks of the opponents." Although the governor was calling himself "a friend of the Sikhs, his Government is organising forces to kill the reform movement. He is following the old, old policy of rallying the so-called moderates and crushing the extremists." Hailey must have recognized that much of this article came uncomfortably close to plagiarism – he was reading his adversaries' mail; were they perhaps reading his? In any case he wrote a quite extraordinary and very puzzling document, apparently a private letter to the editor, that is, Panikkar.[41]

Although he appreciated much of what the author said, Hailey wrote, the information was out of date. If the two pending gurdwara civil suits should lead to wholesale beatings or bloodshed, then the confrontation might indeed go on indefinitely; yet "we, on the Government side, have learnt our lesson." Humaneness apart, "mere prudence and ordinary caution would prevent our taking any action which would once again unite the Sikh villager against us." As Panikkar realized, he continued – if it *was* Panikkar – the Birdwood negotiations had broken down because the extremists had never intended to reach a settlement. (Neither had the government, but Hailey was not being quite *that* candid.) Instead the Akalis had wanted a temporary respite, releases from jail, and the chance to reorganize. Their literature had referred continually to their successes but – here Hailey might have been quoting Panikkar's own report to Gandhi – never to their aims. The loyalist committees that "M. S." called Machiavellian were composed of moderates who had been afraid to stand up. He had of course done his best to encourage them, and they were succeeding because people were tired of futile morchas. After all the government was only carrying out the law.

"I have not myself regarded this conflict simply as one between Government

---

[40] Panikkar to Mangal Singh, 18 August 1924; Mangal Singh to Daulat, 21 August 1924, *Akali Papers*, pp. 122–4; Panikkar, *Autobiography*, p. 49.
[41] Clipping dated 7 October 1924 and attached Hailey note, n.d., HPI/2C. Although this was not the most complete explanation of his policy, it was the most direct and the most passionate, the sort of spontaneous articulation one writes in the first instance for oneself. No addressee is given; I have inferred Panikkar. It would not be surprising if Hailey decided not to send it, since he would have known it would undoubtedly be shown to Mangal Singh – although it is also possible that was just what he intended.

and a band of extremist politicians," Hailey asserted. Much graver issues were involved. He sympathized with people who wanted to clean up corruption and have their religious institutions run properly. He felt still more in tune with those who disliked lawyers. "It would . . . be disastrous if we ever allowed one community in India to dominate the rights of minority sections by force," however, "or to oust by mass action individuals who have clearly defined legal rights." Ironically, if the Sikhs had ever taken the trouble to read the much-maligned bill of 1922 they would have discovered that it was actually "a concession which in any other country would probably leave the ordinary man aghast at the disregard shown for vested rights."

On the contrary, "the Sikh has been entirely contemptuous of the claims of law, and has unfortunately been encouraged to believe that he was strong enough to force the hand of Government." In ordinary life, Hailey continued, resorting to a string of stereotypes, the Sikh was "obstinate, obtuse and unreasoning, and his one solution for domestic quarrels or for disputes with neighbours is the . . . bludgeon or the axe." Even educated Sikhs lacked "the slightest recognition that the claims of the State or of Society must on occasion override religious considerations." But even that was not quite the point. "We are not . . . fighting their religious claims or the political aspirations of their leaders," he concluded, but rather a dangerous mentality. "I for one would agree to no form of compromise which would leave the Sikhs to the belief that they could override at will the rights of other communities."[42]

Late in October, as he came down from the hills to make his formal entry into Lahore, Hailey took stock. He thought he had made a good beginning. The Akalis' enthusiasm had apparently been waning even before he took over. Although they had used his own reputation as a rallying cry, so far they had not been able to rekindle it. Despite his tour through the Sikh districts and his deliberately provocative civil suits, no serious incidents had occurred. On the other hand, although the loyalist associations had been useful propaganda tools, he had to admit that they had been unable to exert much impact on ordinary villagers.[43] The campaign was far from finished, he realized. But perhaps his opponents were starting to wear down.

In December 1924, presiding over a unity conference in Lahore, Gandhi located the root cause of all India's communal problem in the Punjab. When he convened the Legislative Council in November Hailey had said much the same thing. Compared with the larger Hindu–Muslim strife, he pointed out, the Sikh impasse was a comparatively minor skirmish. Yet crucial principles were involved in it. Especially in the Punjab, where communal passions were so intense, no group could be allowed to gain its objectives by force. That, he stressed, appealing for a settlement, was really the only principle at stake. He was neither attacking the Sikhs' religion nor blocking their legitimate political

---

[42] Hailey note, ibid.
[43] Hailey to Muddiman, 29 October 1924, HPI/6C.

aspirations. Even the most intransigent bureaucrat took no pleasure in seeing ignorant people put themselves in jail for an object they could easily gain by legislative means. The official mind was not "so obstinately obscurantist that it can be devoid of sympathy with those who are prepared to make genuine sacrifices to secure the reform of their religious institutions, or to purify the management of their shrines." But he must and would enforce the law.[44]

The government would not introduce a gurdwara bill itself, Hailey declared. If Sikhs wanted to draft a private measure, however, his officers would be ready to help them. He would not presume to dictate terms – but might just sketch a few guidelines: (1) The community itself must agree. (2) Since no community or section could be judge in its own cause, specific cases must be decided by independent arbitration. (3) Yet, recognizing changes that had occurred "in the religious conditions of a community," the arbitration tribunal could be given wide powers. (4) Finally, endowment funds must be spent for religious purposes, they must be subject to audit, and their accounts must be published. All in all it was a good conciliatory speech. For once Lahore's nationalist, Hindu newspaper, the *Tribune*, applauded him.[45]

The governor's main fear, he confided, was outside interference.[46] There were several attempts. In November, as Mangal Singh had forecast, Pandit Malaviya first tried to introduce a gurdwara bill in the assembly, then turned up in Lahore to offer himself as mediator. The governor's private secretary curtly declined an interview.[47] Next, at the Lahore unity conference early in December, Gandhi tried once more to repair the strained Akali–Congress relations. Sikhs should not be duped by Hailey, he declared at the Golden Temple; they knew he meant to crush their movement.[48] As Hailey predicted, however, the Akalis would not soon forgive the Mahatma for what they regarded as his sellout of the previous spring.[49] A third initiative came in March 1925 from Jinnah, who convinced Lord Reading that prison conditions in the Nabha princely state were a serious problem and that he was only trying to help. If his own efforts failed, Sir Malcolm replied, Jinnah's considerable talents might be called upon.[50] Malaviya, Gandhi, and finally Jinnah had tried to intervene. Hailey had successfully parried all three.[51]

By March 1925 Hailey was already fairly close to success. The process had had two stages, he explained. The first was forming the anti-Akali associations,

[44] Speech of 9 November 1924, *Tribune*, 11 November 1924.
[45] Ibid., 12–13 November 1924.
[46] Hailey to Sir Reginald Mant, 9 October 1924, HPI/6C.
[47] Malaviya to Hailey and D. Pott to Malaviya, 26 November 1924, ibid.
[48] 6 December 1924, CWMG, *25*, 399–400.
[49] Hailey to Reading, 22 January 1925, HPI/7A.
[50] Hailey–Reading correspondence, 19–27 March 1925, ibid.
[51] In my judgment the evidence does not support the interpretation of Mohinder Singh, *Akali Movement*, p. 135, that "the moves of Malaviya and Jinnah seem to have compelled Hailey to change his earlier policy of allowing the movement to prolong itself indefinitely and not to compromise with the Akalis on the Gurdwara Bill issue." That had not been his policy, and he blocked the two leaders quite effectively.

for though "they owe their existence to our instigation, and continue under our support . . . I could not neglect this obvious means." The second, more difficult step was to split the opposition, separating "the reconcilable from the irreconcilable elements among the Akali or pro-Akali sections of the Sikhs." The former "realize that they cannot succeed by physical violence, and can no longer hope to force the hand of Government." His strategy had been to behave as though gurdwara reform were really the only problem, with legislation constituting the obvious and easy remedy. He had repeated that point at every opportunity, making clear that otherwise the present law would be implemented, meaning that in due course mahants might well repossess gurdwaras they had lost earlier in the agitation.[52]

Since December Sikh members of the Legislative Council (MLCs) had been talking with H. W. Emerson and other officials.[53] The discussions were going slowly, but time seemed to be on Hailey's side and he was inclined not to press. By March 1925, however, he had a first draft of a bill in hand. It was a draftsman's nightmare, he apologized as he sent it to Delhi for approval.[54] For one thing the slate was not clean. A gurdwara act had been passed in 1922 and, although it had been temporary and had never been put into effect, it remained as a model, its outstanding feature being a central Sikh commission with sweeping powers including control of disputed shrines. It was typical of the Sikhs' "lack of statesmanship and foresight," he observed, that they had never put that bill into effect, for "they would have secured infinitely more than we are now prepared to give them."[55]

Moreover, despite the fact that the hereditary rights of mahants had been confirmed by civil courts, the SGPC were in physical possession of many disputed shrines. Sikhism was not a doctrinally unified religion, Hailey continued, but contained as many as twenty-six distinct sections, and the modern reform movement dated only from the late nineteenth century. Even as early as the 1911 census, however, well before the gurdwara controversy, the orthodox Amritdhari group had already constituted 90 percent of Punjab Sikhs. Despite the danger of recognizing a strong theocratic institution by statute, the bill must therefore concede a central managing agency the SGPC would dominate.[56]

Although the situation looked promising, success depended on tense discussions that were occurring among Sikh MLCs and the jailed leaders of the SGPC at Lahore Fort. Hailey could only wait them out. No hint whatever should be given that the introduction of the bill was a government triumph, he ordered, while it must be reiterated that he had never permitted negotiations on

---

52 Hailey to Reading, 22 January 1925, HPI/7A.
53 See the correspondence, December 1924–April 1925, between Emerson and Jodh Singh, who acted as emissary between the Sikh MLCs and the SGPC leaders in Lahore Fort, *Akali Papers*, pp. 137–51. Emerson was instrumental in arranging the Gandhi–Irwin Pact in 1931.
54 Hailey to Muddiman, 19 March 1925, HPI/7A.
55 Hailey to L. Rushbrook-Williams, 20 April 1925, HPI/7B.
56 Hailey note, n.d. [11 April 1925 added in pencil], ibid.

such issues as the release of prisoners.[57] He watched the negotiations closely. At first the jail contingent supported the bill; opposition emerged from the militants popularly called the Akali Dal; the moderates seemed likely to cave in; then they rallied. Face-saving conditions were put forward, but this time the SGPC did not say the bill would be withdrawn if they were not met. To Hailey's sharp eye the most hopeful sign of a break was that among the terms "there is no mention of the unfortunate Maharaja of Nabha."[58]

A year earlier Hailey had deprecated a premature settlement the Sikhs would not logically accept. Since then he had played a waiting game. The government "could have 'stonewalled' for years without great damage to ourselves," he confided. Now he wanted to move ahead: "Once you get a movement for recovery of good-will started, it is dangerous to allow it to get stale." Yet intervention, either through increased pressure or concessions, might backfire, so the Sikhs must be left to themselves.[59] Hailey hoped to "send the Akali Dal and the Extremists to Coventry." If the gurdwara bill should succeed in solving the Sikh question it would validate a novel political experiment: "Frame your own legislative solution, but manoeuvre your opponents into putting it forward as their own."[60]

Only at the last moment did an anti-Akali opposition begin to organize. Meeting a deputation of mahants from the Udasi sect, Hailey recognized that their claim that any gurdwara founded before the time of the Tenth Guru in the late eighteenth century should be classed as Hindu had both history and law in its favor. He could only square his conscience, he confessed, by reflecting that to ignore the plain fact of the ascendancy of orthodox, Amritdhari Sikhs would be like "those who during the Reformation period, insisted that the Protestant Englishman should be content to see his cathedrals in the hands of Roman priests."[61] Belatedly, and only after the gurdwara bill was safely in committee, he corresponded with the Maharaja of Patiala, supposedly the most powerful Sikh of all, whom he had ignored for the same reason he had resisted Malaviya and Jinnah, because he wanted a settlement that depended on no outside authority.[62]

On 7 July 1925 a special session of the Punjab Legislative Council passed the Gurdwara Act unanimously. In his concluding speech the governor tried to make the most of it, advising Sikhs to think earnestly and farsightedly about their community's future: "It cannot stand alone; its welfare and its progress" were tied to the Punjab as a whole.[63] He came armed with more than a lecture.

---

57 Hailey to Rushbrook-Williams, 20 April 1925, ibid.
58 Hailey to Muddiman, 2 May 1925, ibid.
59 Hailey to Craik, 9 May 1925, ibid.
60 Hailey to de Montmorency, 11 May 1925, ibid.
61 Hailey note, 6 May 1925, ibid.
62 Hailey to Patiala, 17 June 1925, ibid., and Hailey to Hirtzel, 23 September 1925, HPI/8A. See Barbara N. Ramusack's excellent article, "Maharajas and Gurdwaras: Patiala and the Sikh Community," in Jeffrey, ed., *People, Princes and Paramount Power*, pp. 170–204.
63 Punjab Legislative Council Debates, 8, 1301 ff.

Throughout the confrontation, insisting that the religious question must be negotiated separately, he had permitted no conditions. He was not frightened of making concessions, he explained, but only if they were certain to succeed.[64] Early in June, when it seemed that extremists might yet block the bill, he had refused releases of prisoners. The bill was only a means, he reasoned, the end being a change in mentality; concessions should therefore come after the bill rather than before.[65]

Now was the time. Both the SGPC and Akali Dal were being taken off the list of illegal associations, Hailey announced. There would be releases but no general amnesty. Prisoners would merely be asked to agree in writing that they would accept the gurdwara bill and "refrain from resort to other courses."[66] A few days later in conversation Hailey casually threw in another concession. Although he had recognized the practical supremacy of the SGPC, he had refused to permit it to be named as the central managing agency, thus maintaining the fiction that the bill had been negotiated with all Sikhs. Now he agreed that the central body might call itself what it liked. After all, he was quoted, "what was in a name?"[67]

Of the thirty-six prisoners in Lahore Fort, nineteen agreed to accept Hailey's condition to abide by the act and give up direct action; they were released late in July. The remaining seventeen insisted that no Sikh should be required to give any written undertaking whatever, refused to sign, and served the balance of their sentences. The recriminations between these two factions were bitter and prolonged.[68] Just as Hailey had intended, his apparently innocuous condition effectively split the Akali movement for a generation. When next the Sikh community felt itself under severe attack, during World War II and the partition crisis, the Akali Dal would have to be rebuilt essentially afresh. Yet there would also be continuity. Its control over gurdwaras and their substantial endowments gave the SGPC, and thus any faction that could dominate it, an important power base. And the acknowledged Sikh leader in 1947, the man who drew his sword and shouted, "Death to Pakistan," was one of the irreconcilables of July 1925. His name was Master Tara Singh.[69]

The Gurdwara Act of 1925 was universally regarded as a triumph, the only question being to whom the glory belonged. The SGPC and most Indian newspapers called it the victory of a heroic, nonviolent campaign in which the Sikhs overcame all obstacles a tyrannical government had put before them. Gandhi, for whom the agitation had become embarrassing, welcomed the set-

[64] Hailey to Hirtzel, 26 May 1925, HPI/7B.   [65] Hailey to H. D. Craik, 9 May 1925, ibid.
[66] Punjab LegCo Debates, *8*, 1301 ff.   [67] N.d. [11 July 1925], *Akali Papers*, pp. 157–8.
[68] "Akalis," wrote Khushwant Singh, "who had won their bitter struggle against the mahants and the government over control of their shrines, now turned their venom against each other." (*A History of the Sikhs*, 2 vols. [Princeton, N.J.: Princeton University Press, 1963–6], 2:213.)
[69] See particularly the last two chapters of Mohinder Singh's *Akali Struggle: A Retrospect*, which from the perspective of the late 1980s stressed the importance of internal politics within the Sikh community after 1925.

tlement and advised prisoners to accept the conditions.[70] British conservatives feted Hailey like a conquering general. The Akalis had been no bogey, Sir Michael O'Dwyer wrote admiringly, "but a real hard nut . . . and you have cracked it without using the steam hammer."[71] That was also the verdict of Akali extremists, who admitted that they had "suffered a crushing defeat."[72] Historians also differ only on whether the primary credit (or blame) should go to the Akalis or to Hailey. It is by no means novel to conclude that his confrontation with the Sikhs was one of the most spectacularly successful political operations in the annals of British rule in India. Nor is it unusual to characterize his policy as a classic application of Machiavellian tactics. O'Dwyer was right. Sir Malcolm Hailey set out to turn back what he called a dangerous mentality. He intended to split the Akalis. And he did so.

Ironically, in view of O'Dwyer's own reputation as a heavyhanded autocrat, he was also right in emphasizing that Hailey had cracked the nut without a steam hammer. Force had of course been used, ruthlessly and repeatedly, with the beating of thousands and the deaths of hundreds of religiously motivated and largely nonviolent people. During Hailey's governorship, however, both sides played within implicitly agreed ground rules; although some heads were broken the savage beatings of 1923 were not repeated. He had not condoned the Nankana massacre of 1921. But he had been home member during 1922–4 and he had defended the Jaito firing of February 1924. If necessary he would have done it again. Yet, apart from the notification of the SGPC and Akali Dal as illegal associations in 1923, he worked within the ordinary law, taking pride in not having ruled by ordinance. On the whole the Akali press was allowed to publish its propaganda. The Babbar Akalis had already been suppressed before his arrival. After the turbulence of 1921–3 his own tenure was actually comparatively quiet. If Hailey was skillful he was also lucky.

Hailey's tactics were more than vaguely Machiavellian, in the ordinary sense of ruthlessness conveyed by Gloucester's promise in Shakespeare's *Henry VI, Part 3*, to "set the murderous Machiavel to school." They were *strictly* Machiavellian. After thinking through the problem he settled on a limited and rational objective: not to bring the Sikh community to its knees but to split the Akali movement and overcome what he regarded as its dangerous mentality. He deployed not the full range of his arsenal but weapons precisely calibrated to achieve his object: the loyalist committees, patronage power, court challenges, his own speeches. Maneuvering his opponents into fighting on his own ground, he employed minimum force not to drive them away but to hold them there. Above all, though there was nothing novel about the attempt, he tried to split the Akalis by separating religious and political issues, by perceiving that the gurdwara bill was a means rather than an end.

---

[70] [11 July 1925], CWMG, 27, 361–2.   [71] O'Dwyer to Hailey, 29 March 1925, HPI/7A.
[72] Extract from *Babbar Sher* (Amritsar), 2 August 1925, in report on vernacular press, HPI/5D.

As Hailey put it in an after-dinner speech he was not "by nature, an ascetic; I like good food, good company, and deprecate the overtaxation of liquor." Nor was he immune to flattery. The Punjab press had been portraying him as that most intriguing figure, the arch-oppressor, and he had tried hard to live up to the ideal. According to the press he had succeeded admirably: the Golden Temple bombed, thousands hung to roast over slow fires, his white, tender hands stained red from the blood of saints, his "ravening teeth . . . meeting in the flesh of martyrs." All this sounded very promising and he really must see his dentist about some good ravening teeth. The disappointing truth, however, was that in dealing with the Akalis his administration had "reached the very height of statesmanship; for we have done nothing" – never persecuting, rarely prosecuting, merely upholding the law while making a genuine offer. "I am ashamed to confess to conduct so undramatic," he lamented. "I feel like Nadir Shah caught in the act of wheeling a perambulator. But there the sad fact is!"[73]

Hailey was certainly Machiavellian in the context of *The Prince*. In his big book, the *Discourses on Titus Livy,* however, Machiavelli argued that although a ruler's behavior must be rational – otherwise he will not long remain ruler – the ultimate test of statecraft is whether it promotes or retards the quality he called virtue. Did Sir Malcolm have a moral objective? Historians have not usually thought so. It is therefore perhaps worth repeating Hailey's own spontaneous statement of October 1924: "It would . . . be disastrous if we ever allowed one community in India to dominate the rights of minority sections by force, or to oust by mass action individuals who have clearly defined legal rights." From the perspective of the 1990s the Punjab of the 1920s has an eerie sense of déjà vu. The organizations (SGPC, Akali Dal), places, rhetoric, issues, the blurring of religion and politics, even some of the government's tactics – so much seems the same. The resemblance is of course only superficial. Sir Malcolm Hailey did not have to deal with the contemporary Khalistan movement but with an earlier, much less developed stage. Yet his ideal of a society in which people and groups behave rationally, under and within a rule of law, was and is a moral one – as the Punjab of the late twentieth century makes tragically clear.

In the summer of 1925 Sir Malcolm Hailey's prestige in Britain and even among Indians could hardly have been higher. His own collection of press clippings contains a portrayal written by the Punjab correspondent of the Indian-owned, English-language paper of Allahabad, the *Leader.* It described him as "a strange mixture of the bureaucrat and the publicist, demagogue and autocrat." Fretting at being isolated in the palatial Government House on the Mall in Lahore, whenever possible he liked "to rub shoulders with the people, hobnob with municipal commissioners, shake hands with the secretaries . . . and exchange ideas with the public men." He loved crowds. Wherever he went he entered with zest into the life of the place – no detail too

---

73 Draft dated February 1925, HPA/338. Nadir Shah was the notorious eighteenth-century sacker of Delhi.

insignificant, no inhabitant too mean – and "this becomes him better than his official exclusiveness." Hailey had "solved the Akali problem to all intents and purposes," the writer concluded. Indeed, "he appears to be a ruler fitted for solving political riddles. It is now expected that he will straighten out the Hindu–Mahomedan tangle in the Punjab."[74]

[74] *Leader,* 15 August 1925. Philip Mason, *The Men Who Ruled India,* 2:290, told the story of a police inspector who reported on a demonstration in Lahore, remarking that among the crowd was a disreputable-looking European. The governor had been walking the dog, came upon the marchers, and tagged along out of curiosity. Mason gave no source for the anecdote and the police records remain unavailable. But more than one historian has told me that a story as good as that just *has* to be true.

9

Governor of the Punjab: the communal problem, 1924–1926

"The new communal feeling is political," Sir Malcolm Hailey wrote in July 1924, shortly after he took over the Punjab. The recent removal of the sultan of Turkey by the Atatürk revolution having deprived the Khilafat movement of its raison d'être, he explained, Indian Muslims were looking increasingly at their position in their own country. Some of them were declaring that Old Autocracy was preferable to New Democracy under Hindu domination.[1] Hailey's perception that a largely middle-class, predominantly political, and essentially new political consciousness was maturing in the 1920s is worth emphasizing.

Communalism in twentieth-century India is probably best understood as a clash between fundamentally political ideologies devised for combat in a modern arena.[2] As religions Islam and Hinduism – the first austerely and uncompromisingly monotheistic, the second including monotheistic, polytheistic, and pantheistic tendencies; the first a spear, the second an umbrella – were of course acutely different and perhaps ultimately incompatible. India's medieval history has been written both as a tale of enmity and a story of harmony – there were both. Not until the twentieth century, however, did the two religions become *structurally* antagonistic. Only then did separate communal electorates come into existence, for the purpose of electing explicitly communal representatives.

The categories of British India's electoral system were essentially artificial, assuming complete identity of interests among people who on any grounds other than religion – class, sectional, linguistic, caste – were in fact very disparate. Stereotyping encouraged communal consciousness. Census categories became ideas; ideas were imposed on and merged into reality. Not least among the strengths of communal ideologies was their capacity to obscure the processes

---

[1] Hailey to Chirol, 2 July 1924, HPI/6A.
[2] The best general study is Bipan Chandra, *Communalism in Modern India* (New Delhi: Vikas, 1984). For works on the 1920s see Mushirul Hasan, *Nationalism and Communal Politics in India, 1916–1928* (New Delhi: Manohar, 1979); S. L. Malhotra, *Gandhi: An Experiment with Communal Politics: A Study of Gandhi's Role in Punjab Politics, 1922–1931* (Chandigarh: Panjab University Press, 1975); Prem R. Uprety, *Religion and Politics in Punjab in the 1920s* (New Delhi: Sterling, 1980); David Page, *Prelude to Partition: The Indian Muslims and the Imperial System of Control, 1920–1932* (Delhi: Oxford University Press, 1982); and David Gilmartin, *Empire and Islam: Punjab and the Making of Pakistan* (Berkeley: University of California Press, 1988).

that had created them. Although the leading communal organizations – the Arya Samaj and Hindu Sabha among Hindus, the Aligarh movement among Muslims, the Singh Sabha among Sikhs – emerged only in the late nineteenth century, they soon acquired an aura of permanence. Like most of his contemporaries, Jawaharlal Nehru being a significant exception, Hailey ordinarily behaved as though communalism was the inevitable norm of Indian politics – even though he knew very well that things had not always been just like that.[3]

Hailey was not alone in perceiving that an essentially new disease had invaded the body politic. In 1923 a Congress committee found that Hindu–Muslim relations in the Punjab were so "strained that each community . . . had practically arrayed itself in an armed camp." Having tried to negotiate the outstanding religious issues – atrocities during a Muslim rebellion in Malabar in south India, a riot in the Punjab city of Multan – the committee got nowhere. The reason, they charged, was that middle- and upper-class people were deliberately fanning the flames. "We can only hope," they despaired, "that the people will now take up the settlement of their differences in their own hands and dispense with their so-called representatives."[4]

To Gandhi it seemed "as if God has been dethroned."[5] For three weeks in September 1924 he fasted. After that a unity conference met in Delhi. From the Punjab, however, Hailey noted, virtually nobody came. North India's Muslim agriculturists had long been under Hindu economic domination, he observed, and though canal irrigation and high prices had somewhat improved their economic position, they remained inferior politically. Superior education and organization had enabled Hindus to monopolize administrative positions. It was thus "no mere question of cow-killing, or of shouting the *Azan*," he declared. "We have always had little troubles of this kind, and they always die down after a time." Riots triggered by religious conflict were "not the substance of the situation. The reality is that there is an actual clash of interests between the two communities representing different social standards and ideals." Not that he or his officials liked the tension: "We are bored out of our lives by it, for it comes up in a thousand ways which people in other parts of India do not fully understand. There is no item of our work, from the administration of justice down to the digging of drains, in which we do not have to face troubles arising from communal differences."[6]

Again, Gandhi agreed completely. Communal hostility in the Punjab was

---

3 As Peter Hardy has observed, "whether separatist politics bred separate electorates or separate electorates bred separatist politics is a version of the question about the chicken and the egg." (*The Muslims of British India:* [Cambridge: Cambridge University Press, 1972], pp. 147–8.) Scholars still debate the degree of Muslim opinion that preceded the so-called command performance of 1906 and the creation of separate electorates in 1909. But the Lucknow Pact of 1916, in which the Congress and the Muslim League agreed on precise mathematical formulas for Muslim representation in central and provincial legislatures, was not imposed by the British.

4 Report of Congress Committee, n.d., NML, AICC 3/1923.

5 18 September 1924, and draft resolution on Hindu–Muslim unity, CWMG, *25*, 171–2, 214–5.

6 Hailey to Arthur Moore, 6 October 1924, HPI/6C.

special, he contended; once the two communities came together there, then unity could be achieved all over India.[7] The Punjab was different because, alone among provinces where the reform scheme had been instituted, Hindus were a clear minority. The minister of education, who was responsible for appointments in local government, the educational and medical departments, and admissions to government colleges, was a Muslim, Mian (later Sir) Fazli Husain. Hindus were accusing him of pursuing a frankly communal policy.[8]

Soon after he became governor circumstances forced Hailey to make a quick study of Punjab politics. According to his count the provincial Legislative Council consisted of eleven Sikhs, controlled by the Shiromani Gurdwara Prabandhak Committee (SGPC), all of whom were boycotting; twenty-one Hindus, including nine members of the Swarajist Party, seven Independents, and five Agriculturists; and thirty-four Muslims, four of whom were Khilafatists, the remaining thirty being followers of the minister of education, Fazli Husain. The second minister (for agriculture) was Lal Chand, a Hindu of the Jat (agriculturist) caste, who had agreed to bring his four colleagues into an alliance with Fazli Husain's supporters, forming a rural coalition: the basis of the National Unionist Party that would dominate the politics of the province until 1946, the eve of partition. Along with the official bloc (thirteen government officers, six nominated nonofficials), it added up to a stable working majority.[9] In July 1924, however, the high court in Lahore having ruled in favor of a petition charging Lal Chand with election fraud, Hailey had to find a new minister.

Except for the fact that the parties were communal blocs instead of groups of "friends," a provincial governor's cabinet making rather resembled that of George III in the days of Fox, Pitt, and Lord North. For two months, while factions bargained and maneuvered, Hailey delayed the decision. His first option was a more representative, urban Hindu minister. Although the national Swarajist party had imposed a ban on accepting office, the local men seemed to want power. But the acknowledged Hindu leader, Raja Narendra Nath, whose no-confidence resolution against Fazli Husain had led to a bitter communal debate in 1923, could find no basis for agreement with his adversary.[10] Although a divided cabinet was possible, Hailey reasoned that once Lajpat Rai, the province's most eminent Hindu politician, returned from London, he would surely persuade the Swarajists to walk out. That would leave Narendra Nath with only seven supporters, while the government would remain divided. In the

[7] CWMG, *25,* 411–2.
[8] The reforms had not been instituted in North-West Frontier Province or Baluchistan. Bengal had a slight Muslim majority in population, but not in the Legislative Council.
[9] Hailey note, 15 October 1924, HPI/6B. See the extremely detailed and valuable study by Satya M. Rai, *Legislative Politics and Freedom Struggle in the Panjab, 1897–1947* (New Delhi: Indian Council of Historical Research, 1984).
[10] The debate of 13 and 15 March 1923 is in Punjab LegCo Deb., *4,* 1274 ff. See the analysis in Page, *Prelude to Partition,* pp. 71–2.

end Hailey fell back on what he called a more constitutional choice, another Jat Hindu named Chhotu Ram.[11]

When he opened the Legislative Council in November 1924 Hailey made communalism his centerpiece. Although the problem was not unique to the Punjab or India, he asserted, its ubiquity was striking; in all spheres – social matters, education, law and justice – it intervened. Recently the tension had been exacerbated, first by the war and then by the reforms, which had given majority communities new means to assert their position, challenging minorities to press their claims in turn. The only apparent remedy was to remove the real sources of conflict by lifting backward communities economically and educationally. Building a sense of security would take time, but "we must clearly endure."

The government could do comparatively little, he insisted. Much power and patronage had already been transferred to responsible ministers, the trend would only accelerate as the reform scheme proceeded, and "the minority must recognize that it cannot claim both the progressive extension of democratic institutions and the retention of checks from outside." Although no one thought separate electorates were ideal, they were based on the Lucknow Pact of 1916 between Congress and the Muslim League, and that could not be altered unless the communities themselves demanded it. Both communal voting and representation were transitional, belonging "to the sphere of curative medicine, and our constant endeavour is to promote . . . that state of health . . . which will make such a remedy unnecessary."[12]

In this speech Hailey tried to set a trap. The Swarajists were pressing for more rapid constitutional advance. But that must give more power to the majority, and in the Punjab that majority would obviously be communal, which for the foreseeable future would be entrenched by separate electorates. Though these were recent, and though he called them transitional, they had in fact become an established feature of the political structure, with the force of inertia behind them. Moreover he insisted that the state would remain neutral. How were India's leaders, on whom he placed the entire responsibility for resolving the conflict, to climb out of the pit? In 1929 the frontal attack of Motilal Nehru's report on communal electorates would fail – not because it was based on mistaken premises, but because the initiative had to be taken apart from and indeed against the weight of state power.

Although Hailey's understanding of the communal problem was in some ways strikingly perceptive, settling it was after all not his first priority. Just three days after delivering his Legislative Council speech he wrote a letter that throws the rest of his career in India into bold relief. In June he had expected not only a resurgence of the Akalis' gurdwara campaign but a larger, much more dan-

[11] Hailey note, 15 October 1924, HPI/6B. See Prem Chowdhry, *Punjab Politics: The Role of Sir Chhotu Ram* (New Delhi: Vikas, 1984).
[12] *Tribune*, 11 November 1924.

gerous agitation against a rise in canal-colony water rates. Having learned something from the tax revolt of 1907, however, he had cut the increase some 40 percent. "It is of supreme importance to us to keep the Punjab agriculturalist from agitation," he explained; "I am convinced that the Congress people can never really succeed in being a danger to us until they enlist the services of a physical force brigade." Congress representatives were now at work in rural areas all across north India. "Within the next two or three years," he predicted, "we shall have another big agitation comparable with that of non-cooperation, but on different lines, and worked by men who have no ideal of non-violence." When the showdown came, "I should like to think that . . . the Punjab agri-culturist was apathetic, if . . . not actually hostile, to the movement."[13]

In December 1924 Gandhi came to Lahore to preside over the provincial Congress committee. At the Golden Temple – and his ambiguous relations with the Sikhs analyzed in the preceding chapter seem less mysterious in the context of the larger Hindu–Muslim problem he was trying to resolve – he accused Hailey of plotting to crush the gurdwara reform movement. Next day, identifying the Punjab as the seat of tension all over the country, he declared that the only solution was for one community, that is, Hindus, to surrender to the other. Punjabis were renowned fighters, he asserted. But they should be fighting for essentials: for the honor of their women, for their freedom, not for trifles like seats and jobs.[14]

At Rawalpindi, where he interviewed Hindu refugees from a serious riot at Kohat in North-West Frontier Province, Gandhi accused the government of intensifying the conflict by not maintaining law and order. He proposed a deal: Hindus to concede communal representation and appointments in proportion to population if Muslims would abandon separate electorates. This mediation effort failed; he would try again at the Congress session in Belgaum. Punjab Hindus were getting angry at what they perceived as Gandhi's favoritism toward Muslims, Hailey noted. They had "begun to see that if they are to get protec-tion as a minority, it must be from Government."[15]

An abrupt change in the attitude of Lajpat Rai was both symptomatic and instrumental in raising the temperature. Although Hailey had assumed that a dedicated Swarajist would be returning from London, the man who showed up was well on the way to becoming a fervent communalist. Did not Gandhi realize, Lajpat Rai asked in a series of articles, that the forced removal of Hindus from Kohat raised issues of life and death? The community desperately needed to organize and defend itself. Except among lower-middle class Pun-jabis, however, he saw few signs of "corporate communal life among the Hin-dus of India." The Mahatma must stop urging surrender, he warned, and apply himself to removing the real causes of communal tension.

---

13 Hailey to Hirtzel, 13 November 1924, HPI/6C.
14 7 December 1924, CWMG, *25*, 411–2.
15 Hailey to Muddiman, 11 December 1924, HPI/1C.

By and large, in Lajpat Rai's view, those causes turned out to be the fault of Muslims. Pan-Islamicists rather than Indian nationalists, they insisted that any demand they made was justified on religious grounds and damned all non-believers. Above all their only cure for communal tension was communal representation. Once accept that, he declared, and "there is no chance of its being ever abolished, without a Civil War." Even the outright partition of the Punjab would be preferable. Partition, indeed, might have to be considered wherever there were "compact Muslim communities," with Muslims getting perhaps the North-West Frontier Province, western Punjab, Sind, and eastern Bengal (that is, roughly the moth-eaten Pakistan of 1947). Muslims were demanding a wholesale revision of the Lucknow Pact, Lajpat Rai informed Hindu leaders, while Congress had repeatedly shown itself to be incapable of defending Hindu interests. Fortunately, he asserted, the Hindu Mahasabha would also be meeting in Belgaum.[16]

Lajpat Rai's rhetoric represented only one side of the rising tension. Punjab Muslims held that the Shuddhi (reconversion) and Sangathan (strengthening) movements among Hindus amounted to preparation for organized violence. They too were talking about partition. Dr. Saifuddin Kitchlew, for instance, the same Khilafatist and Congress leader whose arrest at Amritsar in 1919 had triggered the Punjab horrors, was now demanding revision of the Lucknow Pact on the grounds that it discriminated against Punjab Muslims. In Belgaum he attended the Khilafatist conference but not the Congress session. In 1925 this former devoted Gandhian formally resigned from Congress to lead the Tanzim movement, aimed at reinvigorating Islam.[17]

At Belgaum Gandhi tried to reunite a national movement that had degenerated into a morass of competing factions. The communal problem was fundamentally political, he reiterated, "religion has been travestied," and the whole structure of separate electorates and representation ought to be destroyed. The trap Hailey had set in his speech could not be avoided, however, for until their jealousies had been superseded minorities "must be allowed their way. The majority must set the example of self-sacrifice."[18] Also at Belgaum the president of the Mahasabha, Pandit Madan Mohan Malaviya, announced that a committee chaired by Lajpat Rai would represent Hindus at an All-Parties Conference to be held in Delhi.[19] At its session in Bombay, where the tone of communal bitterness matched that of the Mahasabha, the All-India Muslim League also appointed a committee.[20] When the delegations met in Delhi, the

---

[16] Lajpat Rai, series of articles and letter in the *Tribune*, 26 November – 19 December 1924; Page, *Prelude to Partition*, p. 122. Several of the letters are reprinted in Lala Lajpat Rai, *Writings and Speeches*, ed. Vijaya C. Joshi, vol. 2. The Hindu Mahasabha had been founded in 1915 to unify the Hindu communal voice.

[17] Page, *Prelude to Partition*, pp. 103–4.

[18] Statement of 26 December 1924, CWMG, 25, 477–8.

[19] *Tribune*, 30 December 1924.

[20] See Syed S. Pirzada, ed., *Foundations of Pakistan: All-India Muslim League Documents, 1906–1947*, 2 vols. (Karachi: National Publishing House, 1970), 2:1–30.

conference rapidly collapsed. Gandhi tried to negotiate directly with Sir Fazli Husain, but failed. Perhaps it was just as well, the Mahatma said, for at present any compromise would have to be imposed by the government. National unity would "take longer than I had expected." If he were the government he "would do exactly as the British are doing, i.e., try to divide and rule." The communal problem was an "insoluble puzzle. I propose to keep out of it."[21]

For the time being, Hailey observed, "the Congress had disappeared giving place to the Muslim League and the Hindu Mahasabha." Gandhi's proposed bargain would be an insidious trap, he warned, for the burden of carrying it out would be placed on the government, which inevitably would draw the hostility of both communities.[22] Fortunately for the British, he continued, the problem was too deep-seated for paper compromises. Hindus had long "constituted the intelligentzia of the province, dominated its politics, and absorbed a large share in the administration"; they were "the moneyed element, and in Muhammadan districts practically held the finance of the zamindar in their hands." Now that the reforms had given Muslims the balance of political power they had naturally pressed their advantage, "and one does not find it entirely unreasonable if they did so with some acerbity and a sense of triumph."[23] The combination of communal representation and separate electorates had been so vicious, Raja Narendra Nath wrote on behalf of the Hindu Sabha, "that some of us think it would have been better for the province if the Reforms had not been introduced."[24]

Although its bitter political disputes and virulent communal press made the province a powder keg, and despite the fact that major clashes had occurred in all the surrounding areas, the Punjab had experienced no serious riot since Multan in 1922. An outbreak which according to the official statement did *not* happen at Panipat, a predominantly Muslim town in the eastern Punjab, however, demonstrated the potentiality. According to the deputy commissioner only the cool, gallant police had prevented a gentle Muslim procession during the Muharram festival from being attacked by pugnacious Hindus armed with lathis, scythes, and pitchforks. According to the Hindu account Muslim police had lured into the town "innocent Hindu pilgrims . . . peacefully proceeding to the annual Jumna fair," whereupon they attacked them maliciously. In the eyes of local Muslims the Hindu Sabha's pilgrims were "stalwart Hindu Jats . . .

---

[21] Gandhi to Fazli Husain, 2 March; statement of 5 March 1925, CWMG, *26*, 215, 222–3.

[22] Hailey to Sir Verney Lovett, 7 February 1925, HPI/7A. "When I see these constant invitations to Government to interfere in communal matters," he told an Indian moderate, "I can only point to the entire failure of popular leaders in the same direction." Hailey to Sir Dinshaw Wacha, 26 December 1924, HPI/6C.

[23] Hailey to Reading, 22 January 1925, HPI/7A.

[24] Narendra Nath to Lajpat Rai, 18 February 1925, enclosed in Narendra Nath to Craik, 14 April 1925, HPI/7B. See also Punjab memo, 13 August 1924, Reforms Inquiry Committee, PP, 1924–5 [Cmd. 2362], *10*, 671 ff.

tools in the hands of city Banias and the leaders of the Sangathan movement who were the real wire-pullers."[25]

Going to Panipat himself, Hailey listened carefully to both sides. On the way out Hindu villagers crowded about: "His Excellency stopped his car and assured by putting his hands over an old man that justice would be meted out to them." Although eventually the fuss died down, what Hailey called the "little affair at Panipat" had demonstrated "what the communities would do without a restraining hand."[26]

"It was a sad thing," said the Congress president Sarojini Naidu, that Punjab leaders had left "Congress and taken to the unworthy task of pitting one community against another." As the province standing between India and Swaraj, "the Punjab should be ashamed of herself."[27] On the contrary, Lajpat Rai maintained, the Hindu Sabha was not hostile to Congress but only to its present leaders, the Swarajists. Congress had "outlived its usefulness," declared the Sangathan leader, Bhai Parmanend, who charged Gandhi with having encouraged Muslim extremists to raise their demands. The Swarajists were secular, he asserted, not really Hindu at all. What right did they have to represent Hindu constituencies? The community was engaged in a life-or-death struggle: "even Swaraj is the means and self-preservation is the end."[28]

Muslim rhetoric kept in step. The reason for the epidemic of riots, said Shaikh Abdulla of the United Provinces at the Aligarh session of the Muslim League, was that Hindu youths were being trained to match physical strength against the other community, "practically a preparation for civil war." India, observed the League's president, Sir Abdur Rahim of Bengal, had "two distinct communities or peoples," possessing "distinctive culture, civilization and social habits . . . traditions and history . . . ; the fact that they have lived in the same country for nearly a thousand years has contributed hardly anything to their fusion into a nation." The current Hindu insurgence was the most serious challenge Muslims had ever faced, he argued, even surpassing the Christian crusades.[29]

"One is as usual obsessed by the feeling that in spite of much activity, one has really done little," Hailey wrote on the last day of 1925.[30] Some economic schemes were going forward, and financially the province was in the black. Politically things remained comparatively quiet, for the Akali challenge was over and "even the Swarajist Hindus are turning steadily to the side of government, realizing the danger of alienating it in the face of a Muhammadan majority." Congress seemed to realize that at least for the time being it had little chance of

[25] Reports in *Tribune*, 4–19 August 1925.
[26] *Tribune*, 30 August 1925; Hailey to O'Dwyer, 6 August 1925, HPI/7B.
[27] Naidu speech at Gujranwala, *Tribune*, 22 October 1924.
[28] Lajpat Rai letter, ibid., 24 October 1925; Bhai Permanend statement, ibid., 31 October 1925.
[29] Pirzada, *Foundations of Pakistan*, 2:31–69.
[30] Hailey to Vincent, 31 December 1925, HPI/8B.

support for a large-scale confrontation. Although the communal rivalry made governing easier, however, it was also irritating. "One hears of nothing else day and night," he had put it earlier; "it is like staying in a house where the husband and wife are always nagging at each other."[31]

There was of course plenty to do: crime and corruption, agricultural programs, education, the cooperative movement. He had been doing "a most unusual amount of touring, and find it has a good effect in bringing the existence of Government as a personality before the people," to some degree replacing "the ordinary excitement which the agitator and his like pour into their somewhat dull lives." Occasionally life was "a little wanting in pep, and is perhaps a little parochial," he confessed. "I do not know the remedy, unless it is to organize a local revolution!"[32]

Although his province might look on national politics with detachment, Hailey remarked rather complacently at the annual dinner of the European Association at Lahore in February 1926, "if this is isolation nevertheless we are moderately content." In their hearts, he said, Punjabis probably agreed that as long as communal differences persisted a strong administration would be needed. These – the strict impartiality of British governance and tacit Indian consent – were the twin towers of trusteeship: "not a demand for power, [but] an incentive to duty." Hailey's contrast of the Punjab with the rest of India, the *Tribune* commented caustically, was like Sir Michael O'Dwyer's famous boast that he would make the province into India's Ulster.[33]

Indians seemed intent on doing that themselves. Warning Hindus that they were a dying race, Lajpat Rai resigned from the Punjab Congress. In March Motilal Nehru led the Swarajists out of the Legislative Assembly in Delhi, and though the local party followed suit its members were soon back pledging to defend Hindu interests. The Hindu Mahasabha announced it was reserving the right to oppose anti-Hindu candidates – meaning Hindus who in their opinion were not upholding the interests of the community – and demanded that all aspirants for seats sign a pledge. Pandit Malaviya formed a new Nationalist Party.[34] In April Calcutta suffered three severe riots resulting in more than one hundred deaths. Having been killed by Muslim outrages Gandhi's Hindu–Muslim unity had "only lasted like a mid-summer night's dream," sneered the

---

31 Hailey to O'Dwyer, 6 August 1925, HPI/7B.
32 Hailey to Vincent, 31 December 1925, HPI/8B. Among the clippings in the Hailey Collection is the following from the *Bande Mattram* of May 1926. Old women, said the article, were given to inspecting the lines on palms and the soles of children's feet; if the line was long the child would travel far. The lines on Hailey's feet would be long indeed. "Sir Malcolm will be nothing less than 60 years old [in fact he was fifty-four]. People often travel much in youth; but with Sir Malcolm youth and old age are equal. The Punjab has seen many Lt. Governors and Governors, but hardly any one of them ever visited a district more than once. . . . Sir Malcolm has scarcely been 2 years in the Punjab, and there will hardly be any district which he has not visited during this period. In certain districts he has toured not once or twice, but thrice and even four times. Let alone the large cities; he has even penetrated into small villages. Can those young Congress workers, who tour much, vie with this aged Governor?"
33 *Tribune*, 18 February 1926.   34 Ibid., 12 and 23 March 1926.

Hindu Mahasabha leader B. S. Moonje; the present struggle was "nothing less than a kind of civil war." If Indian Muslims "came out in the field with an effective force," answered Abdur Rahman Dojanewi in Delhi, "Lalas would come forward with folded hands and make peace in two hours."[35] Was it not time for the government to stop the inflammatory rhetoric? Unfortunately, Hailey noted somewhat speciously, a great deal of communal agitation could be conducted within the law.[36]

In April 1926 Lord Reading was succeeded by Edward Wood, Lord Irwin (later Lord Halifax), with whom Hailey's relationship would be extremely close. Profoundly disturbed by the rioting – Irwin was deeply religious, and only the most callous of men would have remained unmoved by the Calcutta slaughter – the new viceroy proposed a gesture. It was a good idea, Hailey advised, although because a draft speech had been enclosed it would have been a little awkward for him to have said otherwise. But Irwin should take care to speak as an individual and avoid convening a round-table conference, for that would certainly fail, and it was "a cardinal tenet of our faith that a Viceroy should not be connected with failure." Above all it should be made clear that the communal problem was primarily an Indian responsibility.[37]

A few weeks later the paradox that the province with the most virulent communal problem had remained immune to the epidemic of rioting ended at Rawalpindi. Trouble had been predicted for 20 June, the Muslim festival of Bakr-Id; instead it happened on the fourteenth. As usual apparently trivial causes – a proposed cinema and the playing of music, both near a mosque – led to the clash. Also as usual there were conflicting versions. Muslims accused a Sikh procession of taunting them, said they had borne the insults stoically until attacked, and noted that they had suffered most of the casualties. Sikhs charged that their peaceful procession, which included women singing hymns to God, had been bombarded by brickbats. Hindus alleged that Muslim toughs from outlying villages had burned the central market, Muslim policemen having allowed them to carry gasoline and kerosene openly in handcarts while preventing owners from gaining access to their property. The fire brigades were nowhere in sight. Methab Singh, who came on behalf of the SGPC, found everybody blaming everybody else. In fact, he concluded accurately, the situation was "so complicated that confusion paralyzed reason." The wholesale arson represented "a new and mischievous programme of destruction."[38]

---

35 Ibid., 27 April and 11 May 1926.
36 Hailey to Sir Dinshaw Wacha, 31 July 1926, HPI/9B. During the civil-disobedience campaign of the early 1930s, of course, the UP government under Hailey would prohibit virtually everything referring to Gandhi. See N. Gerald Barrier, *Banned: Controversial Literature and Political Control in British India, 1907–1947* (Columbia: University of Missouri Press, 1974), pp. 116–7.
37 Hailey to de Montmorency (PSV), 10 June 1926, HPI/9B. Irwin gave his speech on communalism on 17 July. See Edward Wood, *Indian Problems* (London: Allen & Unwin, 1932), pp. 231–40. Two days later savage rioting broke out again in Calcutta.
38 *Tribune*, 16–20 June 1926; Kirpal Singh, ed., "Sardar Bahadur Mehtab Singh's Report on Rawalpindi Riots – 1926," *Panjab Past and Present*, 15 (1981), 407–24.

Had the local authorities been caught napping, Hailey asked in Simla? Why had the Sikh procession been permitted to take place without a license? Why had troops not been called out during the intense excitement on the day of the fourteenth? The police were being charged with giving insufficient protection and preventing people from putting out the fires. What had happened to the fire brigades? The Punjab Congress Committee concluded that leaders on all sides had not done enough to curb passions and that the authorities had been far too slow to act.[39] Rebuking local officials on the basis of hindsight was not a step governors took lightly, and Hailey's public statements backed up the Rawalpindi authorities. But his government's quick reaction in the still more serious riot at Lahore in 1927 suggests that in private he largely concurred with the Congress report. He also agreed with Mehtab Singh: The systematic arson of shops and houses of an opposing community at Rawalpindi was a new and sinister feature in communal rioting.[40]

At the height of the outcry over the Rawalpindi riot the Punjab Legislative Council bitterly debated a bill to regulate professional moneylenders, most of whom were Hindu. This was not a communal measure, insisted the mover, Mir Maqbool Mahmood (Muslim); it would merely ensure that, like doctors or lawyers, moneylenders were registered properly and kept regular accounts. It was indeed communal legislation, Pandit Narak Chand (Hindu) replied, based on a mistaken reading of the Koran and branding honest businessmen as Shylocks; had not the *Muslim Outlook* called the bill an essential part of the Tanzim movement to consolidate the Muslim community? Not only was this a communal bill, charged Raja Narendra Nath (Hindu); it was class legislation pitting zamindar against non-zamindar. Of course, Sir Fazli Husain agreed cheerfully; but people who favored representative institutions "will have to abide by the rules ... and carry on the game whether they are winning or losing."[41]

That in essence was what Hailey said himself late in October when, as the 1926 election approached its climax, he dissolved the second reformed Council. Although the government had been accused of "truckling to communal

39 *Tribune*, 21 July 1926.
40 Hailey to Hirtzel, 15 June; Hailey to Crerar, 19 June 1926, HPI/9B. The *Tribune*, 20 June 1926, pointedly contrasted Hailey's willingness to go to the plains in hot weather with Lytton in Bengal who, like the fiddle-playing Roman emperor Nero, had stayed three weeks in Darjeeling while Calcutta tore itself apart.
41 30 June–7 July 1926, Punjab LegCo Debates, 9, 1178 ff. Malcolm Darling, *The Punjab Peasant in Prosperity and Debt*, was quoted by both sides. Supporters of the bill cited his arguments that debt was increasing, that credit was too easy, that too much of it went for unproductive purposes like marriages or funerals, that some moneylenders were unscrupulous, and ordinary record-keeping mixed up principal and interest. Opponents used his points that the maligned village moneylenders lived with their clients, tided them over famines, shared their high risks as no bank would, charged average interest rates (12–15%) which were probably not exorbitant, and above all were irreplaceable. See the critical examination by Mridula Mukherjee, "Commercialization and Agrarian Change in Pre-Independence Punjab," in K. N. Raj et al., *Commercialisation in Indian Agriculture* (New Delhi: Oxford University Press, 1985), pp. 51–104.

ends," he pointed out, it was bound to appoint ministers who could cooperate. If there existed "in the Council a body, whether constituted on communal or other lines, which appears sufficiently united to present on ordinary occasions a working majority," then it was proper to give that party official support. In short, as a student of the eighteenth-century British constitution would have put it, the king's government had to be carried on. Sir Malcolm saw "nothing so far but one of the inevitable consequences of representative government, a reaction in the field of administration to the influence exercised by a majority party" that happened to be constructed on a communal basis. The day would come, "and its coming is our most fervent prayer," when the communal stage of India's political development would have been superseded. But "when it comes, and parties are reconstituted on a new basis, it will still be the will of the majority which will prevail."[42]

Nevertheless, Hailey said that he had been impressed by the heated communal debate on the moneylenders bill, his lawyers had warned him that the drafting was irremediably defective, and there seemed to be a danger that agricultural credit would dry up. Despite the fact that officials had supported the measure through the Council, he had therefore decided that it must be vetoed.[43] There was "much that I should have liked to say about communal differences, on the vexed question of communal representation in our services," he wound up. As any newspaper reader would have known, however – Gandhi himself had reached the same conclusion – for the time being the communal situation had gone past the point of return.

The Indian elections of 1926 were thoroughly communal, the tone being somewhat reminiscent of contests in the same period in the American South. Although comparisons could easily be pushed too far, these two cases do seem to be variations on the theme of how artificially constructed electorates work to shape political discourse. Black voters and candidates as well as many poor whites having been excluded, southern elections were factional struggles within the Democratic party in which white politicians tried to outdo each other in racial invective, the level of racism being in inverse proportion to actual black participation.[44] In British Indian elections, where voters were artificially fenced off into separate electorates, anti-Hindu or anti-Muslim war cries were in fact

---

[42] 25 October 1926, Punjab LegCo Deb., 9, 1797–1810. Many contemporary Indian politicians would have understood the comparison. The *Tribune* had recently printed a long extract from the London *Times* of Sir John Fortescue's revelations concerning George III's role in eighteenth-century elections (growing out of Sir John's editing of the king's correspondence) and had commented on it in a leading article.

[43] Although he promised to bring in an improved bill he left the issue alone, and a Registration of Moneylenders' Bill was finally enacted in 1938. Rai, *Legislative Politics and Freedom Struggle in the Panjab*, pp. 248–9.

[44] See particularly Valdimer O. Key, *Southern Politics in State and Nation* (New York: Knopf, 1949), and J. Morgan Kousser, *The Shaping of Southern Politics: Suffrage Restriction and the Establishment of the One-Party South, 1880–1910* (New Haven, Conn.: Yale University Press, 1974), and my own book, *The Highest Stage of White Supremacy: A Comparative Study of South Africa and the American South* (New York: Cambridge University Press, 1982), especially ch. 1.

weapons for internal skirmishing within communities that were supposedly homogeneous.

In 1926 the leading organizations in all three Punjab communities – the Hindu Sabha, the Khilafat committee, and the Sikh League – demanded loyalty oaths requiring candidates to vote on all communal questions as directed by those bodies. By far the bitterest struggle, which demonstrated that Gandhi's strategy of boycotting the councils had perhaps been right after all, took place between Swarajists and Hindu communalists. "It was simply beyond me to meet the kind of propaganda . . . of the Malaviya-Lala [Lajpat Rai] gang," Motilal Nehru told his son in an often quoted letter; "privately almost every individual voter was told that I was a beef-eater in league with the Moham-madans to legalise cow slaughter. . . . Communal hatred and heavy bribing of the voters was the order of the day."[45]

In December 1926 Hailey gave a convocation address at Punjab University in Lahore, where he was chancellor. His subject was the province fifty years hence. Dismissing what he called short-term issues – by then, he said disarm-ingly, Indians would long since have had self-government – he asked what truly significant changes were going on. The most crucial was education. By 1976 sheer illiteracy would have ended and with it the curse of communalism. For "religion, whose true function is a guide in the conduct of life and thought, steps beyond its sphere when it binds its followers into communities so circum-scribed and defined as to create social divisions and antagonisms." Although faith would not be abandoned, educated people would put religion "in its proper place. . . . That may be hard doctrine to-day," he declared, "but if my vision is correct, it will be the commonplace of the future."

Was Punjab University leading toward this utopian vision? Unfortunately Hailey saw too "few examples of the distinctive University type, the man who knows and shows that . . . he has been 'a citizen of no mean city.'" Indeed the institution itself was communalized, "still in the tribal stage; it needs to be a nation." It was symptomatic that the university did not even have a cricket team. "We desire to present to India," he concluded, "a people fitted to stand in the forefront of her advance, socially united, morally and intellectually equipped to help her master her own destinies."[46] A generously idealistic vision, observed the *Tribune*. But were the people in the governor's utopia free?[47]

45 2 December 1926, Jawaharlal Nehru, ed., *A Bunch of Old Letters* (New York: Asia Publishing House, 1958), pp. 51–2. The Swarajists lost heavily throughout India; in the Punjab Legislative Council they fell from nine members to three.
46 Speech of 23 December 1926, HPI/44.
47 *Tribune*, 25 December 1926.

〜〜

10

Governor of the Punjab: the communal problem, 1927–1928

From his idealistic vision of a society freed from the curse of religion gone wrong, Hailey returned in January 1927 to the humdrum reality of communal politics. The election had virtually wiped out the Swarajists, while the "party" of the Hindu Jat minister Chhotu Ram had been reduced by half, that is, to two. The situation having become ridiculous, Sir Malcolm consulted the two most powerful men in the Legislative Council, Raja Narendra Nath and Sir Fazli Husain, about the option of appointing a third minister. The former told him that urban Hindus would be able to cooperate with rural members. In particular they would not attempt to repeal the Land Alienation Act of 1900, as they had long threatened to do, and they would accept communal representation in district and municipal bodies. Although Sir Fazli objected strenuously Hailey went ahead, dropping Chhotu Ram and naming two new ministers, Manohar Lal (Hindu) and Feroz Khan Noon (Muslim), while retaining Jogendra Singh (Sikh), whom he had appointed in January 1926. His motive, he explained, flatly contradicting his reasoning of September 1924, was to capitalize on the aloofness of provincial Hindus from Congress.[1]

The cabinet shuffle of January 1927 remained controversial. According to Hailey he wanted to hold the scales between contending communities and keep Punjab Hindus separated from Congress. But the biography of Sir Fazli Husain by his son saw a close connection between the veto of the moneylenders bill, the kicking upstairs of Sir Fazli to the post of revenue member in January 1926, and the ministerial appointments of January 1927 – all parts of an alleged campaign to weaken the agrarian or Unionist party.[2] Nothing could have been easier, Hailey commented in the 1960s, stressing his lifelong identification with rural interests ever since his service in the Lower Jhelum canal colony, than to come down heavily for the Unionists and against urban Hindus, but that was not how he had seen his obligation.[3]

---

[1] Hailey note, 27 December 1926, HPI/9C; Hailey to Muddiman, January 1927, HPI/10A. See also Irwin to Birkenhead, 13 January 1927, quoted in Prem Chowdhry, *Punjab Politics: The Role of Sir Chhotu Ram*, pp. 175–6.
[2] Azim Husain, *Fazl-i-Husain: A Political Biography* (Bombay: Longmans, 1946), pp. 160–3. The weakest link is the second. "Apparently," Azim Husain explained, "the Governor outmanoeuvred Fazl-i-Husain who accepted office without resisting."
[3] Hailey to D. Anthony Low, 10 January 1961, HPI/51.

Although the proposition that he was out to weaken Sir Fazli Husain's National Unionist Party is not convincing, Hailey's motives were rather less straightforward than he implied.[4] As recently as his Legislative Council speech of October 1926 he had stressed the imperative need for the government to support a party capable of commanding a working majority – an argument that would have favored the appointment of another rural minister. The real difference between 1924 and 1927 was that in the meantime Punjab Hindu politicians had distanced themselves from Congress. By rewarding them he hoped to maintain the gap. Whereas the utopian convocation speaker had presented a vision of a harmonious society free of religious conflict, the pragmatic governor was reinforcing a structure of politics based on precisely that dynamic. Apparently the cure for communalism was more communalism.

In 1927, owing to his strong influence with the viceroy, Lord Irwin, Hailey's advice on the makeup of the Indian Statutory Commission led to what has been called one of the most colossal blunders in modern British history.[5] Under the Government of India Act (1919) Parliament was to review the constitution within ten years, so a commission needed to be appointed no later than early 1929. That was also the mandatory date for the next British general election, however, which seemed likely to go to Labour. Frightened of the sort of commission a Labour government might appoint, the Conservative secretary of state Lord Birkenhead had therefore been considering appointing it earlier. In August 1926 Hailey noted Birkenhead's reference to the possibility of a royal commission rather than a joint select committee restricted to members of Parliament, which would exclude both British officials and Indians. Even Indians might prefer the latter, he speculated: "At the moment the communal question is even more important than that of the form which constitutional advance might take."[6]

Was Irwin quite sure that the uproar created by conflicting reports by Hindu and Muslim members of a royal commission would not be useful, Birkenhead asked? Parliament needed a detached view, Hailey stressed. Even the most detached British official would be biased in favor of the bureaucracy to which he had given his life, however, while if Indians were included all sections would have to be represented and no appointment would be uncontroversial. On the whole, especially if communal tension remained acute, he thought that opposi-

---

4 Although Chowdhry, *Punjab Politics*, pp. 176–9, noted Hailey's statement that he wanted to keep Punjab Hindu politicians away from the Swarajists, as well as the letter to Low, he nevertheless argued that the governor was indeed bent on weakening the agrarian party. Page, *Prelude to Partition*, pp. 91–3, judged that Hailey's elevation of Sir Fazli to the revenue membership was intended to encourage Hindus to lessen their opposition to government rather than to weaken the Unionists. I agree with Page.
5 The argument concerning Hailey's large role in the decision is made persuasively by Page, *Prelude to Partition*, pp. 153–9.
6 Birkenhead to Reading, 10 December 1925, in second earl of Birkenhead, *F. E.: The Life of F. E. Smith, First Earl of Birkenhead* (London: Eyre & Spottiswoode, 1960), pp. 511–12; Hailey to G. Cunningham (PSV), 21 August 1926, HPI/9C.

tion to an all-British statutory commission might not prove to be serious. Although he did not discount Birkenhead's cynical reasoning, the advantage would be "dialectical rather than substantive, and if such differences exist we ought to be able to prove them without inviting Indians to serve . . . for the purpose of making their dissensions manifest."[7]

With the benefit of hindsight Hailey's counsel was certainly disastrous. It is no wonder, however, that a governor of the Punjab in 1927 would have supposed that communalism had displaced the struggle for swaraj as the controlling force in Indian politics. Numerous politicians on both sides were saying precisely that. Moreover, despite the reinvigoration of the freedom movement and the temporary Hindu–Muslim unity that followed the announcement of the lily-white statutory commission in November, the subsequent failure of the Nehru Report two years later suggests that Hailey may not have been entirely wrong. In any case events soon seemed to confirm his judgment. Early in May, just when he was getting ready to go fishing, there came "a little riot in Lahore."[8]

Lahore was unusual, the governor reported: "no regular riot arising out of a procession or the like."[9] About midnight, 3 May, an assault by a Muslim youth on a Sikh girl had provoked a row between crowds resulting in four Muslim deaths, but police had seemed to have the affair in hand. Next morning, however, warned by the CID to expect trouble at the day's funeral processions, Hailey called in reinforcements. His views were well known, he explained, recapitulating the doctrine of the Punjab school: "I believe in the reassuring effect of an early display of troops." Although the funerals did create several incidents, the real trouble came after the processions broke up, resulting in fourteen corpses and more than a hundred injuries. This kind of violence was hard to combat: "The usual thing is for 3 or 4 men with lathis to fall upon some innocent wayfarer, slaughter him and disappear."[10]

Aided by local guides, soldiers saturated the narrow lanes and alleys of the medieval Old City – a visitor finds it hard to visualize how a riot could possibly be controlled there – enforcing a curfew, while armored cars patrolled the wider streets of nearby Anarkali market and other neighborhoods. Herbert Emerson, the former deputy commissioner of Lahore, took charge; meetings were prohibited and the carrying of lathis and other weapons forbidden. Lest the wholesale arson of Rawalpindi be repeated, Hailey had orders broadcast to the effect that anyone setting fires would be shot on sight.[11] That seemed to

---

[7] Hailey to Irwin, 23 April 1927, HPI/10A.
[8] Hailey to Vincent, 5 May 1927, ibid.   [9] Hailey to Muddiman, 7 May 1927, ibid.
[10] Hailey to Vincent, 5 May 1927, ibid. See also the official report, probably written by Hailey himself, 27 July 1927, NAI HomPol 11/x/1927.
[11] Hailey to Vincent, 5 May 1927, HPI/10A. Hailey particularly praised the town criers, an "efficient and sensible body of men. My wife was in the bazaar yesterday and came back asking if anything fresh had happened, as while she was there, one of the criers issued a proclamation ending up with the words 'Any one who disobeys will be shot immediately.' I had to explain to

have "a somewhat reassuring effect," though he presumed he would be criticized severely for it later on.[12] Well, he sighed, they would get through this somehow, but it would be too hot for fishing: "Religious feeling really has very serious disadvantages."

It still seemed a strange sort of riot, for unlike at Rawalpindi neither open fighting nor a clash between police and people had occurred. Hailey looked deeper. Though Lahore was a "cockpit for the baser kind of communal politicians," though it possessed "a peculiarly vile communal press" as well as several thousand potentially violent railway workers, though numerous near collisions had been averted, and though communal feeling had recently worsened, the city had been relatively quiet. "It is always difficult to calculate the dynamics of rioting," he explained; "one observes all the signs and the portents, but it is not easy to determine the exact temperature at which feelings will boil over; the atmosphere may continue surcharged for prolonged periods without an outburst, unless some chance spark produces a sudden blaze."[13]

Although curfew continued, by 11 May Hailey left for Simla. Late in July he conducted a postmortem: 27 deaths (15 Hindu, 6 Muslim, 6 Sikh) and 272 treated in hospital, all of them casualties of "mob violence, and it is a matter of satisfaction that not a single shot had to be fired." Several points were critical. First the deputy commissioner had been absent taking his family to a hill station, and all his assistants were Indians who could not be reached by telephone. Because Indians however capable were inevitably suspected of bias during a riot, new British recruits to the ICS were urgent. Second, although the police had been criticized for permitting Muslim funeral processions, these had in fact been controlled, strengthening the escorts would have left the Old City unpatrolled, and the real trouble came only after the convoys had broken up. Third, the report quoted headlines from the vernacular press: "The Day of Judgment in Lahore. General Slaughter of Innocent Muslims"; "Muslim Blood Cheaper than Water," and the like. Since the repeal of the Press Act, the report alleged, journalism had become increasingly inflammatory: the more sensational the higher the sales. Fourth, the local leaders having been somewhat less than helpful during the crisis, strong British rule was said to be as essential as ever.

Finally, Lahore indicated that a new type of riot might have become typical. All through the night of 4 May Emerson and police officials had worked out

her that the criers had adopted this common form for all announcements . . . as being on the whole more efficient than 'God save the King.' . . . I never know exactly how far these proclamations are implicitly believed by the population, or whether they merely honour them in the spirit in which they are intended. Every now and then some Babu arrives at the Police Station at 8 o'clock when curfew begins, and insists on being accommodated for the night, lest he should be shot on the way home. . . . The greater number of people seem to take the notice in good part and to obey it without being very seriously alarmed." Hailey to Hirtzel, 10 May 1927, ibid.

[12] This does not seem to have been the case. The *Tribune* criticized the authorities for allowing the processions and the police for communal bias, but praised Hailey for his firm stand in contrast with Lytton's absence from Calcutta.

[13] Hailey to Muddiman, 7 May 1927, HPI/10A.

plans for saturating the streets with troops and guarding against arson. In future such schemes must be developed in advance. "Recent experiences show that on the first outbreak of communal rioting the danger against which the local authorities will have to guard is the clash of large bodies of men or arson and looting by mobs," Hailey's analysis concluded; "if sufficient police or troops are available close at hand, this danger can usually be averted with comparative ease." A more dangerous second stage must then be anticipated: "It is certain that after the first few hours of excitement communal hatred will express itself in the form of murderous assaults on isolated wayfarers. The only method of preventing this form of outrage is intensive patrolling."[14]

One cause of the Lahore riot had been intense Muslim anger over the case of *Rangila Rasul* (Merry Prophet), an anonymous pamphlet in Urdu purporting to describe Muhammad's relations with women. The publisher, a Hindu bookseller, had been given eighteen months. In May 1927, however, the very day of the riot, a subordinate justice in the high court had overturned the conviction on the ground that the law prohibited attacks on classes or races but not satirical writings on the dead. Although he shared the ordinary man's bafflement, Hailey told a Muslim deputation, his lawyers had advised him to leave the *Rangila Rasul* case alone. Instead the journal *Risala Vartman* would be prosecuted for an attack on the Prophet in an article called "A Trip to Hell." If that case too should fail, he would seek to change the law.

"I can only say that the judgment astonishes me," Hailey wrote privately, abruptly summoning the chief justice to return from vacation. Although he was "much too old a hand at these matters to be betrayed into an indiscretion," it had seemed "essential that the local Government should show its hand at once."[15] The Bakr-Id festival had passed peacefully, but Muslims were holding outraged meetings and Muharrum lay ahead. When Muharrum too went by without incident he was "still confident that but for my answer to the deputation . . . we should have had very serious trouble."[16] Although he did not invent the agitation, he was not playing it down either, his object being to persuade the Government of India to permit closer regulation of the communal press. In that he succeeded, the result being a Communal Insults bill enacted by the Legislative Assembly in September.[17]

As Hailey watched Indian politicians maneuver he saw no reason to change his view that communalism was their overriding concern. Jinnah came to Lahore to coax Muslims into accepting the so-called Delhi compromise – separate electorates to be abandoned in return for guaranteed representation, splitting Sind from Bombay, increasing Muslim seats in Bengal, and imple-

[14] NAI HomPol 11/x/1927.
[15] Hailey to Muddiman, 13 June 1927, HPI/10B. See N. Gerald Barrier, *Banned: Controversial Literature and Political Control in British India, 1907–1947*, pp. 99–102, and Gene R. Thursby, *Hindu–Muslim Relations in British India: A Study of Controversy, Conflict, and Communal Movements in Northern India, 1923–1928* (Leiden: Brill, 1975), pp. 40–7.
[16] Hailey to Hirtzel, 23 June and 21 July 1927, HPI/10B, 11A.
[17] Thursby, *Hindu–Muslim Relations*, pp. 64–9.

menting the reform scheme in North-West Frontier Province and Baluchistan – and ran into a stone wall. According to Hailey's information Jinnah was told that Punjab Khilafatists preferred forty more years of bureaucracy to abandoning the communal vote, while Hindus were just as furious at the prospect of putting their fellows in Sind and NWFP into minority positions.[18]

Still hoping to exploit the inevitable bickering, Birkenhead proposed a round-table conference. Whatever they might say in public, Hailey advised the viceroy, many politicians did not really want to resolve the impasse, for they had built their careers on the communal issue. "I should regard Mr. Gandhi as the key of the situation," he concluded; "if he desired to take part (and of course he would have to be allowed to do so, if we are to escape the charge of camouflage), then others would feel constrained to do so." If a conference should be held, however, its very first step would no doubt be to suggest that the government was the main obstacle to unity.[19] Such a trap Hailey hoped to avoid.

Early in July 1927 the *Tribune* reported a rumor that the statutory commission to review the constitution might be all-white, calling the idea so absurd that no sane British government would even consider it.[20] The writer would have been astonished to learn that the absurdity could be largely ascribed to that shrewd political calculator, the governor of the Punjab. In September came yet another conference among Indian factions on the communal problem, resulting in yet another failure. Late in October Lord Irwin told Indian leaders privately that the commission would be chaired by Sir John Simon and composed of two peers and five members of the House of Commons – all white. On 8 November the decision was made public. The reaction to what was said to be a supreme insult was instantaneous, filling the press with calls for boycott and Hindu–Muslim unity.

The gap between public and private positions made the situation hard to evaluate, Hailey advised. But the crucial fact was that a committee of the Punjab Muslim League, chaired by Sir Muhammad Shafi, had voted 22 to 4 to cooperate with the Simon Commission. Moreover, although the Hindu press solidly favored boycott, the two most important Hindu members of the provincial Legislative Council, Raja Narendra Nath and Gokul Chand, feared giving Muslims an advantage and were privately opposed to the campaign. The Muslim position would also probably determine that of the Sikhs.

At last raising his eyes from the communal cesspool of the Punjab, Hailey confessed surprise at the rapidly growing support for boycott, especially from Bengal Muslims, for of course he hoped his province's lead would tip the balance elsewhere. Although he still thought the communal card was there for the playing, doubt had crept in. He could not disregard the possibility that the Punjab Muslim League might "find it difficult to stand out if it finds itself completely isolated," in which case the faction of "Punjab Hindus which is

[18] Hailey to Muddiman, 13 June 1927, HPI/10B.
[19] Hailey note, 25 June 1927, ibid.   [20] *Tribune*, 3 July 1927.

against boycott would lose its chief ground for refusing to join Congress demands."[21] A great deal was riding on Sir Muhammad Shafi.

The vigor of the boycott campaign had been surprising, Hailey wrote in
December. But the composition of the Simon delegation had "really injured the
amour propre of India, and the feeling is so strong that it will for some time to
come override any consideration based on reason, or any calculation of advantages to be derived from cooperation with the Commission." Liberals like
Sapru, even his own revenue member, Sir Fazli Husain, who had opposed
Congress ever since the war, had joined in. Still, the issue had not apparently
attracted ordinary people and it seemed unlikely to "gain the sympathy or the
money of those who made the backbone of the Non-cooperation movement; I
mean the Marwaris, the traders in the town and the smaller professional classes." Nor was everybody as wholehearted as it might appear: "Jinnah was in two
minds . . . up to the very moment he made his announcement."[22]

As well Jinnah might have been, for the Muslim League was on the verge of
schism. During the summer, Hailey explained, the supporters of compromise
had been in the minority; those advocating separate electorates realized that
only the statutory commission could maintain them. Recently Punjab Muslims
had gone en masse to the League's meeting at Delhi, where they elected Sir
Muhammad Shafi as president and named Lahore the site for the annual
convention. Whereupon Jinnah held another meeting, which selected Calcutta.
It seemed likely that Punjab Muslims would stay home, however, "and at the
moment it looks as if they would carry out their long contemplated step of
making a League of Northern India and the Frontier."[23]

That federation, Hailey elaborated, in a comment worth quoting in view of its
bearing on the later Pakistan movement, would "seek to embrace the Punjab,

[21] Hailey tel. to Irwin, 15 November 1927, HPI/11B. In 1955, criticizing a draft Irwin (by then
Lord Halifax) had made of his memoirs, Hailey wrote the deadpan comment: "I agree that the
official world of India was (as far as my recollection goes) almost unanimous in agreeing that a
Commission confined to Members of Parliament was most logical and most appropriate. . . .
What counted with many of us was the obvious difficulty of getting an agreed opinion which
would be accepted by both the Indian Liberal Movements and the more advanced members of
Congress. Some of us thought that the Parliamentary Commission would actually give the
Indian Liberals a better chance of giving expression to their views, and would be more likely to
produce a scheme which would commend itself to Parliament. Most of us would have been glad
if we had been able to find some appropriate position for the Indian Liberals in which they could
exert their moderating influence, but we realized that they had no great courage when it came to
facing the more determined members of Congress." Hailey to Halifax, 8 September 1955,
HPA/339.

[22] Hailey to F. H. Brown, 14 December 1927, HPI/11B. On Sir Fazli's return from overseas late
in November, he denounced the all-white commission. When Hailey called him on the carpet
Sir Fazli offered his resignation; realizing that a powerful Muslim opponent who had quit on
principle would be dangerous, Hailey backed down. See exchange of letters, November–December 1927, ibid. Sir Fazli was a longtime rival of Sir Muhammad Shafi for leadership of the
Punjab Muslim community. He soon came round; in March 1928 he moved the resolution in
favor of cooperation with the commission. The Marwaris were a powerful merchant caste,
including the Bombay financier G. D. Birla, who was Gandhi's largest banker.

[23] Hailey to Brown, 14 December 1927, ibid.

parts of the United Provinces, the North-West Frontier, Baluchistan and Sind; it is part of their programme to secure Sind for the Punjab and to give up to Delhi some of our Hindu districts in the south-east of the Province." These measures, Muslims were saying, were "only a preparation for a larger federation which shall embrace Afghanistan and perhaps Persia." No wonder Hindus regarded "the Punjab as a kind of Ulster, entirely oblivious to national progress in its insistence on its own separate claims. You will notice," Sir Malcolm concluded, "that the dream of the future . . . does not include Bengal. For the moment, the Northern India Muslim has given up his co-religionist . . . as hopeless, and seems to expect no assistance from Bengal in the cause of Islam."[24]

Sure enough, two sections of the Muslim League met late in December. At Calcutta the Jinnah group supported both the boycott of the Simon Commission and the Delhi compromise on separate electorates; in Lahore the Shafi faction favored the opposite. At present, Shafi asserted, joint electorates would simply result in periodic communal outbursts, severely injuring the nationalist cause.[25] In Madras, under the presidency of another Muslim, Dr. M. A. Ansari of Delhi, Congress pressed for Hindu–Muslim unity and the boycott.

As the Simon Commission arrived late in January 1928 the odds in favor of a successful boycott looked good. Not since 1919 had Liberals and members of the Congress shared platforms, while Hindu–Muslim relations were apparently the most cordial in years. Obviously, Lajpat Rai pointed out, Madras and the Punjab had been chosen as the first stops on the tour because the government was counting on internal divisions in those provinces to break up the campaign. In Punjab cities committees were formed and merchants reported brisk sales of black flags. But the Shafi section of the Muslim League remained the key. According to the *Tribune* Hailey went over to Delhi to assure the viceroy that the Punjab would be safe for Simon.[26]

Sir Malcolm had reason to be hopeful. In rapid succession first the Shafi Muslims and then the provincial Hindu Sabha came out against the boycott. For the time being, he wrote the day before the commission arrived, the movement seemed to have lost ground. The boycotters had been "making a dead-set at the Punjab on account of the opposition of our Muslims," and great significance was being attached to the observance of a hartal. Quieter people were at work, however, and though a good many shops would be closed in Amritsar, "I should be astonished if the visitor to Lahore can notice much outward sign."[27]

The hartal was only transitory, Hailey stressed. What mattered was, first, that the movement had united all extremists and some moderates, and second, that it was acquiring an increasingly angry racial tone. "We all prophesied three years ago," he recalled, conveniently forgetting his own role in triggering the

---

24 Hailey to Hirtzel, 15 December 1927, ibid.
25 Reports of the two meetings in Perzada, *Foundations of Pakistan*, 2:108–38. See Muhammad Shafi, *Some Important Indian Problems* (Lahore: Model Electric Press, 1930).
26 *Tribune*, 27–31 January 1928.   27 Hailey to Hirtzel, 2 February 1928, HPI/12A.

confrontation, "that about this time the wave of agitation would arise again," the only question being what form it would take. India was "such a strange country and subject to sudden gusts of emotion that if we get a few untoward incidents on which public feeling can be whipped up, things may further deteriorate." Realizing that they had not yet touched the masses, leaders were searching for a popular issue. The situation reminded him of the early stages of the Rowlatt agitation early in 1919, when nothing seemed to be happening until agitators "managed to get about a series of the most astonishing and impossible lies." There were signs of that now, including persistent rumors of a coming war. Something must clearly "be invented if the boycott agitation is to become anything more than a mere passing and political demonstration."[28]

Early in February 1928 the Simon Commission stopped briefly in the Punjab on its way to Delhi. Although versions of the boycott's effectiveness differed, even the *Tribune* agreed that it had failed dismally in Lahore. The governor was reported to have "addressed a gathering of a few selected persons" in the Legislative Council compound, where he was "understood to have thanked Sir Mahomed Shafi and others for their efforts."[29] Just as Hailey had hoped, the Shafi group's initiative provoked a chain reaction, for the All-India Hindu Mahasabha repudiated the agreement that had been reached between Congress and the Jinnah branch of the Muslim League. Congress, charged the Mahasabha leader B. S. Moonje, had vainly tried to appease Muslims, who had shown repeatedly that only abject surrender would ever satisfy them.[30]

The true test would come when the commission returned in March. Late in February, addressing the European Association, Hailey compared the current agitation with the noncooperation period of the early 1920s. Then the danger had been not so much the actual boycott as "the teaching of the doctrine of bitterness and racial hatred, in the attempt to spread among a quiet and law-abiding people the contempt of law and the invasion of authority," the legacy of which had been intense communal antagonism. There were obvious similarities: racial propaganda, denial of British sovereignty, a boycott bringing together leaders who until recently had been divided. Should communal differences actually be bridged, he remarked affably, "they should hardly regret that a bond of reconciliation had been found in opposition to a measure of His Majesty's Government."

There were also important contrasts with the earlier period, he pointed out: no postwar upheaval, a resolution of what then had been the ambiguous situation of international Islam, a more favorable economic climate. The Simon agitation had not yet stirred the masses, numerous factions had not joined in, "and they are sections to which the wider sphere of political consciousness and political authority resulting from the working of the Reforms scheme has given an importance which they did not then occupy."[31] In March 1925, Birkenhead

---

[28] Ibid.   [29] *Tribune*, 5–7 February 1928.
[30] Ibid., 12 February 1928.   [31] Reports of speech in ibid., 28 February 1928, and HPI/45.

had told Irwin that he placed his "highest and most permanent hopes in the eternity of the communal situation."[32] Albeit somewhat more discreetly – after all, press reporters were present – the governor of the Punjab was saying much the same thing.

When the Simon Commission returned on 10 March Lahore retrieved its honor: a crowd the *Tribune* estimated at thirty thousand shouting "Go Back"; black-turbaned Akalis, Hindu and Muslim volunteers charged by lathi-wielding police; cries of "Shame, Shame" as cars carried people to meet the commissioners.[33] But people did meet them. Some like Shafi and the Hindu Sabha did so publicly, others privately, including some whom Hailey identified as Congress members. On the fourteenth the Legislative Council voted to cooperate. Irwin telegraphed congratulations: "It will be of great value and I know how much it is due to you personally."[34] Still cautious, Hailey decided to delay his leave, which was due in April, deciding instead to take three or four months just before the scheduled end of this service in February 1929.[35] He could only admit, he wrote after the commission's departure, that the agitation had created far more mischief than he could have foreseen six months before: "For the moment the extremists of the two communities are pitting themselves against Government rather than against each other, and our loyalist friends . . . complain that we do nothing actively to counter the attack." If only other provincial legislatures had voted to cooperate.[36]

Hailey's capable chief secretary, Herbert Emerson, wrote an extended appraisal that also played down the boycott itself. The hartal had succeeded only in Amritsar, he argued, neither Muslim leaders nor businessmen had taken part, and most of political Punjab had met the commission. Although the campaign had failed to achieve its tangible object, however, the position was shaky. People had cooperated with the commission for practical reasons, not from any feelings of warmth toward the government. At any moment some minor tremor might have created a landslide in the other direction. At present the rural areas had no overweening popular grievance, politicians were widely distrusted, and recent harvests had been good. Barring untoward incidents, circumstances did not therefore seem favorable for the creation of a mass movement.

That was far from the whole story, Emerson continued. Early in April a National Week conference had been held in Amritsar. The Simon Commission had hardly been mentioned, while communal issues had been raised only as a hook on which to hang communist-style attacks against religion. Resolutions had been passed favoring independence outside the empire "by all possible means." Having recently returned from Russia with a head full of advanced ideas, Jawaharlal Nehru had attended a youth meeting. The result of National Week had been a combination of "certain extremist and revolutionary bodies" –

[32] Quoted by Chandra, *Communalism in Modern India*, p. 244, n. 19.
[33] *Tribune*, 10 March 1928.   [34] Irwin to Hailey, tel., 14 March 1928, HPI/12A.
[35] Hailey note, 17 March 1928, ibid.   [36] Hailey to Irwin, 23 March 1928, ibid.

the Kurti (worker) and Kisan (agricultural laborer) parties, the Naujawan Bharat Sabha (students), and extremist Akalis. This merged organization proposed to establish district branches and carry on propaganda stressing the land question in rural areas, labor and student issues in the cities.

In the short run these developments had frightened people, Emerson explained, very likely strengthening the antiboycott faction. The fact remained that a small extremist group was intent on introducing revolutionary methods into the province. Tracts glorifying violence were circulating. People strongly suspected of involvement in conspiracies were known to have entered the province. Links had apparently been formed with revolutionary groups in Bengal and UP. An important indication of approaching trouble was the fact that, except for Nehru, all-India leaders were keeping their distance. The student organization was particularly dangerous.[37] Emerson's report was not without foundation. Among the delegates at Amritsar was a brilliant, courageous young man whose assassination of a Punjab police official and subsequent execution would soon make him a national hero. His name was Bhagat Singh.[38]

Although Hailey also took the student movement seriously, his main apprehension was that the campaign might be taken into the villages.[39] Agriculturists had "acquired a class consciousness of their own which must find an outlet," he pointed out, and "the political agitator may awake to the fact that he has a very good field open to him for creating trouble among this class." The nub of the problem was that the government's land-revenue system was fundamentally inequitable, for though poorer urban residents escaped income tax "there is no such provision for the rural masses." In time would come demands to place land revenue on a graduated basis too. The complexity would be staggering. "All I can say," he concluded, "is that I hope I shall not have to face this problem in my time."[40]

Face it he would. Along with the civil-disobedience campaign with which it was closely linked, the agrarian problem would dog his every step for the next seven years. As he moved up to Simla for what he presumed would be his last hot weather in India, however, he did not know that. A little row the next time Simon came to town, a few months of leave – and that would be it. At the age of fifty-seven Hailey would have only a five-year term on the secretary of state's advisory council to occupy him. It was a prospect he loathed and dreaded. "I could not . . . face living in England without work," he had written in 1925. "That is one of the real disabilities of an Indian career – if one has been moderately successful, one leaves the country about the age of 55 or 56, just

---

[37] Emerson note, 23 April 1928, HPI/12B. See J. Nehru, "An Appeal to Youth," 18 March 1928, *Selected Works of Jawaharlal Nehru*, ed. S. Gopal et al., 1st series (New Delhi: Orient Longman, 1972–), 3, 179–81.

[38] See particularly Bipan Chandra, "The Ideological Development of the Revolutionary Terrorists in Northern India in the 1920s," in his *Nationalism and Colonialism in Colonial India* (New Delhi: Orient Longman, 1979), pp. 223–51.

[39] Hailey to Crerar, 8 May 1928, HPI/12B.   [40] Hailey to Francis, 10 May 1928, ibid.

when one ought to be of some real use to the world, condemned to cultivate cabbages or to compile jottings for an antiquarian journal."[41] He had not had leave since 1924, however, the Simon agitation must have been exhausting, and his kidney stone may have been acting up. In the middle of May he told Sir Frederick Hirtzel at the India Office that he was feeling seedy.[42] It almost cost him the UP.

In June 1928 the recently appointed governor of the United Provinces, Sir Alexander Muddiman, died suddenly of a heart attack. How quickly things turned around! Only a year ago in Simla, in one of his classic performances, Hailey had helped give Muddiman what Americans call a roast; suddenly, apparently in the prime of life, the man was gone.[43] For several weeks speculation mounted, the obvious candidates to succeed him being Hailey and Sir Montagu Butler, the younger brother of Sir Harcourt who was the most popular UP governor in modern memory. Irwin made up his mind within four days. Although Sir Montagu would have the initial advantage of his brother's reflected glory, Hailey was "the all round better man." The decisive question, the viceroy cabled, was "whether Butler would have been as likely as Hailey to get Punjab straight during last four years, and I have little doubt that great majority of informed opinion out here would answer this question in favour of Hailey." If Hailey were to be chosen, then he would need early leave lest his health should suffer. "He has had only about one year's leave in 33 years," Irwin pointed out, "and I know that he is feeling the strain."[44]

The India Office was also concerned about Sir Malcolm's health. If he were appointed and given leave at once, however, the man in line to be acting governor was the Nawab of Chhatari, who would have to be passed over in this tense period – yet another snub to an Indian. For several weeks, leaving newspapers to speculate that the job might go to someone else after all, Irwin and Birkenhead considered other candidates, none of whom quite seemed to do. At last Birkenhead agreed, on strict condition that Hailey take early leave. "I was concerned solely about his health," the secretary of state explained, based largely on Hailey's own statement to Hirtzel, where he had "made it quite plain that he was feeling the strain, and that his body was rebelling against the tyranny to which he had subjected it during many years of almost uninterrupted work." Sir Malcolm was "not one of those men who is always running over here; he has in fact taken little more than one year's leave in 33 years' service. It is not reasonable to presume upon the public spirit of a man like that."[45]

Hailey accepted with alacrity, telegraphing Hirtzel asking him to inform Lady Hailey (who was in London) "shortly before announcement is made as I have

---

41 Hailey to Sir Theodore Morison, 26 November 1925, HPI/8B.
42 This letter, referred to by Hirtzel as having been dated 14 May, is not in the Hailey Collection and I have not been able to trace it elsewhere. Birkenhead quoted it, however, in his private letter to the viceroy of 26 July.
43 *Tribune*, 17 July 1927.   44 VR to SS, telegram, 23 June 1928, L/PO/8/17 (iii).
45 Birkenhead to Irwin, pvt., 26 July 1928, ibid.

hitherto not spoken to her of possibility of this appointment and she will naturally desire information regarding possible date of my taking leave."[46] Although he was a tired and very possibly a sick man, duty had called, and the salary of ten thousand rupees (£7,500) was of course substantial. Above all he would not be condemned to idleness. Moreover, through his influence his old friend Sir Geoffrey de Montmorency succeeded him in the Punjab.[47] Which merely meant that Hailey would now be governing two provinces, the *Tribune* jeered. The tone of Lahore's leading newspaper had changed abruptly in the past few months. The reason was of course its perception that by pulling strings behind the scenes and finally by playing the trump card of communalism Hailey had turned back the boycott of the Simon Commission. Because he would presumably do the same again Punjab's gain was UP's loss. Although the departing governor's capacities could not be doubted, the paper concluded, neither could his very dubious achievement. Sir Michael O'Dwyer had once boasted that he would make the Punjab India's Ulster. Sir Malcolm Hailey had done it.[48]

Just before departing Hailey spoke at a farewell dinner in Simla. He hardly recognized himself, he said – a dull bureaucrat distinguished only by hard work and a talent for stepping forward when subordinates did well – in the flattering remarks made about him. Fortunately the press had fully recorded his many faults. As Gibbon had remarked of a pope, "rape, incest and adultery were the crimes charged against the Holy Pontiff; the graver charges were suppressed."

They might disagree, he told the Indians present, about means and timing, but not about ends. Although British civil servants might be wrong or unduly cautious, "we are not on that account enemies of India's aspirations or traitors to the salt we have eaten." The province's great continuing failing was communal tension. "It is a favourite fallacy," he asserted, "that these differences somehow suit the obscure purposes of a Machiavellian Government, and are even fostered by its agents." If any one really did wish to perpetuate communal conflict, "then he seems to me to be the victim of intellectual even more than moral iniquity. It is incomprehensible to me that any one, gifted with even the most moderate intelligence, should desire a situation so destructive not only to the orderly progress of India," but to "the comfort and peace of mind of those concerned in the work of administration." This charge "ought definitely to be relegated to the limbo of exploded political fictions."[49]

It was not recorded whether members of the audience blinked in astonishment. Was this the same man who had spoken to the European Association in February? The one who had just defeated the Simon boycott? In fact the governor of the Punjab, or at least part of him, had deeply hated communalism, had been bored by being in a house where husband and wife were always

[46] VR to SS, tel., 23 July 1928, enclosing message from Hailey, HPI/13A.
[47] Irwin had recommended him in March, with Sir Montagu Butler again the second choice. See VR to SS, tel., 19 March 1928, and Irwin to Hailey, 8 May 1928, saying he had done what he could.
[48] *Tribune*, 2 August 1928.   [49] 7 August 1928, HPI/45.

nagging, had been appalled by savage, random murders in Lahore. He did indeed look forward to a future when the curse would be forgotten. Nor had Hailey really played the communal card. Sir Muhammad Shafi and B. S. Moonje had done that – they were not children; he did not hold a gun to their heads – for their own ends. Yet the charge that "British rule and British policy hold a special responsibility for the growth of communalism in modern India" is one a student of Sir Malcolm Hailey cannot deny.[50] In truth, he probably could not have solved the problem – but he never seriously attempted it either. Instead, he watched its dynamics closely and, in pursuit of his first priority – the success of British policy – he did his best to capitalize on it. As long as governors did that as skillfully as he had, what he called political fiction would not soon be put in limbo.

50 Chandra, *Communalism in Modern India*, pp. 237–8.

◇◇

Governor of the United Provinces, 1928–1930

"I naturally cannot help feeling an intruder here," Sir Malcolm Hailey confessed in August 1928, shortly after he took over as governor of the United Provinces of Agra and Oudh. Knowing his new colleagues would resent the appointment of an outsider, he referred frequently to his older brother's long service in the local land and revenue department.[1] Although the Punjab and UP shared a common boundary, Lahore was 750 miles from Lucknow, the capital of Oudh (now Awadh), and 1,000 miles from the capital of Agra, Allahabad. UP was smaller in area than the Punjab, ranking eighth among the Indian provinces. At 50 million, however, including princely states, it had nearly twice the population, a figure second only to Bengal and 10 million more than that of England and Wales. Although UP possessed more prominent cities – Benares (now Varanasi), Aligarh, Cawnpore (now Kanpur), and Agra, as well as the two capitals – it too was predominantly agricultural, with 90 percent of its people living in rural areas.

As he settled into his beautiful summer capital at the hill station of Naini Tal, Hailey discovered some important contrasts. Whereas water rates from canal colonies in previously unproductive desert areas had provided the Punjab a financial bonanza, in UP the vast Sarda canal project was bringing water to districts that were already under cultivation, so the revenue outlook looked relatively bleak. He was struck by differences in protocol. The Punjab had "always been accustomed to something like personal rule," he observed, the governor had to immerse himself in detail and interview numerous people, and ministers tended to refer almost everything for "advice," so that at times it appeared as though the reforms might never have come into effect.[2] UP seemed much more formal. More than style, the prevailing British ideologies also differed subtly. The Punjab school into which Hailey had been indoctrinated stressed paternalism and direct personal contact with peasants and the middling sort of landowners. The controlling ideology of UP stressed an alliance with the big landlord class. Also with roots in the Great Mutiny of 1857–8, it was called the Oudh Policy.

---

[1] Hailey to Verney Lovett, 28 August 1928, HPI/13B.
[2] Hailey to F. H. Brown, 23 August 1928, HPI/13C.

As the British extended their rule after 1820 over what was then the north-west frontier of Bengal they found a ruling class, called *zamindars* in Agra and *taluqdars* in Oudh, presiding over what anthropologists call little kingdoms. Because these local rulers were largely hostile to the British and apparently parasitic, contributing nothing to the greatest happiness of the greatest number, utilitarian administrators wanted to remove them, especially in the princely state of Oudh, and its annexation in 1856 is ordinarily listed as one of the causes of the Mutiny. The Oudh Policy originated in two British perceptions during the uprising: first, that many taluqdars went over to the opposition; second, that tenants whom the British supposed they had freed from their oppression tended to follow them. Fearing a long, bloody, and expensive process of pacification, the British decided to restore those whom they now called "natural leaders" to their former positions, making a "covenant" with a class whose support they regarded as crucial for their rule.[3]

The Punjab school and Oudh Policy reflected the land-tenure and revenue systems of the respective provinces. Although the Punjab had some large land-lords, most of the supporters of Sir Fazli Husain's Unionist Party were more modest landowners, some of whom were self-cultivating, and the government collected its revenue directly from the producers. Like Bengal and Bihar, UP lay in India's zamindari zone, where landlords serving as tax farmers paid a portion of their rent collections to the state. In Oudh especially a tiny number of families owned half the land, and the vast majority of the rural population were tenants and landless laborers. During the decade since 1918 tenancy legislation had damaged the government's relations with landlords, some of whom, perceiving that the future of the British Raj was limited, were negotiating with Swarajists. Hailey found it surprising that the recently published Nehru Report on the constitution, which had recommended universal suffrage (and thus the enfranchisement of some 14 million tenants) as well as the elimination both of separate electorates for Muslims and special representation for landlords, had encountered so little opposition. "I am afraid that I have already been guilty of impressing" the dangers on both groups, he confided.[4]

The new governor's first concern was the Simon Commission, which would return to India in November. The previous February, at the time the Punjab Legislative Council was agreeing to cooperate with the commission, the UP legislature had decided by one vote against doing so. Since then Bombay and Bengal had come into line against the boycott campaign, Madras looked favorable, and Hailey's advisers hoped for a reversal in UP in September. As it did in

---

[3] See Hailey's analysis in his note for the Secretary of State on the Permanent Settlement, 27 June 1933, HPI/32A. For the evolution of the Oudh Policy, see Thomas R. Metcalf, *Aftermath of Revolt: India, 1857–1870* (Princeton, N.J.: Princeton University Press, 1964), and *Land, Land-lords, and the British Raj: Northern India in the Nineteenth Century* (Berkeley: University of California Press, 1979); Peter D. Reeves, "The Landlords' Response to Political Change in the United Provinces of Agra & Oudh, India, 1921–1947" (unpublished Ph.D. dissertation, Australian National University, 1963).

[4] Hailey to Sir Fazli Husain, 25 August 1928, HPI/13B.

the Punjab the government had twenty-three official or nominated members against one hundred elected representatives. What it did not possess was anything like Sir Fazli Husain's solid Muslim bloc. Although most Muslim members of the Legislative Council (MLCs) had voted against boycott, several had not, and under the Lucknow Pact of 1916 they were guaranteed only one-third of the seats.

Indeed the only organized parties were in opposition.[5] Fifty council members, typically landlords who were rather analogous to the "country gentlemen" of eighteenth-century British parliaments, belonged to no party. Like George III a governor needed to appoint ministers who could draw support from this amorphous group. Yet the government had to be carried on and "backwoodsmen" were usually poor debaters and indifferent administrators, far below the caliber of C. Y. Chintamani, the Liberal publisher of the *Leader* (Allahabad), or the Swarajist leader Govind Ballabh Pant. Finding Hindus who were both competent and loyal was particularly difficult. In the early 1920s Sir Harcourt Butler had turned to Chintamani, and though those two men had had a personality conflict Liberals remained in office. In June 1928, two of the three ministers having abstained in the boycott vote, Hailey's predecessor, Sir Alexander Muddiman, had demanded their resignations. One of the two replacements, Raja Jagannath Baksh Singh, representing the Oudh taluqdars, had supported boycott but had since changed his mind.

The governor's dilemma being obvious, people naturally tried to take advantage of it. For some time a young Cawnpore businessman named Charles Allen, son of the longtime publisher of the *Pioneer* (which had recently passed into other hands and become an opposition paper), had been trying to drum up support for a country party. The government, he complained, was neglecting its friends and courting its irreconcilable enemies.[6] Although such a party was badly needed, Hailey agreed, recalling an earlier conversation in Lahore, Allen was distressingly naive: "He would not believe that in politics it is usually necessary to pay a price for support." In Lahore the price demanded by Allen's rather more worldly associates had been an unacceptably large reduction of the land revenue. This time, when Hailey interviewed Allen's friend J. P. Srivastava, it turned out to be ministerial office. The government should withdraw support from Jagannath Baksh Singh, Srivastava urged. Otherwise his own exasperated supporters might just turn around and vote against the Simon Commission.

Such a demonstration would indeed be effective, Hailey remarked dryly, although he would not necessarily learn the lesson "that we ought to have chosen him as Minister instead!"[7] Unfortunately, in talking with Allen, Hailey

---

5 Independent Congress (15), Swarajist (18), Liberals (7), and Independents (9). See Peter D. Reeves et al., *A Handbook to Elections in Uttar Pradesh, 1920–1951* (Delhi: Manohar, 1975), pp. 126–51.
6 At the India Office Birkenhead was saying the same thing. Irwin to Hailey, 7 September 1928, HPI/13C, and enclosed Irwin–Birkenhead correspondence.
7 Hailey to Irwin, 10 September 1928, ibid.

allowed himself to be drawn into an indiscreet discussion of tactics. Ministers from the other side ought not as a rule to be appointed, he said, unless the action well and truly split the opposition. Allen informed Srivastava and the viceroy, Lord Irwin, that the governor was willing to dismiss his minister or at least permit official members of the Legislative Council to vote as they pleased.[8] With a jolt Sir Malcolm realized he was perilously close to becoming implicated in a conspiracy.

Until after the Simon debate he stayed his hand. On 18 September, avoiding direct defeat, Chintamani and Pant led the opposition in a walkout, after which the Council voted to cooperate with the commission. Next morning Hailey told his other two ministers that unless they supported Jagannath Baksh Singh he might have to reconstitute the entire cabinet. The no-confidence vote ended in a tie, which the Council's president broke in favor of the opposition. More vigorous action by the governor, the minister suspected with some justice, would have saved him.[9] Continuing his maneuvering, Allen confided that he had raised pledges of £145,000 toward buying out the *Pioneer* and returning it to progovernment hands. For the moment, however, Hailey had had it with Allen, refusing to see him or answer his letters. At the end of November, however, when Allen invited the Haileys to attend a reception for the Simon Commission at Cawnpore, Sir Malcolm relented.[10] Before he left UP in 1934, Hailey would employ secret-service funds to subsidize Allen's purchase of the *Pioneer*. And Srivastava, after a decent interval, duly became minister of education.

Because the two other ministers were a Muslim and a Sikh the appointee had to be a Hindu – and all the capable Hindus were in opposition. The situation became laughable. One aspirant claimed to have nine staunch supporters; he turned out to have none; his family's fortune had been based on his grandfather's modest service to the British during the Mutiny; now, having been rebuffed, the man would no doubt become a Swarajist. Without enthusiasm Hailey settled on Raja Kushalpal Singh, whose "qualifications are respectability, loyalty and Hinduism; he is, I fear, a poor debater with a very retiring manner." This time the ministers had to sign a joint-responsibility agreement: "If they will not hang together, I will not allow them to hang separately."[11]

The tedious triviality of local politics – personal intrigue, communal squabbles triggering the odd riot, bloodless struggles for office – the mold Indian

---

8 See Allen–Srivastava–Irwin–Hailey correspondence, 12–17 September 1928, ibid.
9 Hailey explained that the government bench had been so concerned about the Simon resolution that it had been unable to organize properly for the no-confidence vote. See Hailey to Irwin, 16 October 1928, HPI/14A. Although he had not wished to be seen to be involved in a conspiracy, he was not unhappy with the result.
10 Hailey to Allen, 18 November 1928, ibid.
11 Hailey to Irwin, 12 and 16 October 1928, ibid. The new minister acquired the nickname "It speaks." Many were sent to prison for bringing the government into contempt, the *Leader* commented (10 December 1928). "But here are Ministers who actually bring it into increasing contempt almost every day of a Council session."

nationalists charged was Britain's real objective in encouraging provincial autonomy, was a facade behind which larger forces driven by intense feelings were at work. In October 1928 the Simon Commission landed in Bombay: more hartals, black flags, cries of "Shame" and "Go Back." At Lahore, where the boycott had fizzled in March, mounted police swinging lathis charged, severely beating Lajpat Rai and allegedly contributing to his death in December. UP was next. In Agra, where the authorities expected two or three hundred, the crowd was nearer two thousand. At Cawnpore demonstrators gave the commissioners a scare. In Lucknow Jawaharlal Nehru and Govind Ballabh Pant were beaten in a lathi charge, the latter seriously, and rattled police threw brickbats.[12] Officials seemed to have lost their senses, Nehru reported: "The place was like a fortress. Perhaps this is only an exhibition of Haileyism. Anyway I am quite content with it. It has done more good to our public life than anything we could have done."[13]

Sir Malcolm was indeed displaying a degree of personal truculence not seen since the firing at Jaito in February 1924, which had also taken place just before a long-deferred leave. "It must be recognized that *no* explanation" of police behavior in Lucknow would satisfy the opposition, he noted, so "the only thing to do is to stand the racket." He was not swayed "because Govind Ballabh Pant gets hit instead of mere Ram Baksh." Talk of an impartial inquiry seemed "absurd for there is nothing to enquire about." If police fired and killed people, that would of course need looking into, "but here so far as I know there has not been a single hospital case."[14]

Although the Simon boycott got most of the headlines, a small peasant movement two thousand miles away in Gujarat was in some ways a good deal more portentous. Late in 1927 the Bombay government had announced a 30 percent increase in the revenue settlement for Bardoli tahsil, the same section where Gandhi had intended to launch a no-tax campaign in 1922. Led by Vallabhbhai Patel, peasants refused to pay and launched civil disobedience, which the Bombay government met with force. During the summer of 1928, however, Irwin became convinced that the tax settlement had indeed been faulty. An independent inquiry was agreed to, which eventually recommended a substantial revision in favor of the peasants. The Bardoli satyagraha "proved that the power of the people is greater than that of the State," Gandhi put it, "as conclusively as that two and two make four." Although an approaching All-Parties conference might achieve some constitutional advance, "the way to organic swaraj . . . lies through Bardoli."[15]

12 Hailey to Crerar, 6 December 1928, HPI/14B.
13 Nehru to Subhas Chandra Bose, 6 December 1928, *SWJN*, 3:120. See also reports in the *Leader*, 1 December 1928 and after, as well as descriptions of the lathi charge, *SWJN*, 3:106–18, and *An Autobiography*, pp. 177–81.
14 Hailey note, 3 December 1928, UP GA Dept, 566/1928.
15 Statements of 19 and 28 August 1928, CWMG, 37:190–1, 214. On the Bardoli movement, see the contemporary account by Gandhi's private secretary, Mahadev Desai, *The Story of Bardoli* (Ahmedabad: Navajivan Press, 1929), and more recent works by D. N. Dhanagare, *Peasant*

India was full of Bardolis. The land-revenue system was an obvious target for the agitator, Irwin observed, and Bardoli had shown how much inflammable material was lying around.[16] Urban agitation was far less dangerous than rural, Hailey agreed, remembering as usual the Punjab canal-colony tax revolt of 1907. The threat might be more acute in communities of small or middling landowners like Gujarat or the Punjab than in zamindari regions like UP, he supposed, provided that in the latter all reasonable demands of tenants had been satisfied. Although tenant grievances had sparked an agrarian conflagration as recently as 1921, however, he believed that the Agra and Oudh tenancy acts of 1926, which had been passed over strenuous landlord opposition, had probably relieved the situation.[17]

That of course would have been profoundly mistaken, and as Hailey learned more about the UP he changed his mind. In the Punjab, he reflected, "we had a province of middle class and small landlords," many of whom were self-cultivating. There were a few big landowners but "not of the major zamindar type, nor had they and their families enjoyed their wealth long enough to give them the characteristics of a special class or to dissociate them from a close interest in the cultivation of their own land." The canal colonies had raised the demand for tenants, strengthening their bargaining power. In general the Punjab's rural population was therefore more homogeneous, "keener, more energetic and more responsible in the political sense." Moreover, although communalism was sometimes embarrassing, it "placed Government in a strong situation as holding the balance of power between the parties." Even Hindus had been unable to maintain consistent opposition, for they had "to depend on Government if they were to maintain their position vis a vis the Muslims."

In short, Hailey could not "help feeling that the swarajist had a good case when he took up the cause of the tenant in 1920–21 and urged him to non-cooperation," forcing the government to enact tenancy legislation, which in turn alienated landlords. Moreover, "the Hindu is in such predominance that he does not fear a combination of the Muslims with Government." In UP there were "none of those arguments which we were able to utilise in the Punjab in order to bring the Hindu to some extent to our side." All of which constituted perhaps as candid an explanation of communalism as a tool of divide and rule as can be imagined.

"Our only hope of political stability lies in welding together the zamindar and rural interest and in giving it greater vitality," Hailey concluded.[18] His stren-

---

Movements in India, 1920–1950 (Delhi: Oxford University Press, 1983), pp. 88–110; Shirin Mehta, *The Peasantry and Nationalism: A Study of the Bardoli Satyagraha* (New Delhi: Manohar, 1984); and Krishan Dutt, *Sardar Patel in the Bardoli Movement* (Meerut: Anu, 1986).
16 Irwin to Hailey, 6 September 1928, HPI/13C. See also "Lessons of Bardoli," NAI HomPol 197/1928.
17 Hailey to Irwin, 9 September 1928, HPI/13C. The UP revenue department also judged that Bardoli was unlikely to have much impact on a system dominated by big landlords. Letter of 17 November 1928, UP SR Rev 391/1928.
18 Hailey to Irwin, 16 October 1928, HPI/14A.

uous but ultimately unsuccessful campaign to build a strong landlord party would be the central theme of his governorship. As he himself put it in the early 1960s, his job in UP had been to counteract the growing power of Congress, which had attracted large numbers of city dwellers and tenants, and had even persuaded many zamindars to contribute money and political support as a hedge against the government's inevitable departure. The fact, however, was that zamindars were Britain's only conceivable allies. Although he had no choice but to try and weld them together into a cohesive conservative party, he acted with a strong sense of fatalism.[19]

Throughout his governorship Sir Malcolm Hailey's attitudes toward the landlord–tenant problem in UP would be profoundly though by no means uncharacteristically ambiguous. In private his analyses of the zamindari system would sometimes sound as though they might have been written by a Swarajist. Indeed, they strikingly resembled the views of his arch-nemesis, Jawaharlal Nehru. Publicly Hailey talked to landlords like a Dutch uncle. The taluqdar class, he told the British India Association in Lucknow, stood "in special relation to the British Government as owners of estates which have been formally confirmed to you by the covenant of 1859." Although landlords were pressing for both constitutional advancement and guarantees of their own positions, he pointed out, these claims were rapidly becoming contradictory. Leading republicans were also preaching communism, including the confiscation and redistribution of property.

Elsewhere, he noted, "a landed aristocracy has had to meet, as you will have to meet, the impact of popular institutions." The British ruling class had met the challenge head-on, drilling "its sons in public affairs," closing ranks, managing estates responsibly, gaining influence in the press. UP zamindars must do the same. They should also choose their allies wisely. "Your lot must lie with one side or the other," he warned, "and I do not see how any member of your order can reasonably ask the protection of the British Parliament if he allies himself to those whose steps are leading them to demand complete independence of its control."[20]

In December 1928 Hailey went on leave, his first since 1924. Although he was glad enough to go home, he confided, he himself did not really need a break. Lady Hailey had been in bad health for some time, however, she had lost weight alarmingly, and the break simply could not be postponed any longer.[21] They were off to Switzerland. He would see if at fifty-seven he was too old to learn skiing: "I am sure it would give sincere pleasure to the *Pioneer* [newspaper] if it were announced that I had been buried in the snow!"[22]

---

19 Hailey to D. Anthony Low, 19 January 1961, HPI/51.
20 Speech of 4 December 1928, HPI/46.
21 De Montmorency to Hailey, 2 September 1928, HPI/13C; Hailey to de Montmorency, 1 December 1928, HPI/14B.
22 Hailey to Birdwood, 17 December 1928, ibid. The time in Switzerland was not enough. When Sir Malcolm returned in April 1929 he came alone; Lady Hailey rejoined him later in the summer.

By the time Hailey returned in April 1929 the political atmosphere had heated up substantially. At Calcutta Gandhi had averted a split in Congress by giving the British an ultimatum: India must receive dominion status within one year, or it would declare independence unilaterally.[23] Under the leadership of Jawaharlal Nehru Congress was rejuvenating its organization and preparing to renew the struggle.[24] Since the extremists seemed intent on making trouble, Irwin wrote, "as and when opportunity offers, we ought to try and hit them."[25] Strikes in Bombay, Calcutta, and elsewhere threatened to make it a two-front war. Two fronts, but so far not three. Although droughts and plagues of locusts had given UP farmers two bad years in a row, Acting Governor Sir George Lambert reported, so far there had been no appreciable agrarian agitation.[26]

"The younger politicians are openly advocating a kind of blood and revolutionary campaign," Hailey observed; "there is no longer any talk of 'soul force' or passive resistance." In a way, that simplified matters, it being "easier to deal with incitements to violence, and with actual violence itself, than with widespread passive resistance," as long as outbreaks remained isolated rather than becoming widespread as in Ireland.[27] On the whole he was skeptical – and Gandhi or Jawaharlal would have agreed with him – of Congress's ability to agitate effectively on constitutional issues alone; a popular platform based on issues closer to the lives of ordinary people would be needed. A governor of UP could have little doubt about what that organizing focus was likely to be. The agrarian situation continued to deteriorate, Hailey now believed that landlords were typically "bad and oppressive," and Gandhi was planning a tour of the province in October.[28]

Predictably the Government of India prepared for the approaching challenge with a combination of coercion and conciliation. Along with the Lahore and Meerut conspiracy cases, which were designed to attack the revolutionary-terrorist movement and the labor left, it introduced a Public Safety Act that Jawaharlal called broad enough to include just about anything.[29] Meanwhile

---

23 Gandhi interview to press, 2 January 1929, CWMG, *38*, 315–17.
24 Nehru letters of March 1929, SWJN, *4*, 141–3. See also Judith M. Brown, *Gandhi and Civil Disobedience: The Mahatma in Indian Politics, 1928–1934*, and Gyanendra Pandey, *The Ascendancy of the Congress in Uttar Pradesh, 1926–1934: A Study in Imperfect Mobilization* (Delhi: Oxford University Press, 1978).
25 Irwin to Hailey, 10 January 29, HPI/15A.
26 Lambert to Hailey, 4 February 1929, ibid. The wave of strikes was matched – or more than matched – by the government's onslaught against the Indian labor movement in the important conspiracy trial of Communist and other union leaders, which eventually resulted in long prison terms. Because the case was being heard in Meerut Hailey had direct responsibility for the prisoners. The affair was badly managed, he reported, "for though I approve of trying Communists, I believe that the lines on which it is being run, which are frankly a general propaganda against the whole Communist or Bolshevist doctrine throughout the world, are a mistake. The trial will be greatly prolonged . . . and for publicity purposes it will be a failure." Hailey to O'Dwyer, 11 July 1929, HPI/15B.
27 Hailey to Hammond (governor of Assam), 2 August 1929, ibid.
28 Hailey to Sir Stanley Reed, 31 July 1929, ibid.
29 Nehru note [October] 1929, NML, AICC 6/1929.

Irwin spent most of the summer of 1929 in England consulting with the new Labour secretary of state, William Wedgwood Benn, the result being a declaration, which Hailey urged should be made as full-blooded as possible, reaffirming that dominion status was indeed Britain's long-range goal for India and promising a round-table conference.[30]

Although Irwin's pronouncement drew support from Liberals, Muslims, and moderate members of Congress, the Congress working committee laid down conditions: dominion status to be agreed in advance, general amnesty, and predominant representation for Congress at the conference.[31] In December 1929 Gandhi and Motilal Nehru met the viceroy, who told them that the British Parliament must remain unfettered. At the Congress session in Lahore, proclaiming himself both a republican and a socialist, Jawaharlal asserted that the goal was no longer dominion status but full independence; nonviolence was only a tactic. Gandhi's resolution deploring a bomb attack on the viceroy's train passed, but only narrowly.

Early in January 1930 the Congress working committee authorized Gandhi to launch civil disobedience as and when he thought advisable. Independence Day, 26 January, was marked by hartals and demonstrations across the country. On the thirtieth Gandhi issued his eleven points – if they were going all out for independence, Jawaharlal objected, why bother with points at all? Early in March the Mahatma informed Irwin that he would break the salt laws, receiving the curt reply that the viceroy regretted he had decided on a course so full of potentiality for violence. "Either we shall win the goal for which we are marching or die in the attempt," Gandhi declared just before he set out on his march to the sea. "There can be no turning back."[32]

Hailey watched the unfolding drama as a keen student of political behavior. Until lately, he told the Oxford historian Reginald Coupland, he had not taken the independence question very seriously. But a "younger and more hotheaded section is getting hold of Congress." Their militancy disturbed their elders, who realized that violence would actually ease the government's difficulty, "for then it becomes a simple police matter and we can easily take the upper hand." The really dangerous problem, he pointed out repeatedly, was agrarian. In UP large numbers of tenants were being "rack-rented and badly treated by their landlords; and if the agitator should get hold of them as he did in 1921, he would have a good case." Moreover "the landlord . . . can put on the screw by all manner of illegal means, and tenants are afraid to come to the Courts." Hailey also knew, however, that poor oppressed peasants do not ordinarily lead revolu-

---

[30] Hailey note, June 1929, HPI/16A. "I do not myself see any harm" he told the diehard O'Dwyer, "if it is made clear that Dominion Status must be achieved . . . by a series of constitutional developments and [not] by the bang of a drum"; it seemed wise "to provide an occasional landing stage for more sober people to rest on while the Extremist is being swept down the tide." Hailey to O'Dwyer, 4 October 1929, ibid.

[31] Text of Delhi Manifesto, 1 November 1929, SWJN, *4*, 165–6.

[32] CWMG, *43*, 45.

tions. They would become involved only "if there is something like an all-India movement, affecting the popular imagination, like that of 1921–22." Notwithstanding the independence rhetoric, he saw little sign of that.[33]

Hailey's eye was on the rural situation. Although Gandhi's tour of UP drew large crowds and raised a good deal of money, his speeches were surprisingly moderate, hardly mentioning the tenant problem. Travelling through the same districts a few weeks later Hailey found them quiet and peaceful.[34] It was all very puzzling. If Congress was in earnest, he asked himself, why was the government's obvious weak point being neglected? Repeatedly he warned peasants against outside agitators; the government would listen only to authentic representatives from the tenant class itself.[35]

In the period before the salt march Hailey gave three important speeches. The first, a supposedly nonpartisan address at Allahabad University in November 1929, on the modest subject of the future of Asia, was one of his best. The Socratic inquirer, he said, concerned with the biology of a society, would note that the potent combination of industrialization, democracy and education had transformed the West and was now revolutionizing Asia. Observing also the growth of national consciousness the philosopher would not be unduly disturbed by India's diversity: "You can of course have a considerable degree of unity without uniformity." It was however hard to determine the extent to which nationalism had "yet become a dynamic fact in India at large, or how far it is likely to constitute a unifying and compelling principle in the near future." The philosopher would not restrict the inquiry to the attainment of self-government, but would ask: freedom for what? What kind of civilization would an independent India want to be? Europeans had not of course thought things out in that way, but neither had they had a model of a modern society before them.

India had the chance and therefore the obligation to think critically and make rational choices, Hailey continued. The future lay with Indian intellectuals. The trouble was that they were so totally preoccupied with the present. To claim that he was equally interested would of course sound insincere, but "if ever we could stand aloof, we cannot do so today, when the air is full of hope and expectation, and the watchers in the tower cry to you tidings of the breaking of the dawn."[36] It is deeply ironic that the most thoughtful answers to the speaker's questions would one day be given by the man who had presided at the Lahore Congress in 1929 – but only after men like Malcolm Hailey had given him sabbatical leaves by putting him in jail.[37]

In a more explicitly political address at the Muslim University in Aligarh, Sir Malcolm spoke to the communalist. "Your religious life is the soul of your

33 Hailey to Coupland, 3 September 1929, HPI/16A.
34 Hailey to Irwin, 18 November 1929, ibid.
35 *Leader*, 28 November 1929.   36 Speech of 30 November 1929, HPI/47.
37 I am referring to Jawaharlal Nehru, *The Discovery of India*, which was written in internment during World War II.

culture," he observed. "You have a philosophy and literature of your own, which is part of the life of your community." Speaking as "a candid observer, and one whom certainly no one could accuse of lack of friendship," he urged that what Muslim India needed most was leadership. Otherwise, the implication was clear – for though the majority of Muslim leaders were aloof, others were ranging in and with Congress – the very survival of the community was in danger.[38]

What did practical men make of the current scene, Hailey asked at the Upper India Chamber of Commerce in Cawnpore? Although the objective of dominion status had been laid down unequivocally, extremists were claiming immediate independence and threatening another round of lawlessness. Had Congress forgotten its own inquiry of 1922 into civil disobedience? Gandhi's earlier campaign had been financed by Indian businessmen whose books must still show the enormous cost. The governor hoped that "the word will go round the bazaars that it is unwise to supply the sinews of war to any party which may again misuse them with such disastrous results." He would not discuss how the government might respond: "Personally I should prefer to see India itself kill the new movement with ridicule."[39]

India did not kill it with ridicule. Indeed the salt march of 1930 remains one of the most dramatic, moving stories of the twentieth century. Before the year was out Hailey would recognize that the question he had posed in his convocation address – how mature, dynamic, and permanent was Indian national consciousness? – had been passionately answered. At the time, however, Gandhi's tactic seemed a strange one, for though the salt tax might remind Europeans of the Old Regime in France, it made little difference to the ordinary Indian. It seemed that way to Jawaharlal Nehru too. Indeed, the perceptions of Nehru and Hailey, intense opponents representing contrasting perspectives and profoundly different worlds, were often strikingly alike. "We were bewildered," Nehru recalled later, "and could not quite fit in a national struggle with common salt." Only after seeing Gandhi "staff in hand, marching . . . with firm step and a peaceful but undaunted look" did he feel "abashed and ashamed for having questioned the efficacy of this method" when the Mahatma first proposed it.[40] And he was never quite convinced.

For some time Hailey had felt that although there had been good reasons for caution, the government's reaction to the noncooperation campaign of 1920–2 had been too slow. "The name of Government will be mud in India unless we show a firm hand this time," he warned.[41] Yet premature action could push potential allies into the arms of extremists and build opposition in Britain,

[38] Speech of 25 January 1930, *Leader*, 30 January 1930.
[39] Speech of 23 January 1930, ibid., 29 January 1930.
[40] *Autobiography*, pp. 210–3. Early in February 1930, in a speech at Rae Bareli, he advised tenants to withhold enhancements of rent. D. N. Dhanagare, *Agrarian Movements and Gandhian Politics* (Agra: Agra University Press, 1975), p. 99, and *Peasant Movements in India, 1920–1950*, p. 121, takes this speech as the effective beginning of the no-rent campaign in Oudh. I agree with Pandey, *Ascendancy of Congress in Uttar Pradesh*, that it did not start until October.
[41] Hailey to de Montmorency, 16 January 1930, HPI/17A.

where the Labour Party was in power. Gandhi delivered his salt ultimatum on 5 March. Not believing for a minute that salt was really going to be the driving issue in a national movement, Hailey searched for a more logical strategy. He found it in the speeches and intercepted correspondence of Nehru, who of course was trying to do precisely the same thing.

In his own speeches Nehru was stressing peasant grievances, urging the abolition of the zamindar class, and trying in general to push Congress toward a more radical economic program. To the provincial committees he outlined a three-stage strategy. The first phase would belong to Gandhi, ending with his arrest. The second, directed by the provincial committees, would widen into a mass movement and attack other targets. The third, when the Congress leaders would all be in jail, would become full civil disobedience, which might "involve non-payment of taxes, of land revenue or rent." Ordinarily, another working-committee circular advised, "a no-tax campaign should follow the salt campaign."[42]

Although this scheme was undoubtedly a good deal tidier than Gandhi's – playing chess with a man who apparently did not plot series of moves could be harder – to a governor sitting on top of a revenue system like the UP's Nehru's model made perfect sense. From Hailey's perspective Gandhi's stroll to the coast had come as a relief. Everything should be done to drag the salt phase out as long as possible. He thought like Jawaharlal. If *he* were getting up a revolution he would go for the jugular.

And there was no doubt where that was. It was "common enough to find land near a village which pays rent of Rs. 18 to Rs. 24 a bigha," Hailey explained, "whereas the landlord pays to Government only Rs. 2 or thereabouts per bigha as land revenue." Getting hold of this the agitator "tells the cultivator that there are parts of the world where the landlord does not exist as an intermediary between the cultivator and the State, and suggests that in a socialistic or communistic country the landlord would be got rid of and the tenant would pay only the Rs. 2 land revenue . . . to the State itself." The agitator would point out further, "with great justice, that the landlord is an uneconomical factor, for he does nothing whatever for the tenant," neither building him a house nor providing tools, "and any occasional benefit . . . is outweighed by the fact that whenever he has a marriage, or a death, or a visit from a Governor, or an accident to his motor car, he makes an illegal levy from the cultivator to pay for it."

What argument could be used to persuade tenants that the agitator was wrong, Hailey asked rhetorically? "I know of none myself." Warnings about social chaos would leave peasants cold. "I have spent a good deal of my life in India among the cultivators," he concluded, "and I believe there is only one argument which we can use in a province such as this, and that is the simple argument that Government is strong enough to down the agitator and is going to do so."[43]

[42] Circular letters of 22 February and 15 March 1930, SWJN, *4*, 271–9.
[43] Hailey to Hirtzel, 4 April 1930, HPI/17B.

On 6 April 1930 Gandhi reached the sea. He had caught the government on the horns of a dilemma: damned if they arrested him, damned if they didn't.[44] It would be hard to overstate the damage to the government's prestige, Hailey agreed, admitting that the tactic had been surprisingly successful: first Bardoli, now this. Indeed the government presented "the picture of a person once dignified if unwieldy, but now entirely without position or respect, because its beard is pulled and its hat knocked over its eyes by every urchin in the street." Losing face would make it "more difficult to 'hold' our general population. The East has far more respect for a ruler who misuses his powers than for one which allows his authority to be flouted."[45] Gandhi's symbolic launching having been completed, Jawaharlal's scheme called for the campaign to intensify quickly. Now, Hailey thought, was the time to bring it quickly to a head. Although Irwin decided to leave Gandhi alone for the time being, permission came from Delhi to move against the leaders. "I have no objection," Hailey directed in a handwritten note, "to giving simple imprisonment to old men like Moti Lal [Nehru]."[46]

---

[44] CWMG, *43*, 200.

[45] Hailey to Hirtzel, 4 April 1930, HPI/17B. "It is hard for any one not actually in India to realize the effect of the Bardoli decision," he told his older brother. "It is quoted against us everywhere by landlords who openly give it as their reason for philandering with Congress rather than supporting Government. If we were to have any fresh tragedy of this kind we should 'lose face' so much that it would be difficult to claim support from anyone."

[46] Note of 9 April 1930, ibid.

〜〜

12

Governor of the United Provinces: civil disobedience and Round Table Conference, 1930–1931

The flame from Gujarat spread across urban India, as Jawaharlal Nehru put it, like a prairie fire.[1] He himself received six months' imprisonment. Early in May Gandhi delivered a challenge the government could not refuse, when he vowed to take possession of a salt works in Surat; this time he was interned under an old state prisoners act, which denied him the opportunity to make a statement in court. With the poet Sarojini Naidu leading instead, satyagrahis marched in orderly rows to the gates, where they were beaten senseless and carried away on stretchers. Witnessing the repetitions, an American newspaper correspondent felt a strange surge of anger not only against the police but against the demonstrators.[2] In Sholapur district, Bombay presidency, martial law was declared, Bombay city was reported to be effectively in Congress hands, and Indian capitalists filled Congress coffers.[3] At Chittagong in Bengal revolutionaries made a daring attack on an arsenal. At Peshawar in North-West Frontier Province, Indian troops at first fired on Muslim Red Shirts led by Gandhi's disciple Abdul Ghaffar Khan. Then, ominously, they refused.[4]

In the United Provinces, where proper salt could not be made, the manufacturing ritual was farcical but, since the object was to show contempt for the government, no less effective. Liquor and foreign-cloth shops were picketed, schools and municipal buildings flew Congress flags, forest laws were broken, and Congress volunteers directed traffic. The young and the female participated widely, the early 1930s being pivotal in the political awakening of Indian women.[5] By March 1931, when the Gandhi–Irwin pact was declared, the

---

[1] Jawaharlal Nehru, *An Autobiography*, pp. 212–13.
[2] Webb Miller, *I Found No Peace: The Journal of a Foreign Correspondent* (New York: Simon & Schuster, 1936), pp. 189–99.
[3] Note of Sir Harry Haig, 13 June 1930, quoted by Judith M. Brown, *Gandhi and Civil Disobedience*, p. 135.
[4] See Stephen A. Rittenberg, *Ethnicity, Nationalism, and the Pakhtuns* (Durham, NC: Carolina Academic Press, 1988). See also Hailey to Hirtzel, 8 May 1930, HPI/18A, and Hailey–Birdwood correspondence, 12 and 14 May 1930, ibid.
[5] See Radha K. Sharma, *Nationalism, Social Reform and Indian Women: A Study of the Interaction Between Our National Movement and the Movement of Social Reform Among Indian Women, 1921–1937* (Patna: Janaki Prakashan, 1981).

government counted sixty thousand convictions, Congress ninety thousand. Although the tactics and strength varied from place to place, Hailey explained candidly in a speech that November, the British were facing a sustained emotional wave of unprecedented magnitude and intensity.[6]

UP had several firing incidents and numerous beatings, but no violent outbursts on the scale of those in Bombay, Peshawar, or Chittagong. Nehru's efforts to revitalize the Congress organization having succeeded, in all the urban areas it mounted a strong challenge. Even in Naini Tal, Hailey reported, small boys carrying flags shouted slogans.[7] The government struck back in a wide variety of ways: parents required to guarantee children's good behavior,[8] lists prepared to screen applicants for government jobs,[9] grants withheld from schools flying the Congress flag, district boards superseded,[10] government employees forbidden to attend Congress meetings, pensions withdrawn.[11] By late June, when the ill but feisty Motilal Nehru joined his son in jail, some 750 people had already been given prison terms. Early in July the UP government declared the Congress working committee in Allahabad illegal, searched its offices, and seized its papers. District by district, local committees were attacked in turn. Through the long hot summer of 1930, however, one facet was conspicuously absent. There was no rent strike.[12]

From the beginning, Hailey explained to his district officers, still echoing Jawaharlal's working-committee circulars, the salt phase had clearly been intended only as a prelude, for it focused on an issue that to ordinary Indians was insignificant. Unlike the noncooperation movement of the early 1920s, however, this campaign involved clear if technical violations of the ordinary law, which gave the government the chance to pick off leaders when and where it chose. Experience indicated that agitation could not continue for any extended period, and already there were signs that Congress's financial and organiza-

---

[6] Transcript in HPI/48. The best general and comparative study is Brown, *Gandhi and Civil Disobedience*, though I agree with her Indian critics that it doesn't sound all that much like a national movement. See also the excellent short survey by Mridula Mukherjee in Bipan Chandra et al., *India's Struggle for Independence, 1857–1947*, pp. 270–83.

[7] Hailey to Irwin, 25 April 1930, HPI/17B.

[8] A conference of school superintendents at Benares protested that although they favored maintaining discipline, the strong feelings of the community should be considered. Some parents were participating in civil disobedience and the vast majority sympathized with its goals. Respected leaders such as Pandit Malaviya, who had recently become a member of the Congress working committee, were being arrested daily: "The school authorities will be helpless witnesses . . . because it will not be possible to force them [students] to remain at study." *Leader*, 13 July 1930.

[9] Hailey note, 8 August 1930, UP GA [General Administration] Dept 241/1930.

[10] In the case of Rae Bareli district board, for instance, the government justified the action on grounds of financial insolvency; in effect the board had become a local Congress committee.

[11] In a case of one seventy-year-old man who had been convicted for civil disobedience and sentenced to six months rigorous imprisonment, the pension was eventually restored – as an act of mercy! UP GA Dept 283/1930.

[12] This point, again, follows Gyanendra Pandey, *The Ascendancy of the Congress in Uttar Pradesh, 1926–1934*, pp. 43–4, who argues that Congress intentionally held back on no-rent in order to avoid alienating landlords and splitting the movement.

tional resources were being squeezed. Hailey's strategy was therefore to pin Congress to the salt issue as long as possible.[13]

The timing of Gandhi's arrest was crucial. Looking back on 1921–2, Hailey advised the viceroy, Lord Irwin, "we were continually hoping that agitation would wear itself out . . . ; we had seen 1919 and Amritsar; there was a very genuine fear that decisive action might precipitate outbreaks the suppression of which might again produce incidents so difficult to live down and so damaging to our reputation among Indians." Could agitation today – without strong Muslim support and given the lapse of time since General Dyer's massacre at Jallianwala Bagh – possibly achieve what it had then? Objectively, perhaps not. Yet "there is a new and somewhat potent factor. The bazaars ring with talk of Independence and Revolution; and when Revolution becomes the talk of the street corner," people might indeed act violently. The psychology of the mass movement was like a "nerve storm; the more quickly it reaches its height the more rapid will be its decline. Last time it had a long ascending curve and a slow decline." Hailey's instinct was "to bring it as rapidly as possible to a head." Now that Gandhi had pledged to achieve independence, "there seems to be even for him no going back merely because violence takes place. He has not done a single day's fast for Chittagong."[14]

Hailey's other main concern was the attitude of Muslims, for Nationalist Muslims had a substantial following in UP.[15] Noting that local Muslims were complaining about police brutality, fearing that the deaths at Peshawar in the North-West Frontier Province might create an emotional landslide like the Khilafat agitation a decade earlier, he ordered an independent inquiry into a firing incident at Lucknow.[16] District commissioners were ordered to take particular pains to keep Muslims away from salt demonstrations.[17] He would try to persuade his superiors to make a definitive declaration on the protection of minorities, he promised his home member the Nawab of Chhatari, for "the Muslim position . . . is one to which . . . I attach the very greatest importance."[18]

The Congress working committee must have been pleased with the first six weeks, Hailey wrote entertainingly to Irwin from his sickbed late in May. People

---

[13] Hailey to DCs, 17 April 1930, HPI/17B.   [14] Hailey to Irwin, 25 April 1930, ibid.

[15] See Pandey, *Ascendancy of Congress in Uttar Pradesh*, pp. 106–13; David Page, *Prelude to Partition: The Indian Muslims and the Imperial System of Control, 1920–1932*, pp. 197–220. For the historical background see Francis Robinson, *Separatism Among Indian Muslims: The Politics of the United Provinces' Muslims, 1860–1923* (Cambridge: Cambridge University Press, 1974).

[16] Hailey to de Montmorency, 5 June 1930, HPI/18B. He told Irwin candidly that the police's forcible breaking up of a peaceable demonstration had been a great mistake. Hailey to Irwin, 9 June 1930, ibid. The inquiry eventually concluded that the firing had been justified.

[17] Ch. Comm. Allahabad to Ch.Sec., UP, 9 May 1930, UP GA Dept. 241/1930.

[18] Hailey to Chhatari, 1 May 1930 ibid. "We have for some time been calling the attention of all district officers to the necessity of using their influence to keep Muslims straight," Hailey told the home member; "we have issued confidential orders that prosecutions under the Sarda [child marriage] Act are not to be entertained, if these can possibly be avoided." Hailey to Haig, 10 May 1930, ibid.

with a general-staff conception of strategy and tactics might think differently of course. So might those who took Congress rhetoric seriously: "We talk about waging a war of Independence without meaning in the slightest that it shall really be a war, or even intending to gain Independence by it." Grand phrases resounded "about sacrificing the life-blood of our youth," alarming "people who do not know that our real meaning is only that we shall have a very large number of demonstrations, and a great mass of violent writing and speaking, and that a few hundred people shall go to prison for short terms." In fact, he reasoned, the object of the campaign was not to bring the government down – that was not practical politics – but to emphasize Congress's organizational strength, demonstrate its large popular following, and hustle the British into making some concessions. Although "the General Staff would think this a very poor display of objective, with hopelessly ill-defined lines of attack on a very nebulous front," that was probably all Congress had ever really had in mind.[19]

Some British officials thought Congress had not been pressed hard enough, others that the agitation was beginning to decline, still others that a gesture of appeasement would end it at once. As for the first, although it might seem incongruous to defer the "crushing blow at their centre," suppose Congress were outlawed? The government would get prisoners and records but no money, it would be hard to answer the charge "that we are fighting nationalism, not civil disobedience," and in any case Congress would soon be legal again. "I would go a long way to suffocate it and be done with it," Hailey asserted, "but it hardly seems worth while making a lot of trouble merely in order to give it a mild dose of laughing gas."

On the other hand, Sir Malcolm continued, people accustomed to Western psychology were often misled into thinking that conciliatory gestures could resolve serious problems. Indians had "developed an almost religious veneration for Queen Victoria," for instance, "the kind of thing which the Victorians, secure not only in their own consciences but also in the strength which Britain still occupied in India, did remarkably well." In the current atmosphere, however, altruism would be interpreted as weakness. "I myself jib nervously at the very notion of bargaining with these gentlemen," he concluded. "I would as soon sup with Old Nick, and indeed much rather, for our own particular Satan has often shown himself a bit of a sportsman, and notoriously sticks to his bargains."

Precisely as he had reasoned during his confrontation with the Sikhs in 1924, when the decision had been his own, in advising the viceroy Hailey deprecated either wholesale repression or conciliation. That left steady, gradually increasing pressure. He had "so often seen Governments . . . do the wrong thing," he

---

[19] Hailey to Irwin, 23 May 1930, HPI/18A. Thinking at first it was flu, he had gone on tour without consulting a doctor, trusting in what he called the genial warmth of May. "Even the Indian Sun however is not what it was in pre-Reform days," he lamented, and he had been "so broken in my manhood that I surrendered myself to a doctor," whose concoctions had finished him properly. It turned out to be malaria. See Hailey to de Montmorency, 5 June 1930, ibid.

wrote, "just when a little quiet persistence or . . . genuine obstinacy would have brought success." It was wrong to think in terms of victory, he emphasized, for "that would involve an almost impossible effort to smash opposition permanently or an equally impossible effort to win a goodwill which we ought to know that we actually can never capture."[20]

Just when steady pressure seemed to be having some success, Hailey began to receive mixed signals. From London came word that the Labour cabinet was ignoring the Simon report and leaning toward sweeping concessions. Press leaks from Delhi suggested that a deal with Congress was being considered. On the other hand, despite Hailey's advice that local conditions did not necessitate any dramatic escalation of repression, he was ordered to declare the working committee unlawful.[21] Hailey proposed to arrest Motilal Nehru, was told to stay his hand while a feeler was being checked out, then ordered to arrest everyone in sight. What in the world, Hailey asked Sir Geoffrey de Montmorency of the Punjab in some perplexity as they prepared for a conference in Simla, was going on?[22]

At Simla governors gave situation reports. Madras: civil disobedience declining rather satisfactorily. Bengal: likewise; rise in terrorism expected. Bombay: position truly desperate; stock exchange rarely open; businessmen "supporting the movement do not mind if they are broken, provided that Government is broken also." Punjab: improving except for Amritsar. Hailey on UP: signs of Congress weariness; despite a sharp decline in agricultural prices, rents coming in fairly well; "nothing serious in the way of a no-tax or no-rent campaign. In fact, the Congress has temporarily given up this idea, holding out hopes for the next harvest." On the whole, Hailey thought, "if the Muhammadans keep on the right side, and we continue steady pressure . . . after two or three months the movement will definitely be beaten." When it did end, the governors agreed, there should be no general amnesty.[23]

Although the formal meeting was somewhat reassuring, private conversations revealed that Irwin, Finance Member Sir George Schuster, and others, with eyes on the coming Round Table Conference in London, seemed to be going soft on the constitution. "The prospect makes one very unhappy," Hailey confided. "I almost begin to wish that I had left India two years ago instead of staying on to face a new order of things to which I feel that I am both by temperament and tradition unsuited." The younger generation might adapt, "but I fear that my own back is too stiff to bow to them either with comfort to myself or satisfaction to the circumstances!"[24]

---

20 Ibid.
21 Once Congress as a whole was declared unlawful, Hailey pointed out, little space would remain short of martial law. Hailey to Irwin, 25 June 1930, HPI/18B.
22 Hailey to de Montmorency, 11 July 1930, HPI/19A. See also notes on discussions re views of UP Govt. to be presented to the Government of India, UP GA Dept 507/1930.
23 Proceedings of Governors' Conference, 23 July 1930, HPI/19A.
24 Hailey to Sir Theodore Morison, 6 August 1930, ibid.

As Hailey had forecast there were mediation efforts. Because the Round Table Conference in London would be severely discredited unless Congress were known to have rejected reasonable offers, the Nehrus and other leaders were permitted to meet Gandhi. Also as Hailey had foreseen the ante had risen considerably. Congress's demands now included the right to secede from the empire, complete responsible government including defense and finance, Gandhi's eleven points, and the referral of India's national debt to an international tribunal. Even if the terms were accepted, the working committee insisted, peaceful picketing must be allowed to continue, the salt laws would not be enforced, and all prisoners not convicted of violent crimes would be released at once without condition. Hailey was relieved the terms were so clearly unacceptable. So was Jawaharlal: "I delight in warfare," he wrote; "it makes me feel that I am alive."[25]

Like most British officials Hailey had badly underestimated the strength of Congress's organization, which he conceded was much improved over the non-cooperation period.[26] But more than organization was involved. First, the agitation had attracted "the wide sympathy of Hindus as a genuine Hindu movement," which had been reinforced by the refusal of Muslims as a body to participate; there were "few Hindus, even among loyalists and officials, who have not some kind of pride in the solidarity which has been shown." Second, the movement reflected "a recognition by the middle classes of the difficult economic conditions in which they are placed and the apparent hopelessness of their outlook" – that is, precisely the social dynamics that were driving communalism. Third was Bombay, where businessmen believed passionately that the city's commercial depression was the result of British currency and fiscal policy. The Indian capitalist class seemed willing to make huge sacrifices if they could win finance and commerce ministers responsible to the national Legislative Assembly.[27]

Although officials in north India regarded urban agitation as routine, Hailey observed, "we remembered the agrarian agitation of the non-cooperation period and realized that the agitator really has a first class field for work among the tenants." Congress's ultimate objective, he had learned from Nehru's circulars, "was a no-rent and no-revenue campaign, and it was a fear of this which really made us take the opportunity offered by the Salt Act agitation to attempt to

---

[25] Hailey to de Montmorency, 6 September 1930, HPI/19B; Nehru to Gandhi, 28 July 1930, CWMG, *44*, 467–8.

[26] Hailey to Sir Verney Lovett, 3 July 1930, HPI/19A.

[27] Hailey to Sir Denys Bray, 14 August 1930, ibid. On the role of the capitalist class see A. D. Gordon, *Businessmen and Politics: Rising Nationalism and a Modernising Economy in Bombay, 1918–1933* (New Delhi: Manohar, 1978); Claude Markovits, *Indian Business and Nationalist Politics, 1931–1939: The Indigenous Capitalist Class and the Rise of the Congress Party* (Cambridge: Cambridge University Press, 1985); B. R. Tomlinson, *The Political Economy of the Raj, 1914–1947: The Economics of Decolonization in India;* Aditya Mukherjee, "Indian Capitalists and the National Movement," in Chandra et al., *India's Struggle for Independence*, pp. 375–85; and Amiya K. Bagchi, *Private Investment in India, 1900–1939* (Cambridge: Cambridge University Press, 1972).

forestall Congress by arresting its leaders and breaking up its organization." So far the government's strategy had managed to contain the movement. Early in July he had sensed that enthusiasm might be waning. Once more, however, he had been too optimistic. Demonstrations were broken up only to re-form the next day; successive groups of leaders were arrested, but others replaced them. The civil-disobedience movement had demonstrated an impressive capacity to sustain and renew itself, and some district officers felt that villagers were becoming involved. Although he himself did not expect serious trouble in the near future, he concluded, "if the agitation is prolonged over the winter, I should begin to feel some real anxiety as to the results."[28]

Weary of the campaign of attrition, disillusioned by signs of weakness above him, fighting off malaria and very likely a urinary tract problem, Hailey's mood had darkened considerably. At Simla he had argued that reviving the wartime emergency measures would confirm Congress's claim to have made the country ungovernable. Early in September, again sensing a lull, thinking the time ripe for a strong counterattack, in rapid succession he asked for an ordinance to control local boards and for authority to round up Congress volunteers. It was now Irwin who complained of mixed signals.[29]

Also in September Hailey learned that the India Office had requested his attendance at the Round Table Conference in November. He would of course enjoy going home for roast beef and Christmas pudding, he wrote, though seeing former colleagues like Sir Michael O'Dwyer or Sir Reginald Craddock would put him in "the equivocal position of a young lady who has to face a severe family circle with a confession that she has lost her virtue." Perhaps he could just sit back and answer technical questions. The worst of it was that he would be unable to try out a new shotgun, and "unthinking people will have shot all the duck by the time I get back!"[30]

The lull continued. Although Hailey expected a slight revival as leaders' prison terms expired, "of course, we shall do our best to sweep them up again."[31] Jawaharlal Nehru was released on 11 October. Three days later Hailey wrote that "we have got to a definite period of stagnation as regards Congress agitation." Hence "we have decided somewhat to intensify pressure in places where agitation really appears to be a nuisance, while leaving the rest of the province to the ordinary routine procedure." Most important, he saw no signs whatever that Congress was likely to succeed "in any widespread campaign for non-payment of rent or revenue."

The really serious problem, Sir Malcolm noted, was not Congress agitation but a sharp fall in farm prices the true magnitude of which had only recently

---

28 Hailey to Bray, 14 August 1930, HPI/19A.
29 Irwin to Hailey, 20–21 September 1930, HPI/19B.
30 Hailey to de Montmorency, 16 September, and to Sir Findlater Stewart, 25 September 1930, ibid. Having taken long leave so recently he had to resign formally; once again Sir George Lambert replaced him.
31 Hailey to de Montmorency, 2 October 1930, ibid.

become apparent. Several district officers were reporting that "at the rates now prevailing for cotton, wheat, etc., the cultivator simply cannot afford to pay the existing rates of rent." Revenue could not be reduced unless rents were lowered too, but that would "involve great friction and something like a minor social upheaval" with the landlord class. The causes of this depression were obscure and its duration was impossible to prophesy. It was bad luck "that this economic trouble should supervene at the moment when we are battling with difficult political conditions, but there it is." One could "only pray that the international financial Pandits will find some way of mobilizing the gold reserve and restore world peace!"[32]

On 16 October Hailey left for England. Three days later Nehru was back in jail. He had had a reasonably busy week, proclaiming his admiration for the condemned hero Bhagat Singh and inspiring the UP Congress committee "to launch a no-tax campaign in the province whenever and wherever it was possible [giving] district Congress committees freedom of action."[33] In the context of an accelerating world economic crisis, the civil-disobedience movement in UP was about to move into an entirely new phase. The long-deferred no-rent campaign had come at last. Once more Hailey had miscalculated and the UP government was caught off guard.

∞∞∞∞∞∞

By refusing to end civil disobedience in August 1930 Congress had hoped to condemn the subsequent Round Table Conference to irrelevance. As with the council boycott of the early 1920s, however, the strategy had mixed results, balancing the benefits of a declining level of agitation against the costs of leaving political space unoccupied. To some extent Congress dominated the proceedings like Banquo's ghost. Managing to fill the vacuum, however, the British authorities kept the timing and direction of the constitution-making process largely in their own hands. As a key participant behind the scenes in 1930, as adviser to the Conservative secretary of state, Sir Samuel Hoare, before the Parliamentary committee of 1933, and helping with the final passage of the Government of India Act of 1935 through Parliament, Hailey was to play an important role.

The Round Table Conference of 1930 was dominated by two events that took place during the initial skirmishing. First, Indian Liberals tried to present a united demand for immediate recognition of dominion status, failing which the entire Indian delegation would walk out. Despite Jinnah's efforts to negotiate, however – Jinnah, Hailey remarked maliciously, was as slippery as the eels his forefathers had sold in the Bombay market – Muslim delegates insisted on

---

[32] Hailey to Crerar, 14 October 1930, ibid.
[33] Report of speech, 18 October, *Leader*, 20 October 1930.

separate electorates, which Moonje and the Hindu Mahasabha rejected. Second, delegates from the princely states came up with a sketch for a federal constitution. Hoping to hide their inability to break the communal deadlock, Sir Tej Bahadur Sapru and other Indian delegates welcomed the idea. So did Hailey, who advised that neither dyarchy nor any other steps toward responsible government at the center should be conceded in any other context. A federal assembly, he pointed out, where the princes would be heavily represented and where the viceroy would nominate many members, would be much more conservative than a legislature restricted to British India alone, which Congress would inevitably dominate. Federalism might be a red herring, he observed – or a fishable salmon.[34] As Sir Samuel Hoare noted, the federal formula might "make it possible to give a semblance of responsible government and yet retain in our hands the realities and verities of British control."[35]

Moreover, by making constitutional advance somewhat more palatable to the British Liberal and especially the Conservative delegation, the federal scheme might enable the Labour government to avoid open conflict with the opposing front benches. Ever since the general election of June 1929, when it received three hundred thousand fewer popular votes but twenty more seats than the Conservatives, leaving the fifty-nine Liberals with the balance of power, Labour had held office only because its opponents had chosen not to defeat it on a vote of confidence. As usual some Labour ministers wished to fight and die for a true socialist platform, while others wanted to be seen to govern responsibly – the classic pattern of the left, turning anti-imperialists into colonial reformers. The doctrinaire group, Hailey noted contemptuously, included Secretary of State for India William Wedgwood Benn, and the foreign secretary, Arthur Henderson.[36] Fortunately, in Hailey's view, the prime minister, James Ramsay MacDonald, was "earnest and sympathetic," a master of the "supreme task of saying nothing, at satisfying length, but saying it very nicely."[37]

The Simon Commission having recommended provincial autonomy but no ministerial responsibility at the center, Irwin had drawn up a scheme for some-

---

34 See particularly Samuel Hoare, note of Hailey's views, 13 November 1930, Templewood Collection, MSS EUR E 240/52B; Hailey to Irwin, 14 November 1930, HPI/34; Hailey note on federation, n.d. [18 November 1930], HPI/31A.

35 Hoare memo for shadow cabinet, 12 December 1930, quoted by Carl Bridge, *Holding India to the Empire: The British Conservative Party and the 1935 Constitution* (New Delhi: Sterling, 1986), pp. 56–8. See also Stuart Ball, *Baldwin and the Conservative Party: The Crisis of 1929–1931* (New Haven, Conn.: Yale University Press, 1988), and J. A. Cross, *Sir Samuel Hoare: A Political Biography* (London: Cape, 1977).

36 Benn was naive and out of his depth, Hailey thought. And "Henderson shows not only a complete ignorance of the questions at issue and an entire disinclination to accept advice from anyone, but in the Committee itself preserves the impassivity of a cod-fish on a fish-monger's slab." Hailey to Irwin, 10 December 1930, HPI/34. On the Labour Party see Partha S. Gupta, *Imperialism and the British Labour Movement, 1914–1964*, especially pp. 102–18, 201–24, and Mesbahuddin Ahmed, *The British Labour Party and the Indian Independence Movement, 1917–1939*.

37 Hailey to Irwin, 27 November 1930, HPI/34.

thing he called responsive government, which managed to avoid the word dyarchy and featured a unitary government composed of officials and non-official Indians who might be members of the legislature – actually it sounded a lot like dyarchy.[38] Sending the delegates back to face Congress with less would presumably be disastrous, while a revolt from Labour's left wing could be expected. Moreover, Hailey said in a speech at Oxford's Raleigh Club, there could be no doubt of the sophisticated organization and deep emotion of the civil-disobedience campaign, which had captured the soul of Hindu India.[39] On the other hand, he told Irwin, the deep hostility of Conservatives to the whole notion of dominion status needed to be experienced first-hand in order to be understood. MacDonald's task was therefore delicate: enough progress to help the Government of India in its struggle with Congress, but not enough to cause defeat at home.

At the outset, Hailey reported, Indian delegates having protested that he and Sir Charles Innes (Burma) should not have been present, his role was restricted to that of unofficial adviser. As he saw it, notwithstanding his early books that had made British authorities in India regard him with suspicion, MacDonald's views were extremely sound.[40] Moreover the prime minister understood the vital importance of detail. Each morning he met with a small group of officials at Number 10 Downing Street, discussed the day's business, and handed out documents for drafting. While Henderson was put in charge of the federal subcommittee, MacDonald grasped the nub of the problem and chaired the one on minorities. Like most of the Labour Party, Hailey thought, Wedgwood Benn was inclined to pay too much attention to the numerical majority of Hindus. Although they might have more heads, Hailey reminded him, resorting to a stereotype, Muslims "always showed their superiority when it came to breaking them" and that after all was "the ultimate sanction in politics."[41]

The communal problem also helped explain why provincial governors needed to have specifically defined powers. At Parliamentary question time, Hailey warned, for instance after a riot, it would not be enough to say that a minister's resignation had been requested. Perhaps it was as well, Hailey reported after what he called a deplorable fracas among the delegates at the prime minister's house at Chequers, that Labour ministers "should see India for once

---

[38] See report of the Indian Statutory Commission, PP, 1929–30 [Cmd. 3568–9, 3572], XI, XII; Irwin note on central government, August 1930, HPI/19B.

[39] Transcript of late November 1930, HPI/48. In this speech Hailey admitted candidly that Edwin Montagu had undoubtedly intended a good deal more progress toward responsible government at both the central and provincial levels than had actually taken place, warned that it was hard to overestimate the intensity with which Indians wanted recognition that they were not a subject country, and explained that federalism seemed a way out of the difficulty by providing the possibility of a conservative legislature the British could live with.

[40] See James Ramsay MacDonald, *The Awakening of India* (London: Hodder & Stoughton, 1910), and *The Government of India* (London: Swarthmore Press, 1919).

[41] Hailey to Irwin, 10 December 1930, HPI/34.

in its fez and dhoti [a loose lower garment, worn especially by male Hindus] instead of a top-hat and frock-coat."[42]

All told, Hailey confided, he had not worked as hard since long ago when he was in the secretariat at Calcutta – and at the end of the day he had to face an orgy of alcohol, spiced food, and still more voluble Indians. Although he got Christmas Day off, the next day he returned to help prepare MacDonald's concluding statement – "short and sufficiently indefinite to avoid difficult implications," saying that it was hoped to entrust the governance of India at all levels to executives responsible to legislatures, subject to safeguards during a transitional period of unspecified length – the sort of thing, he had already observed, that MacDonald did very well. The conference finally ended in the middle of January, after which Hailey went into hospital for an operation. Although no diagnosis of the affliction is available, both his history of kidney stone and his reticence in describing the symptoms – 9 December: "I have been rather bad with the complaint you know of." 18 February: "Owing to the delay I seem to have been badly poisoned." – suggest prostate or other blockage of the urinary tract. In any case he would have been in extreme pain for several months.[43]

Although such urological operations (if that is what it was) are now routine for older men, as of 1931 they were comparatively recent and difficult.[44] Hailey was unable to leave England until late in March, and even then it was against medical advice. He therefore observed from afar the dramatic Gandhi–Irwin pact of early March 1931, when the Mahatma suddenly asked to see the viceroy on the eve of the latter's retirement, and then negotiated an end to the civil-disobedience campaign with what seemed like amazing faith and patience.[45]

When Hailey returned many things would be much the same. In UP the slump in agricultural prices had worsened further. People at the India Office were so absorbed by the civil-disobedience movement, he had noted, "that they cannot realise that our real difficulty is really going to be agrarian."[46] Tenants were reportedly still withholding their rents, although it was hard to tell whether they were doing so for political reasons or because they were in fact unable to pay. Now, overnight, the political situation had altered entirely. Although Hailey knew he would be facing acute economic pressure, at least for the time being there would be something at least resembling political peace. Already, however, the Gandhi–Irwin settlement was being roundly condemned by both extremes:

---

[42] Hailey to Irwin, 15 December 1930, ibid. The meeting had shown the "worst side of Indian politics," MacDonald noted tersely in his diary; "India was not considered. It was communalism & proportions of reserved seats." Quoted by David Marquand, *Ramsay MacDonald* (London: Cape, 1977), pp. 581–2.

[43] Hailey to Sir George Lambert, 9 December 1930, HPI/19B; Hailey to Irwin, 18 February 1931, HPI/34.

[44] I very much appreciate the advice of Dr. John Grimes.

[45] See Sarvepalli Gopal, *The Viceroyalty of Lord Irwin, 1926–1931* (Oxford: Clarendon Press, 1957).

[46] Hailey to de Montmorency, 13 November 1930, HPI/19B.

by the Indian left as a sellout, by Churchill and other diehards as a nauseating spectacle.

"I think then this," Hailey wrote to Irwin from his nursing home: "If we were to have negotiations for peace at all, then it is a very successful result and a triumph for you," the obvious question being "whether we have not permanently injured ourselves by admitting Congress to the position of making a Treaty with us." Time would tell. But the Round Table Conference, and indeed the logic of the whole reform scheme ever since the Montagu declaration of 1917, had pointed toward negotiation, "and I cannot quite think of anyone else who could have carried it through."[47] Hailey doubted peace would last. So did Jawaharlal Nehru, in despair at having seen Gandhi suspend agitation once more just when it seemed to be approaching a climax. Was this how the world ended – not with a bang but a whimper?[48]

[47] Hailey to Irwin, 6 March 1931, Halifax Collection, MSS EUR C 152/19. "I agree with you that the big question is as you state it," Irwin replied, "namely, have we done damage by according the recognition to Congress involved in direct negotiation? I was fully alive to it, but I could not feel that, after everything that had happened at the Conference and since, any other course was open to me when Gandhi himself asked to see me. And I have always thought that discussion about peace terms would in some form and at some point become inevitable." Irwin to Hailey, 20 March 1931, HPI/34.

[48] Nehru, *Autobiography*, p. 259.

13

Governor of the United Provinces: 1931, year of crisis

Late in April 1931, disregarding doctor's advice that he needed six months to convalesce, Hailey returned to India. At once he was confronted by two crises: first, the aftermath of a horrible communal riot that had taken place in Cawnpore at the end of March; second, the catastrophic impact of the world-wide depression on the local agrarian economy. Also in April Irwin was replaced by Lord Willingdon, and though the new viceroy did not renounce the pact with Congress he was skeptical of it and intent on returning India to normalcy. Before the year was out civil disobedience would resume. The year 1931 would rank as one of the most intense, pivotal ones in the history of modern India. Although Hailey avoided public criticism of the acting governor, Sir George Lambert, who stayed on as finance member, he quickly became convinced that he had not returned a day too soon.

The Cawnpore riot had been triggered by the local Congress committee's pressure on Muslim merchants to observe hartal on 24 March, the day after the national hero Bhagat Singh was hanged in Lahore for the assassination of a Punjab police official. It was one of the worst communal conflicts of the entire interwar period, resulting in more than four hundred deaths and at least twelve hundred serious injuries. For four terrifying days, while individuals were murdered at random in alleyways and arsonists burned houses with people trapped inside them, the city was effectively in the hands of *goondas* (criminal elements) of both communities. Cawnpore was deserted and lifeless, British businessmen reported a week later, the people apprehensive and sullen. Plunder, arson, and slaughter had stopped, not because the strong arm of law had been reasserted, but because the mob had spent its energy.[1] Stating that the small police force had been overwhelmed by quite unpredictable circumstances, Lambert gave the local authorities a strong vote of confidence. As criticism mounted from all sides, however, he ordered a public inquiry. Naturally, Congress was holding one too.

By the time Hailey returned the press was printing long extracts from the

---

[1] Sir Thomas Smith and others to Lambert, 5 April, and Lambert to Smith, 10 April 1931, UP Police 1263/1931. The best account of the riot is the introduction to N. Gerald Barrier, ed., *Roots of Communal Politics*, pp. 8–27, the Congress report on the riot that was published and immediately banned in 1933.

official hearing, where Europeans and Indians alike were testifying to the savagery and the breakdown of control. Hindus charged the Muslim-dominated police with direct instigation or, at best, letting the two sides go to it. Muslims complained about Hindu magistrates. British military witnesses asserted that the police had been apathetic and dilatory, squatting idly while murder and arson were being committed in plain sight. Although the indiscriminate, decentralized pattern – little real fighting, isolated individuals slaughtered by small groups, women and children burned alive – to some extent accounted for the lack of police firing, Hailey realized that the evidence was irrefutable. Somehow that mob ought to have been stopped in those first crucial hours before the situation got out of hand.[2]

In the middle of May, in an action Indians appreciated and remembered, for he was obviously far from recovered, Hailey went down into the furnace of the plains. "The by-ways of Cawnpore are not very sweet smelling at the best of times," he reported, "and there still lingers a nasty odour about the houses in which corpses had been left for any length of time."[3] Talks with Muslim and Hindu deputations, worried British mill owners, and local officials all confirmed his judgment that civil authority had indeed broken down deplorably.[4] He was therefore prepared for the inquiry report, which censured the district magistrate, J. F. Sale, and found that the police had not done their duty. Those two conclusions, which followed inescapably from the widely publicized evidence, were common to both the official and the eventual Congress report. Where the two documents differed was on the long-range causes. The official version cited the atmosphere of lawlessness during the civil-disobedience campaign and the deterioration in police morale after the Gandhi–Irwin pact. The Congress report blamed the government's policy of divide and rule.[5]

Hailey's official reaction was a skillful if transparent exercise in damage control. He too pointed to the civil-disobedience movement. Not only had it aimed to paralyze government – was he admitting that it had succeeded? – but, especially in Cawnpore, Muslims had regarded it as an exclusively Hindu affair. He himself ought to have been tougher. It was one thing to allow fairly wide latitude to demonstrators in Allahabad or Lucknow, quite another in such a notorious mill town and cocaine-smuggling center. Noting that Sale had committed errors in judgment and had lost the confidence of both communities, Hailey abruptly removed him from office. But he refused to accept the sug-

---

[2] Hailey to Dawson, 26 April and Hailey to Willingdon, 27 April 1931, HPI/20.

[3] Hailey to Stephenson, 19 May 1931, ibid. A few days after his arrival he went riding, but overdid it. By the end of May he was able to work at normal pace, but not until January 1932 could he ride comfortably. See Hailey to de Montmorency, 29 April, and Hailey to Gwynn, 26 May 1931, ibid.; Hailey to Irwin, 2 January 1932, HPI/23A.

[4] Hailey note, 18 May 1931, UP Police 1263/1931.

[5] Barrier, *Roots of Communal Violence*. To Nehru's displeasure the report turned into a rambling treatise the object of which was to demonstrate that on the whole communal relations had historically been amicable. Although Nehru agreed with the thesis, he did not think a report on a riot the proper place to make the case. See note of 31 October 1931, SWJN, 5, 264–7.

gestion that the Gandhi–Irwin pact had so affected the police that it had neglected its duty.[6] Having expected only an ordinary demonstration, he concluded, the understrength force had simply been overwhelmed by an explosion of unforeseen ferocity.

Then citing what he called a compelling need to cut government expenditure, he postponed the June meeting of the Legislative Council. Announcing decisions quickly, he told Sale, had been essential for "the object which we had primarily in view, namely, to bring discussion on the matter to an end as soon as possible."[7] Nevertheless, controversy continued. Indians charged that the official inquiry and Hailey's resolution had been a whitewash. English diehards interpreted Hailey's statement as an attack on Irwin's appeasement of Congress. Like General Dyer, they alleged, Sale was being made a scapegoat. "I do not think I [had] quite probed the depths of iniquity of which English politicians are capable," Hailey fumed. If he had meant to criticize Irwin he would have said so.[8]

Did the horrifying pattern of indiscriminate carnage indicate a new kind of riot, an India Office official asked? It was much like Lahore in 1927, Hailey reflected, except that in the Punjab capital "the authorities got the upper hand from the first. That . . . is the real explanation of Cawnpore." The man on the spot had acted timidly, failing to alert the provincial government to the gravity of the situation. Knowing Sale to be earnest but indecisive the government ought to have sent a stronger man: "It was just the initial loss of control and failure to act promptly and decisively which produced such an appalling crop of murders."[9] Hailey omitted one obvious difference. In 1927 he himself had been on the scene.

∽∽∽∽∽∽∽

Late in May 1931, a few days after his visit to Cawnpore, Hailey had what seems to have been his only face-to-face confrontation with Mahatma Gandhi. Their meeting centered on the UP's economic crisis. Since the previous October, when Hailey had suddenly noticed a sharp downturn in agricultural prices just before he left for London, the situation had worsened. According to the price tables, using 1873 as the base-100 year, the general index had fallen from 203 (1929) to 171 (1930) and 127 (1931), while wheat had decreased from

[6] Resolution of 9 June 1931, HPI/21A.
[7] Hailey to Sale, 22 June 1931, ibid.
[8] Hailey to Brown, 1 July, and Hailey to O'Dwyer, 3 July 1931, ibid.
[9] Hailey to Stewart, 8 June 1931, ibid. Would Hailey's presence in UP have made any difference? Although local officials might well have been more confident that they would be backed if they took firm measures, the course of events on the crucial afternoon of the twenty-fourth would probably not have been affected, and he would not have been able to reach the city until at least the twenty-fifth. On the other hand, supposing he had realized the degree of danger, he would probably have sent in massive military reinforcements the previous evening with orders to fire on sight. My hunch is that it would have been a good deal worse than Lahore, but not as bad as it was.

262 (1929) to 172 (1930) and 134 (1931): a slump of about 50 percent over the two-year period.[10]

The agricultural economy of north-central India had long since been integrated into the capitalist world system. The government's land revenue and most rents were collected in money; cultivators had largely switched from subsistence to cash crops such as wheat, rice, and sugarcane. Yet the penetration of capitalism had not resulted in consolidation and the scale of production remained small. In Oudh and the overcrowded eastern section of Agra average holdings were 3 to 4 acres, compared with 5.5 to 10.5 in the somewhat less congested, better irrigated, more prosperous west. Even in normal times, the UP Banking Enquiry had reported just before the slump, the average peasant lived at or perilously near the margin of subsistence. All agrarian classes, zamindars as well as tenants, carried a huge and growing burden of indebtedness, 38 percent of which was classed as unproductive.[11]

The ruinous, cascading effects of the depression in a UP village are portrayed in Premchand's brilliant contemporary Hindi novel *Godan*.[12] Facing eviction if they defaulted on rents, tenants dug up coins, sold ornaments and farm animals. Some gave up, deserted holdings their families had farmed for generations, and joined the ranks of seasonal laborers. Well-to-do moneylenders harassed clients, humbler ones shared the fate of their debtors, and credit dried up. Struggling to maintain status zamindars mortgaged land still more heavily if they could manage to find a creditor, pressed their agents to collect rents more efficiently – and the agents squeezed the tenants. Merchants, laborers, railway workers, barbers: all classes and castes suffered. Emotions alternated between hopelessness and anger born of a sense of injustice. The depression was not just another act of God. It was man-made. The one bright spot was that, crops having become virtually unsalable, peasants may actually have eaten a little better.[13]

If rents could not be collected then the provincial government would go to the wall too. Under the zamindari system revenue was a fixed portion of rent, nominally 40 percent, although *nazrana* (entry) and illegal fees brought the rate down to about 30 percent. The government's ability to give direct relief to tenants was therefore limited. Over the three decades since 1900 rents had risen more than eight times faster than revenue, increasing dramatically during the boom of World War I. The land revenue was more than half the provincial government's income and it had no reserve. The result, a report of 1934 concluded, was that officials had been in no position and in no hurry to resolve the crisis. They had hoped it would go away.[14]

[10] Department of Commercial Intelligence and Statistics, Government of India, *Statistical Abstract for British India, 1924–1934* (Delhi: Govt. Printer, 1936), p. 816.
[11] Report on the Present Economic Situation in the United Provinces, 1933, HPI/29C.
[12] Dhanput R. Srivastava [Premchand], *Godan: The Gift of a Cow*, tr. Gordon C. Roadarmel (Bloomington: Indiana University Press, 1968).
[13] Jawaharlal Nehru, *An Autobiography*, pp. 277–8.
[14] A. A. Waugh, note, 30 August 1934, "Rent and Revenue Problems," HPI/29C.

In December 1930, while Hailey was away in England, facing the sharp, uncertain fall in prices and the short, intense rent strike, the government had remitted 10 lakhs of revenue, or about four annas in the rupee (R1 = 16 annas), an amount the 1934 report called hardly worth mentioning. By March 1931, however, the true gravity and likely duration of the slump had become evident. Pointing to the vast disparities as between different regions and classes of tenants, however, Sir George Lambert decided against general relief and restricted remissions to the neediest cases, whose rents were to be taken back to the level of 1915.[15] Despite the no-rent campaign of November 1930 through early March 1931, by the time Hailey returned coercive pressure by landlords' agents and police had succeeded in collecting about 75 percent of rent demands.

Now the trouble with this approach was very simple. The price index for wheat in 1915 had been 227. To find a year comparable to the figure of 134 for 1931 one had to go back to the turn of the century. Recalling that rents had risen faster than revenue, if those too were taken back to that level, then under the strictly proportionate remission formula on which the landlord-dominated legislature was insisting, the government would swiftly be reduced to bankruptcy. The more Hailey studied the problem the more brutally clear it became. Rent strike or no rent strike, if prices stayed where they were tenants would just not be able to pay. Moreover Congress leaders could do their sums as well as he could. They had staked out a position as a peasants' party and the no-rent campaign had given the freedom struggle for the first time a rural, truly national dimension. From their opposing perspectives Hailey and Nehru had alike concluded that the obsolete, fundamentally inequitable zamindari system provided a fertile field for sustained agitation. Gandhi's salt march had puzzled both men. Both of them had wondered why the obvious target was being neglected.

A few days after the Delhi settlement Nehru sent out another of his lucid circular letters. The Gandhi–Irwin pact was only a truce, he stressed, during which Congress must "consolidate the position gained . . . during the past year . . . in the rural areas."[16] Throughout the UP, district Congress committees inquired into conditions, reported atrocities, circulated form petitions on which peasants certified their inability to meet rents, sometimes negotiated compromises, and called on tenants to pay "what they could afford" – perhaps eight annas in the rupee. Was this not merely a no-rent campaign in a different form, Gandhi was asked? Although he could never give up Congress's primary function, the Mahatma replied, "to speak for and represent the peasantry," he agreed to have a frank talk with Hailey.[17] "I do not love the idea of negotia-

15 Lambert speech, 31 March 1931, UP LegCo Debates, *50*, 886 ff. For the rabi, or spring, harvest Rs. 60 lakhs were remitted in revenue, causing rents to be reduced by Rs. 207 lakhs. Waugh note, HPI/29C.
16 Letter to provincial committees, 10 March 1931, SWJN, *4*, 488–90. See also Pant to T. Sloan (Revenue Secretary), 20 March 1931, UP SR Rev. 465/1931.
17 H. W. Emerson note of interview, 7 April and Gandhi to Emerson, 9 April 1931, CWMG, *45*, 450–8, 404–5.

tions," Sir Malcolm observed, "but since we have made the Delhi Settlement I think we must work it for all it is worth and endeavour to get him to throw his weight against those who are now agitating the tenants."[18]

For the best of reasons Hailey delayed. Before meeting Gandhi, he explained, he needed to clear his conscience and convince himself "that we are not prosecuting people for giving what after all is only reasonable advice."[19] Rents were "undoubtedly high," he wrote in one of a series of private letters to the prime minister, Ramsay MacDonald. Peasants understood very well that only their agitation of 1921 had begun to raise them from their earlier positions as virtually helpless tenants at will, "liable to uncontrolled rack-renting by the landlord." Naturally they would perceive that renewed pressure would bring further rewards. Even if Congress recalled its volunteers tomorrow, the anti-landlord propaganda had already spread, and in any case tenants had minds of their own. "Our agrarian system is admittedly far from ideal," he admitted, "partly the result of historical growths, partly due to the congestion of population which has placed unusual power in the hands of landlords, who in return have done very little for tenants, and partly due to our own revenue system." In time "we may perhaps have to contemplate . . . making changes." But that "would involve not only a recasting of our own finances but the complete revision of the old standing relations between tenant and landlord."[20]

On 20 May 1931 Gandhi and Hailey had their meeting in Naini Tal. Both men evidently did their best to avoid anything that might increase hostility. The fact that the Mahatma stayed at a village on another mountain three miles off meant that people who came to do *darshan* (obeisance) to him caused little trouble. For his part Hailey waived the rules outlawing motor cars and the holding of demonstrations on the Mall, and had a hockey match postponed so a meeting could be held on the Flats. Gandhi was an arresting personality who put his case well, Hailey reported; "one has to think out three moves ahead when one is talking to him."[21] Hailey was one of India's strongest, most effective governors, was Gandhi's summation; if he wished he could be a force for justice.[22]

Hailey avoided the issue of whether the Gandhi–Irwin pact had recognized Congress's claim to represent the Indian people, stressing instead the danger that tenants would refuse to pay rents and resort to violence when landlords tried to collect: "I naturally quoted Chauri Chaura to him." Gandhi freely admitted the risk, denied Congress was still engaged in a subterranean no-rent campaign, and seemed aghast when shown evidence from one district that implied it. Congress was "quite opposed to the idea of actually starting a parallel government or anything of the kind," he declared. Although he argued that only effective cooperation from Congress would persuade tenants to pay, he

[18] Hailey to H.R.C. Hailey, 30 April 1931, HPI/20.
[19] Hailey to Emerson, 27 April 1931, ibid.
[20] Hailey to MacDonald, 17 May 1931, ibid.   [21] Hailey to Stewart, 20 May 1931, ibid.
[22] Gandhi interview on train to *Bombay Chronicle*, 29 August 1931, CWMG, *47*, 380.

could not promise that. Nor would he use his influence unless he had something more definite than a mere official announcement that remissions at a level to be determined by the government would be granted.[23] It is worth noting that at this stage neither Gandhi nor Nehru's briefing notes mentioned what would soon become the major plank in Congress's platform: "fair rent."

The government might simply accept Congress's figures, Gandhi suggested, or cooperate with Congress in a public inquiry. The problem was far too complex to fit any simple formula, Hailey replied. And the model Gandhi no doubt had in mind, the famous Champaran Commission of 1917 in Bihar that had resulted from his very first Indian satyagraha, was inappropriate for an entire province of 6 million tenants. Besides, inquiry would mean delay with the likelihood that no money would be obtained at all, and if peasants paid nothing this harvest they would be doubly hard to persuade next time. Surely the best course would be to proceed cautiously with collections, treating cases of genuine hardship with leniency. "We left the matter at that . . . not . . . very satisfactory conclusion," Hailey reported, "for I did not get his definite engagement."[24]

Three days after their meeting Gandhi sent a "Dear Friend" letter, enclosing a draft manifesto, "To the Kisans [tenants] of U.P." The no-rent campaign having definitely been called off, the draft declared, Congress was recommending rent reductions of eight annas for statutory and four for occupancy tenants. Although Congress was authorizing collections to start at once, he hoped that tenants unable to pay would be carried over until the next harvest, that those who had been ejected from their holdings would be reinstated, and that the government would make corresponding remissions to zamindars. Congress did not seek to harm zamindars or destroy property, the statement stressed: "We aim only at its lawful use." He hoped the governor would not find the manifesto embarrassing, Gandhi added privately. Although he had not been able to call the government's relief program sufficient, he had had to say something, and if Hailey could find a better way he would cooperate if he could. "I have arranged," the Mahatma concluded, "unless you would have me do otherwise, to leave Naini Tal this afternoon at 3 p.m."[25]

Gandhi "wanted to go down hill, and I did not want to stop him," Hailey put it, and he replied by return of courier. Although the draft manifesto had much to commend it, he wrote, especially its directives that tenants should start paying and avoid violence, he could not agree to an across-the-board reduction of 25–50 percent. Tenants would naturally take the minimum to be the maximum, and if rents did not come in now they would never be gathered at all. Collections were now under way and the results would be watched extremely

[23] Hailey note re conversation, 20 May 1931, HPI/20, printed in CWMG, *46*, 417–19. Chauri Chaura was the incident of 1922 in which two dozen policemen had been burned alive, after which Gandhi had suspended civil disobedience.

[24] Hailey to Stewart, 23 May 1931, HPI/20.

[25] Gandhi to Hailey, 23 May 1931, CWMG, *46*, 199–203.

carefully.[26] Avoiding the trap, he had been careful not to concede to Congress "the position of a kind of arbiter between tenants and landlords." Although the Mahatma would now publish his manifesto, at least he had not allowed himself to be sucked in. "One can easily see that if one begins any form of association," he added sarcastically, "one may be intrigued into perfectly dreadful developments; and I do not think that I am clever enough to enter into any sort of partnership with such a genius as he is."[27]

Yet Gandhi had given the impression that he thought Congress had established its position throughout India during the agitation, that it therefore had more to gain than lose by maintaining the truce, and that if it played its hand carefully it might "eventually succeed in swamping completely all other elements in politics," becoming the sole representative of India rather than merely one of the parties.[28] It was precisely that kind of recognition that Hailey was determined if possible to avoid.

And so, Gandhi having departed, rent collections proceeded, provoking confrontations between crowds of peasants, landlords' agents, and police officials – it was sometimes hard to tell the difference – numerous assaults, several murders, and frequent firing incidents. A full-fledged agrarian revolution seemed to be very close. "As the pressure of landlord plus government grew on the peasantry," Nehru wrote, "and thousands of tenants were ejected and had their little property seized, a situation developed which in most other countries would have resulted in a big peasant rising."[29] That of course was a partisan statement written by a man in jail. Gyanendra Pandey's detailed case studies of Agra and Rae Bareli districts have demonstrated persuasively, however, that the degree of violence and oppression that summer was indeed extraordinary.[30]

The evidence in the Hailey papers is largely consistent with his statement to Gandhi that, the adequacy of the government's rent-remission program being admittedly questionable, the collection process would be monitored carefully. "I have not tried to force the pace," he asserted, "because it seemed to me advisable to take advantage of the fact that there was less agitation in the east and west of the province." He wanted to avoid another Bardoli test case in the central zone, with tenants in other areas awaiting the result before paying up. Although he did not "expect to get through . . . without the outbreak of open trouble," he was trying to circumvent it.[31] Landlords would not be allowed "to suppose that we shall support them in collecting the last penny," he confided. "We shall confine our efforts to seeing that a good beginning is made and leave the landlords to adjust the rest with tenants."[32]

26 Hailey to Gandhi, 23 May 1931, HPI/20.
27 Hailey to de Montmorency, 24 May 1931, ibid.
28 Hailey to Lord Peel, 25 May 1931, ibid.
29 Nehru, *Autobiography,* pp. 277–8.
30 Gyanendra Pandey, *The Ascendancy of the Congress in Uttar Pradesh, 1926–1934: A Study in Imperfect Mobilization,* pp. 170–87.
31 Hailey to Dawson, 7 June 1931, HPI/20.
32 Hailey to Stewart, 8 June 1931, ibid.

Between the relatively benign, carefully regulated process described in Hailey's papers and the reign of terror reported by Congress sources and largely confirmed by Pandey there is an obvious discrepancy.[33] Perhaps the governor in his hill station did not know what was going on. Perhaps, like Henry II or Ronald Reagan, he sent signals his subordinates could conveniently "misinterpret." Perhaps in some places the situation simply got out of hand. Nehru naturally assumed that having got rid of Gandhi the government had changed its policy. A general campaign seemed to be in existence, he said in June after two months' absence, officials having joined big zamindars in a concerted effort to crush tenants and destroy Congress in the countryside, with the zamindars' agents doing most of the dirty work and officials giving the lead.[34] The government also suspected conspiracy. The climate of lawlessness during the civil-disobedience campaign had created a dangerous mentality among peasants, Hailey thought. Although Gandhi and other Congress leaders might have intended to observe the Delhi pact and avoid class war, the underlings were another matter and the antilandlord propaganda never really stopped.[35]

In July the chief secretary Jagdish Prasad read out to the Legislative Council an address for Hailey, who was laid up with the flu. It was the speech of a statesman, comparable to the one he had made to the Sikhs in 1925. The situation was grim: prices at the level of 1901–5 compared with inflated rents so that "the accepted foundation or existing rentals has more or less collapsed." The impact on the province's finances was extreme. Whereas a surplus of 23 lakhs had been projected, the remission program had produced a deficit of at least 175, it might well go higher, and all signs indicated that it would be recurring. Assuming the Council would provide statutory authority, Hailey asked – so far the state had been acting by executive decree – how should the problem be handled? Should existing rents be reduced to correspond with price changes? Should a minimum be set? Or should an effort be made to ascertain "a fair, full rental for each class of soil in different areas"? The last proposal, he added, would break sharply with tradition, substituting cumbersome tribunals for the self-regulating process of supply and demand. Or should the state

---

33 Although he did not deny this judgment of the prevalence of violence in eastern and central UP, Philip Mason stressed that in western districts where he was serving at the time the theme of class hatred could easily be overstated. "I spent much of the winters of 1930–32 in tents in the villages," he wrote, "and the scene was one of great peace; there were still cases of idyllic relationships between a small zamindar owning perhaps most of one or two villages and his tenants would go out and beat for him if he went shooting (and also give evidence for him in a dispute in the Law Courts), while he would protect them in a variety of ways."

34 Nehru to Jagdish Prasad, 27 June 1931, SWJN, 5, 96–8.

35 UP statement regarding no-rent campaign, 15 December 1931, HPI/29B. This was of course a retrospective analysis written after the Delhi settlement had broken down. It was, however, consistent with Hailey's private opinion at the time, as well as his speech of July to the Legislative Council. "The Congress leadership," wrote Pandey, most of whom were lawyers or zamindars, "hardly wished to see the world turned upside down, more especially when there was the possibility of settling important constitutional issues round the conference table." *Ascendancy of Congress*, p. 181.

simply rely on landlords to agree on reductions? That at least "would preserve the proper and traditional relations of landlord and tenants." But would all the landlords go along?

The government was being accused of joining landlords in a campaign of terrorism, Hailey concluded, but the breach of the Gandhi–Irwin pact would "not be from our side." What amounted to a Congress army had invaded the villages and, though he was not questioning the genuine sympathy of the leaders for the peasants, they might have been a bit more discreet. For "tenants, already intensely troubled by the economic stress, were told that landlords are parasites, that their only hope for the future is a peasants and workers republic which will abolish landlords, and that landlords who resist Congress now will be 'swept beyond the seven seas.'" Here was "a purely economic trouble which, if not properly handled, may lead to a social upheaval. Let us, in Heaven's name, keep politics out of it."[36]

Once again Hailey's private views were strikingly close to Nehru's. Land-lord–tenant relations were not exactly cordial at the best of times, he explained, for absentee landlords were essentially aliens, whereas tenants were often low-caste and treated as such. Indeed, "the East being what it is," landlords would actually be surprised if tenants paid up without coercion: "You may calculate the matter in terms of slaps to the rupee." And the landlords' compulsion in turn "reacts on Government, which I suppose is partly the result of our own unwisdom in claiming here all the position and attributes of God Almighty himself."[37]

Although he might have been surprised at the candor, Nehru would have accepted all that completely. And Sir Malcolm would have agreed with several of Nehru's later judgments: that in this extreme crisis the normal level of violence inevitably rose, that peasants reacted differently to natural and man-made catastrophes, that the raised consciousness of tenants and the presence of numerous Congress workers meant that incidents ordinarily confined within the village were broadcast to the world.[38] Hailey would also have endorsed Nehru's statement early in April that most of the difficulty had resulted from the inability of the UP government to make its mind up.[39] The blunt truth, Hailey observed, was that Congress had been badly hurt before the Gandhi–Irwin pact. But the UP agrarian problem had offered an inviting field, and the acting governor, Sir George Lambert, had been late in moving. While the government waffled Congress had stolen a march.[40]

Hailey agreed with Nehru on still another point. Although his Legislative Council speech had casually mentioned fair rent as a possibility, he had not urged radical changes in the zamindari system. Yet he understood very well that wholesale alterations were necessary and inevitable. Shortly before his speech

[36] 20 July 1931, UP LegCo Debates, *51*, 28 ff.
[37] Hailey to Gwynn, 10 September 1931, HPI/22.　　[38] Nehru, *Autobiography*, pp. 303–4.
[39] Nehru note, 18 April, and speech of 28 July 1931, SWJN, *5*, 70–8, 105–6.
[40] Hailey to Dawson, 15 August 1931, HPI/21B; also Hailey to Crerar, 2 May 1931, HPI/20.

he had sent to the Dominions Office in London for a stack of books. He was reading up the history of Irish land law.

In the late summer of 1931 the fragile truce seemed to be collapsing. UP was not the only problem. Bengal had an upsurge in terrorism, there were repeated firings on Abdul Ghaffar Khan's Red Shirts in North-West Frontier Province, and the Bardoli test case persisted in Bombay. Ostensibly the focus was Gandhi's negotiation with the viceroy, Lord Willingdon, on whether he would go to the second Round Table Conference. If not, then a renewal of civil disobedience seemed likely. The Government of India sent to London a batch of emergency ordinances it had prepared just before the Gandhi–Irwin pact amounting, as one official put it, to civil martial law.[41] Using the Labour government's anxiety for his attendance as a bargaining chip Gandhi delayed his departure. Late in August Congress leaders met Willingdon in Simla. If necessary, Hailey advised, he would agree to an independent inquiry into the UP agrarian problem.

It proved not to be necessary, for Gandhi made Bardoli his sticking point, letting Hailey off the hook. "There was an immense field for him in this province," Sir Malcolm sighed with relief, "and if had seriously settled down in our midst . . . he would have found a great deal of material with which he could have made most efficient play."[42] Throughout the summer Hailey's object had "been to ride him off the UP. I was delighted when he got wrapped up in his funny little problem about his eleven little villages in Gujarat; I was still more delighted when he went home [England]." It was "the mercy of heaven that they have concentrated on a tahsil in Bombay when they might have been playing havoc with six or seven million tenants in the U.P."[43] To all of which Nehru would have agreed emphatically.[44]

By the time Gandhi reached London a severe sterling crisis had brought down the Labour minority government, which was replaced by a coalition. Although MacDonald was still prime minister the cabinet was dominated by Conservatives, including Sir Samuel Hoare as secretary of state. During the summer the Mahatma had been able to exploit Labour's belief that Congress's cooperation was essential. He could no longer do that. At the Round Table Conference he pleaded his case eloquently. In London's East End, as well as in Lancashire where the Indian boycott had exacerbated depression and unemployment in the cotton industry, he scored publicity successes. Communal

---

[41] D. Anthony Low, "'Civil Martial Law': The Government of India and the Civil Disobedience Movements, 1930–34," in Low, ed., *Congress and the Raj: Facets of the Indian Struggle, 1917–1947* (London: Arnold-Heinemann, 1977), pp. 165–98.

[42] Hailey to Gwynn, 10 September 1931, HPI/22.

[43] Hailey to Haig, 10 October 1931, ibid. On the authority of Sir Frederick Pedler, who was Hailey's private secretary in the Congo and during his first African tour in the early 1940s, Robert D. Pearce, *The Turning Point in Africa: British Colonial Policy 1938–48* (London: Cass, 1982), p. 43, asserted that Hailey helped persuade Gandhi to attend the Round Table Conference. Although Sir Frederick told me the same thing, he was unable to identify his source (i.e., whether it was Hailey himself), and I do not believe the evidence supports it.

[44] See Nehru's extremely guarded press statement, 31 August 1931, SWJN, *5*, 18–9.

rivalry was still there for the government to exploit, however, and he got no-where.

Meanwhile the UP agrarian crisis continued to simmer. Now that they had managed to collect most of their rents through government assistance, Hailey reported, landlords were predictably complaining that they need never have been reduced at all. After firming up slightly prices fell again. Obviously the next harvest would see still more remissions. The Legislative Council's agrarian committee invited the Congress leader Govind Ballabh Pant to join, but he refused to be co-opted. In September Congress published its own report, calling the government's relief program pitiful, describing numerous atrocities by landlords' agents, and advocating a concept so far only hinted at: fair rent.[45] Politically the situation was tense but quiet. Although they were being squeezed ever harder, Nehru reported to Gandhi, peasants seemed fatalistic.[46]

If wholesale evictions and beatings continued, Congress leaders threatened, tenants and therefore the Congress itself would have to resort to satyagraha whether Gandhi was present or not. The truce had been only "a phase of the fight," Nehru said, "a change of tactics."[47] The Legislative Council's agrarian committee recommended an increase in relief but no major changes. Rent notices were being distributed, and some tenants were being warned that re-missions would be canceled unless full payment was received within a month. Collections for the kharif, or autumn, harvest were due to begin on 1 December. Pointing out that a different formula was being used there, the local Congress committee of Allahabad district asked the president, Vallabhbhai Patel, for permission to begin satyagraha. Nehru cabled Gandhi that "decision likely have far-reaching consequences but question payment or withholding payment must be decided soon. Vital urgent problem for kisans admitting no delay."

"You should unhesitatingly take necessary steps meet every situation," Gandhi replied, adding ambiguously: "Expect nothing here."[48] Nehru warned the viceroy that tenants in Allahabad district might have to be advised not to pay pending negotiations for relief. Not only should remissions be larger but they should be calculated on an entirely different basis: fair rent.[49] On 23 October the kisan conference at Allahabad formally approved a no-rent resolution. Congress had put the machinery in motion. It was up to the UP government.

Meanwhile, having gone through the books from the Dominions Office,

45 UP Congress Committee, *Agrarian Distress in the United Provinces* (1931; reprinted New Delhi: Prabhu, n.d.).
46 Nehru to Gandhi, 1 September 1931, SWJN, 5, 28–30.
47 Patel to Emerson, 15 September, NML, AICC G7/1931; Nehru speech, 24 September 1931, SWJN, 5, 128.
48 Cables of 15–16 October 1931, ibid., 5, 155. When Gandhi's cable was intercepted the last sentence was read as meaning that he had already decided the Round Table Conference would fail. He said it meant only that he could not make a decision on agrarian problems in UP from London.
49 Nehru to Mieville (PSV), 16 October, NML, AICC, G7/1931. Nehru speeches at kisan conference, Allahabad, 23 October 1931, SWJN 5, 162–3.

Hailey had written a comparative note on Irish land law. He found the parallels striking. As in UP, Irish landlord–tenant relations had traditionally been regulated by custom rather than by contract. Asserting the doctrine of free trade on behalf of absentee English landlords, early-nineteenth-century Parliaments had whittled away at the rights of tenants, so that by the time of the potato famine of the 1840s they had possessed essentially none at all. That was the basis of Ireland's agrarian problem. The long depression that began in the 1870s and the simultaneous agitation of the Land League had forced from Parliament a series of acts giving tenants what were called the three *F*'s – fixity of tenure, free sale, and fair rents. Eventually tribunals had defined fair rent as "how much an occupying tenant working the holding with reasonable skill and industry could make out of the farm."

That definition, Hailey noted, was very close to that of Gandhi, who had said that fair rent would be a reasonable percentage of any surplus above the costs of subsistence and production. In retrospect, once the three F's had been attained, the other steps in the Irish sequence now seemed natural and inevitable. A land commission was created and Parliament was further compelled to give tenants the chance to gain proprietary rights. An act of 1903 enabled the commission to purchase estates and transfer them to tenants, who bought their holdings by making annuity payments into a sinking fund that in turn financed further acquisitions.

Once the state began to intervene in landlord–tenant relations, Hailey asked, was there any point at which the sequence ending in the abolition of the landlord system could be stopped? So far the UP had reached only the first stage, the recent Tenancy Acts having involved the state in regulating rents, which landlords could raise only at specified intervals. Although the depression was forcing the government to intervene further, so far it had deliberately avoided anything beyond a simple formula comparing existing rents to price levels. For any scheme enabling tenants to buy their holdings gradually, however, the calculation of fair or economic rents would be essential. The state could not invest huge sums "based on rack rents which could not be collected at all or collected only under constant pressure," he pointed out, implicitly admitting the massive structural oppressiveness of the whole zamindari system. Yet the Irish Free State now contained only 1.5 million cropped acres, compared with 35 million acres under cultivation and 6–7 million tenants in his own province. "Heaven forbid that in our own time we should have to fix 'economic' rents," he concluded. "But will our successors be able to resist their demand?"[50]

---

[50] Hailey note, 28 October 1931, HPI/22. Hailey's main source was Richard R. Cherry, *The Irish Land Law and Land Purchase Acts* (3rd ed.; Dublin: Falconer, 1903). Although this is not the place to pursue the point in detail, Hailey's note embodies an earlier interpretation differing sharply from that of recent historians of Ireland, who have argued that absentee landlordism was far less significant *economically* than used to be supposed. Rents tended to be uneconomic, while middling Irish farmers (who operated on narrower margins and who were tenants themselves)

The question was rhetorical. By 1931 Hailey already knew how it would all come out: the UP tenancy act of 1937, the zamindari abolition committee of 1946 leading to the end of the system with compensation in 1952, court challenges being finally resolved in the early 1960s. His Irish note fully confirms Nehru's assertion that Sir Malcolm realized the zamindari system "cannot work and . . . is collapsing," that "this system is utterly divorced from modern conditions and is bound to topple over because of its inherent instability. All the world over one can see this process going on."[51]

In public, of course, Hailey was saying exactly the opposite. Arguing that large-scale changes could not be undertaken during an emergency – although his own analysis of the Irish story showed that only a crisis could produce the necessary energy – he made no move whatever toward developing a land-purchase scheme. Instead he called that "a doctrine of defeatism. My object is to seek a means by which we can defer even the thought of it for a couple of generations." Again Nehru understood the reason perfectly. Landlords "are at the moment the one class which is pre-eminently interested in the British connexion," Hailey wrote in 1933, and the fact "that their motives are interested does not impair the strength of their feelings."[52] Even if they were compensated fairly, land purchase would eliminate the landlords as a class. Although they might be decadent, although they might at times be fractious and troublesome, they happened to be the only friends in sight. Having peered into the bleak future of his allies, the governor returned to what his own analysis and logic had shown him must ultimately be a losing battle to preserve them.

When his officials met the Congress negotiators early in November, they encountered a demand that rent remissions be doubled. In fact, Hailey sensed, the Congress was quite uninterested in figures at all. Instead the representatives were insisting that the state create tribunals to determine fair rents, pending which the tenants should withhold payments. "We might as well announce at once that no rents should be paid on *kharif* at all," he declared.[53] These

---

were more likely to evict than big English landlords; the poorest rural Irish were not tenants but landless laborers; landlords were a target primarily for political reasons, not because they were particularly rapacious but because they were English. See particularly Barbara L. Solow, *The Land Question and the Irish Economy, 1870–1903.* (Cambridge, MA: Harvard University Press, 1971), Cormac O Gráda, *Ireland Before and After the Famine: Explorations in Economic History, 1800–1925* (Manchester, U.K.: Manchester University Press, 1988), and T. W. Moody et al., eds., *A New History of Ireland* (Oxford: Clarendon Press, 1976–), vol. 5. The relationship between Irish and Indian land legislation would repay much closer study. See Clive J. Dewey, "Celtic Agrarian Legislation and the Celtic Revival: Historicist Implications of Gladstone's Irish and Scottish Land Acts, 1870–1886," *Past and Present,* No. 64 (August 1974), 30–70.

51 Nehru press statement, 20 December 1931, and Nehru to Sir Rampal Singh (Oudh taluqdar), 5 November 1931, SWJN, 5, 309–10, 170–2. See also Nehru to J. T. Gwynn (the *Manchester Guardian* correspondent who was also a correspondent of Hailey), 2 November 1933, SWJN, 6, 52–7: "The zamindari system . . . is hard hit. The British Government is in a quandary. Politically it supports the zamindars in order to draw them to itself. Economically the zamindars are a nuisance to government and are no longer required . . . and yet for reasons of state policy he has to be patted on the back."

52 Hailey note, 27 June 1933, HPI/32A.   53 Hailey to Crerar, 9 November 1931, HPI/22.

demands were not intended to be met, he concluded. Were Gandhi's lieutenants deliberately creating a confrontation from which the Mahatma would be unable to extricate himself when he returned from England?[54] Yet the 1 December deadline was as crucial to Nehru as it was to Hailey. If the government succeeded this time in collecting rents at a level of remissions Congress had maintained was insufficient, tenants would be demoralized. The effort to make Congress a strong peasant party would be weakened or even destroyed.

Late in November the Allahabad district committee of Congress advised tenants to hold back rents pending negotiations. Hailey suspended discussions until that advice was withdrawn. But he did not take the further step of putting emergency powers into effect. Collections would not begin until 1 December, he pointed out. The provincial Congress committee would meet shortly afterward, it just might back down, and in any case he wanted the issue to be as clear as possible. Until an all-out no-rent campaign was actually launched, he advised, he could hold out. Both the British and Indian governments, he reasoned, would want to postpone open conflict at least until the Round Table Conference in London was over.[55]

It turned out that Hailey's superiors were at least as bellicose as Congress. In the event of a direct challenge, secretary of state and viceroy agreed, "an effective reply should be given at the first possible moment."[56] On 5 December the UP Congress committee approved withholding rents in four districts pending negotiations. Although Hailey would have been willing to wait a bit longer, New Delhi urged him on. The issue was still not as clear as he would like, he reflected. Whereas the campaign of 1930 had unambiguously aimed to bring down the government, this time "Congress is ostensibly advising people not to pay . . . until adequate reductions have been made . . . to meet the economic situation. In many European countries there would be some hesitation in penal-

---

54 Nehru's denial of the charge that he and other Congress leaders acted behind Gandhi's back strikes me as persuasive (*Autobiography*, pp. 286–92). He also maintained that "the U.P. Committee never started a no-tax campaign in 1931," and that even if it had, the peasants were acting defensively for economic reasons (ibid., pp. 298–9). In a judiciously argued and impressively documented chapter, Sarvepalli Gopal, *Jawaharlal Nehru: A Biography*, 3 vols. (Delhi: Oxford University Press, 1975–), 1:154–71, largely supported Nehru's version, arguing that Willingdon and Emerson helped Hailey overcome his initial misgivings. Robin J. Moore, *The Crisis of Indian Unity, 1917–1940* (Oxford: Clarendon Press, 1974), p. 243, concluded that "Jawaharlal was spoiling for a fight. He would leave Gandhi as little opening as possible to pursue the way of co-operation." Judith M. Brown, *Gandhi and Civil Disobedience: The Mahatma in Indian Politics, 1928–34*, pp. 267–71, stressed Nehru's fear lest Congress should lose its position with the peasantry. It seems to me that Nehru was trying to avoid abandoning the tenants with whom he sympathized and whose support he understood to be vital for Congress, but that he probably did not intend an all-India confrontation at this point. As Hailey suggested, what Nehru wanted was a limited and protracted test case, another Bardoli, and that concerned Sir Malcolm a good deal more than outright civil disobedience.

55 Hailey to de Montmorency, 3 December 1931, HPI/22.

56 Quoted by Low, "Civil Martial Law," pp. 172–3. Although Hoare had found Gandhi friendly "there was not a dog's earthly of satisfying his demand." Hoare to Willingdon, 3 December 1931, quoted by Brown, *Gandhi and Civil Disobedience*, p. 252.

ising an agitation on such grounds." His case would be that Congress's action was "tainted by political motives" and that agitation would foment class war.[57]

On 13 December the UP ordinance was promulgated, providing sweeping powers against no-rent agitation and propaganda. On the seventeenth Willingdon laid out his plans. Formally the government would wait for the Congress working committee's meeting of the twenty-ninth, just after Gandhi's return, unless Congress took any one of a list of steps. It took most of them. By the time Gandhi arrived in Bombay a number of leaders had already been arrested. The working committee declared civil disobedience. Willingdon refused to see the Mahatma unless he disavowed his comrades, and Gandhi too went to jail.

"The Delhi Pact . . . is dead and gone," Willingdon crowed, wiping off his own hands, "murdered by Jawaharlal and Abdul Ghaffar [Khan]."[58] Irwin's approach "was a good thing only if it was successful," was Hailey's less gleeful verdict. Because it had not succeeded "I suppose therefore we must agree that it was a mistake."[59] He was less definite about who had held the knife. Gandhi had probably intended, after his fashion, to cooperate, but "elements here . . . had been more or less deliberately attempting to force his hand." Yet Hailey admitted that the Congress working committee had controlled neither the Bengal terrorists nor the Red Shirts in North-West Frontier Province. The central directorship *had* identified closely with the rural movement in UP and, although he could not make quite up his mind whether the decision had been intended as a declaration of hostilities, had given local committees their heads. On the other hand Congress had surely not expected the government to react so quickly. Although he himself had hesitated, he divulged to Irwin, "I may say in confidence that the Government of India did not share my doubts."[60]

This time there was no ambiguity about the signals. "Congress is being hit hard and straight," a junior official wrote home. Although that official's own area, Rae Bareli, the center of agitation in 1921 and recently a special target of Nehru's, remained surprisingly quiet, "tenants are not paying their rents, partly no doubt to be attributed to financial stress, but they are going to be made to all right."[61] Employing the sweeping emergency powers, Hailey reported late in December, he had prohibited meetings and made some arrests. But he was not really having much trouble. By and large tenants were paying up, apparently demonstrating – though of course the reasoning was circular – the sufficiency

---

57 Hailey to Mieville, 6 December 1931, HPI/22. The widely published statement of 15 December 1931, is in HPI/29B. Privately, then, Hailey did not directly contradict Nehru's argument that Congress had not in fact launched a no-rent campaign in 1931. Nehru speech, 20 December 1931, and Nehru to K. M. Munshi, 29 April 1940, SWJN, 5, 309–10 579–80; *Autobiography*, pp. 311–12. I think there was a campaign, but that Nehru and the Congress hoped to keep it local, low-key, and protracted – in other words, a Bardoli.
58 Willingdon to Hoare, 26 December 1931, Moore, *Crisis*, pp. 246–7.
59 Hailey to Hirtzel, 22 December 1931, HPI/22.
60 Hailey to Irwin, 2 January 1931, HPI/23A.
61 A. P. Hume letter home, 18 December 1931, Hume Collection, IOL, MSS EUR D. 724/3.

of the government's rent remissions.[62] At the moment, he judged, even Congress workers themselves seemed to have little enthusiasm. Except for a couple of districts, he stated a month later, the no-rent campaign no longer existed.[63] Although Nehru later claimed that tenants were actually more active and disciplined than earlier – what was different was the severity of government repression – his fear that successful collections would demoralize them and weaken Congress's position in rural areas seemed to have been fully justified.[64] As an official report put it later, "when at last Congressmen definitely launched their 'no-rent' campaign in the autumn of 1931, they found, not for the first time, that they had 'missed the bus.' "[65]

Hailey was winning. As he began what he supposed would be his last year of service, however, he was depressed. The government's mentality disturbed him. Although the challenge could not have been avoided, he wrote, "as soon as the fight begins we once again get into an atmosphere of militarism in which the only objective is the destruction of the enemy. But in a civil contest one does not destroy the enemy and has ultimately to find some way of resuming the decencies of life with him." The judgment that, after all the angry rhetoric and violence that had gone on during this long and eventful year, this was still a civil contest is both striking and questionable. (The best evidence for it is the degree of personal respect which, after all, these adamant opponents still maintained for one another.)[66] To Hailey the long-term prospect remained as grim as ever. Where would loyalists and moderates, weakened by their long dependency, still under the delusion that the government would always be there to protect them, be in five years' time? Congress could be beaten this time and the vacuum might perhaps be filled in thirty to forty years. But the constitution under a new Government of India Act, providing provincial autonomy and supposedly leading toward a full-fledged federal dominion, was to take effect in 1935.[67]

Hailey's dark, introspective mood was reflected in a remarkable letter written to, of all people, Katherine Mayo, the American author of a controversial exposé of Indian sexual mores which Indians called "that filthy book."[68] The

---

62 Hailey to de Montmorency, 23 December 1931, HPI/22.
63 Hailey to Stewart, 19 January 1932, HPI/23A.
64 *Autobiography*, p. 331.
65 Waugh note, 30 August 1934, HPI/29C.
66 Although numerous quotations could be introduced in support, I shall restrict myself to one example. In 1934 Nehru was moved to a prison in UP so that he might see his wife, Kamala, who was suffering from tuberculosis; eventually he was released so that he might accompany her to Germany, where she died. In November he wrote to discountenance efforts to gain his release, adding that "I am very grateful to the Provincial Government for the facilities that have been granted to me during the last three months for spending some days with my wife, seeing her occasionally later on, and receiving reports of her condition. I am particularly grateful to Sir Malcolm Hailey for the personal interest he has taken in the matter. It was very good of him to direct, as I learnt later, that everything should be done to facilitate my wife's journey to Bhowali." Nehru to Jagdish Prasad, 5 November 1934, SWJN, 6, 301–2. On the whole each man recognized that the other had a job to do.
67 Hailey to Irwin, 2 January 1932, HPI/23A.
68 See Katherine Mayo, *Mother India* (London: Cape, 1927), a lurid and sensational account of cruel practices, which the author ascribed entirely to child marriage and caste, although they are

British were "rather a timid administration," he admitted, awed by being an alien government and therefore much too cautious in dealing with questions affecting religion or social customs, "mistrustful of our civilization, or careless in the face of things which we knew to be involving great misery" to India's millions. Compared with the robust Christianity of some of their predecessors his own generation had copped out, leaving India to improve itself. Yet, he continued in the vein of his Allahabad convocation address of 1928, Indian intellectuals were wholly preoccupied with political questions. They had not really confronted the problem either.

That was perhaps why Mayo's *Mother India* had so shocked both officials and Indians. The book had shattered a conspiracy of silence, revealing much "we both of us were uniting, perhaps from different motives, to keep somewhat in the background." In such a heated atmosphere "you certainly presented to the world, in a form which could not escape its attention, the fact that we were both neglecting fundamentals." Mayo had "hit us both, but undoubtedly you hit India hardest; for what you revealed of Indian institutions and character was the gravest blow to its party of advance at what they felt to be an inopportune moment," the review by the Simon Commission. Although on balance he believed she had done good, the long uphill battle to raise the status of women had barely begun.

abundant in all and certainly in British or American societies. She drew some of her most shocking material from evidence provided by Indian social reformers during the debate on the Sarda Act of the late 1920s, which raised the age of consent to fourteen. The discussion of her book coincided with the Simon Commission's tour of India, leading Indians to charge that British officials had conspired to prejudice Anglo-American opinion against them. See Manoranjan Jha, *Katherine Mayo and India* (New Delhi: People's Publishing House, 1971). Mayo had already written a book on American administration in the Philippines, with a preface by Hailey's friend Lionel Curtis, who perhaps suggested she write to the governor. In January 1925 (HPI/9A), realizing the importance of influencing American opinion, Hailey replied encouragingly. In November she and a friend turned up in London, where the Foreign Office described them as being interested in promoting "a good understanding between England and America" (FO to Home Department, Government of India, 4 November 1925, HomPol 40/1926). When she toured the Punjab early in 1926 Hailey directed that she be given all possible support. "I cannot but believe that the glorious truth of Britain's attitude & achievement in this dark country must shine through," she wrote after leaving; "my mind is full of reverence & pride, in the beauty of what Englishmen are doing here" (Mayo to Hailey, Lucknow, 15 February 1926, HPI/9A) – which must have made Sir Malcolm fairly confident that her account might be at least mildly favorable. In August 1927, her book now published, she feared she might have overdone it: "Perhaps 'Mother India' is abhorrent to you, in India. . . . I know she is hideous. Her first sections are made of the very stuff that I have most keenly avoided, in thought & word, all my previous life." But she could *not* avoid, she said, and above all she had tried to be clear (Mayo to Hailey, 18 August 1927, HPI/11A). (In fact she succeeded in removing any evidence of avoidance, and lack of clarity was not among the book's shortcomings.) On the conspiracy thesis, the evidence indicates that Hailey and other officials were indeed attempting to influence American opinion in Britain's favor. When Mayo's tour was being arranged in 1925, however, the statutory commission was still supposedly four years away. Gandhi called the book a "drain inspector's report" that Westerners should avoid although Indians should read it intensely (CWMG, *34*, 539–47). Nehru said that, although her writing was full of transparent overstatements and outright falsehood – individual cases being taken as typical – the kernel of truth hurt (SWJN, *3*, 395–400).

"As I grow older," Hailey reflected, "I see more and more the immense difficulties of our position." The British were trying to transfer "liberal institutions . . . largely based on the experiences of an industrial people" to a "vast agricultural population which lacks the facility for the rapid formation of mass feeling on which such institutions must depend." (Did not the civil-disobedience movement refute that argument?) Given a clean slate they might well choose to retrace their steps and "attempt to build up a new India based on the essentials of its own conditions." But "we should have to build a wall round India and ask the world not to look over it for another hundred years."

At present "we are once more engaged in fighting an agitation for civil disobedience," he continued. "I suppose that the world . . . must look on this . . . with something like amazement." Having welcomed Gandhi to the Round Table Conference and promised responsible government, "within a month we are putting every member of Congress in prison by means of regulations, ordinances and all manner of things that to the outside world must reek of the middle ages." This was not the government's choice, he insisted, Congress having forced the confrontation "by a singular combination of conceit, futility and unreasonableness." The trouble was that Britain was "entirely devoid of any real solution for the future." The conflict "would be not only justifiable but even salutary if we felt that there were any prospect that we were creating in India a strong and responsible body of opinion which under the new constitution would take over the fight from us and show itself determined to suppress all these subversive doctrines."[69] As Sir Malcolm Hailey's Irish note showed he understood thoroughly, however, that was quite unlikely to happen.

[69] Hailey to Mayo, 10 January 1932, HPI/23A. It is interesting that he read *Mother India* as a criticism of British rule rather than an apologia; it troubled his conscience. See also Hailey to Eleanor Rathbone, 16 April 1934, HPI/27B, Labour MP and author of a book on child marriage that Indian reformers did not find objectionable.

14

〰〰〰〰〰〰〰〰〰〰〰〰〰〰〰〰〰〰〰〰〰〰〰〰〰

Governor of the United Provinces: winding down, 1932–1934

At an Indian Civil Service dinner in Lucknow in February 1932 Hailey spoke of trying times just past and still more difficult ones ahead. Although he noted that the current civil-disobedience campaign was being contained successfully, within two or three years the new constitution would bring provincial autonomy and an extension of popular institutions. By then either a strong and responsible conservative party dedicated to maintaining the British connection would have been constructed or power would have to be handed over to a Congress controlled by its left wing. If Providence decreed the second alternative, then he hoped England would recognize that the work of their great and noble service was finished: "It must march out with the honours of war, with its flag still flying. . . . If that be the manner of our ending, then it will be no unfitting end."[1] Such a defeatist outlook was all very well for famous old men at the end of their careers, one of his audience grumbled later.[2]

Compared with 1930, Hailey judged, 1932 was a damp squib.[3] The difference in government policy must be stressed, for whereas in 1930 repression had built up gradually, now the mailed fist struck hard from the first. As Gandhi wrote in despair, the array of special ordinances made it virtually impossible to sustain the sort of popular, open, quasi-legal, nonviolent movement Congress represented.[4] A measure of the continuing threat was that in June 1932 Hailey listed twenty districts where he thought the no-rent campaign would reappear in strength if emergency powers were withdrawn.[5] Although the 1934 elections would demonstrate once more Congress's recuperative powers, by the summer of 1932 the confrontation had degenerated into a stalemate.

On the government side what Hailey called the general staff mentality persisted. Having joined battle with Congress, wrote the Conservative secretary of

---

[1] Speech of 4 February 1932, HPI/48.
[2] A. P. Hume to his parents, 3 September 1932, Hume Collection, IOL MSS EUR D 724/4.
[3] See Judith M. Brown, *Gandhi and Civil Disobedience: The Mahatma in Indian Politics, 1928–34*, pp. 292–9, and Gyanendra Pandey, *The Ascendancy of the Congress in Uttar Pradesh, 1926–1934: A Study in Imperfect Mobilization*, pp. 192–3. Contradicting Hailey's assertion that the no-rent campaign practically did not exist, however, most of the prisoners in UP were tenants and agricultural laborers.
[4] Statement of 11 March 1932, CWMG, 49, 190–3.
[5] Hailey note, 24 June 1932, UP HomPol 1911/1932.

state, Sir Samuel Hoare, the government must make clear it meant to push on to victory. Then what, asked the Labour prime minister, Ramsay MacDonald? Would a time come when talks with Gandhi were resumed? Or must he be kept in prison more or less indefinitely while the government went on smashing Congress? Anything resembling negotiations, the viceroy Lord Willingdon maintained, would upset the government's Indian supporters and shake the confidence of the police and army.[6] He was pursuing what he called a dual policy: pulverize Congress and proceed with constitutional advance on Britain's own terms. Hailey remained uncomfortable. "We may drift into the condition of Ireland," he worried, "where we had an insurgent left wing fighting the Executive and the great mass of public opinion disinterested and demoralised!"[7]

Yet Hailey also shrank from the logical alternative, another pact with Gandhi, for there was really nothing the government could offer the Congress left wing. Nehru seemed not to be thinking about "responsible government at all," Hailey thought. "His ambition is some form of Leninism in which intellectuals of his type would exercise power for the benefit of the masses but without the necessity of depending on the votes of the landed or middle classes."[8] Attacking Congress was not enough, Hailey reiterated. The government must strive to create a well-organized party capable of dominating the legislatures and taking office under the new constitution.

Using the threat of a renewed no-rent campaign and Nehru's socialist program as targets, at countless meetings Hailey preached the same theme: The new constitution was coming sooner than they realized; the victors in the first election would have the advantage; people like themselves with a stake in the country, national patriots who differed with Congress only on methods, must organize. But landlords and other loyalists resembled the chessplayers in Premchand's short story of mid-nineteenth-century Lucknow, too absorbed by the game on the board to take in the fact that they were in mortal danger on a real battlefield, maintaining a "pathetic belief that somehow or other . . . there will be a 'government' which will come to their aid."[9] A generation ago, before the historic split of 1907, Congress had been pursuing what at least in retrospect

---

6 Hoare to Hailey, 9 February 1932, HPI/23A; MacDonald to Willingdon, 31 March 1932, quoted by D. Anthony Low, "'Civil Martial Law': The Government of India and the Civil Disobedience Movements, 1930–34," p. 177.

7 Hailey to Dawson, 21 February 1932, HPI/23A.

8 Hailey to Hoare, 28 February 1932, ibid., reporting a discussion with the historian Edward J. Thompson, a close friend of the Nehrus; see Thompson to Hailey, 25 February, ibid. Although Hailey's use of the Leninism label was intended to be abusive, Nehru was in fact attracted to the Russian model. Moreover a directorate composed of Congress intellectuals was reasonably close to the situation during the first couple of decades after independence in 1947. Under the circumstances it is hard to see how it could have happened otherwise, the remarkable thing being that democracy has worked as long and as well as it has. Hailey did not of course foresee, and there is no reason to think Jawaharlal did either, what in fact transpired: a Nehru dynasty unto the third generation.

9 Hailey to Seton, 2 February 1932, HPI/23A. See Dhanput R. Srivastava [Premchand], *The Chess-Players*, tr. Gurdial Mallik (New Delhi: Orient, 1967). The comparison with Premchand is my own.

struck the governor as quite reasonable objectives: Indianization of the army and bureaucracy, gradual transfer of power to representative legislatures, local control over finance and tariffs. In contrast the Congress of the 1930s was being driven by the acute discontent of the lower middle class, "educated just enough to be conscious of the fact that it has poor standards of living and poor opportunities of improving them." These social dynamics had "very dangerous possibilities."[10]

The effort to build a conservative party would come to nothing unless landlords could be restored to financial solvency and local power. Could rural areas be controlled any longer without special powers? asked the home member, the Nawab of Chhatari, who was one of the wealthiest taluqdars in Oudh. Either tenants must be made so content that they would not listen to propaganda, he believed, or the government must provide landlords with enough muscle to enable them to dominate their little kingdoms as of old. But the first alternative seemed hopeless, for the more security the tenants gained the better Congress seemed to do with them. Either the government should develop a land-purchase program or it should allow zamindars to eject tenants for engaging in any political agitation whatever.

Forfeiting tenants' rights merely for supporting Congress seemed a bit reactionary, Hailey responded mildly. Admittedly improvement in their legal rights had not insulated tenants against agitation. In fact, he pointed out, the reforms had stopped well short of truly stable tenure. Provided they paid their rents, under the tenancy acts they could not lawfully be ejected. Recently, however, when the fall in prices had made rents unpayable, tenants had been "ejected in considerable numbers."[11] (So much for his testimony to Gandhi the previous August that the number of evictions was not abnormal.) Moreover the imposition of entry and other fees, sometimes amounting to two years' rent, made nonsense of legal entitlements. No wonder tenants with firmer tenures were more likely to support Congress, Sir Malcolm observed. They had more to lose.

Since 1900, he continued, rents had more than doubled, no corrective machinery existed, and state intervention created hostility on both sides. Bad as things were now it would be criminal to hand the issue unresolved to a popular government, which would be dominated by one class or the other. Hailey suggested a fluctuating scheme, rents being separated into fixed and annually adjusted parts, the latter moving either automatically with the price index number or according to the decision of a tribunal. If it were a tribunal, however, sooner or later the pressure for fair rents would become irresistible. A land-purchase system on the Irish model, relieving landlords of the whole revenue-collecting hassle, might be superficially attractive. Irish landlords were recovering only half their former income, however, and the abolition of land-bank bonds had recently become a hot issue. He hoped to postpone the evil day as

[10] Hailey to Haig, 21 June 1932, HPI/24B.
[11] Notes of Chhatari, 24 June, and Hailey, 1 August 1932, HPI/29B.

long as possible. The policy must be twofold: removing grievances agitators might exploit and instilling in landlords a sense of the obligations of land-ownership. There might still be time "for the large zamindar to create for himself the position which was once occupied by the old-fashioned Squire in English village life."[12]

At the 1931 Round Table Conference, where Gandhi failed to reach agree-ment with Muslims and other minorities, it was understood that Prime Minister Ramsay MacDonald might have to decide the communal question himself. In March 1932 Gandhi warned Hoare that he was adamantly opposed to reserved seats for Depressed Classes (untouchables), on the grounds that Hinduism would be split irrevocably and that the efforts of Hindu reformers would be doomed to failure. On this issue of principle, he insisted, there could be no compromise; he must fast unto death. When the decision was announced in August Gandhi renewed his threat. Really the little man was impossible, Willingdon fumed.[13] As the fast neared Hailey grew apprehensive: If Gandhi died people would forget the exact reason; he would not have martyred himself to preserve the unity of Hinduism but in protest against British policy. The weapon had always been available; the wonder was that he had never used it before. "On a cold-blooded calculation," Hailey reasoned, "we should lose less by his death than by allowing India to believe that he has forced the hand of HMG by the threat of suicide."[14]

Gandhi's fast threw Hindu India into what Hailey called an emotional orgy. As temples were thrown open and well restrictions relaxed, the Mahatma and the Depressed Classes leader Dr. B. R. Ambedkar reached a compromise. Gandhi declared that henceforth he would work solely on behalf of *Harijans* (children of God). Perhaps the government could use this emotional outpouring to escape from the impasse, it was suggested. "We can . . . do without the goodwill of Congress," Sir Harry Haig responded coldly, "and in fact I do not believe for a moment that we shall ever have it, but we cannot afford to do without the confidence of those who have supported us in the long struggle against the Congress."[15] Many Congress leaders, Hailey thought, actually pre-ferred to have Gandhi in jail.[16]

Apart from a little mild blackmail from landlords in the Legislative Council, who threatened to hold up the UP special powers bill unless they received

---

[12] Hailey note, 1 August 1932, ibid. See also Hailey to Sir Michael Keane (Assam), 23 July 1932, HPI/24C.

[13] Gandhi to Hoare, 1 March 1932, CWMG, *49*, 190–3; Willingdon to Hailey, 23 August 1932, HPI/24D.

[14] Hailey to Willingdon, 13 September, Hailey to Irwin, 18 September 1932, HPI/24E. Although this bloodless calculation is shocking, it needs to be compared with Nehru's mixed reactions: intense annoyance at Gandhi's sacrifice on what seemed to him a side issue, concern about the effect of the hunger strike on public life in the future, and afterward admiration. Again he was never quite convinced. Jail diary, 22 September 1932, *SWJN*, 5, 407–10.

[15] Haig note of 28 December 1932, quoted by Robin J. Moore, *The Crisis of Indian Unity, 1917–1940*, p. 289. The Gandhi–Ambedkar negotiations are in CWMG, *51*.

[16] Hailey telegram to Willingdon, 20 December 1932, HPI/25A.

proportionate remissions of revenue in return for the rent they were losing, very little seemed to be going on. The sterile, pointless stalemate continued. Someday Congress would become legal again, Hailey recognized; even now it was "really the only party on the scene."[17] In November 1932 he agreed to stay on until 1934. The following March he was asked to go to England to advise the Parliamentary committee on the constitution. No one else, Hoare reasoned, could answer the diehards so effectively. The recently issued white paper containing the government's proposals, Hailey quipped, resembled a will that left everything to the heir and then added twenty pages of separate bequests.[18]

At the end of April Hailey reached England, where he compared himself to Dr. Jekyll and Mr. Hyde, for though in India one heard nothing but the inadequacy of the government's proposals, "here one plunges suddenly into an atmosphere of suspicion and even resentment at their scope."[19] Now the ICS's acknowledged elder statesman, his role would be to reinforce Hoare's argument that the new constitution would provide "adequate safeguards . . . against Congress gaining the upper hand."[20] Although Hoare wrote glowingly of Hailey's help that summer, his presence went largely unrecorded in the official record.[21] The Hailey Collection contains notes on various subjects: the relationship between center and provinces, finance, law and order, the land-revenue system. These tend to show that though his mind was perhaps becoming increasingly comfortable at the level of detail, a trait that would become still more pronounced as he aged, it had lost none of its penetration and incisiveness.

The fact of the matter was that in the mid-1930s, nearly twenty years after the Montagu declaration and despite the well-advanced Indianization of the army and civil service, the British government was still not convinced a full transfer of power was either essential or inevitable. The new constitution was being deliberately designed to delay independence and preserve British influence in south Asia as long as possible. Hailey was a civil servant whose duty was to carry out that policy. Although he possessed a strong sense of fatalism and had deepened his respect for Indian nationalism and the sophistication of Congress, emotionally he had not yet crossed that gap either. His objective was still to fight back the Congress. That would require finesse and attention to psychology. Indians were not going to obtain what they had been promised in 1917. But neither could the British appear to be standing still. During the summer of 1933 Hailey was therefore defending proposals for change that would be substantial – but not *too* substantial. Although he was not an entirely

---

17 Hailey to Irwin, 12 January 1933, HPI/25B.
18 Hoare telegram to Willingdon, n.d., enclosed in Willingdon to Hailey, 12 March, HPI/25C; Hailey to Keane, 25 March 1933, ibid.
19 Hailey to Willingdon, 26 April 1933, HPI/34.
20 Hoare statement to cabinet, 10 March 1933, quoted by Carl Bridge, *Holding India to the Empire: The British Conservative Party and the 1935 Constitution*, pp. 88–9.
21 Samuel Hoare [Viscount Templewood], *Nine Troubled Years* (London: Collins, 1954), pp. 84–5.

free agent his arguments reflected his understanding of the nature, dynamics, and likely future of the imperial enterprise he had been serving for nearly forty years.

If civil servants of his own generation seemed more advanced than their predecessors, Hailey observed in a House of Commons committee room in June 1933, it was not because they were "idealists, or defeatists, or cowed by agitation," but because they recognized how much had changed. A constitution must have the cooperation of ordinary, law-abiding people, even the most loyal Indians had been infected by "the growth of a spirit of self-respect," and the present halfway, dyarchical system no longer worked. Members of Parliament needed to imagine a government in a permanent minority in the body voting its supplies, facing criticism that was necessarily irresponsible precisely because the legislature's powers were not final.

This profound structural weakness, Hailey maintained, was "destroying that general atmosphere which is so essential to good government in the East." How was it that solitary officers in districts as large as some countries – torn by communal difficulties, visited by epidemics or natural disasters, subject to economic problems beyond the conception of people who had not seen them – were able to persuade people to accept their orders? Districts in the UP averaged a million people and just seven hundred locally recruited police; troops were used only during acute disturbances. The British Raj "depended on the atmosphere of authority which we have built up mainly on a general reputation for good work, but partly on respect for the ultimate source of strength which we have purposely kept in the background." By exposing the irremovable and supposedly invincible government to continual ridicule, dyarchy was undermining the foundation of British hegemony.

Diehards behaved as though the slate were clean, Hailey continued. Yet much power had already been transferred to provincial ministers and a good deal of Indianization had taken place. Although some officials disliked the prospect of advance, most of them thought it inevitable and no one believed the clock could be turned back. Except for emergency powers, he insisted, provincial autonomy must be full, including responsibility for law and order. Although reserved departments not responsible to the legislature would continue in the Government of India in finance, foreign relations, and defense, other departments could be transferred at the center as well. Geometric logic mattered less than functionality; a government with limited powers that worked would be better than one with larger prerogatives that did not.[22]

In a fascinating talk on "India – 1983" at the Royal Empire Society's summer school in Oxford, Hailey's canvas was larger and his thoughts more speculative. Fifty years on, he cautioned, historians would no doubt find that existing forces had operated unexpectedly or that external eruptions like the Great War or internal political upheavals had changed things beyond recognition. Although

---

22 Speech of 21 June 1933, HPI/49.

anything might happen, then, "we have for our present purpose to assume that India, safeguarded as in the past by the British connection, will keep its frame-work intact."[23]

Capital would continue to expand, Hailey predicted,and though the country would not industrialize enough to alter its predominantly agrarian character, manufacturing interests would increasingly challenge the ascendancy of the landed classes. Although the depression had interrupted the process, the increasing money value of their products had raised both the living standards and the political consciousness of cultivators. Whereas previous tenant movements had sought to secure stable tenure, increasingly they would be demanding state-controlled rents. Hailey summarized his Irish note, spelling out the sequence: fixed tenure – fair rents – land purchase. In India landlords were already being called parasitic, the depression had forced state intervention, and the pressure for fair rents would eventually become irresistible. Indeed the consequences of a huge, politically active peasant class in a province like UP or the Punjab would be hard to exaggerate. Having begun to approach natural limits the expansion of irrigation, and therefore of agriculture, would slow, while growth would be challenged severely by overpopulation. In short India seemed headed for a Malthusian trap. Serious, widespread poverty would remain the dominant feature.[24] Hailey did not indicate what the state would or could do about it. Compared with his championship of colonial welfare and development after 1938, his conception of the obligations of trusteeship remained limited.

Noting that communalism was largely the result of secular causes, Hailey included religion under the social heading. Both major religions were being rapidly transformed. The caste and joint-family systems, which he called the two distinguishing features of Hinduism, were gradually disintegrating, while Muslims now saw themselves as a distinct culture. He also stressed the untouchables' campaign and the women's movement, expecting both to quicken and increase their political clout. Contemporary India's most striking characteristic, however, its affinity for mass movements, had become apparent only

23 Sir Malcolm Hailey, "India – 1983," *Asiatic Review*, *100* (1933), 620–32. Bridge, *Holding India to the Empire*, p. 154, quoted this sentence as evidence that "to the Conservative and official mind in the 1930s the British Raj in some form was expected to last for generations into the indefinite future." As far as Hailey is concerned this strikes me as overstated. His job in 1933 was to persuade Conservatives that the India bill was safe; he could hardly have said the Raj would end in fifteen years or so. The context of the speech is clear from a letter in which he complained that the press had misquoted remarks during a supposedly off-the-record discussion: "I purposely chose as the subject of the paper the title 'India 1983,' so as to avoid discussing present proposals, and devoted myself entirely to analysing the different forces that would operate in that period. I made this as objective as possible." Hailey to Stewart, 25 July 1933, HPI/26B.

24 Until the late 1960s these predictions seemed valid. Since then, however, not only irrigation but the better seeds, fertilizers, and techniques of the Green Revolution have improved the agrarian situation, while Indian industrialization has boomed. Poverty remains serious and widespread. It is worth repeating the argument of many economists that the population density of Europe and Japan is higher than India's: the crucial equation is not absolute population, but population compared to the base of production and services.

recently. During the past generation the control of public opinion had passed from a small intelligentsia to the lower middle class. "Economic conditions press with particular hardship on this class in the East," he warned. Though it was customary to suggest that India might become Leninist, it was just as likely to go fascist.[25]

Half a century earlier John Strachey had stated confidently that no such country as India existed.[26] How strange that sounded now. The subcontinent's many peoples, communities, and linguistic groups notwithstanding, no one could deny the dynamic power of nationalist feelings in contemporary India. Even if a British Raj still existed in some form in 1983, it would have altered beyond recognition, and the process of indigenization would have been virtually completed. He would be a bold man indeed who would predict the shape and texture of Indian civilization.[27]

In the summer of 1933 Lady Hailey's illness reached a crisis. In May she went into a nursing home in Harley Street, it was touch and go whether she would be able to return to India at all, and when she did she had to have a nurse-companion.[28] In a decision to be discussed in Chapter 15, Hailey settled the question of what to do after retirement by accepting the directorship of the *African Survey*. Meanwhile the joint-select committee on the new constitution dragged on into the autumn.[29] Having expected to be in England only a couple of months he finally left early in November.

During Hailey's absence civil disobedience had remained at a token level – "no ripple of any sort in any part of the country," Willingdon reported; "the peace of the cemetery," Gandhi called it – and the impasse continued.[30] In May the Mahatma fasted again, this time in atonement for untouchability, and the government released him. He would not formally call off civil disobedience, however, and Willingdon was "brutal enough to say that I don't feel much inclined to start negotiating with the commander of a defeated force."[31] Declaring that ordinance rule was destroying the freedom movement by driving it into secrecy, Gandhi called off mass civil disobedience but continued it individually. Early in August he was again arrested, fasted, again released – and still no negotiations.

Congress leaders were apparently tiring of Gandhi, looking for a chance to ditch him, and searching for a more promising strategy. To Hailey the situation looked much like 1924. If the Swaraj Party were revived, he observed, the government would come off badly in the next elections.[32] Worse, Congress

---

25 Nehru noted Hailey's prediction and said he might well be right. *Autobiography*, pp. 590–1.
26 John Strachey, *India* (London: K. Paul, Trench, 1888).
27 Hailey, "India" (1933), 620–32.
28 Hailey to Srivastava, 25 May, and Hailey to Clay, 1 June 1933, HPI/26A. No information is available on the precise nature of the illness.
29 The Haileys had to take their August holiday in Ireland; otherwise he would have had to pay a full year's British income tax. Hailey to L. A. Bates, 3 August 1933, HPI/26B.
30 Gandhi to C. F. Andrews, 15 June 1933, CWMG, *55*, 196–9.
31 Willingdon to Hailey, 23 June 1933, HPI/34.   32 Hailey to Clay, 1 June 1933, HPI/26A.

might return to the agrarian problem, and he preferred full-scale civil disobedience to a subterranean no-rent campaign.[33] Much would depend on Nehru's attitude when he came out of jail. As for Gandhi, Hailey observed cynically, "I think that the world would be well rid of such a troublesome person and should be glad to see him starve himself out of life." On the other hand he realized the Mahatma's value to the government; while he was on the scene, Congress would remain practically immobilized.[34]

After his release late in August Nehru exchanged published letters with Gandhi, wrote articles analyzing Indian economic problems in the context of the collapsing capitalist world system, and urged Congress to adopt a more radical program, including the expropriation of landlords and large mill-owners.[35] Hailey found these ideas disturbing, not so much because they were Bolshie as because he thought them politically shrewd. Nehru was a realist, he observed: "he would never have agreed himself to purely political demonstrations, such as the Salt Campaign, and he is much too wise to mix himself up in the mazes of untouchability. It will always be his inclination to take up some concrete issue such as agrarian relations." As always Nehru could do "a great deal there, without bringing himself within reach of the Law, and we may find it difficult to check him."[36]

If Gandhi were such an asset and the alternatives so much worse, should not he be helped to maintain his leadership? The Mahatma's policy had always been to attack the government while simultaneously negotiating with it, Home Member Sir Harry Haig reasoned, the strength of recent British policy having been to decline this halfway position.[37] Although Willingdon might call Gandhi a beaten general, however, the army was still there and the government remained reluctant to face it. As Hailey had written in 1932, "we know that the spirit which inspires Congress movements is there just the same."[38]

When Hailey returned to India late in November 1933 rumors were circulating that, notwithstanding the convention against members of the Indian Civil Service becoming viceroy, Hailey would succeed Willingdon.[39] Reports reached the Indian press, where they persisted even after the announcement of his acceptance of the directorship of the *African Survey*. To Hailey the political situation looked much as it had in London. "I think that Nehru . . . is really on the right track," he wrote the very day the Congress leader was arrested yet

---

[33] Hailey to Willingdon, 15 July 1933, HPI/34.

[34] Hailey to Chhatari, 8 September 1933, HPI/26B.

[35] Nehru–Gandhi correspondence in SWJN, 5, 526–30, and CWMG, 55, 426–30; articles in SWJN, 6, 1–16. See also Nehru's amusing parody of Hailey, ibid., 5, 561–2.

[36] Hailey to Chhatari, 29 September 1933, HPI/26C.

[37] Haig note, 15 November 1933, quoted by Low, "Civil Martial Law," p. 186.

[38] Hailey to Irwin, 3 November 1932, HPI/25A.

[39] Keane to Hailey, 10 December 1933, HPI/27A. In his *Dictionary of National Biography* article Philip Mason said it was common knowledge that Hailey would have been offered the position except for his wife's eccentricity. There will perhaps be little disagreement that he would have been a better viceroy than Lord Linlithgow.

again in Calcutta; "he realises that the major problems of India are at present not political but economic." The government had kept hoping for a rise in prices. Even if it came, however, "it would really be only a palliative, for no one could pretend that the conditions of tenants or lower middle classes had ever been satisfactory; "the problem goes much deeper."[40] Really, it was getting harder to answer Jawaharlal all the time.

Even though his own analysis suggested moving toward an end of the zamindari system, Hailey continued to try to shore it up. Landlords had long been heavily indebted, the depression had worsened the situation, and without state intervention many estates would pass to moneylenders. When the landlord-dominated Legislative Council threatened to hold up the emergency powers bill in December 1931, he interpreted the action as a desperate cry for help. He responded by asking for agrarian-indebtedness legislation, which went ahead during his absence in London, and just after his return the Council passed a measure requiring agricultural loans to be renegotiated on terms more favorable to borrowers. Unfortunately, he concluded, the bill had gone too far; if past contracts were revised too drastically "nobody will ever lend money again."[41]

It was his own fault, Hailey chided himself, for ever allowing the bill to be presented in the first place. Hard-pressed landlords had pinned their hopes on this measure; he had vetoed it; now he was being portrayed as a crony of the moneylenders. To an old Punjabi, he confessed, that was the bitterest pill: "I never thought I should sink so low!"[42] He could console himself only by hoping a future government would be just as stubborn if one day a Swarajist majority proposed to reduce all rents.[43] Whereupon, having learned that as expected the current home member Sir Harry Haig would succeed him in December, Sir Malcolm went fishing. It would be his last hot weather in Naini Tal.

With elections scheduled for the late autumn of 1934, Congress began to organize a Swarajist party to fight them. "I quite see that this will be disappointing," Hailey told his education minister, "but it is something that we had always foreseen and cannot very well avoid."[44] The day of reckoning he had long warned about was at hand. The delay in the new constitution resulting from the diehard revolt in Britain was unfortunate, he asserted, for the Indian political stagnation was about over. The resurgence of the Swarajists was only one indication. Rising communal tension was always part of the beginning as well as the end of periodic waves of agitation, and several minor incidents had occurred. Some British officials would be surprised at Congress's showing in the 1934 elections. Despite its recent disorganization and financial exhaustion, however, Hailey recognized that it remained the only organized party. Although he admitted that his campaign to promote a landlord organization, including

[40] Hailey to Irwin, 19 January 1934, HPI/27A.
[41] Hailey to Chhatari, 8 February 1934, ibid.
[42] Hailey to de Montmorency, 14 April 1934, ibid.
[43] Hailey to Willingdon, 14 March 1934, HPI/27B.
[44] Hailey to Srivastava, 11 April 1934, ibid.

providing secret-service money to a syndicate to take over the *Pioneer* news-paper, had gone beyond the detached role the government should play, despite "anything we can do *sub rosa*," his heart had never really been in it. He realized that he had failed.[45]

Besides handicapping his attempt to stimulate their electioneering, Hailey's deteriorating relations with landlords distressed him personally. That summer he took a final shot at the indebtedness problem. Once more he put forward an automatically fluctuating scheme. Landlords objected to its complexity, how-ever, and a meeting of district officers was divided. Reluctantly Hailey left things as they were. The untidiness nauseated his administrator's stomach. Directing that a thick file be prepared on the subject, he wrote a handing-over note for his successor. "The larger landlord takes no part in the economy of production," it asserted; "one does not say it publicly, but in the economic sense he is really a drain . . . since he takes off a considerable part of the produce of the land and gives back to the land and its cultivator nothing in return." Would a more equitable rent system be economically beneficial? Did the landlord's rake-off so impair the cultivator's mentality and physical capacity as to prevent proper development of the soil?

Hailey left these rhetorical questions unanswered. But the file for Haig included his Irish note of 1931. Once more he went through the sequence: fixed tenure – fair rent – land purchase. Ever since late 1930, he stressed, the driving force in the agrarian crisis had not been Congress agitation but the sheer economic plight of tenants. Even now rents were hard to collect, not because tenants were defiant but simply because they had been pushed beyond their means. The demise of the zamindari system might be distant, "though I am wont to think myself that even the best established institutions will crumble quickly under the force of modern economic pressure."[46] Once more Nehru would have been surprised, at least by the candor. And he might have reflected on the deep irony that Sir Malcolm Hailey had put him in jail for pressing ideas that, apart from the conclusions, sounded so remarkably like his own.

Meanwhile the Congress electoral campaign proceeded. Persuading the movement to fight the elections as a body instead of through a separate Swara-jist party, Ghandi averted a recurrence of the split of the 1920s. Although he would still not formally abandon civil disobedience, the government declared that it had been withdrawn in effect, and Ghandi announced his retirement. Like Gladstone he would be back. The election returns were even worse than Hailey had expected. Not only were conservatives swamped in Hindu constitu-encies but Nationalist Muslims did well against the Muslim League. Prospects for the crucial provincial contests under the new constitution looked grim.[47]

---

45 Hailey [to Hoare?], 3 May 1934, HPI/27C.
46 Hailey note for Haig, 31 August 1934, HPI/29C.
47 Hailey to Willingdon, 9 November 1934, HPI/28A. For election analyses see Moore, *Crisis of Indian Unity*, p. 305, and Peter D. Reeves et al., *A Handbook to Elections in Uttar Pradesh, 1920–1951*, pp. 246–7.

After their defeat landlords would at last begin to exert themselves. By the time Hailey left India, however, it was apparent that his attempt to build a viable alternative to Congress had misfired.

Late in October 1934, aged sixty-two and at the end of a forty-year career that had spanned the birth, childhood, and maturity of a national struggle for freedom, Sir Malcolm Hailey came down from Naini Tal and prepared to leave India. Or, as Indian Liberals sometimes observed, two men made the trip in the same body: the Machiavellian politician and the philosophical statesman.

The politician made the rounds of the counterrevolutionary elements the Government of India Act was being designed to entrench. At the Agra Zamindars' Association in Allahabad Hailey promised that the government would do all it could to protect its allies. Even so, the landlord class faced a time of troubles. "You will hear that the existence of the landlord has no economic justification since he takes a considerable share of the production of the land while contributing little to it," Hailey warned, presumably reading from his own private notes. The only remedy for a zamindar class threatened by socialist doctrines of land expropriation was to organize and defend itself politically.[48] Although he had long since ceased to believe it would fly, he tried to give the landlord party one last push.

At a banquet in the princely state of Benares Hailey observed that although the new federal constitution would protect their position in the central government, the internal evolution of the states themselves remained uncertain. Most people seemed to expect them to develop representative institutions. Whether those alien grafts from Westminster would succeed in British India, however, itself remained in doubt. Autocracy was "a principle which is firmly seated in the Indian States," he pointed out; "round it burn the sacred fires of an age-long tradition," and it should be given a fair chance first. Autocratic rule, "informed by wisdom, exercised in moderation, and vitalized by a spirit of service to the interests of the subject, may well prove that it can make an appeal in India as strong as that of representative and responsible institutions."[49] This spirited defense brings to mind Nehru's classic paradox of how the representatives of the advanced, dynamic West allied themselves with the most reactionary forces of the backward, stagnant East.[50] It might have been Joseph the Second.[51]

The statesman gave the convocation speech at Lucknow University. He had received the invitation in the Kumaun hills, he said, where "the old gods dwelt; and I seemed very near to the elemental things of India," far from the usual convocation subjects, "in a mood that even made me doubt if I could find any matter on which I could address you." But he had cocked one ear toward Germany, where they were burning books and persecuting Jews, and the other

[48] Speech of 10 November 1934, HPI/49.
[49] Speech of 5 November 1934, ibid.   [50] Jawaharlal Nehru, *The Discovery of India*.
[51] Joseph II of Austria is often regarded as the prototype of the eighteenth-century doctrine of enlightened despotism.

toward Calcutta, where he thought he heard an echo. Although European learning, culture, government, and law might be good in themselves, he quoted, all of them were said to be so many "fetters of our servitude. . . . Take them beyond the seas so that we . . . may . . . not be accursed with . . . either your goodness or your evil." Granted that Indian nationalism was inevitable and healthy. Granted that the rejection of European culture was in part a natural response to British arrogance. Granted that, to say the least, the British reaction to the Great Rebellion of 1857 had been too prolonged. Granted as well that the movement to promote vernacular languages and Indian culture should become still stronger. The fact remained that the country could not afford to discard its one lingua franca, English. And the most intense patriotism would never succeed in nationalizing science.

The speaker described the phenomenon the world of the 1930s was learning to call totalitarianism, a concerted drive "to smash down any show of difference of opinion, and to regiment every aspect of the individual life. The press is silenced; minorities are banished or suppressed; the teaching of philosophy or history is regulated by a State censorship; public opinion is reduced to a mechanised mass mentality." Fate (or if not fate, his listeners may have muttered, then Robert Clive) had brought India "into contact with that form of European thought which has proved itself most resistant to these Caesaristic tendencies." For all their faults the British had invented the concept of His Majesty's loyal opposition, implying tolerance, individual initiative rather than mass mentality, and truly popular sovereignty. Politicians might malign the new constitution. But "the philosopher will see in [it] the Empire's challenge to the spirit of the world's new tyrannies."[52] That has not in fact been the verdict of historians on the stillborn Government of India Act of 1935, and some of the audience must have wondered whether this was the same governor who had been ruling under repressive emergency powers. But there was truth in what he said.

∞∞∞∞∞∞

By the time of his retirement in December 1934 Sir Malcolm Hailey was commonly acknowledged to be the most distinguished representative of the Indian Civil Service of his generation or even of the twentieth century. This judgment would be confirmed by his prime minister and his king, who elevated him to the House of Lords, by retired colleagues who elected him repeatedly to the presidency of their association, and finally by the service's historian.[53] Ever since the age of forty he had occupied an extraordinary variety of important positions: commissioner of Delhi, finance and then home member of the Government of India, and finally governor of Punjab and UP, the two most pres-

---

52 Speech of 26 November 1934, HPI/49.
53 Philip Mason, *The Men Who Ruled India*, 2:288–91.

tigious governorships open to the ICS. He had advised five viceroys and, it was widely assumed, but for his wife's extreme eccentricity and tragic illness he would have been the first member of the ICS since Lord Lawrence to reach the pinnacle himself. Already it was becoming difficult to separate man from legend. In its twilight era the Indian Civil Service needed a heroic figure – and Hailey was it.

This had been no foregone conclusion. During his first two decades in India, serving as colonization officer in the western Punjab between two stints in the bureaucracy, he impressed his superiors and earned rapid promotions. After all, however, compared with the "adventures" of men like Jan Smuts, Cecil Rhodes, or Frederick Lugard, his early career was not really exceptional. By 1910, when he was thirty-eight, although it would have been reasonable to predict he would probably retire as governor of the Punjab, he had given no indication of escaping the mold of an extremely competent but not truly extraordinary bureaucrat.

Apart from his escapes from plague and typhoid, for in the days before antibiotics few of his contemporaries could have served an appreciable time in India without some close calls, Hailey had several strokes of good luck. First, his membership of the preparation committee for the Durbar of 1911 enabled him to catch the eye of Lord Hardinge, who vaulted him over numerous men with longer seniority in making him commissioner of Delhi. Second, despite the fact that he wrote the Punjab government's official account of the Jallianwala Bagh massacre of 1919, he was not required to testify before the Hunter Committee and therefore managed to avoid too close an identification with Sir Michael O'Dwyer's unpopular regime. Third, because the India Office's controlling role in Indian finance was well understood, he largely escaped direct responsibility for the currency fiasco during his period as finance member in the early 1920s.

It is easy to slide into the assumption that eminence is ordained, forgetting the crucial role of contingency. A case in point would be Sir John Thompson, who had been chief secretary of the Punjab in 1919, the year Hailey wrote the Jallianwala Bagh report and then became finance member. "An able officer with a grievance," Sir Fazli Husain noted in his diary after talking with him in 1931; "1919 Disturbances did him [in] as he was so closely associated with Sir Michael O'Dwyer." Subsequently, after Sir Edward Maclagan had refused him a top position in the Punjab administration, Thompson had become permanent secretary in the political department, where he was thought to have succeeded "till the Princes got against him," so that he wound up as chief commissioner of Delhi, the post Hailey had occupied as long ago as 1912.[54]

Part of the explanation of why Hailey became a benchmark for his service, then, lies in his ubiquity, his sheer longevity at the top. If he got some breaks, however, he made the most of them. As finance and especially home member in

[54] Fazl-i-Husain, *Diary and Notes of Mian Fazl-i-Husain*, ed. Waheed Ahmad (Lahore: University of Punjab Press, 1977), pp. 73–4.

the reformed Legislative Assembly he displayed considerable parliamentary talent. It is hard to recall a more successful political exercise than his confrontation with the Sikhs during the gurdwara agitation of the mid-1920s, which more than any other achievement solidified his reputation. By the early 1930s he had already become, as he put it, an ancient monument.[55] In the UP he did not achieve his goals of beating back the Congress challenge and building a conservative landlord party as a viable alternative. Even there, however, his success in outlasting an intense civil-disobedience campaign and preventing an agrarian revolution was thought to outweigh his failures. In the end the mystique of the Indian Civil Service – its prestige, its hegemony, its ultimately preposterous claim to govern a vast, complex, and alien subcontinent – rested on its aura of competence. And it was competence, above all, that Hailey exuded and personified. In him myth and reality merged.

Two themes stand out. The first concerns the strength and persistence of the ideas of the Punjab school into which Hailey had been indoctrinated under S. S. Thorburn, and which had then been strongly reinforced during his formative adult experience in the Jhelum canal colony. As he himself testified frequently, no matter how high and mighty he became he never lost his sense of close identification with rural people. Since landlords were the only class allies the British had in India, that affinity was partly a matter of attending to business. But for Hailey it was genuine and intensely emotional. In important ways – his championship of colonial development, his eventual advocacy of the philosophy if not the doxology of indirect rule, his effort to prevent the peasantry from becoming heavily indebted to an indigenous moneylending class – the Punjab doctrines would resurface frequently during the African phase of his life that lay ahead.

The second theme concerns Hailey's ambiguous, contradictory approach to Indian political questions. Intellectually, at least as early as 1914 he had recognized that Indian nationalism was an integral part of an Asian revolution and that ultimately it must succeed. Probably more clearly than most of his colleagues, he had understood that the most Britain could hope to achieve was a series of orderly retreats. Emotionally, however, he could never quite accept that. Nor did he ever reconcile himself to Congress's claim to be the authentic embodiment of a national freedom movement. Although part of him hated communalism passionately, he used it astutely as one of the most potent weapons in his arsenal. Most striking, however, were the remarkable parallels between his reasoning and that of his adversary Jawaharlal Nehru: on Gandhi's salt march, on the future of the zamindari system, on the high revolutionary potential of the no-rent campaign. The fundamental ambiguity of the man, which personified so well the contradictory nature of the empire he served and represented, would also reappear frequently during the African phase of his career.

[55] Hailey to Sir John Thompson, 14 July 1932, HPI/24C.

∞∞∞∞∞∞

Of all the assessments that appeared late in 1934 the one Hailey prized most was in C. Y. Chintamani's *Leader.* In the margin of the clipping he noted: "This is an Indian paper, very anti-government and generally abusive." What, the editorial asked, were Sir Malcolm's political opinions? As commissioner of wartime Delhi, as finance member presiding over a currency disaster that had cost Indian taxpayers millions, as home member making a false and damaging distinction between responsible government and dominion status, as the adroit manipulator of communal rivalries who had cajoled the Punjab into cooperating with the Simon Commission – at the time of his appointment in 1928 Hailey's record had made the UP apprehensive. Since then he had attacked the civil-disobedience campaign with a panoply of repressive ordinances and had played a large role in shaping a new constitution the reactionary features of which were anathema to Indian nationalists. Although he might not be a diehard or a last-ditcher, the writer concluded, he was no closet supporter of the Indian freedom struggle either.

As a governor, the editorial said, he was one of the best. With a keen, alert mind, he was "uniformly industrious and turns every minute to account. Un-usually endowed with the capacity of administration, he has shown that he . . . can be . . . a statesman when he chooses." Wherever or whenever he was needed, as so conspicuously after the Cawnpore riot of 1931 when he had been convalescing from a serious operation, "there the hour found Sir Malcolm, the summer heat of May or June did not matter, and in disregard of every consider-ation of personal comfort. Duty has never called without instant response."[56]

On 5 December 1934, "amidst scenes of oriental splendour, with decorated gates, bunting, flags, floral decorations . . . elephants . . . students and [other] people lined up all along the route," Sir Malcolm and Lady Hailey left Luck-now.[57] Next day in Allahabad he handed over to Sir Harry Haig. From the railway station, where a seventeen-gun salute boomed, he left for Delhi and Bombay. Thirty-five years later, as stipulated in his will, his ashes would be placed in the grave of his daughter Gemma at Simla, where his wife's had been since 1939. He would think often of India. But he did not look back. And he would not return.

[56] *Leader,* 7 December 1934.   [57] Ibid.

15

~~~~~~

Surveyor of Africa, 1935–1939

Early in December 1934 the Haileys left India for Kenya, where Sir Malcolm had intended to combine a fishing holiday with an introductory tour of eastern and southern Africa. In Delhi, however, on the way out, he agreed to represent the Government of India during the final passage of the new constitution through Parliament. Cutting the trip short, they arrived in London early in February. Almost at once Lady Hailey's health broke down and Ann Wright, a friend of Gemma's who had been serving as nurse-companion, had to be sent for. Wright would stay on until Lady Hailey's death from a heart attack in 1939. After that she would play the same role in Lord Hailey's life. Although there is no direct evidence, the fact that he worked and traveled with hardly a break throughout the late 1930s makes it likely that the last years of the marriage were distant and strained.

Seizing on every possible excuse – a threat from the princes to stay out of the federation, the Legislative Assembly's recent rejection of the budget, endless technicalities – Churchill and the diehards fought the new constitution clause by clause. The one benefit, Hailey wrote, was that by thoroughly boring the public the interminable debate had all but finished India as a live issue in British politics.[1] Not until July 1935 was he able to secure his release from the India Office. Only then, a year behind schedule, was he able to turn his full attention to Africa – to what, although of course he did not know this, would amount almost to a second career.

While he was in England during the summer of 1933, it will be recalled, Hailey had been approached by his old friend Lionel Curtis about directing the *African Survey*, which was to be sponsored by the Carnegie Corporation. Although Hailey's African phase would last nearly thirty years and is actually more widely known than his Indian career, at the time his expectations were limited. The new job should be interesting, he wrote in October 1934, a few weeks before he left India, "but I would not have taken it had I seen any future in England for the retired service Governor. You know his fate." If India were on the boil he might be consulted; otherwise he was ignored. He still hankered after responsible, continuous work, and saw no prospect of getting it. Having

---

[1] Hailey to Mieville, 8 April 1935, HPI/28B.

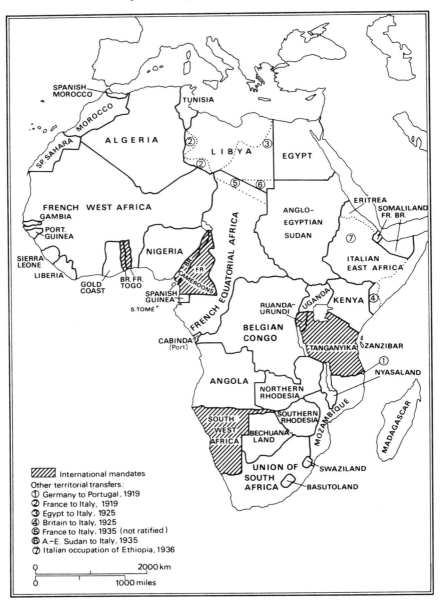

Africa in 1939

been in India seemed positively detrimental: "No doubt this is our own fault; we all bore people with our Indian experiences . . . ; I do not wonder that the world looks askance at us." Naturally enough people at home could not tell the difference between a man who had governed provinces larger than England and a lieutenant colonel who wrote letters to newspapers from the backwoods of Devon: "They were both of them something in India and that is about the end of it."[2]

Ever since its publication in 1938 the *African Survey* has been regarded as a significant landmark in helping to define and legitimize the field of African studies, as well as in the evolution of the Commonwealth. It was a pivotal work, looking both ways. Pointing forward, it became associated almost at once with the theme of activist, constructive trusteeship, with the wartime colonial reform movement and the Colonial Development and Welfare acts of 1940 and 1945, with the replacement of the doctrine of indirect rule by that of partnership, and indirectly with the postwar transfer of power.[3] But the *Survey* also looked backward, culminating the interwar generation's discussion of African problems: race, culture, primitiveness, and what would later be called colonial dependency. In order to lay a foundation for the last quarter-century of Hailey's public life, that debate needs to be briefly sketched.

Apart from a few mavericks like Norman Leys, the radical doctor whose views now seem so sound and sensible, the British climate of opinion toward Africa between the wars was shaped by the interaction between two schools.[4] The first was that of the White Man's Countries, dominating southern as well as much of central and eastern Africa. It stressed economic development through white initiative, white capital, and white management of migrant black labor, segregation, white monopoly of political power, and the evolution of Africans "on their own lines." The second school was that of the Tropical Dependency, centering in West Africa, Uganda, and the mandate in Tanganyika. It featured peasant production, protection of Africans from white ownership of land and other essential means of production, and indirect rule. Although the relationship between the two schools became increasingly antagonistic, they drew on a common bank of scientific and anthropological theory, employed common language, and shared the elementary assumption, based either on race or on culture, that African peoples were fundamentally different. From that assumption it followed that Africans ought to be treated differently

---

[2] Hailey to Brown, 25 October 1934, HPI/28A.

[3] The standard study of this ideology is John M. Lee, *Colonial Development and Good Government: A Study of the Ideas Expressed by the British Official Classes in Planning Decolonization, 1939–1964* (Oxford: Clarendon Press, 1967). "Lord Hailey," writes Lee (p. 15), "was the leading exponent of the new faith."

[4] Norman M. Leys, *Kenya* (London: Hogarth, 1924), was a best seller, going into three editions in three years. Leys wrote two other books, *A Last Chance in Kenya* (London: Hogarth, 1931) and *The Colour Bar in East Africa* (London: Hogarth, 1941). See also my book on his controversy with J. H. Oldham, *By Kenya Possessed: The Correspondence of Norman Leys and J. H. Oldham* (Chicago: University of Chicago Press, 1976).

and had a different future. Agreeing that Africans ought to "develop on their own lines," the two schools differed mainly on the end. Both thought that would be a long way off.

More than schools, these were ideologies in the Marxist sense, composed of layer upon layer of mystification, flexible and absorptive, incorporating internal debates that strengthened instead of destroying them. The South African school included a Cape liberal tradition, based on the so-called color-blind franchise of 1852 and encapsulated in the slogan commonly associated with Cecil Rhodes: "Equal rights for all civilized men." Missionaries like Arthur S. Cripps of Southern Rhodesia urged segregation, by which they meant equitable territorial division. The recognized champion of the West African school, Lord Lugard, also favored segregation, meaning separate urban areas for Africans and whites, which he justified on grounds of health. That school contained both autocrats like Lugard, with his well-known lack of sympathy with the aspirations of educated Africans, and truly progressive governors like Sir William MacGregor in Lagos or Sir Gordon Guggisberg in the Gold Coast. Although the South African school centered in the Union and other White Man's Countries it remained a significant tendency in British thought.[5]

Many institutions and associations were engaged in this dialogue: the Royal African Society, geographical, anthropological, and other scholarly groups, the Empire Marketing Board, South Africa House, the Labour Party's Fabian Colonial Bureau, missionary societies, the merged Anti-Slavery and Aborigines Protection Society. But the single most influential organization was the International Institute of African Languages and Cultures, formed in 1925 by a group of missionaries led by Joseph H. Oldham. At first it focused exclusively on languages. Seeking official cooperation and sponsorship, however, Oldham brought in Lugard, whose *Dual Mandate* (1922) had already become the classic

---

5 The classic analysis is Sir W. Keith Hancock, *Survey of British Commonwealth Affairs*, 2 vols. (London: Oxford University Press, 1937–41), vol. 2. pt. 2. The best general surveys are Penelope Hetherington, *British Paternalism and Africa, 1920–1940* (London: Cass, 1978), and Paul B. Rich, *Race and Empire in British Politics* (Cambridge: Cambridge University Press, 1986). The former is based entirely on published sources; the latter has extensive archival research but omits the central role of Oldham. On science see Nancy Stepan, *The Idea of Race in Science: Great Britain, 1800–1960* (New York: Archon, 1982). On anthropology see Adam Kuper, *Anthropologists and Anthropology: The British School, 1922–1972* (New York: Pica, 1973), and the symposium edited by Talal Asad, *Anthropology and the Colonial Connection* (London: Ithaca Press, 1975). On the South African school see particularly Martin Legassick, "British Hegemony and the Origins of South Africa, 1901–1914," "The Making of South African 'Native Policy,' 1903–1923," and "The Rise of Modern South African Liberalism: Its Assumptions and Its Social Base" (London: Institute of Commonwealth Studies, University of London, 1970–3), and Paul B. Rich, *White Power and the Liberal Conscience: Racial Segregation and South African Liberalism* (Manchester: Manchester University Press, 1984). The standard work on Lugard is Margery Perham, *Lugard*, 2 vols. (London, Collins, 1956–60). For critical analyses of indirect rule see I. F. Nicolson, *The Administration of Nigeria, 1900–1960* (Oxford: Clarendon Press, 1969); John E. Flint, "Nigeria: The Colonial Experience, 1880–1914," in Lewis Gann and Peter Duignan, eds., *Colonialism in Africa*, 5 vols. (Cambridge: Cambridge University Press, 1969–), 1:220–60, and "Frederick Lugard: The Making of an Autocrat (1858–1943)," in Gann and Duignan, eds., *African Proconsuls: European Governors in Africa* (New York: Free Press, 1978), pp. 290–312.

articulation of trusteeship and indirect rule. Lugard became the institute's first chairman and its purview broadened to include cultures. Oldham also recruited Bronislaw Malinowski of the London School of Economics, who advocated what he called practical anthropology.[6] The institute thus became a triple alliance of entrepreneurs, each with his own agenda: Oldham's of modernizing Christianity in Africa, Lugard's of promoting his versions of indirect rule and trusteeship, Malinowski's of obtaining financial support for his students. The institute also drew in liberals from southern Africa and the Negro education establishment in the United States.[7] But the central force was Oldham. As a Rockefeller Foundation official noted, he was "*the* man to see."[8]

A study of its director is not an appropriate place for a detailed study of the origins of the *African Survey*.[9] Suffice it to say that although credit for inspiring the project has ordinarily been given to South Africa's General Jan C. Smuts, who suggested it while he was delivering the Rhodes lectures at Oxford in 1929, the true founding father was Oldham. As early as 1925, in an attempt to short-circuit the intense, emotional controversy over Kenya, Oldham proposed to the Rockefeller Foundation a survey that would expose East Africa to "the assembly and dispassionate study of the facts." Within the past half century, he stressed, a new continent had been incorporated into the capitalist world system. Powerful economic forces interacting with political problems of colonial rule, racial tensions arising "when two diverse stocks live side by side," the impact of a progressive, complex civilization on mainly primitive peoples – the world was "confronted, as it were overnight, with a problem of almost unparalleled complexity and difficulty, and all on a gigantic scale."[10]

The American foundation held back, however, and Oldham was shrewd enough not to push too hard. Meanwhile the International African Institute went forward. By 1929, when Smuts gave his lectures, advocating South Africa's version of segregation as a model for export to British colonies to the

   6 Frederick D. Lugard, *The Dual Mandate in British Tropical Africa* (1922; 5th ed., ed. Margery Perham; London: Cass, 1965). This period in Lugard's career is covered briefly but with insight in Perham, *Lugard*, vol. 2, chs. 31 and 32. See Malinowski's "Memorandum on Colonial Research," Christmas, 1927, presumably written for Oldham, Malinowski Papers, London School of Economics, 1969 Addenda, Item 5, and his article "Practical Anthropology," *Africa*, 2 (1929), 22–38, which any academic will recognize as a standard grant proposal.
   7 See Kenneth J. King, *Pan-Africanism and Education: A Study of Philanthropy and Education in the Southern States of America and East Africa* (Oxford: Clarendon Press, 1971).
   8 Note by John Van Sickle on interview with Malinowski, n.d. [1931], Rockefeller Foundation, New York, Project Files.
   9 See my article "Lord Hailey and the Making of the African Survey," *African Affairs*, 88 (October 1989), 481–505.
  10 Oldham to Woods, 29 June 1925, Laura Spelman Rockefeller Memorial Collection, Rockefeller Foundation Archives, New York, 3/85. See also Oldham's note of conversation with Dr. Abraham Flexner, 4 February 1925, Oldham Papers (RH), MSS Afr s 1829/1/5. Smuts's paternity has already been questioned by John D. Hargreaves, "History: African and Contemporary," Presidential Address, African Studies Association, United Kingdom, September 1973, *African Research and Documentation*, 1 (1973), 3–8, and Kenneth Robinson, "Experts, Colonialists, and Africanists, 1895–1960," in J. C. Stone, ed., *Experts in Africa* (Aberdeen: Aberdeen University African Studies Group, 1980), pp. 55–74.

north and adding in the discussion that Oxford should turn from Greece to Africa and "let science speak," Oldham's institute was already well along on a proposal to Rockefeller for a five-year development grant.[11]

The so-called Oxford Project was short-lived and essentially without issue, for the attempt of Smuts and Lord Lothian to raise funds for it got nowhere. After learning that Rockefeller support for two such similar projects was quite unlikely, the Oxford and London groups merged. In April 1931 the Rockefeller Foundation formally rejected the Oxford proposal, accepting the International African Institute's instead. Oldham then drew up a plan not for a half-baked study center but for something much like the eventual *African Survey*, that is, a comparative investigation of major problems, current research, and future needs, which the Carnegie Corporation agreed to back.[12] This project, he assured the Colonial Office, had nothing to do with the earlier one associated with Smuts.[13] As an official noted, the undertaking ought to be called the Chatham House project rather than "the Oxford Scheme which is no longer connected with Oxford."[14]

Although the selection committee's ideal profile – a public figure previously uninvolved in African controversy rather than an academic – fit Hailey exactly, the search for a director took two frustrating years. In May 1933, just when the group was despairing of ever finding the right man, Hailey had a talk with Lionel Curtis, spent a weekend at Lord Lothian's country house in Norfolk, and said that if the job were offered he would take it. Carnegie and the Colonial Office would jump at Hailey, Curtis remarked; he was progressive, had "taken a leading and most courageous part in the movement for giving self-government to the Indians," and would confront Africa with a mind that was fresh and still vigorous.[15] The committee and Dr. Frederick Keppel, president of the Car-

---

11 See "Report on the condition in the Rockefeller interests supplied confidentially to B. Malinowski by an American Observer," and Malinowski memorandum "On the Scheme for African Research," 1929, Malinowski Papers, 114.

12 Memo (clearly by Oldham), n.d. [but 1931], Oldham Papers (RH), MSS Afr s 1829/2/4. This would seem to be the memorandum enclosed in Oldham to Lothian, 19 May 1931, just before the first meeting with Keppel, Lothian Papers, GD 40/17/259. Oldham had attacked Smuts's advocacy of South Africa as a model for east Africa while welcoming his support for research. See Joseph H. Oldham, *White and Black in Africa: A Critical Examination of the Rhodes Lectures of General Smuts* (London: Longmans, Green, 1930).

13 Passfield note, 20 May 1931, CO 323/1115/80018 (1931).

14 Tomlinson note, 17 June 1932, CO 323/1166/90033 (1932). Chatham House was the home of the Royal Institute of International Affairs.

15 Curtis to Oldham, 29 May 1933, Oldham Papers, MSS Afr s 1829/2/5. Three other offers had been made: Sir William Marris (a former Indian governor); Sir George Schuster (finance member of the Government of India); and Whitney Shephardson (an American with close Rockefeller connections). Inevitably one of the best qualified, Margery Perham, was thought more appropriate for secretary, which she declined. Although W. M. Macmillan, the distinguished historian of South African race relations, later charged he had been led to believe he would be selected, he was not seriously considered, on the undoubtedly correct grounds that his passionate stand against segregation would antagonize South Africa and white settlers. See William M. Macmillan, *My South African Years: An Autobiography* (Cape Town: Philip, 1975), pp. 202–3, 242–5, and Mona Macmillan, *Champion of Africa: The Second Phase of the Work of W.*

negie Corporation, rapidly approved.[16] Hailey lunched with Lugard and Oldham, either of whom might have made things extremely awkward for him.[17] In July the offer was formally accepted. Hailey's sovereign merit, Curtis put it, was that although he knew as much as anyone could about governing the diverse peoples of a subcontinent, he would bring to Africa an absolutely fresh mind.[18]

At the planning conference Curtis stressed the continental dimension, the biologist Julian Huxley the need for a broad ecological outlook. To Lugard the aim should be an opinion, clear and unequivocal, concerning the political position Africans would ultimately occupy. Quoting the phrase of the American journalist Walter Lippmann, "the discipline of objective information," Oldham suggested three divisions: natural sciences, economics, and the "human element." Listening intently, Hailey tried to visualize the final report. It might be "a survey of existing knowledge," he said, "pointing out the lacunae and suggesting possible ways of supplying the knowledge that was lacking." Or it "might consider the problems with which the administration was faced and try to suggest remedies." But those objectives were quite different. Which was it to be? Lord Lothian cited the Simon report on India. But the Simon Commission had had to answer only the single question of whether the constitutional advance of a centralized government should proceed, Hailey objected. Several powers were governing Africa and conditions differed widely. The only common theme, he suggested naively, was the Bantu problem.

Next day they discussed details. Hailey explained that he could not begin before September 1934. (In fact it would be nearly a year after that.) Meanwhile a secretary would be hired and various experts would begin writing drafts or separate volumes on science, economics, and "human problems." Once he began to work full time he would consider the preliminary material, select what seemed the outstanding problems, spend four to six months on intensive read-

M. Macmillan, 1934–1974 (Long Wittenham: Swindon Press, 1985), pp. 75, 108–9. There is some justice in Macmillan's comment that his own book, *Africa Emergent: A Survey of Social, Political, and Economic Trends in British Africa* (London: Faber & Faber, 1938), which was commissioned as a preparatory study for the *Survey,* where it was not acknowledged, turned out to be a good deal closer to the original model of a report that could be sold for a few shillings at railway stalls, besides being considerably more readable.

[16] Keppel's suspicion that Hailey might be too old was dispelled on meeting him: "It is evident he is not only in first-rate physical condition but at the height of his intellectual powers." Keppel to R. M. Lester, 24 June 1933, Carnegie Corporation archives.

[17] See Oldham, list of persons, n.d., and of books, 19 July 1933, and Hailey to Oldham, 1 July 1933, Oldham Papers (RH), MSS Afr s 1829/1/3. "It would have needed very little original sin in a man of his position as *the* great ex-administrator and authority upon Africa," Margery Perham wrote, if Lugard "had shown some slight sense of disinheritance at the irruption into his field of an administrator from India . . . to whom Africa was a virgin field. But Lugard quickly appreciated Lord Hailey's almost superhuman powers of absorption and synthesis" (*Lugard,* 2:698–700). Along with Prime Minister James Ramsay MacDonald, Lugard was to sponsor Hailey's application to the prestigious Athenaeum Club. See Hailey to MacDonald, 3 September 1936, MacDonald Papers, PRO 30/69/1446.

[18] Curtis to Carr-Saunders, 29 June 1933, Lothian Papers, GD 40/17/121.

ing and consultation, then go to Africa to investigate on the spot. The report itself, he stressed, "should be short so that it would be read."[19]

The text of the *African Survey* would eventually amount to 1,662 pages – the index took it to 1,837 – and readability has not ordinarily been regarded as one of its more conspicuous characteristics. Obviously something fairly drastic happened to Hailey's projection. Part of the explanation lies in the difficult, painful relationship that developed between the man – his mind, his personality, his basic outlook on his craft – and his subject. But much of the problem was apparent in his very first reaction. As he had noted, the project might be a survey of existing conditions, an identification of problems, or a policy statement, but those were very different aims. His conundrum had not been resolved at the meeting and it never would be.

Ultimately the Colonial Office would lend its own people to the frantic effort to complete the *Survey*, embrace the volume as the raison d'être of empire, and repeatedly call upon its director as adviser and troubleshooter. At the time the project was being launched, however, officials were profoundly suspicious of meddling anthropologists, especially if they came from the London School of Economics, which was one of the reasons the selection committee had wanted a man like Hailey in the first place.[20] The announcement that a heaven-born Indian Civil Servant would conduct the investigation naturally caused some concern in Africa. How would the Government of India react, one governor complained, if some ex-African officer were chosen "to tour India . . . with a view to ascertaining how far the resources of modern knowledge are being utilised . . . and what need there is for further research"? Would Hailey be reporting to Lord Lugard? Suppose he found fault with policies? Would subordinates be free to criticize? If not, what value could there be in questioning them? He was thankful that a man of Hailey's stature was going to do the job, Sir Cecil Bottomley of the Colonial Office responded.[21]

Although Hailey had hoped to do a good deal of African work during his last year in India, not surprisingly he could never find the time. Nevertheless the *Survey* began to take shape. Margery Perham's friend Hilda Matheson, who had worked in the BBC, was hired as secretary, though executive manager would have been a more appropriate job description. Arrangements were made to use forthcoming work by W. M. Macmillan (social and economic), Perham (a general survey of native administration rather than the more restricted study she actually wrote on Nigeria), and Diedrich Westermann (anthropology). Although there were apparently problems with it, the Cambridge biologist E. B. Worth-

[19] Notes of informal discussions, 15–16 July 1933, CO 847/2/4204.

[20] See for instance minutes of Sir George Fiddian and J. W. Flood, July 1933, CO 847/2/4204.

[21] Sir Hubert Young to Bottomley, 5 June, and Bottomley to Young, 23 July 1934, CO 847/3/24207. Heaven-born: Higher castes in Hinduism are twice-born, which is celebrated by rituals, not unlike the way evangelical Christians are born again. Indian Civil Servants were ironically said to be heaven born, meaning not born of women.

ington wrote the first draft of a report on science.[22] A Jewish refugee from Berlin, Charlotte Leubuscher, who had published extensively on South Africa, was engaged to do an economic study. But the director himself had yet to come to grips with the project. Until early in July 1935 he remained preoccupied with India and he left for Africa in the middle of August. He had to do some fairly frantic reading on the boat.

It was therefore only on the way to Cape Town that Hailey could devote himself to becoming an Africanist. That a man of sixty-three should even have attempted such retooling is remarkable. To be sure the job was much less daunting than it would be now. In 1935, the year Hailey began, the distinguished missionary-anthropologist Edwin Smith surveyed the science of man in Africa, including geography, demography, and linguistics as well as anthropology, asking "What do we know of Africa? . . . Very little as yet. Whatever department we examine the tale is much the same. . . . We have only scratched the surface of things."[23]

The fields Smith surveyed were actually some of the better developed. A few other missionaries were competent amateurs, several colonial officials were recognized anthropologists, and colonial governments had begun to employ professionals. Economics was a good deal thinner.[24] As Hailey himself later complained, apart from South Africa there was little history of any quality.[25] Scientific journals contained African materials and some fields had standard works. Colonial Office advisory committees had produced reports on education, soil erosion, tsetse fly, and so on. Several colonies had "Notes and Records." What did not exist, and the gap naturally struck Hailey at once, was anything comparable to the wealth of detailed material on India, systematically gathered over several generations, district by district, in censuses, gazetteers, geological surveys, or revenue-settlement reports.

---

[22] Edgard B. Worthington, *Science in Africa* (London: Oxford University Press, 1938); criticisms in CO 847/4/47002 and CO 847/4/47002/1 (1935). In his memoirs Macmillan explained his bitter disappointment at not being chosen as director, but there is no evidence that he was seriously considered. See John E. Flint, "Macmillan as a Critic of Empire: The impact of an Historian on Colonial Policy," in Hugh Macmillan and Shula Marks, eds., *Africa and Empire: W. M. Macmillan, Historian and Social Critic* (London: Temple Smith, 1989), pp. 212–31. I have found no evidence to explain why Macmillan's *Africa Emergent* was not acknowledged in the *African Survey*.

[23] Edwin W. Smith, "Africa: What do we Know of it?," Presidential Address, *Journal of the Royal Anthropological Institute*, 65 (1935), 1–81.

[24] Allan MacPhee, *The Economic Revolution in British West Africa* (1926; reprinted New York, Negro Universities Press [1970]), and Lillian C. A. Knowles, *The Economic Development of the British Overseas Empire* (London: Routledge & Sons, 1924–) come to mind; but apart from Sally Herbert Frankel's excellent book, *Capital Investment in Africa* (London: Oxford University Press, 1938), which was commissioned as a specialist volume for the *Survey*, the economics chapters in Hailey's volume (written by E. A. C. Robinson of Cambridge University) listed virtually no secondary works at all.

[25] Hailey to Malcolm MacDonald, 2 January 1938, CO 847/16/47117, urging a "connected scheme embracing the history of all the African Colonies," a project that would finally be realized half a century later in the multivolume *Cambridge History of Africa*.

Although Hailey's working notes from the 1930s have not survived, masses of them from later on do exist.[26] These show how he went about his work, methodically tackling piles of books, articles, reports, and (by then) Colonial Office files; writing longhand summaries of individual documents and synthetic memoranda on special subjects, some short, others ranging to ten pages or so; clear, detailed, getting the main point, capable of being used by others as well as by the writer: the sort of précis he had been taught to do at school and in the secretariat in Calcutta, notes like the one on the Sikhs in 1924 or on Irish land law in 1931. Hailey worked at Africa as he had at India – long, hard, compulsively. He was already an expert on colonial governance. Although superficial comparisons could cause problems, a Nigerian district was not very different from one in the Punjab; a man who had dealt with music before mosques knew that messing about with African customs could cause trouble; an adviser on the 1935 constitution did not have to stretch to comprehend indirect rule.

By the autumn of 1936, when he began to draft the *Survey*, Hailey had already gone a long way toward retooling himself. He would of course never be an expert geologist, linguist, epidemiologist, or ethnographer. He was a generalist, shaped by a heavily classical Victorian education and then by his Indian career – not so much the unusual diversity of his positions as simply the multitude of subjects to which he had had to turn his hand routinely. To say that he became an Africanist means no more than that he became competent in the vocabulary and literature of the subject, capable of evaluating and comparing, able to plan, criticize, and edit the work of others. By 1936 he would probably not have said that the common theme of Africa was the "Bantu problem," for by then he would have known that the Bantu languages are only one of several groups – although he might still have said "native problem." The difficulty Hailey would have with the *African Survey* did not result from lack of competence in a field he had turned to only recently. It was that of writing a book at all.

During his tour of 1935–6 Hailey spent a month in South Africa before moving more rapidly through Central and East Africa – Lusaka, Salisbury, Zomba, Dar-es-Salaam, Nairobi, Entebbe – reaching Khartoum by January. Breaking off to fly to England to see Lady Hailey and talk with the *Survey* committee, he returned through Kenya before proceeding to the Congo, Nigeria, and the Gold Coast, reaching Senegal by June. As had been his practice ever since his trip to Japan in 1918 he kept a travel journal, but only the southern African portion of it has survived.[27] His secretary, Donald Malcolm, a young man in the Tanganyika service, also kept a diary, but it is disappointing.[28]

---

[26] One collection is in the papers of Sir Frederick Pedler, RH MSS Afr s 1814; another is in the Public Record Office, CO 1018.

[27] The itinerary is in CO 847/4/4702 (1935). A typescript of the journal is in the Worthington Papers, RH, MSS Afr s 1425/1/1. There are some interesting anecdotes in Worthington's memoirs, *The Ecological Century: A Personal Appraisal* (Oxford: Clarendon Press, 1983). On one occasion Worthington was trying to siphon gasoline, sucked it into his lungs, and would have died except that the quick-thinking Hailey gave him a bear hug, forcing air into his chest.

[28] Donald Malcolm Papers, RH, MSS Afr s 1444.

Lord Hailey and the Asantehene of Asante, Gold Coast

Several journal entries deserve quoting. At the missionary college for Africans at Fort Hare: "Discussed . . . question of mentality, particularly in regard to physiological facts of adolescent period: I quoted Fraser [Alexander Fraser, principal of Achimota College in the Gold Coast and Oldham's brother-in-law] that there was sex obsession at puberty and post puberty period which needed to be overcome by insistence on games, manual work and other interests." Donald Malcolm, quoting Hailey at Johannesburg: "If there were 2 mil. Pathans in S. A. instead of 8 mil. placid Bantu the whites would either have to mend their methods or they wouldn't survive a week." Hailey himself at Bloemfontein: "If the segregation policy were carried out with goodwill, and in a liberal and enlightened manner, it might confer . . . more [immediate] benefits on Na[tive]s than the continued efforts of their friends to maintain a losing fight for assimilation." By the time the *Survey* appeared such naive preconceptions as these had largely been abandoned. The basic assumption of the volume was that there was nothing distinctive about the African mentality, and though judgments were avoided segregation was largely demystified.[29]

---

[29] Hailey entries of 24 and 26 September 1935; Malcolm entry of 11 October 1935. Although by 1938 Hailey had improved his knowledge of South African history, the *Survey* downplayed the

Taking notes

Although the work was absorbing, Hailey wrote from Rhodesia to a friend, Africa – its dust, its rough roads, its sweat, its flies – was hard going.[30] The man who just a few years earlier had never blinked at touring the Indian plains in June was actually complaining about the weather! By Christmas, having done Kenya, they were in Entebbe. Characteristically, and rather pathetically, Hailey worked away on Christmas morning. His young comrade hung up a stocking and put a present in it.

Two statements bear on the difficulties Hailey would have with the *Survey.* First a conversation with Smuts: "I put [to] him question whether our Report might go beyond the merely 'objective' and suggest lines and policy suitable for

long military struggle of the nineteenth century. It concluded that no reliable data existed on racial mentalities or personalities.

30 Hailey to Sir Findlater Stewart, Ndola, 1 November 1935, Stewart Papers (IOL) MSS EUR D 890/9.

Fishing

adoption; he went beyond my own tentative suggestion and thought it would be a mistake not to make such suggestions, with a guard on language and expression."[31] Second a letter from Nairobi wishing he could keep his nose out of details.[32] In 1933 Hailey had asked whether his report should survey knowledge and problems or offer recommendations for policy. Already it was turning into both -- and more.

In January 1936, as planned, Hailey flew to London to see his wife, returning to Uganda late in February. Within a few days a letter from Donald Malcolm hinted that his chief was considering breaking off the tour. Lothian wrote, but decided not to send, a warning that omitting West Africa would destroy the project's greatest strength, its continental dimension. Someone Hailey's age might be feeling the uncertainty of time and the need to set down what he had to say, Curtis reasoned. The man was just bursting to write, Hilda Matheson reported. That was precisely the danger, Lothian thought: "He has looked at Africa hitherto almost entirely through a white man's eyes. He is saturated with the Union–Rhodesia–Kenya point of view with nothing but Tanganyika as a corrective." Yet there were "two other Africas . . . , the black Africa under our control which is going to be self-governing on its own account without white

---

31 Hailey journal, Pretoria, 2 October 1935, Worthington Papers, MSS Afr s 1425/1.
32 Hailey to Lothian, 22 December 1935, Lothian Papers, GD 40/17/127.

residents and . . . the Africa under French and Belgian control about which we know very little."[33]

By June, having completed the originally projected tour of West Africa which had been none too exhaustive to begin with, Hailey was back in London, where he learned he was to be given one of the few peerages ever conferred on Indian Civil Servants. The full title would be Baron Hailey of Shahpur and Newport Pagnell.[34] The district and retired soldiers' boards of Sargodha, in the Jhelum canal colony, expressed gratitude for the inclusion of Shahpur district in the title.[35] Not since John Lawrence, founder of the Punjab school and the only ICS man ever to become viceroy, had anyone been more deserving, Sir Michael O'Dwyer wrote; all old Punjabis would rejoice. "It was good to give & wise to take it," said Hailey's closest friend Sir Geoffrey de Montmorency.[36]

Having dreaded being put out to pasture, Lord Hailey did not want for opportunities. Twice he was asked to chair the Palestine Commission. He got Palestine aplenty when he succeeded Lord Lugard in the autumn of 1936 as British representative on the League of Nations Permanent Mandates Commission.[37] Hailey was not a wealthy man, his wife's medical bills must have been mounting alarmingly, and company directorships were there for the taking. He was offered Kenya, which he was told badly needed an overhaul by a first-class administrator.[38] He also had to decline an invitation to take charge of the durbar for the coronation of Edward VIII. When he had agreed to direct the *Survey*, he explained in November 1936, he had supposed that only a few months would be needed after his tour. But writing was turning out to be much harder than expected. The field was enormous, the sort of ready-made material available in India was nonexistent, and he did not expect to finish until a year later.[39]

That was a severe understatement. In September 1936 Lothian found Hailey

---

33 Lothian to Hailey, 12 March 1936 (not sent), Lothian Papers, ibid.; Curtis to Lothian, 13 March 1936; Lothian to Curtis, 16 March 1936, ibid./128; Hailey to Lothian, 2 April 1936, ibid.
34 Hailey to Stewart, 20 June [1936], HPI/28B.
35 Resolutions of 12 August and 6 October 1936, ibid.
36 O'Dwyer to Hailey, 23 June, and de Montmorency to Hailey, [24 June 1936], ibid.
37 Apart from joking that he wondered why Lugard regarded deafness as a handicap (Hailey to Matheson, Geneva [8 March 1937], Lothian papers, GD 40/17/127), there are virtually no references in Hailey's private papers to his service on the Mandates Commission. The Mandates Commission's published *Proceedings* tend to show that when he did attend, he was well prepared. It was at this point that he read the annual reports, and so on, from South Africa's mandate in South-West Africa, on which he drew for the report he wrote for Smuts in 1946. The most interesting discussions were on Palestine, which he naturally understood as a manifestation of a problem with which he was very familiar: communalism. See particularly his fascinating cross-examination of British officials after the Arab disturbances of 1936: What warning had been received? How good was the criminal intelligence department? On whose authority was firing permitted? Was the use of blanks prohibited as they were in India? (32nd Session, 30 July – 8 August 1937). As might be expected, the proceedings also tend to show that although he tried to display detachment, he ordinarily supported his government's line, for instance, on the necessity for partitioning Palestine.
38 Sir William Ormsby-Gore to Hailey, 24 June 1936, HPI/28B.
39 Hailey to [the viceroy, Lord Linlithgow?], 24 November 1936, ibid.

"in the depths of gloom. He feels he cannot do the Report. What has really happened is that he became so interested in the detail when he was in Africa that by the time he came home he had subconsciously intended to write a book which could only be done in five years."[40] Although Hailey himself now realized this was impossible he had not really adjusted to the sort of book that might be finished in a month or two. The project had become rather a nightmare, Hilda Matheson reported. Curtis was advising "a Durham Report for Africa, something which could be printed on 200 pages of large type, calling attention to the future development of Africa & postulating the chief requirements of knowledge or the application of it in the logic of the future. . . . Anything over & above this must be in appendices, the book could be written in a few weeks, etc., etc." Yet "Hailey feels, & rightly insists, that he can't write what he calls a 'Curtis book,'" she explained. "He can't prophesy, he can only state facts & suggest inferences. And he can't bear to state them in a half-baked form, or as mere generalisations; they must be accurate & be clearly based on knowledge." High expectations had raised the pressure: "Some quality of 'pronouncement' will be given to the Report just because it comes at this time & is by Lord Hailey. The problem is to know how far Lord Hailey's minimum standards can be kept down to proportions which can be written & revised in the time & at the cost available & which will not be too big to sell."[41]

Of the planned twenty-two chapters, Matheson reported, Hailey was writing Law and Justice himself. Lucy Mair, already a highly regarded anthropologist at the London School of Economics, had handed in material for Land and was working on Native Administration. Several other specialists had been taken on, John Keith, formerly of the Tanganyika service, was helping with the drafting, and Hailey was proposing to pay Granville St. John Orde-Browne, author of *The African Labourer* (1933), out of his own pocket. The director himself was deeply depressed and showing signs of overwork. And the Carnegie grant would run out in March 1937.

Finally daylight came and the enterprise began to take shape. "The Lionel Curtis type of prophetic utterances was never possible for Lord Hailey," Matheson explained, "nor was a mere plan for research." Instead the book would be "a close analysis of first principles, & a factual description of the fundamental issues which will contribute something new & something of permanent value to African study." The approach would be strictly empirical. "Facts are dynamite," she quoted her boss, "propaganda is smoke." She now hoped the *Survey* might be finished by the later summer of 1937. Carnegie, which had already given an additional £3000, would have to be asked for still more cash.[42]

During 1937 Hailey gave two addresses bearing on the *Survey:* "Nationalism in Africa" at the Royal Empire Society in January, and "African Problems and

---

[40] Lothian to Curtis, 14 September 1936, Lothian Papers, GD 40/17/127.
[41] Matheson to Oldham, 29 September 1936, Oldham Papers (RH) MSS Afr s 1829/1/3.
[42] Ibid.

Indian Analogies" at Oxford in July. The first argued against the proposition that African institutions were unique. Their peculiarity lay not in their nature "but in the circumstances in which we encounter them." The second talk mildly criticized indirect rule. He did not see how such a system could possibly be a preparation for self-government, which the British had always defined as responsible government on parliamentary lines. Both papers explored the question of incipient African nationalism. If as yet there were "few signs of that nationalistic feeling which has become so strong a feature in India," he observed, "they will come in time; they arrive in the course of nature; and nothing you can do, and no variety or system of rule that you can adopt, will prevent their eventual growth."[43] These speeches show that the comparative perspective, many of the basic assumptions, and the pragmatic philosophy which were to inform not only the *Survey* but the important native-administration report of 1941 were already in Lord Hailey's head. No one who heard him would have suspected that he was having any trouble mastering his new field, let alone that he was in the middle of a severe psychological and physical crisis.

Although only a few scraps of correspondence have survived, they tell the story. By November 1936 there were already signs of an approaching breakdown, but Hailey refused to see a doctor. "He says he knows exactly what you will say and that he cannot take that advice," Lothian told Hailey's physician, Lord Dawson of Penn; "he says that he has always had to eat his own troubles in the past and he is going to continue to do so."[44] The following March Hailey wrote Matheson from Geneva. "I fear that I must realize that I have taken on a task . . . heavier than I realized, and that I am much to blame for failing to see in time the scope it was assuming. I have begun to be doubtful of my ability to carry it through at all, in any time," he confessed. "I cannot commit myself to hasty generalizations or unchecked statements; I have not that gift of self-confidence which makes some people preach well on things of which they know nothing. In fact, I am not really fit for a work of this scale. If I could honestly give it up I should do so tomorrow."[45]

Early in October 1937, when he was once again in Switzerland for the Mandates Commission, Hailey "collapsed in a serious nervous breakdown." He was put to bed in a sanitarium, a crisis occurred, and for several days he was near death. After conferring with his Swiss medical colleagues Dawson advised that he should probably recover, but would be unable to do anything taxing for

---

43 William Malcolm Hailey, "Nationalism in Africa," *Journal of the African Society, 36* (1937), 134–47, and unpublished Oxford lecture of 13 July 1937, Hailey Papers (RH), MSS Brit Emp s 338. I therefore disagree with Robert D. Pearce, *The Turning Point in Africa: British Colonial Policy, 1938–48* (London: Cass, 1982), p. 52, who maintained that Hailey "was not one of those who believed that nationalism would arise in Africa in the course of nature." Although I discuss the point later on, it perhaps bears stressing that whereas in the second edition of the *Survey* published in 1956 Hailey insisted on "Africanism," he had no problems with "nationalism" in the 1930s.

44 Lothian to Dawson, 25 November 1936, Lothian papers, GD 40/17/127.

45 Hailey to Matheson, [18 March 1937], ibid.

some time. A sympathetic Dr. Keppel cabled that Hailey should be kept from any strain: "After all books like babies must be weaned."[46] By January the patient was recuperating slowly and was moved to the south of France.[47] At this point the *Survey* committee decided to go ahead and have the whole report put into galleys on the assumption that by summer Hailey might be able to proof-read, do a few revisions, and help with the conclusions.[48] By March he was well enough to travel. No one would even consider asking him to do anything now, Lothian wrote, requesting that he please stay abroad and build his strength so he could begin work on the proofs in May or June. "I hope that you will feel able to fall in with these ideas," Lothian concluded, implying his lack of confidence; "I have no doubt that 'Hailey on Africa' is going to be a lasting and memorable contribution to the future of Africa, especially if it can receive the finishing touches from your hand."[49]

Early in May 1938 Matheson took some proofs to the south of France and, though she reported Hailey irritable he did begin to do a few revisions. After that his recovery proceeded more rapidly. In June Lothian scolded the colonial secretary, Malcolm MacDonald, who had asked Hailey to go to Geneva again. It had been "the extra burden of the Mandates Commission," Lothian explained, "which finally broke him down" after months of overwork on the *Survey*, and "for some days the doctors despaired of his life. After six months of complete prostration and great pain he has been slowly crawling back to life on the Riviera, and as an experiment we have been during the last three or four weeks sending him some galley proofs of the *Survey* partly for his expert revision but also to accustom him to beginning to do a little work again."[50] Late in July Hailey returned to London and was said to be in fine form, touching up the concluding chapters.[51] The volume was published in October. The evidence is therefore clear. Although he planned and launched it, Lord Hailey personally wrote only a fraction of the *African Survey*.[52]

Because no medical diagnosis of the illness of 1937–8 is available, the generic term "breakdown" cannot be improved upon and there is too much credible evidence not to accept the ascription to overwork. Nevertheless a degree of skepticism seems warranted. One had supposed that work was mother's milk to the man, and he certainly scribbled away at a fair pace for twenty-five years or so after his recovery. An acquaintance in India surmised that it must be his old

---

46 Lothian to Keppel, 8 November 1937, ibid./129; Keppel cable to Lothian, 16 November 1937, Carnegie Corporation archives.

47 Matheson to Lothian, 30 January 1938, Lothian papers, GD 40/17/129.

48 Lothian to Hailey, 14 February 1938, ibid.

49 Lothian to Hailey, 18 March 1938, ibid., addressed to a hotel in Italy. I have found no letters from Hailey himself during this period, though several are mentioned in other correspondence.

50 Lothian to MacDonald, 8 June 1938, GD 40/17/130. MacDonald wrote back lamely that Hailey's own statement that he was fine had persuaded him to ask him to return to Geneva instead of resigning as he had offered to do in May. Hailey attended the session.

51 Matheson to Lothian, 27 July 1938, Lothian Papers GD 40/17/130.

52 The 1938 edition included a long list of people who contributed material; the 1957 edition was more explicit in stating that they had in fact done the bulk of the writing.

affliction.[53] In view of Hailey's medical history – that is, his operation probably for kidney stone, enlarged prostate, or blockage of the urinary tract in 1931 – that sounds possible, but it is only a layman's guess and there is no evidence to substantiate it. If it was overwork then anxiety, depression, and despair must have aggravated the condition enormously.

In fact the *Survey* itself seems to provide important clues. In November 1937, on receiving word of Lord Hailey's condition, Hilda Matheson had given a reassuring progress report. The most crucial sections were nearly complete, she said, and most of the rest could probably be finished within the next few months, though there would of course have to be a fair bit of revision.[54] That, Sir Frederick Pedler recalled half a century later, was putting it mildly. In November 1937 he was released temporarily from the Colonial Office to take over the editorship of the *Survey* – on strict condition that his name not appear in the list of acknowledgments or anywhere else in the book. After meeting with the staff Pedler went through the material which, incomplete as it was, he calculated at perhaps a million words, far beyond Oxford University Press's maximum. Some pieces were polished but too long, others rough and full of holes.[55] As Lothian summed up later, "parts of the Report were in no state to submit to any editor and . . . Mr. Pedler often had to deal with material that was scarcely in first draft."[56]

Somehow the *Survey* team met the deadline. The Pedler Collection at Rhodes House contains a pile of notes and letters showing how he went through the individual chapters, about one a week, checking doubtful points with experts.[57] Keith, who had been helping Hailey with the writing before the collapse, continued to do most of the drafting. Since the galley proofs themselves are not available the extent of Hailey's revisions cannot be precisely determined. The suggestion that the volume might be published just as it stood provoked him to exert his will, Matheson commented; some galleys came back altered virtually

---

53 Jim [Wright] to Hailey, 20 January 1938, HPI/28C. Worry about Lady Hailey may also have been a factor, though I doubt a truly debilitating one.

54 More precisely, of the twenty-three chapters now projected (not counting the conclusion), nine were in printed drafts, three practically complete, seven in varying stages of preparation, four untouched. Progress report, 5 November 1937, Oldham Papers (RH) MSS Afr s 1829/1/3. The printed pieces dealt with African society, including population, social anthropology, and languages; the urban section of native administration; education; the state and the land; private rights in land; and water supply, minerals and mining, cooperative organization, and labor. Nearly completed were law and justice, taxation, transport, and part II of native administration. Chapters being drafted were descriptive (physical, racial, etc.), systems of government, health (being written by Dr. William Kauntze of the Uganda medical service), agriculture and animal husbandry, forestry, erosion, and two chapters on economic development (E.A.G. Robinson of Cambridge).

55 Interview, 13 November 1986. At the time Pedler was serving as private secretary to the Parliamentary undersecretary, Lord De La Warr, who was away in Australia. The conditions are spelled out in Matheson to De La Warr, 24 November 1937, CO 847/8/47002. So far as I can determine Pedler's role was not revealed to Dr. Keppel.

56 Lothian to De La Warr, 22 March 1938, Pedler Papers (RH) MSS Afr s 1814/4 (FP9).

57 Ibid., 1814/4 (FP8/5).

beyond recognition, and he far exceeded the allowed scale of corrections.[58] It is not surprising that the *Survey* was uneven. The wonder is that the quality control was as high as it was.

From the preceding discussion it seems clear that the student of Lord Hailey should begin the *Survey* where he did: with Chapter 7, "Law and Justice," a subject that had long interested him in India and the only one he did from scratch.[59] It is a model essay of fifty-four pages, tightly written, broadly comparative, theoretical, and admirably unified. Using the Roman and British Indian examples, he put the problem of the transmission of a legal system into historical context. Then a smooth transition: Unlike the historian a student of jurisprudence in Africa could observe a living process. Yet now a new factor had to be considered, for law had "become the means of expressing the changes which a community deems best suited to improve its social and material life." In Africa the law imposed by European powers was passing beyond the first phase of an instrument to secure order into a more extended one, which would require legislation appropriate to new conditions.[60] After this statement of the *Survey*'s largely implicit thesis that the aim and test of colonialism in Africa was its contribution to development, Hailey stated incisively that very little in African law was peculiarly African. If it showed no distinctive racial genius, however, one feature "must be unique. The strength with which new forces from many angles are playing on African social institutions can have no parallel in history." Although there was nothing very novel about this introduction, it did possess synthetic mastery, and the Indian comparison gave it a fresh, personal perspective.

The next two sections of the chapter are surveys – the Union, the British Central, East, and West African colonies, French West Africa, the French and Belgian Congo – typical of the rest of the volume. But these are comparatively short, the detail not being allowed to overwhelm the theme. Section 4 contains one of the few persuasive descriptive passages in the entire volume, an eyewitness account of a native court where complainants appeared before judges who knew them intimately, where perjury was rare, where unhampered by formal rules a straightforward and intelligible search was conducted for the truth. This scene contrasted sharply with a court administered by Europeans, where evidence was given through an interpreter and according to "rules of admissible

---

58 Matheson to Oldham, 15 July 1938, Oldham Papers, (RH) MSS Afr s 1829/1/3.

59 Even here Hailey used a research assistant, J. L. Krige, a South African lawyer with training in anthropology. The recently opened Lugard Papers at Rhodes House bear out Perham's statement that he gave Hailey as much help as he could and loaned him revised chapters of the *Dual Mandate*, including one on law and justice.I have compared the two versions and it seems to me that Hailey owed little or nothing to Lugard, who told Margery Perham that the *African Survey* was probably the best available source on that subject, for it was "Hailey's special hobby." Lugard to Perham, 2 December 1942, (RH) MSS Perham 22/4.

60 William Malcolm Hailey, *An African Survey: A Study of Problems Arising in Africa South of the Sahara* (London: Oxford University Press, 1938), pp. 261–6.

evidence [which] must often seem to the African to have been designed to hamper the discovery of the facts," perjury being ubiquitous because witnesses did not feel the community's presence and because the court's oaths lacked authenticity.[61] Then a section on punishment, the main problem being that European concepts of sin, guilt, deterrence, and rehabilitation all had little relevance. In Africa, Hailey concluded, "we have still the opportunity . . . of considering questions of principle and their practical application, based on the only standard which we can now regard as properly applicable, namely, the social value of the institution we are creating."[62]

If the reader moves directly from Law and Justice to the two other core chapters of the volume – 6, Systems of Government, and 9, Native Administration – the problems that faced and eventually broke Lord Hailey seem apparent. It is not that anything was glaringly wrong with the material. The sections on South Africa, for instance, avoided the myth enshrined in standard works of the period that white occupation had occurred prior to or simultaneous with that of "the Bantu," made clear the degree of discrimination that permeated segregation and showed the system to be economically unviable. Although the treatment of indirect rule in Nigeria and Lugard's role in shaping it was certainly favorable, some criticisms were made, especially of the failure to provide openings for educated Africans.[63]

There was no lack of competence on the part of those who did the work; Lucy Mair and Charlotte Leubuscher, for instance, were proficient, well-published scholars. It is as essays that the chapters fall down. The theoretical perspective, thematic unity, control and subordination of detail apparent in Law and Justice are not there. Words like "relentless" and "pedestrian" come to mind. The material was all right. But it was not Hailey's, driven by his own conceptualization, based on his own reading of the sources, seen through the lens of his own experience. Without ever thinking much about it everyone had assumed he would be able to turn other people's work into something not only good but his own. This would seem to have been his dilemma in September 1936 when Lothian found him in despair. Doggedly, silently, through a wretched, lonely, painful year he struggled to resolve it. Eventually – the first time in his life he had ever come close to failing at anything – it overwhelmed him.

---

[61] Ibid., pp. 297–8. Indian historians will recognize this anti-lawyer passage as typical of the Punjab school to which Hailey belonged; in the Nigerian context it was also anti-southern, which may be why it was omitted from the second edition.

[62] Ibid., pp. 309–15.

[63] "One of the great questions under indirect rule," Pedler wrote to Matheson, "is whether the African of European university education is ever to receive an appointment under the European administration. This is a major point of principle; it involves the question of whether the native authorities are to progress by the employment of better educated men until they can dispense with the present administrative guidance, or whether the administration is to be envisaged as a permanent frame. . . . Do you know whether Lord Hailey had any views on this point?" Pedler to Matheson, 27 January 1938, Pedler Papers (RH) MSS Afr s 1814/4 (FP9).

That a volume of more than 1,600 pages might have posed some reasonably challenging problems must strike any reader of the *Survey* as obvious. Why, notwithstanding his recognition from the very beginning that the objectives were confused, did Hailey underestimate the job so badly? The ready explanation that after a distinguished career in which success had followed success he might have grown a bit cocky may have something in it – but probably not much. The hypothesis based on his newness to the field has already been rejected. He might of course have traveled and read more, but he knew enough. The basic fact, after all, is that although he had been writing constantly throughout his career, he had never attempted a real book before. Moreover he was trying to make a book out of other people's material, working against a deadline that was wholly unrealistic for the only kind of study a man of his attitudes and temperament could do.

Among Hailey's Indian papers is a letter of 1930 to a contemporary from Corpus Christi acknowledging the receipt of a book, a treatise in psychology. He would not be able to say what he thought of it, he apologized, because his opinion would be amateurish. "I think I realize now," he added, "that even if I had adopted a different walk of life and given myself to something which required a little deeper thinking and more sustained application, I could never really have done any good or original work."[64] At first blush this sentence by a renowned Indian governor might seem like false modesty. Read retrospectively, with the hindsight of the crisis of the *African Survey*, it sounds like honest introspection. As a machine for organizing, sifting, and penetrating masses of detail Hailey's mind was truly first class. Although his Thal report of 1900 suggests it might have become so, after a lifetime in administration it was not truly original.

An African Survey appeared in October 1938, the month Neville Chamberlain returned from his ill-fated negotiations with Hitler at Munich. The critical response was overwhelmingly favorable.[65] Indeed the merits of the volume were substantial. As a general overview it easily superseded Lugard's *Dual Mandate* (1922) or Raymond Leslie Buell's *Native Problem in Africa* (1928), and as late as the 1990s the second edition was still being consulted as a standard reference work on the continent during the colonial era. A comparison with Sir Keith Hancock's *Survey of British Commonwealth Affairs* (1938–42), which was being written at Chatham House at the same time Hailey's volume was being prepared, or with Gunnar Myrdal's *American Dilemma* (1944), the influential survey of race relations also sponsored by the Carnegie Corporation, however,

---

[64] Hailey to Arthur H. B. Allen, 19 February 1930, HPI/17A. The book was *Pleasure and Instinct: A Study in the Psychology of Human Action* (London: Kegan Paul, 1930). I must add that, after looking over the book in much the same way Hailey must have, I wouldn't know what to say about it either.

[65] Important reviews include Reginald Coupland, "The Hailey Survey," *Africa*, *12* (January 1939), 1–10.

highlights the difference between a workmanlike but on the whole rather uninspired compilation and truly first-class books – original, artistic, brilliant, and incisive.[66]

At the time of its publication two powerful currents were converging to lift the historical significance of the *Survey* far above the intrinsic qualities of the volume itself. First, the British Africanist establishment, which had been struggling for recognition for more than a decade, saw itself defined and stamped with authoritative approval as a valuable and legitimate field of study.[67] Second, Hailey himself soon came to be regarded as a principal spokesman for colonial reform and development, which in turn became *the* prevailing rationale and ideology of empire during and after World War II. The reputation of the *Survey,* and indeed of Lord Hailey as an Africanist, would thus be deliberately and systematically inflated. Although Lord Lothian's preface mentioned that the director had been ill, the understatement was deft, covering up the fact that Hailey had been flat on his back during most of the last year while Pedler and the team were meeting the production schedule. The fact that the volume differed so dramatically from the short, readable book originally planned was soon overlooked. Even Hailey himself remarked that no one had ever intended it to be read.[68] His contemporary verdict is disarming. "I regret that I did not plan the work out more carefully," he confessed; "I could have made it much shorter, and a great deal more to the point."[69] Also on the mark is the criticism of Norman Leys that in Hailey's "immense book I couldn't find a single mention of what Africans themselves think or wish."[70]

The colonial-reform doctrine that the object and justification of colonialism must be its contribution to the material betterment of backward peoples, with which Hailey soon became identified, was only implicit in the volume itself. His postpublication campaign was a good deal more aggressive. Like others he used the *Survey* as a symbol that "spoke for itself." At Chatham House in December he called for an end to laissez-faire, for the application to the colonial empire of the expanded role of the state that had developed in Britain itself during the depression. "I sometimes wish that we could place our hands on our hearts a little less," he said, "and set them to explore our pockets a little more." Promising eventual self-government was all very well, he argued. But Africa's first

---

[66] In 1946, replying to a questionnaire concerning the nature and role of anthropology, Hailey faulted Myrdal's *American Dilemma* for having deliberately set out to influence policy. "I thought that it would have had a far greater value if it had been less tendentious and more objective," he wrote. "It is not indeed so much a scientific study of the negro problem as a direct attack on the opponents of negro rights." I presume most readers would agree with Myrdal's verdict that opponents of Negro rights *were* the problem. Hailey also argued that Malinowski's advocacy of indirect rule impaired his value as an anthropologist. Hailey reply to circular from International African Institute, 3 April 1946, HPA/343.

[67] This point is made by Hargreaves, "History: African and Contemporary."

[68] "Lord Hailey Always Keeps on Working," *West Africa* (November 1948).

[69] Hailey to MacDonald, 14 November 1938, CO 847/11/47070.

[70] Leys to Thomas Jones, 10 September 1941, Jones Papers, National Library of Wales, W12.

priority must be decent health, nutritional, and living standards, for which massive aid would be required.[71]

When Hailey talked with Malcolm MacDonald at the Colonial Office, he found himself preaching to the converted.[72] During an earlier stint at the Colonial Office in 1935 MacDonald had already concluded that a much more forceful program of development was needed if Britain were to justify its refusal to transfer the three so-called High Commission territories to South Africa.[73] Meanwhile, a wave of serious riots had occurred in the West Indies, a royal commission had investigated deteriorating economic conditions in "the British shop-window for the U.S.A.," and it was expected to recommend a substantially larger British commitment.[74] MacDonald was therefore only waiting for further ammunition. By the middle of January 1939 the Colonial Office had already prepared a draft to the Treasury requesting that Hailey's proposal for research be expanded to include the whole colonial empire and funded at half a million pounds a year.[75] In September, shortly after the outbreak of war, the proposal was strengthened and enlarged, the result being the Colonial Welfare and Development Act of 1940. Lord Hailey had been just in time to catch the tide.

∞∞∞∞∞∞∞

Late in January 1939 Alexandra Hailey died from a heart attack. The *Times* printed two notices, one from the Haileys' old friend Sir Geoffrey de Montmorency, the other anonymous (almost certainly a woman). Both recalled earlier, happier times. Sir Geoffrey maintained that although voluntary service was expected of British official wives in India, she had thrown herself into a variety of causes with an unusual degree of commitment. The anonymous writer described a young woman a man could fall in love with: "her lithe frame, her sure foot and true eye, her nerve which no sudden catastrophe could shake, and the piquancy of her small features, crowned by her glorious hair. She did not look athletic, but she could ride any horse, however wild, climb any peak, and swim with the grace and ease of an otter," and she had a beautiful soprano. "Those early years of her marriage were perhaps the happiest of her life," the writer continued, "when she and her husband and child lived in the remote

---

71 William Malcolm Hailey, "Some Problems Dealt with in the 'African Survey'," *International Affairs, 18*, (1939), 194–210.
72 Minutes of CO discussion, 20 December 1938, CO 847/13/47097.
73 Letter of MacDonald, 1970, cited by David J. Morgan, *The Official History of Colonial Development*, 5 vols. (Atlantic Highlands, N.J.: Humanities Press, 1980), 1:xiv–xv.
74 Sir John Campbell, 23 May 1938, quoted by Stephen Constantine, *The Making of British Colonial Development Policy, 1914–1940* (London: Cass, 1984), p. 235. See also William M. Macmillan's influential book, *Warnings from the West Indies: A Tract for Africa and the Empire* (London: Faber, 1936).
75 Draft memorandum, 26 January 39, CO 847/13/47097.

districts of India" in the Punjab canal colony, "without the intrusion of place and pomp."[76] After a funeral service attended by a long list of Anglo-Indian and British official families the body was cremated and the ashes sent to Simla to be placed in the grave of her daughter, Gemma.

Lady Hailey's health having been precarious for years, presumably her husband's feelings were a mixture of sorrow and relief at a sudden but not unexpected end. But there is no basis for speculation, save for a comment in his diary two years later when he was in Africa: "It is a great grief that I am not able after all to be home, as I had hoped, for the 30th, a day when above all dates I could have wished to be in England."[77] Partly because the times were so tense, but largely because he was constitutionally incapable of enduring a long period of inactivity, he kept working without a break. The previous September, during the war scare leading up to Chamberlain's sellout at Munich, he had written to everyone he knew who might be able to employ his services. Early in 1939 he took on two difficult and sensitive assignments, agreeing to chair both an air-raid shelter conference and a coordinating committee on refugees.

Although the earlier panic had dissipated, the British public's concern about the threat of air bombing remained intense. Especially in view of revelations about the nation's woeful unpreparedness, which had been employed in defense of Chamberlain's appeasement policy, the obvious question was whether the government's civil-defense program was at all adequate. The conference went over the whole field thoroughly: deep versus shallow shelters, their relationship to antiaircraft defense, blackout and evacuation procedures, lessons from the German raids on Barcelona. Deep, impenetrable shelters, safe against 500-pound bombs, could undoubtedly be constructed, the report concluded. But were they practical? Could people get to them in the estimated warning time of seven minutes, especially at night? Could they be built in time to be used? How much investment was justified in relation to other war costs? Many shallow but accessible shelters were preferable to a few completely safe ones, the conference concluded: "If experience in Barcelona has taught us anything, it is the danger to persons thronging the streets."[78] (Ironically, the London Underground system was ruled out except for treatment of casualties.) In short, noted Sir John Anderson, for whom the famous back-garden air-raid shelters were named, the Hailey report "provided the strongest justification for the present Government policy."[79]

The refugee committee was a reconstituted version of an earlier body. Ever since Hitler had taken power in 1933 each successive tightening of Nazi per-

---

[76] Letters in the *Times*, 2 February 1939.
[77] Hailey, Congo Diary, Pedler Papers, RH MSS Afr s 1814/23 (FP54).
[78] Cmd. 6006. For the background see Terence H. O'Brien, *Civil Defence* (London: HMSO, 1955), especially pp. 191–2, a volume in the United Kingdom Civil Series of the official *History of the Second World War*.
[79] Minutes of meeting of subcommittee of Committee of Imperial Defence, 14 April 1939, CAB 16/197.

secution had resulted in a fresh wave of immigrants, most (but not all) of whom were Jews. Like other industrialized countries Britain had refused to accept more than a few thousand and, lest liberality toward refugees encourage still harsher German treatment or raise an anti-Semitic storm at home, had committed no public funds. Although no other country had done much more, Eleanor Rathbone's indictment was hard to answer: "If the British Government feels itself too weak to be courageous, at least it might show itself merciful."[80] In May 1938 the Home Office had set up a committee to link the various refugee organizations and help deal with mounting visa applications. In October the committee announced that the government's selective immigration policy had broken down. In December, after the terrorism of Kristallnacht, it rejected the principle that the refugee problem must be handled privately. Lord Baldwin, the Archbishop of Canterbury, and the Catholic Cardinal Hinsley launched an appeal. But still no public money was forthcoming.

There the matter stood when Hailey agreed to chair a new coordinating committee. Seeing thousands of people in distress, always realizing that those were the lucky ones and that hundreds of thousands more were trapped inside the Third Reich, for whom he could do nothing: it was a harrowing experience.[81] Behind the scenes his organization discreetly urged the Home Office to loosen restrictions and cut delays. "Great care . . . was being taken," said the chairman of the Inter-Government Committee on Refugees, Earl Winterton, "to see that refugees . . . did not take employment which could be filled by British people."[82] In March Hailey resigned from the Mandates Commission, most likely because he felt a conflict of interest between membership of a commission that was discussing Britain's refusal to increase the immigration of Jews into Palestine and his chairmanship of the refugee coordinating committee.[83] Then in June, for what were said to be personal reasons, he resigned from the latter committee.[84] His frustration was obvious. Was this the fate of

---

[80] Rathbone letter to Manchester *Guardian*, 23 May 1938, quoted in A. J. Sherman, *Island Refuge: Britain and Refugees from the Third Reich, 1933–1939* (Berkeley: University of California Press, 1973), p. 111. The Home Office had stressed the continuing high rate of unemployment. Still bent on appeasement the Foreign Office had shrunk from criticizing Germany. The Colonial Office walked a tightrope between Zionism and Arab resistance, trying to restrict immigration to Palestine while pointing to the limited capacity for absorption in tropical colonies.

[81] Speech in House of Lords, 17 December 1941, Parliamentary Debates (Lords), *121*, 349–52. Throughout the late 1930s, when Hailey was British representative on the Mandates Commission, he kept his attitudes on foreign policy to himself. Although he was certainly closer on Indian questions to appeasers like Halifax (the former Lord Irwin), Lothian, or Sir Samuel Hoare than he was to the diehard Churchill, his mind and conscience were his own and it would be dangerous to leap to conclusions.

[82] The *Times*, 17 February 1939.

[83] In May Hailey gave two talks on the BBC on the Palestine issue, explaining that he could understand why Jews were so angry at the recent White Paper curtailing immigration (HPA/334). He may also have been uncomfortable at the prospect of having to support Chamberlain's offer to include the return of Germany's former colonies as part of his appeasement deal. In December 1939 Hailey returned to Geneva for what would prove to be the commission's last session.

[84] The *Times*, 23 June 1939.

ancient monuments? Was his reputation for integrity and efficiency to be used as an inevitably wasting asset every time the powers-that-be wished to offer the public a palliative?

On 5 September 1939, two days after Britain declared war, MacDonald asked Hailey to come to the Colonial Office. The war effort notwithstanding, said the colonial secretary, a strong colonial development policy would need to be pursued. Although Hailey might well be asked to play a part, he noted, "there was a particular piece of work which I thought wanted doing, and which he might prefer to do. It was time we got our minds clearer as to the objects of our native policy in Africa." What exactly was indirect rule driving at? In colonies with substantial European populations how could the interests of Africans be protected? Unless objectives were clarified now, steps might be taken that would be difficult to retrace. More specifically, the outbreak of the war having interrupted discussions with the prime minister of Southern Rhodesia, Godfrey Huggins, MacDonald wanted Hailey to look quietly into the policies of Southern Rhodesia, Northern Rhodesia, and Nyasaland and report on the long-heated question of Central African amalgamation.

Hailey replied that he "was prepared to do whatever work was most useful," MacDonald's note continued. "He was a man with no private attachments now; his wife was dead and his son was doing war service. He was free to work in London or on the continent of Europe, or in Africa, or anywhere."[85] Relieved and reinvigorated, the old man was looking forward to a good war.

---

[85] MacDonald note, 5 September 1939, CO 847/15/47100/1 (39).

❁❁❁❁❁❁❁❁❁❁❁❁❁❁❁❁❁❁❁❁❁❁❁❁❁❁❁❁❁❁❁❁❁❁❁❁❁❁❁

16

Two missions to Africa, 1939–1940

In October 1939 Lord Hailey joined a distinguished group of officials and scholars at London's Carlton Hotel. The subject was Africa and World War II. A generation earlier he himself had seen Indian nationalism transformed by global conflict. In Africa too World War I had been a powerful catalyst, increasing the range and pace of colonialism while simultaneously stimulating the growth of African political consciousness. This time the impact would be still more powerful. The colonial secretary, Malcolm MacDonald, identified three main problems. First, hoping to determine where indirect rule was heading and prevent unwise wartime concessions to white settlers in East and Central Africa, he intended sending someone out to investigate. Second, in order to cut costs as well as to encourage their political advance, Africans should be employed at all levels throughout the government services. Third was the land question, although the local variations were so wide that a series of regional inquiries would probably be required to deal with it.

White settlers were the most urgent problem, Lord Lugard declared. For several years now, especially in Kenya, they had been having things far too much their own way; if the British continued along the same lines people would doubt the sincerity of their trusteeship. Since parliamentary institutions were fundamentally unsuited to Africans, he felt, indirect rule ought to aim at gradually assimilating small units into central councils. Educated Africans were pressing hard for unofficial majorities in legislative councils, Hailey pointed out, leaving colonial governments dangerously exposed. He agreed with MacDonald's skepticism about whether indirect rule could be squared with the goal of ultimate self-government. But he also shared Lugard's doubts about transplanting the Westminster model into such uncongenial environments.

The academics spoke up. "We had been letting economic forces rip," Margery Perham asserted; it was high time to bring them under control. The war provided a chance to put dependent colonies on a proper moral footing, said her colleague at Oxford, Reginald Coupland. Delaying self-government had alienated Indian intellectuals; now was the time to win educated Africans over by bringing them into the process. The direction of political development had to be decided first, Hailey objected. Once begin to nominate African legislative council representatives and elections would follow inevitably. African political life had two planes, Perham observed. At the tribal level, which corresponded to the reality of African life, the pace of education through indirect rule must necessarily be slow. Meanwhile the intelligentsia naturally wanted to take over the artificial European state system; "we shall probably give in to them too soon."

Africa needed something really big like the American Tennessee Valley Authority project, the biologist Julian Huxley suggested. Ever since 1931, Keith Hancock rejoined, Britain had virtually stopped exporting capital; it lacked the resources for a huge enterprise like that. Although the Commonwealth's natural tendency during wartime would be to build tariff walls still higher, that would be entirely the wrong direction. There was no alternative to internationalizing the empire, he concluded; "we cannot develop it economically ourselves."[1]

The Carlton Hotel conference was symptomatic of what MacDonald called a seething of thought. Although the Colonial Office had already recommended colonial-development legislation, after the declaration of war in September it put the case more forcefully. Demands for international control of colonies were likely, the Treasury was told, recurring unrest in the West Indies or elsewhere could be extremely embarrassing, and a well-funded campaign to improve the living standards of colonial people would do much for Britain's image in America.[2] The Colonial Welfare and Development Act of 1940 would commit £5 million a year for ten years, including half a million for research. That legislation, Hailey later reflected, had opened an entirely new era in colonial history.[3] Other problems, such as deteriorating race relations and the color bar in government services, were being scrutinized.[4] Hailey's mild criticisms of indirect rule provoked private comments in the Colonial Office that were far less guarded.[5] In short, if the discussions during the early years of the war did not add up to a revolution, there was a sharp difference in tone.[6]

Hailey spent the first months of the war as a volunteer in the Ministry of Information. In an attempt to ascertain the morale on the home front he made a tour of factory towns in the Midlands and the North; it may have been his first

---

[1] 6 October 1939, CO 847/17/47135. Cf. William Roger Louis, *Imperialism at Bay, 1941–1945: The United States and the Decolonization of the British Empire* (Oxford: Clarendon Press, 1977), pp. 103–5 and John E. Flint, "Planned Decolonization and Its Failure in British Africa," *African Affairs, 82* (1983), 389–412.

[2] Note for the Chancellor of the Exchequer, [September 1939], CO 847/15/47100/1. See Stephen Constantine, *The Making of British Colonial Policy, 1914–1940*, pp. 238–61.

[3] Hailey to Sir Charles Jeffries, 10 October 1963, HPA/343.

[4] Margery Perham proposed cultural centers, though they sounded rather like the bridge party in E. M. Forster's *A Passage to India.*

[5] Minutes by Sir George Bushe and Sir Arthur Dawe, January 1939, CO 847/13/47091/2.

[6] See John E. Flint, "Planned Decolonization" and "Scandal at the Bristol Hotel: Some Thoughts on Racial Discrimination in Britain and West Africa and Its Relationship to the Planning of Decolonisation, 1939–1947," *Journal of Imperial and Commonwealth History, 12* (1983), 74–93, and the rejoinder by Robert Pearce, "The Colonial Office and Planned Decolonization in Africa," *African Affairs, 83* (1984), 77–94.

direct exposure to the English working class.[7] In October, though neither he nor MacDonald can have been in any doubt about it, he agreed to go to Africa.[8] In January 1940, shortly before leaving, he conferred with the Colonial Office. To him there were two main areas for investigation: (1) how native administration worked on the ground, where and in what ways it was defective, and (2) the constitutional field including connections between central and local political systems and the employment of educated Africans.

The meeting then turned to the secret part of Hailey's assignment: Central Africa. Ever since the 1920s the issue of closer union of Southern and Northern Rhodesia, perhaps to include Nyasaland, had brought the West and South African schools into head-on collision. Early in 1939 a commission chaired by Lord Bledisloe had argued that a solid bloc of British territory in that part of the continent would have enormous economic, administrative, and strategic advantages. But the respective native policies – parallel development in Southern Rhodesia, indirect rule and trusteeship in the other two territories – appeared to be in conflict, and as long as those programs remained fluid amalgamation would be premature. But the door was not closed, Southern Rhodesia's prime minister Dr. Godfrey Huggins continued to press his case, and the outbreak of war broke off a conference in London. A single man of unimpeachable integrity and authority, he and MacDonald agreed, would be better than yet another commission.

As Hailey saw it the evidence was already overwhelming. Not only were the policies different, there was absolutely nothing ill-defined or tentative about them, and "the most that might be possible would be a piece of constitutional carpentry." The question was whether the obvious incompatibility was to be decisive. In the long run, he thought, the more crucial problem was not Central Africa itself but the danger that white Rhodesians would decide to "go south."[9] Huggins would have been horrified. Although Hailey would change his mind on the last point, he had already articulated the rest of his conclusions.

On 1 February 1940, after a rough flight from Casablanca, cruising at the heady pace of 180 miles an hour, Hailey and his private secretary, Frederick Pedler, the man who had finished off the *African Survey* in 1938, arrived at Dakar, Senegal. The last time he left Africa, Hailey wrote in his diary, he had sworn never again to come within reach of the mosquito. Having taken his quinine, however, "here I am preparing to anoint my feet with eucalyptus oil."

---

7 Described in broadcast from Accra, 21 March 1940, HPA/334. I have not been able to trace the report he said he had written.
8 In addition to his pension, his annual salary would be £2,000.
9 Note of CO discussion, 5 January 1940, CO 847/15/47100/1. See Martin Chanock, *Unconsummated Union: Britain, Rhodesia, and South Africa, 1900–1945* (Manchester: Manchester University Press, 1977). Lewis H. Gann and Michael Gelfand, *Huggins of Rhodesia: The Man and His Country* (London: Allen & Unwin, 1964). The conferences are recorded in DO 35/824/R8/106, 216, 219, 223. See also the C.O. précis enclosed in J. J. Paskin to Hailey, 24 November 1939, HPA/342.

The humidity was like coming to Bombay from the dry heat of north India. Gradually becoming acclimitized he settled down to work in Lagos, reading files and holding interviews. "White & Black alike," Pedler noted, "when they have had their half-hour with Hailey, feel they have been speaking to a great man."[10] At Lagos and Accra Hailey gave upbeat radio talks. "We are fighting for what we believe to be the peace of mind of mankind," he declared, "and to safeguard those decencies in human relations which are the lifeblood of our own type of civilization."[11]

Lord Hailey's tour of 1940 has been colorfully described as "perhaps the last of the epic and eccentric 'travels in Africa' genre, though this frail old man's adventures were in rickety aeroplanes rather than picturesque canoes and steamboats."[12] Although he had apparently recovered fully from his breakdown two years earlier, it had clearly taken something out of him. On his sixty-eighth birthday he reflected on his aging. "I am a little dismayed at the falling off in my own powers of work compared with 1935," he wrote; "I cannot do half what I did then." Might it be the damp heat? "But I do tire more easily," he answered, "and I could not carry on at all if I did not insist on taking a good sleep after lunch." Either he had not recovered from the airplane, he mused, or he was growing deaf, his new teeth were causing problems, and in Ibadan he noted people's concern when he had a nasty fall.[13] Pedler noted a tendency toward garrulousness: "Hailey gets more and more talkative, often wearisomely."[14]

Although the comparison with the intrepid explorer of the 1890s and founder of the Royal African Society Mary Kingsley is appealing, "frail old man" is overstated. Hailey remained an avid fisherman and vigorous walker, rising early at sea for several miles on deck and taking long hikes alone on land. Pedler noted no lack of stamina, and a reader of Hailey's output would hardly be aware of any either. Moreover, although in some ways Hailey was indeed eccentric, the tour was well organized, efficient, and methodical. He was no longer an apprentice. This time his focus, the machinery of native administration, was much narrower than before and it was well within his ken. Pedler, who made copious notes and drafted most of the report, was an effective number two. The tour of 1940 was the work of pros.

As usual Hailey kept a travel journal. Several features deserve stressing. First, his report of 1941 would conclude that although political consciousness

---

[10] Pedler to his wife, 1 February and n.d. [mid-February 1940], Pedler Papers, RH, MSS Afr s 1814/6 (FP12). Hailey journal entry, 2 February, HPA/342.

[11] Transcripts in HPA/334. "I witnessed the scene in the House of Commons," he recalled, "when Mr. Chamberlain announced that he had been invited to visit Munich [a] sudden display of emotion . . . surely unparalleled in the history of Parliament." In justice to Churchill, "whose wisdom I have not always admired, . . . he seemed then to shake that massive head and contract those heavy brows with an air of caution and foreboding." Hailey also remembered "that sea of upturned faces in the pouring rain at Heston aerodrome, watching for the landing of the Prime Minister," who believed he had secured the peace.

[12] Flint, "Planned Decolonization," p. 406.   [13] Hailey diary, 13 February 1940, HPA/342.

[14] Pedler diary of Congo mission, 2 August 1940, MSS Afr s 1814/18 (FP38).

was on the rise, he had found nothing resembling mature nationalism anywhere except in West African coastal cities and perhaps Kenya. The diary makes clear he looked for it. Everywhere he talked with Africans – chiefs, newspaper editors, teachers, leaders of political associations or youth movements; if a local Gandhi sought an interview he made a point of seeing him. On the whole, however, the speeches and manifestoes, even the newspapers, struck him as moderate. A man accustomed to the *Bombay Chronicle* could take the *West African Pilot* in stride.

"The African intellectuals cannot at present compete with the Indian, and may never do so," Hailey remarked after attending a village council in south-eastern Nigeria, "but the ordinary peasant is egalitarian; he is as good as his neighbour, and likes to show it; he can keep his independence and respect in the face of authority. If his practical ability and sense of business were anything like his deliberative capacity, he would do well." He was still more impressed by West African women. "I always enjoy the sight of the busy African market," he wrote, "mainly because I have such an admiration for the African women of this part of the world – cheerful people, broadbacked and bountifully bosomed, self-confident and holding their own with the men in buying and selling, or swinging along the roads with that gay toss of posterior protuberances which Africans consider one of the chief charms of womenkind."[15]

Second, the journal shows that the future chairman of the Institute of Race Relations was not immune from the common prejudice of the period. It was comparatively mild – a few "joking" comparisons of Negroid and monkey faces, a couple of notations about smells.[16] Virtually nothing like it appears in his Indian papers, however, so that even this degree of nonmalignant prejudice was reserved for Africans. Moreover, although his attitudes do need to be recorded, they seem to have made little practical difference. Prejudice did not prevent him from listening carefully to educated Africans like J. B. Danquah, who after all held a London Ph.D. The fundamental axiom of the *African Survey* had been that literally nothing about Africa was either unique or racially determined. That was Hailey's rational view – and he was among the more rational of men.

Hailey took Africans seriously. One illustration is his role in resolving a long-standing dispute between the Gold Coast government and the state of Ashanti over lands that had been seized after the war of 1900. Ashanti's Golden Stool must have reminded him of the Sikhs' Golden Temple at Amritsar, symbolizing sores to be lanced rather than being allowed to fester, and he worked to gain the confidence of Prempeh, the Asantehene.[17] (The governor, Sir Arnold Hodson, was actually the pricklier character; Hailey brought him round by showing him a way to improve his fishing rig.) A better example is the investigation of the

---

15 Entries of 19 and 26 February 1940, HPA/342.
16 See especially the entries of 13 February and 3 March 1940, HPA/342.
17 Sir Frederick Pedler, "Lord Hailey: His Contribution to Africa," *Journal of the Royal Society of Arts, 118* (July 1970), 484–92. See Hailey's interview with Danquah, Pedler Papers, MSS Afr s 1814/8 (FP16).

amalgamation issue in Central Africa. As they read legislative council debates he and Pedler made pointed comments. On the scene, as well as later in the report, Hailey stressed the industrial color bar. His interviews with whites in Northern Rhodesia – notably with Roy Welensky, other railway union leaders, and the Midland Farmers Association – were especially instructive. If such men were allowed to have their way, he concluded, the consequences for Africans would be serious. A note of an interview with African teachers was also telling. One of them, though obviously intimidated, blurted out that unlike in the south, in Northern Rhodesia "we are a little bit free."[18]

Finally, Hailey's journals and notes show a man becoming engaged emotionally as well as intellectually with the subject of African local government. How institutions worked, how they fitted into a people's way of life, had always fascinated him. Long ago his settlement report on the desert area of the western Punjab had demonstrated a flair for anthropology. Now, in Tanganyika, he tried his hand again.[19] His mild and very typical prejudices were no bar, as Kipling wrote of the Elephant's Child, to his "'Satiable Curtiosity." Increasingly the former Indian Civil Servant was becoming committed to the African colonial service, deepening his sympathy and respect. As he talked with men like Sir Bernard Bourdillon of Nigeria or Sir Philip Mitchell of Uganda, as he read their dispatches and reports, he grew closer to them.[20] He had begun as a critic of indirect rule and, especially when he met it in the form of a doctrine, he remained one. As he came to see pieces of working administrative machinery for which no ready substitutes were available, however, he began to grow more conservative. If he never worshiped at the Lugardian shrine, neither did he want to discard the scheme entirely.

Completing their tour late in June 1940, the two investigators departed from the continent via Cape Town. There Hailey talked with Smuts, who was once again prime minister after the epic parliamentary struggle with General J. B. Hertzog that had brought South Africa into the war. The conversation changed Hailey's perspective. Earlier he had assumed that if amalgamation were denied them Southern Rhodesian whites might well go south. The Union's eyes were on East rather than Central Africa, Smuts argued persuasively. Neither he nor

---

[18] Interviews of May 1940, Pedler Papers, MSS Afr s 1814/10 (FP20).

[19] See his note "The Village Community in the Sukuma: Tribal Organization," n.d., perhaps written on the ship back from Cape Town. The note, he explained, was written "not by a specialist, but by one who has for sympathetic and professional reasons an interest in getting to know the African better." Pedler's comment, dated 2 August 1940, reveals something of the relationship the two men had developed: "Most interesting and well-informed: but as a description of *modern* Sukumaland there can be little doubt that this underrates the functions of chiefs & headmen."

[20] See Hailey's marginal note, n.d., on Bourdillon's Memo on Future Political Development in Nigeria (1939), Pedler Papers, MSS Afr s 1814/6 (FP13), calling him a man of courage. The interview with Mitchell is the only one with a governor that is recorded *in extenso*. Ibid./1814/14 (FP27).

the so-called purified Afrikaner nationalists under Dr. D. F. Malan wanted to upset the Union's internal political situation by incorporating another predominantly English-speaking province.[21]

Hailey and Pedler arrived back in London the last week in July. During their absence the war had changed dramatically, the Germans having routed the Belgians in two weeks and the French in six, and Churchill having replaced Chamberlain as prime minister. The British expeditionary force had been fortunate to escape from Dunkirk; the Battle of Britain had begun; if the Germans won command of the air invasion was expected momentarily. Hailey had left a war of preparations. He returned to an island alone, bombarded, and under siege.

Three weeks later Hailey and Pedler, along with a Foreign Office economics expert named Charles Thorley, left Liverpool by ship for the Belgian Congo, charged with helping Governor-General Pierre Ryckmans keep the territory out of German hands. After Belgian king Léopold III's capitulation Ryckmans had broadcast his intention to maintain the alliance with Britain in the hope of ultimately liberating his homeland.[22] But his lines of authority were ambiguous and his economic problems serious, for although the two governments had signed a financial agreement it did not cover the colony's agricultural and mineral products.[23] With its home and most of the European market cut off, with mounting and virtually unsalable products, the Congo faced economic strangulation.

The Congo was part of a larger puzzle in which for strategic reasons France's colonies were a great deal more important. On 23 June, the same day it released the French from their pledge not to negotiate a separate peace, the Churchill cabinet called on French colonial governors to continue the war, guaranteeing salaries and pensions and promising to treat French possessions as members of the sterling bloc. From London the then unknown Colonel Charles de Gaulle appealed to soldiers in the colonies to join the Free French. Most of the empire remained behind Vichy, however, and the British attack on their fleet early in July so angered the French that even a declaration of war seemed possible. For the next two years the British would be pursuing two completely contra-

---

[21] N. Tait minute, 13 August 1940, CO 795/115/45104.

[22] See William B. Norton, "Pierre Ryckmans (1891–1959)," in Lewis H. Gann and Peter Duignan, eds., *African Proconsuls: European Governors in Africa*, pp. 391–411, and the same author's "Belgian-French Relations During World War II as Seen by Governor General Ryckmans," Académie Royale des Sciences d'Outre-Mer, *Le Congo Belge durant la Seconde Guerre Mondiale: Recueil d'études* (Bruxelles: Académie Royale des Sciences d'Outre-Mer, 1983), pp. 285–311. On the Belgian situation see Jean Stengers, *Léopold III et le Gouvernement: Les Deux Politiques Belges de 1940* (Paris: Gembloux, 1980).

[23] Under the agreement the British Treasury made an interest-free advance of £3 million to the Belgians in exchange for 360 million Belgian francs, the latter to be used for purchases in Belgium and the Congo. Text of 24 May 1940 in FO 371/24274. The best analysis of the economic context is Bruce Fetter, "Changing War Aims: Central Africa's Role, 1940–41, As Seen from Léopoldville," *African Affairs, 87* (1988), 377–92.

dictory policies with regard to French Africa.[24] The first, primarily Churchill's, was to encourage the Gaullist movement to establish an African toehold and gradually wean the colonies away from Vichy. The second, primarily Lord Halifax's though Churchill supported it as well, was to negotiate with Vichy and its supporters in Africa, maintain the colonies' neutrality and, once the momentum shifted, hope to move them and eventually unoccupied France itself back into the Allied camp. From either perspective, however, the most important French dependencies were in the west and north. French Equatorial Africa was comparatively marginal. And it was already under British economic control.

So was the Congo. The closer one got to it, however, the larger it loomed. With the British retreating before the Italians in Somaliland, governors in East Africa worried about their rear.[25] To the British consul in Léopoldville, James Joint, the Congo's potential significance as a southern Atlantic communications center was being overlooked. While Britain was awaiting direct invasion, he argued, "German policy is clearly quietly to consolidate their hold on the French African Empire." Brazzaville just across the river might soon be enemy territory.[26] Having recently replaced Malcolm MacDonald as colonial secretary, Lord Lloyd agreed with Joint. A military mission was dispatched and Congo officials were sounded out about a visit by "some prominent British personage."[27] A former governor of Bombay and lately one of the diehard opponents of Indian constitutional advance, Lloyd had in mind "a great authority on Africa and a personal friend of the Governor General of the Congo."[28] Which was how, in August 1940, Lord Hailey found himself on a boat back to Africa.

The Belgians suspected that the British might be plotting to take over the Congo themselves. He would provide all the necessary economic data, the Belgian colonial minister Albert de Vleeschauwer objected; why was an on-the-spot inquiry necessary? According to Hailey's instructions his mission would be described as economic, the political side being kept secret. Like other tropical territories, the directive continued, loss of markets and accumulating commodity surpluses had brought the Congo to the verge of collapse. Britain had conferred most-favored-nation treatment, but that might not be enough. Politically it was hoped that Hailey's prestige, authority, and friendship with the governor-general would encourage him to continue his nominal role as a belligerent, although in practice neutrality was the most that could realistically be hoped for. The assignment was described as temporary, but no terminal date was given and much of the scope was left to Hailey's discretion. His job, in

---

[24] See particularly Desmond Dinan, *The Politics of Persuasion: British Policy and French African Neutrality, 1940–1942* (New York: University Press of America, 1988), and R. T. Thomas, *Britain and Vichy: The Dilemma of Anglo-French Relations, 1940–2* (New York: St. Martin's, 1979).
[25] Tel., Gov of Kenya to SS, encl. in CO to FO, 27 June 1940, FO 371/24282.
[26] Tel., Consul-General Léopoldville (James Joint) to FO, 14 August 1940, ibid.
[27] Minutes of meeting at CO, 12 July 1940, ibid.
[28] FO note, 26 July 1940, FO 371/24283. The appointment is not mentioned in John Charmley, *Lord Lloyd and the Decline of the British Empire* (New York: St. Martin's, 1987).

short, was to keep Ryckmans' back stiff and, within the limits of concessions the British found themselves prepared to make, give him all possible support.[29]

In turn Hailey wrote out guidelines for his subordinates' informal conversations: (1) Future of Congo: Annexation was one of Germany's war aims; "quote the Mittelafrika map" from World War I. (2) Future of French Equatorial Africa: "Be vague. We must wait and see how successful General de Gaulle is going to be in re-establishing France." (3) British Africa: "Talk confidently of large reinforcements." (4) Congo products: Britain wanted something over half its peacetime exports of gold, diamonds, copper, and cobalt. Although agricultural products were not wanted, Britain might help dispose of surpluses. (5) War situation: "Optimism and assurance are essential. . . . It is not just England that is fighting Germany & Italy, but the British Empire, a 1/4 of the world." (6) How long would it last? "Avoid expressing views . . . Britain's great advantage lies in her ability to make it a long war and to wage it with constantly increasing strength."[30]

On the trip Hailey dutifully took his exercise, told Pedler stories about General Dyer and Amritsar, and the two men pegged away at the report from their earlier tour. A former aide-de-camp treated Hailey as though he were still governor of the United Provinces: "This flattersome, and unless the authors of the Prayer Book have made a mistake, even the Deity likes a little flattery." On 29 August, off Accra, word came of a Gaullist coup in Brazzaville, Chad, and the Cameroons. At Lagos he saw Governor Bernard Bourdillon of Nigeria, who told him how he had helped Edgard de Larminat, Philippe de Hauteclocque Leclerc, and the other Gaullists plan their move. Although it had been no part of his mission, Hailey realized that "if we are to help to consolidate the hold of De Gaulle's party on these areas, we must give it prompt economic assistance."[31]

Issuing guidelines for conversations was all very well, Pedler and Thorley must have joked once they reached the Congo, where it turned out that, to put it charitably, the Old Man's French was a little rusty. When a local official came on board to deliver a greeting from Ryckmans, Hailey "mumbled something which nobody could hear but which appeared to have something to do with trains to Leopoldville."[32] Once the mission got to the capital Hailey learned of Consul

[29] FO final instructions, 14 August 1940, FO 371/24283. The problem of surpluses may surprise readers accustomed to thinking of severe shortages of raw materials such as rubber, but these did not occur until after the Japanese conquest of Southeast Asia in 1942; at this stage in the war tropical colonies were a mixed blessing. See Fetter, "Changing War Aims."

[30] "Directions given by Lord Hailey for the attitude to be adopted by all members of the Mission in *non-official* conversations with Belgians and other non-British nationals," n.d., Pedler Papers, MSS Afr s 1814/18/FP37.

[31] Hailey diary, 18–31 August 1940, in Pedler Papers, MSS Afr s 1814/23/FP54. Pedler diary, 18 August 1940, ibid./1814/18/FP38.

[32] Later, when told it had been arranged for them to stay at a dubious hotel, "Hailey said curtly, we would sleep on board." Once more Pedler and Thorley to the rescue: "We did sleep on board, but without causing offence." Pedler diary, 4 September 1940. A few weeks later, after he had had more practice, Hailey gave a five-minute broadcast, remarking that Pedler with every show of sincerity said it had gone well.

Joint's crucial role in helping de Larminat take power in Brazzaville. At their first interview Ryckmans was impressive: "He knows all the facts and figures and does not talk the kind of 'bla' which many Latins indulge in." The Belgian clearly felt he had been given enough promises and wanted action. "Hitherto, he has always acted under orders from Brussels," Hailey pointed out; "the Congo is like a subsidiary company of which the major control is in the hands of a parent company."[33] Now that Ryckmans was on his own he had to make good. And unless his exports started moving he would be in trouble.

The Battle of Britain was nearing a climax. On 8 September came word of a big air raid in London: horrible, Hailey noted, though his committee in 1939 had estimated that the deaths might go as high as ten thousand per attack. On the eleventh he heard a radio broadcast of Churchill's warning that invasion might be close. Hailey spent the day across the river at Brazzaville, where de Larminat was welcoming the governor of Chad, Félix Eboué, the courageous black Frenchman from Martinique who was the first colonial governor to go over to de Gaulle. Having met Eboué in 1936 in the French Sudan, Hailey described him as an old friend.[34] De Larminat struck him as intelligent and hard to rattle, a man well worth supporting.[35]

Once negotiations began Ryckmans grew more difficult, harping on the devaluation of the Congo franc and refusing even to discuss a plan under which Britain would buy some but not all of the surpluses: "He just would not play." Was Ryckmans perhaps taking the reports of a German invasion of Britain seriously? Hailey asked himself. Or, like Indian politicians, was he "making a great show of complaints, good or bad, real or unreal, in order to build up a bargaining counter"? Either way, Hailey sympathized with him: "I think myself that HMG [His Majesty's Government] has been mean in wanting to take up his gold."[36]

Haggling with Ryckmans was at least what the mission was supposed to be about. Hailey had no express authority to deal with the Free French at all. De Larminat and Eboué were in such urgent need of cash, however, that he had had to give a personal guarantee for the princely sounding sum of 1.5 million A.E.F. (French Equatorial Africa) francs.[37] This step seemed the more essential a few days later when the joint Anglo-Free French attack on Dakar failed

---

[33] Hailey diary, 7 September 1940.

[34] Brian Weinstein's excellent biography, *Eboué* (New York: Oxford University Press, 1972), 256–61, which was written before Hailey's diary became available, speculated that when Hailey described Eboué as a friend to de Gaulle later on he was being diplomatic: "They were not real friends." In fact he did call him a friend well before he met de Gaulle. Nevertheless I am inclined to agree with Weinstein; Hailey had friendly relations with many, but few "real friends."

[35] De Larminat's memoirs gave some credit to Joint and Bourdillon but did not mention Hailey at all. Edgard de Larminat, *Chroniques Irrévérencieuses* (Paris: Plon, 1962), pp. 121–222.

[36] Hailey diary, 31 October 1940.

[37] Hailey diary, 18 and 23 September 1940. Hailey personal telegram to Halifax, 18 September 1940, FO 371/24332, and private letter of 29 September 1940, FO 371/24286. Although Hailey was not a rich man he would certainly have been good for it; at the exchange rate of 176.6 it came to a little under £8,500.

disastrously.[38] "I thought myself," Hailey noted, "that the navy had given up the idea that they could dominate from the sea a powerfully defended position on land."[39] Dakar proved what Bourdillon had observed in July: "The name de Gaulle cuts no ice locally."[40] Only in the backwater of Equatorial Africa, where the British navy was unchallenged, had the Free French so far managed to make any show at all.

Late in October, when de Gaulle himself came to Brazzaville, in full dress in the heat of the afternoon sun Hailey crossed the Stanley Pool to see him. De Gaulle wanted to make Eboué governor-general, he learned, "but hesitates as Eboué is negro (so do I. It would create a difficult situation both in A.E.F. and Leopoldville)." Nevertheless Hailey endorsed Eboué. Recognizing the man's courage and ability as well as the damage a rejection of a black man would do to the assimilationist rhetoric of French colonialism, de Gaulle went ahead.[41] The talk ranged far beyond the Congo. Hailey proposed unifying the British command in Africa. De Gaulle handed Consul Joint a telegram for transmission to London: a curious document, Hailey mused, addressing the American government as though from a duly constituted head of state. Clearly the man was keen on his independence "but this is going rather far." Yet the Frenchman did not seem arrogant. "I think he is honest and personally unpretentious," was Hailey's surprising summation. There was no doubting the capacity for leadership: "He *is* indeed to my mind a man who inspires confidence. But it is curious that he seems to retain some mistrust of Great Britain, and cannot believe that we have no desire to turn the present difficulties of France to our own account."[42]

Shortly after seeing de Gaulle, Hailey flew to Lagos, where he laid before a military conference a scheme for a unified African command. Going well beyond what he had proposed to de Gaulle, he called for a single Allied authority to include the Free French, Congo, and South Africa. Already the lack of central planning was causing problems, he argued. He himself, the head of an economic mission, had had to press London for a decision on whether the Congo should undertake any sort of military role in North Africa. Was anybody coordinating de Gaulle's activities? Or was the Free French leader a loose cannon? Without central direction the allied territories would "continue to present . . . the picture of a number of detached units, imperfectly acquainted with each others' needs and resources," depending on orders from a wide array

---

38 See Arthur Marder, *Operation "Menace": The Dakar Expedition and the Dudley North Affair* (London: Oxford University Press, 1976).
39 Hailey diary, 4 October 1940.
40 Telegram, Bourdillon (Nigeria) to SS Colonies, 26 July 1940, FO 371/24329.
41 Hailey diary, 25 October 1940. Hailey and de Gaulle were quite right about local prejudice – not least from Mme. Ryckmans, who discovered that she had to take her children for a holiday instead of attending a dinner party Hailey gave for the Eboués.
42 Hailey dairy, 31 December 1940 – 6 January 1941. Hailey did not know of the continuing relations with Vichy or of the depth of Foreign Office hostility to de Gaulle. For that matter he did not learn until later of evidence showing how defeatist the Belgian ministers had been in June.

of authorities in Europe.[43] Hailey's thinking about regional planning for colonial areas, which would loom so large in his proposals at the important Pacific Conference at Mont Tremblant late in 1942, effectively began two years earlier in the Congo.

For some time Hailey had been urging London to decide whether the Congo ought to send a unit to Somaliland. In August, when his instructions were being drafted, the Foreign Office had presumed that most Belgians were supporting their king and that pressure for more active belligerency would do more harm than good. Besides, British military authorities were skeptical of the fighting capacities of the Belgian and Congolese forces, and indifferent troops would be worse than none. In September, however, the local press began to attack Ryckmans for passivity. The local government was bound by its tradition of subordination, Hailey advised, and incapable of taking the initiative. The British must make up their own minds.[44]

Although de Gaulle's visit had stirred up some patriotic impatience, only after Hailey returned from Lagos did he realize that Ryckmans took the threat of a coup seriously; indeed he was strongly considering resignation. In London, discounting the War Office's low opinion of Congo soldiers, the Foreign Office persuaded the Belgian ministers to declare war on Italy. The Congo would send a small contingent now and train a larger force for use later on.[45] It was enough to persuade Ryckmans to stay on.[46] Hailey was revising his earlier opinion of the governor-general: "He has *not* shown as much initiative & sense of direction as he should have done; has got unduly rattled at the criticism & attacks; has permitted dangerous license to some of his military officers; has been hasty at one time and undignified about his [possible] departure. Not as big a man as I hoped."[47]

By late November a draft economic agreement had been worked out. An important day, Hailey observed on the twenty-eighth, when one Foreign Office telegram thanked him for the draft agreement and another acknowledged what was said to be a valuable proposal on unified command.[48] In fact both messages were misleading. Once de Gaulle was confronted with the proposal for military concentration going far beyond what Hailey had sketched for him in Brazzaville, he opposed it emphatically.[49] And, though their own political muscle

43 Hailey note, 5 November 1940, FO 371/24826. See John Kent, "Anglo-French Colonial Co-Operation 1939–49," *Journal of Imperial and Commonwealth History, 17* (1988), 55–82.
44 Hailey to Halifax, pvt., 29 September 1940, FO 371/24286; Hailey diary, 14 October 1940.
45 Hailey to Halifax, pvt., 1 November 1940, FO 371/24286.
46 Minutes on Hailey telegram to FO, 19 November 1940, ibid. Although it is a very minor criticism of what strikes me as an excellent article, Fetter seems to me mistaken in suggesting that the need for a decision to forestall the threat of a coup against Ryckmans was the reason Hailey flew to Lagos. He did not take it seriously until after his return, and even then it was primarily Ryckmans' response that alarmed Hailey rather than the threat itself. See Fetter, "Changing War Aims," p. 389. Hailey went to Lagos to present his unified command scheme.
47 Hailey diary, 22 November 1940.
48 Hailey diary, 28 November 1940.
49 General Sir Edward Spears note, 8 December 1940, FO 371/24286.

was hardly comparable, the Belgians were also raising difficulties. In any case the final economic treaty concerning the Congo would have to be negotiated in London. Early in December Hailey told the Foreign Office that private reasons required him to leave by the end of the month. "I am wasting time," he complained.[50]

Where another man might have killed time reading detective stories, Hailey kept busy doing a note on native administration in the Congo.[51] He and Pedler continued to work on the report for the Colonial Office. Exploring nearby plantations and villages, the daily walks grew longer. Once, when the boss had not returned by dark, Pedler took a couple of Africans with him, eventually finding an indignant Hailey, who said he knew exactly where he was. Another time Hailey insisted on an excursion to the Sanga Falls. Although it was thought to be forty-five kilometers away it turned out to be ninety; a cloudburst came and both cars got stuck. In varying stages of undress – one man starkers except for a pipe – they finally managed to dig them out; that night Hailey wrote up the incident with relish.[52] The sketch an Indian journalist had written in the 1920s about the governor of the Punjab – curious, interested, escaping Government House whenever possible to mingle with people, a cross between a demagogue and a Machiavellian politician – still held true.

Early in January 1941, leaving Pedler behind to wind up the economic part of the mission, Hailey flew to Lagos, only to discover that he had a low priority for scarce air space. A week later, after falling asleep on the beach and blistering himself badly, he made it as far as Freetown. But he was bumped again and finally arrived in England early in February by ship. "I came home in a blizzard," he wrote to Pedler; "if it has not been very comfortable, it at all events has secured us peaceful nights." London did not seem much changed, he added with characteristic understatement, but "City is very badly knocked about."[53]

---

50 Hailey diary, 14–20 December 1940.
51 Hailey diary, 10 December 1940. The note has not survived. See also the diary entry of 4 October 1940.
52 Hailey diary, 1 December, Pedler diary, 5 December 1940.
53 Hailey to Pedler, 13 January and 5 February 1941, Pedler Papers, 1814/19/FP38. He meant the City of London, in other words, the financial district.

17

A report and a vision, 1941–1942

In February 1941, shortly after returning to London, Lord Hailey handed in the report on "Native Administration and Political Development," which he and Pedler had completed in the Congo. In some ways it was his most significant publication, outranking even the *African Survey*, for it helped set the framework for British official thinking on African affairs through the rest of the war and anticipated the early stages of decolonization. It contained a long introduction, colony-by-colony examinations, a survey of Southern Rhodesia, and a separate note on amalgamation. Although an edited version was distributed to members of the colonial service, the Rhodesian sections remained unpublished.[1]

Wartime Africa was changing dramatically, the report began. One of the causes was British public opinion. The first stages of colonial rule, which had secured law and order, built elementary communications, and practiced trusteeship with a severely limited concept of the role of the state, had now been superseded. During the depression of the 1930s Britain had redefined the state as an instrument for social welfare; in 1940 the Colonial Welfare and Development Act had extended that concept to the colonies. "The improvement of the economic and social life of the colonial population is an essential part of the policy, to which we stand committed, of fitting them to achieve a self-governing status," the report declared. Unless social and political development advanced together, however, self-government would remain a cruel illusion.

Could the British "be sure of the continuance of that degree of acquiescence in our rule which is a necessary condition of administrative progress?" the report asked. Although unrest in the colonial situation was often assumed to be

---

[1] The standard edition is William Malcolm Hailey, *Native Administration and Political Development in British Tropical Africa*, ed. Anthony H. M. Kirk-Greene (Nendeln: Kraus Reprint, 1979), with an excellent introduction by the editor. For other analyses of the report see Robert D. Pearce, *The Turning Point in Africa: British Colonial Policy, 1938–48*, ch. 3, and John E. Flint, "Planned Decolonization and Its Failure in British Africa," 389–412. Flint called it a blueprint for virtually everything important in colonial reform down to 1948, including the Creech Jones dispatch of 1947 on local government. Although Pearce agreed the document was important, he stressed internal ambiguity, denied it was a blueprint, and argued that some of the most crucial developments during the war, especially the appointments of West Africans to executive councils and the granting of unofficial majorities, overturned Hailey's ideas decisively.

artificial, generated and sustained by the agitation of an unrepresentative educated elite, the dynamics were far more general. In India, for instance, a large
middle class had become aware that its standard of living lagged behind that of
comparable classes elsewhere; cities contained masses of people living at the
subsistence level; rural areas had numerous "tenants living in serfdom to landlords, and of landlords living in serfdom to moneylenders." In Africa too an
educated middle class was emerging. There too economic grievances could fuel
anger that would be expressed in racial or nationalist terms. Educated people
were the natural leaders. Once they were well and truly alienated, agitation
became normal.

In South Africa, where legal African opposition was virtually impossible, that
might already be the case. So far, however, Hailey saw few signs of well-
organized, cross-tribal unity with wide popular support. True nationalism might
require a new generation of leaders. In the British colonies he had found even
less evidence of antagonistic racial feelings. Apart from the Gold Coast or
Sierra Leone, the comparatively few associations that did exist were local or
sectional. Although he had looked hard for it, Hailey had found little of what
could realistically be called either nationalism or pan-Africanism.

Such feelings would emerge in due course, for nationalism was the logical,
inevitable antithesis of colonial rule. As he had done so frequently in India
Hailey quoted John Stuart Mill: "In a few generations identity of situation often
produces harmony of feeling, and the different races come towards each other
as fellow countrymen." Although compared with India pan-African solidarity
faced powerful obstacles, especially "the lack of a common culture" and the fact
that there was not one colonial power but four, even so "the existence of alien
rule must in time have something of the same result in unifying African sentiment." The impact of World War I – involving massive movements of foreign
and African troops, accelerating demands for labor, broadening political consciousness – had been considerable, and the present conflict would be still
more momentous.[2]

Neither direct nor indirect rule was a precise term, Hailey observed, turning
to the machinery of administration. The first implied a highly developed bureaucracy like British India's, largely composed of Indians but controlled from
the top; no African regime had anything like that. Indirect rule had been
applied to situations as different as Malaya and Buganda, the authoritarian
emirates of Northern Nigeria, and the amorphous Ibo communities of the
southeast. Whereas the terms suggested two opposing systems, the reality was a
broad spectrum. Kenya, for instance, was said not to have indirect rule. But it
did not have direct rule either, for chiefly families were employed as government agents and local tribal councils expressed African opinion. Although to
indirect rulers everything in Kenya was suspect, its innovations might well be

[2] Report, pp. 7–10.

adapted in other places where tribal structures were weak. Adherence to tradition was not an end, Hailey insisted, but only a means for securing popular acceptance.

Where was indirect rule going? Malcolm MacDonald had asked. One school, which included all educated Africans, saw native authorities only as auxiliaries for local government and perceived the future entirely in terms of parliamentary institutions at the center. Others, including Lord Lugard and Margery Perham, stressed the evolution of traditional institutions, while some officials in Northern Nigeria regarded emirates essentially as sovereign states. The first perspective was probably right, Hailey argued. The overemphasis on tradition was resulting in serious fragmentation of authority. As the drive for economic development grew more intense the inefficiency of anachronistic units would become increasingly debilitating. Above all fragmentation was incompatible with the goal of self-government. "If these organisations were in truth destined to take over the government of the country," then the claim that educated Africans should participate in "their own institutions" might have some validity. Those organizations were obviously not so destined, however, and educated Africans understood that very well. Change could not be restricted entirely to what Perham called the plane of tribal reality. Room would have to be made for African participation at the center.[3]

In India, Hailey had long believed, the most serious British error had been to refuse the political class's first demand, which had been indigenization of the bureaucracy. Instead the reform scheme had extended parliamentary institutions, which had no counterpart in India's political experience, while severely limiting their power and sense of responsibility. Mill's dictum was that *alien* rule produced nationalism. But suppose the bureaucracy had been Indian? Suppose the indigenization program of the 1930s had got well under way several decades earlier? Congress extremism after 1907 might have been headed off or at least slowed down. Already West African newspapers showed that educated Africans were also demanding high administrative appointments, not merely in service departments but as district officers responsible for governing. "It is in our readiness to admit Africans to such posts," Hailey argued, "that they will see the sincerity of our declared policy of opening to them the road to self-government."[4]

No doubt must be left. Self-government, with Africans playing important and increasing roles, was the goal and purpose of British policy. Two outstanding, closely related problems were involved: time and form. Beneath the rhetoric of

---

[3] Ibid., p. 45. Cf. Flint's perceptive observation that "an elaboration of indirect rule institutions could, at most, have led to 'self-administration' of small units and the creation of a permanent need for a cadre of colonial service personnel to co-ordinate. . . . The concept had a good deal in common with that of the 'Bantustans' in South Africa today." "Planned Decolonisation," p. 392, n. 3.

[4] Report, pp. 47–8.

trusteeship the prevailing assumption had always been that African capacities were so minimal that time was essentially unlimited. That premise too was dangerously mistaken. So far African agitation was largely potential. But pressure would accelerate during the war, combining with forces in Britain to step up the pace. The predictable result would be premature concessions. Unless a clear view were developed now of the form self-governing institutions ought to have, steps might be taken that would be regretted later.

The obvious model, the report observed, drawn from British experience, already in place in the dominions and promised to India, was parliamentary institutions leading to full responsible government. There was another school of thought, however, neither alarmist nor mistrustful, which held that the Westminster prototype was totally unsuited to African conditions. Although Lugard and the indirect rulers had never spelled out their vision, although Hailey had already concluded that it was not really a scheme for self-government, he shared their doubts. He suspected that the use of traditional institutions had helped cushion Africans against the shock of rapid Westernization. During the tour his respect for native authorities – for the Africans who composed them, for the officers who supervised them – had deepened, and his Indian experience had reinforced the feeling. Recognizing that the clock could not be turned back, he had nonetheless been profoundly skeptical about whether the Westminster system would succeed in Asia. Was it likely, he had asked, that a constitution evolved over centuries in a small, urban, industrial, homogeneous society would be suitable for a country that was none of those? Africa lacked a common culture, he believed, its communications, economic base, and education were all more primitive than India's, and it was still more ethnically divided. The grounds for anxiety seemed strong.

The real difficulty was not the mere existence of a legislature, Hailey suggested, for a central lawmaking body had to be somewhere, but how it was selected and how it should relate to the executive. Indirect election might be preferable. Where traditional native authorities were working well, conferences of chiefs could be formed. In urban areas elected township authorities could be developed. Where traditional institutions were weak, local councils like Kenya's could be created. All these various bodies would select representatives to regional councils, which would do the same for the central legislature, from which members of the governor's executive council would be drawn.

Methodically but measurably the machine would start to move. Beginning from the bottom election would replace selection. At every level African power and responsibility would increase. Some such scheme, Hailey believed, might produce a more stable executive than a cabinet immediately responsible to a directly elected parliament. That was probably as far as constitution-mongering ought to go at this stage, he concluded. Although the British ought to have some idea where they were going it would be wrong to make the plan too tight and coherent. Remaining pragmatic, they should watch Africans for cues: "The drama of Africa's political evolution is not of the type which can be handed ready-made by the playwright for the actors. Its action will be largely developed by the actors themselves."[5]

Had this metaphorical flourish masked a fundamental contradiction? Had Hailey discarded indirect rule only to reintroduce it in a slightly modified form? Although the report could certainly be read that way, not really. True, existing native authorities led by chiefs were part of his scheme, but so were township and local councils, neither of which were traditional. More significant, Hailey's projection would link locality, province, and center. Although the indirect rulers had used the word "federation" they had not developed linkages; their forecast was decentralized but not truly federal. Whereas their idea was static his had at least the potentiality of movement. Above all he urged that Africans should be brought into important decision-making positions at every level. If that could be achieved in time, he hoped, the apparently inevitable estrangement between Britain and political Africa might yet be avoided.

The trouble was that legislative councils already existed. In the Gold Coast and Nigeria Africans were calling for unofficial majorities and membership of executive councils. If the British were convinced that that was the only road to self-government, Hailey advised, then such steps should be taken soon. Unofficial majorities would short-circuit the process, however, precluding any alternative to responsible government. Moreover the demand for them had come most forcefully not from West Africans but from white settlers in East and Central Africa, where legislatures contained no Africans at all. Although he opposed unofficial majorities, at this point he did not object to unofficial executive councilors. Nominees would no doubt represent sectional interests or political associations, but sooner or later that problem must be faced.[6]

The weakness of all gradual approaches, including Hailey's, was time. He knew it was limited. He knew that a race would have to be run against growing pressure from strikes, riots, tax revolts, ethnic or agrarian disturbances, mounting racial solidarity and anger. He had been through all that before. What he could not have foreseen was how differently Britain would respond after World War II to what, from the perspective of India during the interwar period, would after all be a fairly early stage of nationalism. He set no definite timetable. Like most of the Colonial Office he was probably thinking of a generation in West Africa, considerably longer than that elsewhere.

Good administration enjoying popular support was only a means to the end of improving African living standards, the report insisted, and those were deplorably low. Because African involvement was essential, socioeconomic and political advance must be simultaneous. Hailey urged controlled but resolute development, including the appointment of educated Africans at all levels, which "while leaving an opening for advanced opinion to play its part, would keep the substance of power in the hands of the official Government, until

[5] Ibid., pp. 54–8.   [6] Ibid., pp. 58–61.

258

experience has shown us under what constitutional forms the dependencies can move most securely towards the final stage of self-government."[7]

Although the administrative surveys would have interested the officials concerned, the underlying principles had been covered in the long introduction. The density of detail confirms how engaged Hailey and Pedler had become with the working of native administration on the ground. That point too has been made. The middle section of the report (chapters 2–9) can therefore be skipped, moving directly to chapters 10 (Southern Rhodesia) and 11 (a separate note on amalgamation).

The policies of Northern and Southern Rhodesia differed in practice, Hailey argued, yet the contrast in underlying philosophy was even sharper. Southern Rhodesia called itself a White Man's Country. It sought to guarantee every white person a standard of living that in Europe would be achieved only by skilled workers. There was only one way to secure that objective. The ruling class had to obtain from the rest of the populace enough "unskilled, domestic, or subsidiary labour at wages based on much lower standards of living," while guaranteeing that the latter class would be prevented from competing with less-skilled whites. Although the Bledisloe Commission of 1939 had described this policy as experimental, there was nothing tentative about it. The program had been fully articulated, all important segments of white Rhodesian opinion had embraced it, and only some cataclysm would alter it.[8]

As defined by its prime minister, Dr. Godfrey Huggins, Southern Rhodesia's policy was called parallel development. The favorite metaphor was two pyramids. It was an integrated, systemic whole. In one division Europeans were protected from any competition. In the other Africans were supposedly being given scope for advance "on their own lines." The movement of Africans into white areas was restricted, and more than fifty thousand were convicted of offenses against the pass laws every year. Maize-control regulations favored white farmers. The Industrial Conciliation Act of 1934 required employers in white areas to pay a minimum wage, effectively imposing a color bar that was reinforced by trade-union methods. Directing it all was a white state from which Africans were to be excluded permanently. Especially if investment in the reserves were increased substantially, some Africans would no doubt benefit. But there could be no doubt about the objective. Southern Rhodesia's white settlers were mostly English-speaking and loyal to the British crown. Otherwise the colony was like the Union of South Africa.

In the separate note on amalgamation Hailey stressed that his natural bias favored big political units like the Indian provinces he had governed. According to his investigation, Southern Rhodesia was far outspending its neighbors on African education, health, and so on, he saw little difference in land policies, and he dismissed the argument that the colony's system was unacceptable because it did not follow indirect rule. Instead the crux of the problem was the

[7] Ibid., p. 62.   [8] Ibid., p. 297.

Industrial Conciliation Act. Amalgamation would extend the color bar throughout Northern Rhodesia, especially the copper belt. Thus "the divergence of
native policies . . . remained a factor which, though not necessarily con-
clusive . . . against amalgamation, must be taken into account in weighing [its]
advantages and disadvantages."[9]

Lord Hailey had come out pretty much where he had gone in. The policies
differed more in underlying philosophy than in practice, and although constitutional carpentry might contrive to connect the two colonies, the fundamental
incompatibility would only deepen. Africans would oppose amalgamation bitterly and the industrial color bar would cost them dearly. Yet the contradiction
was not necessarily definitive and, after all, it was not his decision. Those who
made it would have to consider the larger regional context, which his deliberately narrow terms of reference had excluded, of British relations with South
Africa.

Hailey was equivocal about amalgamation. The patriotism of white Rhodesians during the crisis of May–June 1940, when the Germans had overrun
France so rapidly, had deeply impressed him. The native question had divided
Britain from South Africa, he observed at the Colonial Office in August 1941.
It should not be allowed to estrange white Rhodesians too. Yet their enthusiasm
for amalgamation could easily be exaggerated. The most fervent advocates were
actually Northern Rhodesians, especially trade-union leaders bent on applying
the color bar to the copper belt. The color bar was crucial. "It looks as though
in the interest of the black man we ought to make our stand at the Zambesi,"
said the colonial secretary, Lord Moyne. He would not object to amalgamation,
Hailey responded, if the problem of the Industrial Conciliation Act could be
resolved.[10] There the matter rested for the rest of the war. Like the wartime
coalition and the Labour cabinet that succeeded it, Hailey would remain ambivalent.

∞∞∞∞∞∞

In the Romanes lecture of May 1941 at Oxford – as an undergraduate in 1892
he himself had heard Mr. Gladstone give the first in the series – Lord Hailey
explored a problem on which his report had only touched, the implications of
colonial self-government for the Commonwealth. Deftly he sketched the background. The African colonies acquired in the late nineteenth century were
often called the Third British Empire. Although they matched India's size if not
its population, they differed from both India and the white dominions in possessing neither written languages nor recorded history. In governing this new

---

[9] Ibid., pp. 351–2.
[10] Note of meeting in Lord Moyne's room, 13 August 1941, DO 835/265/113036. Moyne had
taken office after Lord Lloyd's death in January 1941.

empire of so-called backward peoples Britain had further developed the concept of trusteeship. Although that doctrine was now regarded as static, in its day it had been dynamic. Its classic statements – Lugard's *Dual Mandate* and the League of Nations charter, both of which stressed the obligation to protect peoples unable to stand by themselves while developing colonial resources for the benefit of mankind – had remained unfulfilled until 1940, when the Colonial Development and Welfare Act had opened a new era. Further, a series of declarations had assured colonies that they could expect responsible self-government once their economic and social development justified it.[11]

It was impossible to predict the timing of independence, he said, using a word that would soon become anathema in official circles. Yet India had been promised dominion status, and recently the term "Commonwealth" had begun to be employed to justify the continuance of dependencies under a power claiming to be waging war for the freedom of all mankind. That word was the result of an entirely separate history of relations between Britain and the white dominions. In the language of General Smuts in 1917, the Balfour Declaration in 1926, and the Statute of Westminster in 1931, the Commonwealth idea had had no relevance to colonies at all. The current usage apparently incorporated the products of all three British empires, looking ultimately to "a projection of the existing Commonwealth, in which such of the Colonies as achieve an autonomous status will rank as equals."[12] Without ever thinking through the problem or consulting his partners, the senior member of a white man's club had decided to admit black, brown, and yellow members. At some point the other parties would presumably have to approve. And the club would need new rules.

The obstacles were severe, Hailey warned. Tropical colonies had no previous contact with British political institutions. Some were artificial units, containing peoples who were mutually hostile; some were too small; some included territories, such as Buganda or the Malay sultanates, whose status was guaranteed by treaty. Others had permanent European minorities. Granting them self-government, as in Southern Rhodesia, would remove Britain's power to prevent the permanent exclusion of Africans from political participation in their own countries. Such difficulties raised questions about the whole idea of colonial self-government. Even the strongest advocates implicitly admitted the need for a period of tutelage. Although the commitment to progress might in some ways be illogical, however, there was no going back on it. The right form for self-governing institutions must therefore be found, while as healthy a balance as possible was maintained between economic and political advance.

The British had always assumed that self-government meant extending their own institutions, Hailey continued. But the parliamentary system required that all elements of a society must agree to entrust decision making to representa-

---

11 William Malcolm Hailey, *The Position of Colonies in a British Commonwealth of Nations* (London: Oxford University Press, 1941), pp. 14–15.
12 Ibid., p. 17.

tives. That was one thing in a homogeneous society. Where deep racial, ethnic, or religious cleavages existed, however, the Westminster model might break down. Finding a viable basis for a truly representative legislature was therefore difficult. Indirect rule, which sought to develop traditional institutions, was the outstanding British alternative. In public Hailey's criticisms were much less pointed than those of his report. He warned that the system would not work where European minorities were strong or traditional authorities weak and mentioned that educated Africans had some objections. But he did not repeat the indictment of his confidential report that the logic of indirect rule pointed not toward self-government but toward enduring stagnation and fragmentation.

Political reform was not enough, Hailey stressed. Truly autonomous nations needed to be self-supporting and therefore of a certain size. The dominions themselves were products of the federation of previously separate territories; presumably the drive toward colonial autonomy would strengthen amalgamation schemes. One could foresee difficulties for the dominions. Would South Africa accept equality with African states? How would colored members of the Commonwealth react to the discriminatory immigration regulations that all the dominions had enacted? Would colonies share the grand imperial vision? The most immediate problem, however, was to keep political advance from outrunning economic change. A time would come when self-government would supersede good government, Hailey concluded. But not yet: "We should not give our native population cause to complain that when they had asked for bread, we had offered them a vote."[13]

Not the least interesting feature of the Romanes lecture is the subject Hailey deliberately excluded, India. Ever since his retirement in 1934 he had maintained a clean break, neither corresponding regularly with serving officials nor speaking on India in the House of Lords. (Indeed, although he had received his peerage in 1936, he made his maiden speech only in 1941.) From time to time, however, he did comment on events. In May 1937, after Congress came to power in seven provinces including the UP, spelling final defeat for his campaign to build a viable alternative, he said the verdict must be accepted. One could only hope that once they took office the more responsible Congress leaders would grow frightened of their left wing.[14] In May 1939 he noted that with the approach of the long-delayed federation the rivalry between Congress and the Muslim League was becoming ever more bitter.[15] That September, stressing the opposition of Congress leaders like Nehru to Nazism, he predicted the country would support the war effort as it had a generation earlier. In October he praised the military classes of north India but acknowledged that Congress's intransigence had forced an impasse.

---

[13] Ibid., p. 41.
[14] Speech at Bombay Dinner, City of London, HPA/338. See also two letters from the Nawab of Chhatari, 28 October 1936 and 22 February 1937, HPI/28C, explaining the continuing weakness of the landlord party; Hailey was not surprised by the result.
[15] Talk of 9 May 1939, HPA/334.

By December he recognized that the deadlock was unlikely to be broken. Civil disobedience seemed probable, further disrupting the war effort and possibly provoking incidents like Jallianwala Bagh in 1919. Only some sort of constituent assembly held any hope, and even that would probably break on the rocks of conflict between Congress and the Muslim League. Britain's objective remained dominion status. But a mere declaration that it would be granted after the war would not be enough.[16]

As long ago as 1917, when Hailey had been commissioner of Delhi, the Montagu declaration had promised progress toward responsible government and dominion status. The Government of India Act of 1919 had lengthened the process indefinitely, and Hailey himself had muddied the waters in 1924 by suggesting that those were two separate stages. In 1929, however, with Hailey advising a full-blooded statement, Irwin had declared that dominion status was indeed Britain's goal. Attending the Round Table Conference of 1930, defending the government's proposals before the Parliamentary committee in 1933, helping push through the Government of India Act of 1935 just after his retirement, Hailey had played a central role in the constitutional negotiations of the 1930s. Not until 1941, however, did he face up to the implications self-governing colonies would pose for the Commonwealth – and then it was not India that dominated his thinking, but Africa.

This gap confirms that in framing Irwin's declaration of 1929 neither the viceroy nor Hailey himself had been moving resolutely toward a multiracial Commonwealth. (After all, even a Commonwealth of fully autonomous white nations was confirmed by statute only in 1931.) It may also support the interpretation that the Act of 1935 was intended not to decolonize but to perpetuate British power in Asia as long as possible. Yet the answer seems to be contained in the one brief statement Hailey did make on the subject. "The position taken by India among the other nations of the Commonwealth," he said in 1939, "will be determined by the character of the elements in India to which the new Constitution gives the chief share in framing her policy."[17] If men like Nehru had a choice, would they not secede at once?

By 1941, having replaced Lugard as the most widely recognized authority on African administration, Hailey had also become one of the leaders of the colonial reform movement. It was a role the old Punjabi, whose title commemorated the bringing forth of an irrigated oasis in a desert, embraced with enthusiasm. Reiterating Britain's commitment to self-government, urging the full participation of educated Africans, he hoped to avoid their alienation. But his first priority was economic and social advance, and that would take time. Foreseeing a race against political demands he knew would ultimately prevail, he included in his native administration report a scheme for linking locality, region, and center. Though he envisaged decolonization, however, he stressed the prepara-

16 Speeches of 18 September, 17 October, and 5 December 1939, ibid.
17 Hailey talk of 9 May 1939, ibid.

tion and the process rather than the end, insisting that self-government should be conferred only on peoples truly capable of standing on their own. The Commonwealth would have to adjust and, if it were to absorb them, dramatically transform itself.

In May 1940 Hailey had assumed direction of the Colonial Office's advisory committee to scrutinize projects under the Colonial Development and Welfare Act. Shortly after turning in his native administration report he also agreed to chair a committee on postwar problems. Over the next two years some 160 memoranda were written on such subjects as secondary industrialization, tariffs, international cooperation, medicine, education, and land tenure. As Flint has observed, these papers show that the Hailey committee recognized the deep structural weaknesses that are now called underdevelopment. They wanted to develop colonial economies not perpetuate their stagnation. If dependency persisted – as it did – it was because the condition was truly structural.[18] Arguing that reliance on the man-on-the-spot had been taken too far, Hailey's own memoranda urged stronger central control. The champion of provincial autonomy in India, the man who had threatened resignation when his superiors meddled with his budget, now exhorted the Colonial Office to take charge.

Colonial planning occupied Hailey through 1941 and 1942, during which Britain won control of its airspace, Hitler invaded Russia, and the Japanese attack on Pearl Harbor at last brought the United States into the war. In August 1941 Churchill and Roosevelt issued the Atlantic Charter, Article 3 of which pledged "to respect the right of all peoples to choose the form of government under which they will live" as well as "to see sovereign rights and self-government restored to those who had been forcibly deprived of them." Did that mean colonies? The charter referred only to Europe, the diehard Churchill declared. British principles, old, unequivocal, and frequently repeated, would continue to guide the steady progress of India and the colonies. Colonial nationalists like Nehru, Azikiwe, or Kenyatta were not convinced. Neither were the Americans.

On 18 February 1942, demonstrating the prestige his name was still thought to have with the military classes, Hailey broadcast to India. Although the statement was obviously propaganda, it showed a sense of identification with the audience it would have been hard to feign. It was the statement of an imperialist, a man's speech meant for men. It was as though he had never left the Jhelum. Since the fall of Singapore on the fifteenth, he said, the public's sense of the disaster had intensified. It meant not only the loss of brave men, many of whom were Indian, valuable arms, raw materials, and a great naval base. The once distant war was now at India's doorstep. The Japanese would say they only meant to drive the British out, leaving Indians and Burmese to govern themselves. Chiang Kai-shek of China could tell them about that.

---

18 Flint, "Planned Decolonisation," pp. 407–8. See particularly the minutes of Sir Sydney Caine and other officials on secondary industrialization, November 1941, CO 852/504/4. The Hailey committee files take up the whole CO 852 series.

Men were judged by how they faced their gravest difficulties, Hailey concluded. Some looked for scapegoats; others met problems head-on. There could be no denying the magnitude of the defeat at Singapore. Yet Russia was now on the move, America with the world's greatest productive capacity was in it to the death, China remained unbroken, and Britain itself was stronger than a year ago. As General Smuts had said recently, war was a risky, up-and-down business. Victory came only at the end.[19]

[19] BBC broadcast transcript, HPA/334.

18

~~~~~~

Adviser and propagandist, 1942–1945

Although Hailey's broadcast after the fall of Singapore did not minimize the military disaster, others drew still more sweeping conclusions. British prestige in Asia, it was said, the hegemony on which the power of men like himself had always rested, had gone forever. Under U.S. leadership, the American columnist Walter Lippmann wrote self-righteously, the Western allies must identify themselves with the Asian struggle for freedom, put off the white man's burden, and purge themselves of the moral taint of imperialism. Whereas the peoples of Burma and Malaya had offered scant resistance, a combined American–Filipino army was still holding out in the Philippines. To Lippmann the difference was obvious. The Americans had set a date for independence.[1]

Did Singapore really demonstrate the failure of civil as well as military policy? asked Hailey soberly in the House of Lords. The fact that a Filipino army was still fighting proved no more than that the Americans had been shrewd enough to train it. The British in India, the French, even the Germans in Tanganyika had done that. Yet the charge that colonial governments had failed to sink roots into the life of the country, as a *Times* editorial had put it, was not easy to dismiss. Those who made it were not thinking of mere acquiescence – obedience to laws, payment of taxes – but of the sort of heroism displayed in the national resistance of the Chinese, Greek, or Russian peoples. That was indeed too high a standard to expect of an alien regime. The problem was not peculiar to the British, however; it was inherent in the condition of dependency. Although it might be long before a plural society like Malaya's, divided as it was into preexisting states as well as by Malay–Chinese–Indian ethnic divisions, could create real nationalism, the lesson was that Britain must continually encourage it. For Hailey Singapore reinforced the case for colonial reform.[2]

By April 1942, when Hailey again spoke in the House of Lords, Sir Stafford Cripps's mission had returned from India in failure. The government had gone

---

[1] *Washington Post*, 21 February 1942, quoted by William Roger Louis, *Imperialism at Bay, 1941–1945: The United States and the Decolonization of the British Empire*, pp. 134–5. As will be apparent from the footnotes, this chapter draws heavily on the superb studies by Louis and by Christopher Thorne, *Allies of a Kind: The United States, Britain and the War Against Japan, 1941–1945* (New York: Oxford University Press, 1978).

[2] 26 February 1942, Great Britain, Parliamentary Debates (Lords), *122*, 129–33.

far to reach a settlement, Hailey observed, even stipulating that provinces might contract out of the union, legitimizing the Muslim League's campaign for Pakistan and perhaps signaling "the end of our vision of [India] as a great unit of Empire strong enough to hold its own in a world that has no place for small and economically insufficient units." Although Indian newspapers were charging the Churchill cabinet with having sabotaged the negotiations just when they were near success, the cause of the breakdown was more fundamental. It was the Congress leaders' realization that not even Cripps would concede them a monopoly of power.[3]

Early in August 1942, when Hailey spoke to the British Council at Oxford, Congress was about to renew civil disobedience, the Government of India having already received approval from London for a sweeping Revolutionary Movements Ordinance. Like Lord Willingdon late in 1931, the government was preparing to beat Congress to the punch. The effect of the campaign would be surprisingly slight, Hailey predicted. Muslims, Liberals, and the army would all oppose it, industrialists and labor would stand aloof, and Congress itself was divided.[4] The echoes sounded familiar. At Lahore University in 1926 he had described communalism as a curse, before tapping it in order to win support for the Simon Commission. Now, although he denounced the Muslim League's Pakistan objective as impractical, he was once more portraying Congress as an exclusively Hindu communal party.

These speeches all reflected the quasi-official position Hailey occupied through the war and beyond. Not until 1947, when he was asked to bring his report of 1941 up-to-date, was he given an assignment like his two missions to Africa in 1940. He remained in charge of committees on postwar reconstruction and research. Although his advice was sought frequently, he was not part of the formal chain of decision making and his policy role depended entirely on the pleasure of the secretary of state. If he should stray beyond acceptable limits it could always be said that he spoke only for himself. In his dual role as adviser and propagandist his semi-independent status was an asset.

As propagandist Hailey coined a new slogan. Indians had long disliked "trusteeship," he asserted; if he were an African he would resent it too. Let the Commonwealth association therefore be described as "senior and junior partners in the same enterprise" rather than the static, paternal relationship between trustee and ward. He urged a colonial supplement to the Atlantic Charter, which would renew the commitment to economic advance as a foundation for self-government. The statement must be honest. If responsible government were thought inappropriate because colonies were poor or because European minorities would be given power, that should be stated frankly. On raising the living standards of primary producing countries to a level nearer that

---

[3] 29 April 1942, Parl. Deb. (Lords), *122*, 770–6.
[4] British Council speech, 4 August 1942, HPA/334.

of industrialized societies, he declared, depended "the contentment or perhaps even the peace of the world."[5]

As adviser Hailey was consulted on Sir Alan Burns's proposal to appoint Africans to the Gold Coast executive council. Ought the British to be training colonial peoples for self-government at all? asked Lord Cranborne. Were colonial rulers merely transients, or did they intend to stay?[6] The "right line of development for Africans," Hailey was quoted, was "to associate them more closely with provincial Councils and with the Administrative Service and gradually build up from below," whereas bringing them into the center too early would "repeat the mistakes made in India." Other colonies were bound to demand equal treatment, and tactically it seemed wrong to move in advance of agitation; better to keep something in reserve.[7] Citing Hailey's authority Cranborne disapproved.[8] Hailey's expertise was Indian, Burns objected, whereas he himself had spent most of his life in colonies of Negroes, who had learned from long experience that riots were the only language governments understood. Concessions ought therefore to be made voluntarily instead of waiting until popular clamor made them necessary.[9] Troublous times lay ahead, warned Sir Bernard Bourdillon of Nigeria; putting Africans onto the executive council would encourage moderates.[10] Facing the combined resistance of his governors, Cranborne reversed himself.[11]

This episode could easily be overdramatized. Hailey gave his opinion only once and then only verbally. Although his report of 1941 had argued that putting nonofficial legislative councilors onto executive councils would be irrevocable and short-circuit the regional councils, he had also said that gaining support from educated Africans was essential. To him it was a question of timing. He had great respect for Bourdillon, whom he called a man of courage, and the need to hearten moderates was an argument he had often used in India himself. If Hailey had been sitting at Cranborne's desk he might well have gone along too. The key point, after all, was not a couple of Africans joining an executive council but the combination of that step with the more important concession of unofficial majorities.[12]

As propagandist Hailey's principal target was the Americans. Despite its

5 20 May 1942, Parl. Deb. (Lords), *122*, 1090–7; address to Anti-Slavery and Aborigines Protection Society, 28 May 1942, HPA/334, a revised version of which appeared as "A Colonial Charter," *Fortnightly* (July 1942), 1–7. How much partnership improved on trusteeship is debatable, for the senior partner would still judge timing. Moreover, as the American Supreme Court Justice Felix Frankfurter pointed out, according to Anglo-American legal tradition a trustee could not judge its own actions. Quoted by Louis, *Imperialism at Bay*, p. 441.
6 Burns to Moyne, 29 January 1942, CO 554/131/33072/42; Cranborne minute, 12 May 1942, CO 554/128/33629A.
7 O.G.R. Williams minute, 13 March 1942, CO 554/131/33072/42.
8 Cranborne to Gold Coast, 19 and 24 June 1942, ibid.
9 Burns to Cranborne, 30 June and 8 July 1942, ibid.
10 Bourdillon to Cranborne, 21 and 18 July 1942, ibid.
11 Cranborne to governors of Nigeria and Gold Coast, 8 September 1942, ibid.
12 Cf. Robert D. Pearce, *The Turning Point in Africa: British Colonial Policy 1938–48*, ch. 4.

impressive record of conquest on the North American continent as well as overseas, the belated entry of the United States into the war intensified a deep-rooted American anticolonialism.[13] Roosevelt himself had strong views, especially against the French. Strident, often badly informed American criticism provoked British defensiveness. Imperialists became still more imperialist, and even the Labour Party's Fabian Colonial Bureau closed ranks. Americans were not fighting to keep Britain's empire together, *Life* magazine said in a famous open letter.[14] Britain would hold its own, Churchill answered; he had not become prime minister to liquidate the empire.

Neither side was monolithic. Some American writers defended the British, while even an imperialist like Lugard called Churchill's declaration unfortunate.[15] Margery Perham pleaded for lowered voices. Americans might be forgiven ignorance about how much the empire had changed, she pointed out; it was less excusable for British leaders not to understand that the empire had become "a self-liquidating concern, dissolving itself by an orderly process into a commonwealth of peoples united by a common ideal of partnership in freedom."[16] That was also Hailey's approach. He too implored Churchill to remove the unfortunate misunderstanding – though after the long struggle of the die-hards against advance in India he of all people knew the prime minister had said exactly what he meant.[17] He too believed that reform was the best response to criticism and that the demand to internationalize colonies needed to be met constructively.

Late in 1942, at the height of the Anglo-American colonial controversy, Hailey made his first trip to North America to chair the British delegation at the conference of the Institute of Pacific Relations at Mont Tremblant, Quebec, returning home in the middle of March. By any standard, let alone for a man of seventy-one, it was a grueling pace.[18] After the conference he took part in the Ministry of Information's campaign to "enlighten" Americans, giving lectures at Brown, Columbia, Chicago, Princeton, and Toronto universities.[19] He also wrote articles on India for *Foreign Affairs* and *Reader's Digest* and talked with numerous people including Roosevelt.[20] In the middle of all that he had to cope

---

[13] The British had not acquired Hong Kong by purchase, Roosevelt pointed out in 1945 to Oliver Stanley, who shot back, "Let me see, Mr. President, that was about the time of the Mexican War." Quoted by Louis, *Imperialism at Bay*, pp. 436–40.

[14] Quoted ibid., pp. 198–200.

[15] Letter in the *Times*, 26 November 1942, quoted ibid., pp. 200–1.

[16] *Times* article, 20 November 1942, reprinted in Margery Perham, *Colonial Sequence*, 2 vols. (London: Methuen, 1967–70), 1:235.

[17] Speech of 6 April 1943, Parl. Deb., *127*, 41–50.

[18] The itinerary is in HPA/Am. s 5.

[19] See William Malcolm Hailey, *Great Britain, India, and the Colonial Dependencies in the Post-War World* (Toronto: University of Toronto Press, 1943) and *The Future of Colonial Peoples* (Princeton, N.J.: Princeton University Press, 1944).

[20] See "India in the Modern World: A British View," *Foreign Affairs*, 21 (April 1943), 401–12. The *Reader's Digest* article, for which he was paid $1,500, never appeared; the draft is in HPA/335.

with the death of his son, Billy, who was killed while on active duty with the Royal Air Force in the Middle East.[21]

The postwar settlement would be unstable, Hailey said at Mont Tremblant, unless it brought a whole new order to the peoples of the Pacific zone. It should raise living standards, helping them escape from their state of economic and political dependency and gain the Four Freedoms. But the foundation of freedom was security, for which regional thinking was essential. Americans regarded the rule of one country over another as inherently wrong and believed the war must liberate dependent peoples. But the British also recognized that the demand for autonomy was bound to be voiced everywhere. Moreover, if colonies sought to pick the fruit of the liberty tree, "it was we who planted it there." The Empire-Commonwealth represented "a procession of peoples in which great distances separate the van from the rearguard." Two principles undergirded British policy: trusteeship or partnership and the tradition that the natural future of a colony was "independent and responsible self-government."

The Philippines were exceptional, Hailey stressed, two centuries of Spanish governance having already laid a basis for self-rule in the islands. In their colonies the British had sought to develop a similar foundation by strengthening local institutions, by gradually substituting native for European administrators, and by creating legislatures with progressively expanding responsibilities. Fault might well be found with the timing of advance or with the absence of a firm date for independence, but surely not with principles or methods. Because self-determination could not rationally mean instant liberation, Hailey tried to explain, there had been some hesitation about extending the precise wording of the Atlantic Charter to dependencies; "but that the *spirit* . . . applies there I have no doubt whatever."[22] Hailey was magnificent, a colleague reported, his only fault being that "he was too obviously head and shoulders above anyone at the Conference: even his accomplished technique could never quite conceal the fact that much of the time he was tucking up his mental trousers to step gingerly through a great deal of intellectual dish-water," making his opponents look like schoolboys, an effect he achieved "in spite of himself, without a trace of condescension."[23]

Although the bias of this appraisal is obvious the conference record tends to confirm it. Hailey's opening statement packed a great deal of the colonial reform program of the past several years – the commitment to colonial develop-

---

21 The *Times*, 8 February 1943. Although the Hailey collection contains no material whatever on his reaction, and only a few scraps of evidence of any kind, it seems apparent that the son had all his life felt himself in the shadow of a famous, masterful, overpowering, and rather undemonstrative father, who may unconsciously have wanted him to follow in his footsteps. If so, the fact that Billy died on active service in wartime may have helped Lord Hailey come to terms with the incompleteness of their relationship.

22 Institute of Pacific Relations, *War and Peace in the Pacific* (New York: Institute of Pacific Relations, 1942), pp. 118–20.

23 D. M. MacDougall to Noel Sabine, 22 December 1943, HPA/Am. s 5.

ment, the firm if cautious support for political advance in the report of 1941, the concept of the Commonwealth as an association of partners, the regional dimension he had been developing since his military-planning proposal in the Congo – into just eight pages. In his proposal for regional councils, and especially his assurance that the spirit if not the letter of the Atlantic Charter applied to the colonial situation, he was to some degree striking out on his own. Churchill, who never recanted his First Minister speech, would not have accepted Hailey's version of his attitude. Nor would the man who had recently become colonial secretary, Oliver Stanley.

Hailey's American lectures repeated themes a British audience would have found familiar. India's fiscal autonomy and accumulation of a large wartime sterling balance had reduced Britain's direct economic interest far below the level Americans might suppose, he maintained. After the Cripps mission there could be no doubt that Britain meant to transfer power; if no date had been set the main reason was conflict among Indians. Colonies too had surprisingly little economic significance, and what backward countries needed was not less but more "exploitation."[24] Self-government must not be a cruel delusion. Difficult problems were involved – poverty, small size and populations, deep internal divisions, European minorities – so the process would take time. He employed the partnership and procession-of-peoples metaphors, articulating an idealistic vision of the Commonwealth as "a union of peoples which is not only a great force in the world but is distinguished by conceptions of social order and of political liberties," fearing comparison with no one. The goal of full membership in such a "commonwealth of free peoples" should inspire colonial citizens "to create for themselves the conditions which justify the grant of independence."[25]

Hailey was only one of a procession of British authorities in a well-orchestrated campaign to stem the tide of American anticolonialism. His lectures were widely reported and his short book *The Future of Colonial Peoples* was published by one of the most prestigious university presses. It would be difficult to measure his impact. There was already an internal American debate, and Hailey provided ammunition to the pro-British faction. The strong and rather hypocritical antiimperial tendency in American thought persisted, however, weakening perceptibly only with the onset of the Cold War in the late 1940s.

Imperialism and colonialism were American catchwords, Hailey reported at Chatham House in March 1943 the day after his return. The key question, however, was the effect American attitudes would have on the wartime alliance and postwar cooperation. If the peace settlement were largely a matter of old-fashioned power politics, then Britain's own capacity and resolve would outweigh perceptions of its morality. In America and elsewhere, however, security

---

24 See also Hailey's article, "Capital and Colonies," an address of 17 June 1943, *Journal of the Royal Society of Arts, 91*, 474–85.

25 Hailey, *Future of Colonial Peoples*, pp. 60–2. Louis, *Imperialism at Bay*, p. 13, calls this the best account of the colonial question during the entire war.

was being defined much more broadly as the removal of internal and international causes of tension. If so the objectives of an international security organization should be two-sided. The United Nations should do more than prevent aggression. It should dedicate itself to improving the living standards of backward peoples everywhere.

Powerful ideals like these underlay American attitudes toward Britain as a colonial power, Hailey continued. Clearly an irredeemably predatory nation would not fit well into such a vision. Although other points – the American habit of rattling eighteenth-century skeletons, Irish-American grievances, the tendency to behave as though Americans "were the sole inheritors of the liberal tradition and the unique possessors of a spirit of moral rectitude, with a mission to teach political ethics to the rest of the world" – might be annoying, they could safely be ignored. If well-informed American opinion was anxious about whether Britain could cooperate in building a better world, however, that could not be neglected.

The tendency at Mont Tremblant to equate backwardness with political dependency was paradoxical, Hailey observed, for of course independent nations including the United States itself contained millions of deprived peoples. So was the identification of the British as the principal culprits rather than the French, Dutch, or Portuguese. His delegation had not found it hard to show that instant liberation would not serve the interests of colonial peoples, however, and Americans generally accepted the concept of "graded political education." The real problem was the Americans' definition of trusteeship, by which they meant "stewardship accountable to the rest of the world." Feeling compelled to make some concessions, and speaking only as private individuals, the British delegation had proposed regional councils. Since the Americans had come with no clear alternative the proposal had been at least a tactical success.

American idealism was not just a pose, Hailey concluded; it was "an integral part of the make-up of what is essentially a large-hearted, a liberal minded and a generous people." And the Americans had no monopoly on idealism. "We have our own vision," he declared, "a society of free peoples," with no room for those "who cannot look forward to political independency, or who are condemned to suffer permanently from economic or social inferiorities," an idea of hope and inspiration "which we can with confidence commend to the rest of the world."[26] Like other ideologies, including the American Dream, the vision he articulated of a new, multiracial Commonwealth, a force for human freedom and dignity in the world, was part propaganda and part genuine belief. Although his Indian convocation addresses had had their idealistic strain, his American speeches went far beyond what he had ever said or thought there. The war did that. Lord Hailey's vision of a new Commonwealth belonged to Britain's finest hour.

---

[26] "The Colonial Problem at the I.P.R. Conference in U.S.A. [*sic*]," Chatham House, 18 March 1943, HPA/335.

When Hailey left for America in November 1942 the themes he would develop there had been thoroughly in line with the Colonial Office's policy. In a way they remained so. An army pamphlet of 1943, for instance, contained a succinct précis of the colonial-reform theme:

We no longer regard the Colonial Empire as a "possession," but as a trust or responsibility. "Imperialism" in the less reputable sense of that term is dead: there is obviously no room for it in the British Commonwealth of equal nations, and it has been superseded by the principle of trusteeship for Colonial peoples. . . . The conception of trusteeship is already passing into the more active one of partnership. . . . Self government is better than good government. . . . We must see if that can become a common Colonial policy accepted by all Colonial responsible powers and concurred in by other nations. Of the cooperation of the United States we may be assured.[27]

During Hailey's absence, however, a shift took place toward Churchill's no-liquidation position. A cabinet committee working on a draft Anglo-American colonial declaration also proposed regional commissions. But the committee's objectives were very different from Hailey's at Mont Tremblant. The phrase "trustee state" was troublesome, wrote Lord Cranborne, implying "impermanence, as if we were only there until our wards had grown up, and must then bundle out willy nilly."[28] Leo Amery at the India Office and the new colonial secretary, Oliver Stanley, also wished to dispel any doubt that Britain would hold its own.

In February 1943 the Americans handed over their own draft "Declaration on National Independence," extending the Atlantic Charter to all peoples, requiring timetables for independence, and proposing an international trusteeship administration to supervise progress. The word "independence," which appeared nineteen times in the American version, was totally unacceptable, the cabinet committee concluded. Even if the phrase "self-government" were substituted, Britain could not agree to timetables. Two days after the committee's decision Hailey was finally given a chance to comment. The American draft had problems of substance and form, he agreed. The substantive points were the mixing up of former Japanese and Italian mandates with British, French, and Dutch colonies and the setting of dates for independence. It was doubtful that rigid timetables represented Roosevelt's view, however – in their conversation the president had spoken of a period of graded education rather than instant liberation – so compromise might be possible. The matter of form was the repeated use of "independence," although of course Hailey had employed that word frequently himself.

To the Americans, Hailey advised, Article 3 of the Atlantic Charter could mean only independence, while the fact that India had been promised dominion

27 *British Way and Purpose* (January 1943), quoted by Thorne, *Allies of a Kind*, p. 343.
28 Comments of January 1943, quoted by Louis, *Imperialism at Bay*, pp. 212–22.

status made substituting "self-government" hazardous. Precisely how did self-government differ from independence? the Americans would ask. Perhaps the phrasing of the Charter itself might be quoted: "the exercise of the right to choose the form of government under which they shall live."[29] Remarking that Hailey had contributed nothing substantial, Colonial Secretary Oliver Stanley ordered that his note should not even be distributed.[30] A number of people, Stanley informed Churchill, including General Smuts and Hailey, had made statements "going rather beyond what we actually have in mind, and I think it would be all to the good if the matter could be put in proper perspective."[31] In July 1943 Stanley told Parliament that the government favored regional commissions, and restated the commitment to progressive implementation of self-governing institutions and the improvement of living standards, but stressed that Britain would remain in sole control.[32] Although Hailey must have felt the statement far too weak, he dutifully broadcast his support to America.[33]

It was an abrupt end of Hailey's period of ascendancy, which had begun after the publication of the *African Survey* in 1938. The Colonial Office's wartime expansion eased him into an annex at York House. Although he continued to chair committees on research and postwar reconstruction, pending the release of experts and the availability of shipping the work of both committees remained on hold. The major planning initiative shifted to insiders like Andrew Cohen and Sir Sydney Caine. Hailey had little to do with working out the UN declaration on the colonial question; again the major role belonged to Colonial Office men, Kenneth Robinson and Sir Hilton Poynton. On African questions Hailey was sometimes consulted but more often not. Finally, in September 1944, on specific instructions from the Colonial Office, Poynton told an American that Hailey was a private individual who spoke only for himself.[34] After the emotional high of his trip to America, when he must have felt he was on an important mission for his country, he was relegated to a kind of limbo. The last two years of the war can therefore be treated rather briefly, summarizing his attitudes on specific issues instead of connecting them to a narrative of events in which, after all, he was playing little part.

India. The responsibility for the breakdown of the 1935 constitution and the mounting communal conflict, Hailey told the House of Lords in April 1943, belonged primarily to Congress. During the Cripps mission, doubting Britain's ability to weather the storm, divided within itself on whether to participate in the war effort, knowing it could not gain support from Muslims, Congress had prepared to renew the campaign not so much for nationalism but, as Gandhi put it, so "Congress would take delivery." Fortunately the hand had been

---

[29] Hailey minute, 5 May 1943, CO 323/1858/9057/B.   [30] Louis, *Imperialism at Bay*, p. 255.
[31] Stanley to Churchill, 9 July 1943, CO 323/1858/9057B.
[32] Louis, *Imperialism at Bay*, pp. 255–8.
[33] Draft of July 1943, HPA/335.   [34] Louis, *Imperialism at Bay*, pp. 384–5.

overplayed and the rebellion had been put down. Admitting Congress to a national government now would confuse the army, undermine the civil service, and let down those who had supported the government. Britain's friends had been greatly tried, Hailey concluded, exactly as he might have done twenty years earlier; they must not be pressed too far. The Americans needed to be told that Britain remained there not for economic advantage but in order to fulfill the vision of leaving behind a great, united nation. Such an attitude might be called prestige or even a form of imperialism, but it was not one American ideals could decry. As long as the Indian question remained unsettled, he concluded, Britain would appear to have faltered in its faith.[35]

When Hailey spoke on India in October 1943 the issue was the Bengal famine, in which perhaps as many as 3 millions died and which, like the surrender at Singapore, called into question the basic competence of British rule. His own generation had taken pride at the disappearance of famine; now once more the specter of starvation was unchained. Normally, he explained, according to the import–export balance if not in meeting modern nutritional standards, India was self-sufficient. The famine was centered in rice-eating Bengal and, though Burma was now occupied by the Japanese, the disruption of imports accounted for only 6 percent of the total. The population explosion was often thought to be crucial – every month at least a third of a million more mouths; yet economists agreed that the increase had been roughly matched by expanding production. There had been no crop failure. Instead the market system had broken down.

During the last war, he continued, inflation had been severe. This time, when the fighting was so much closer, it was bound to be worse. Four-fifths of India's consumers were also producers. Whenever possible peasants kept part of their crop for their own subsistence, and though individual withholdings might be small the effect was significant. The government had had to deal not only with true profiteering but with "a mass of producer-consumers, actuated by motives which could hardly appear to them either unreasonable or illegitimate." But did inflation have to be as high as it was? Why was it concentrated in Bengal, rather than in Bombay or Madras, where the actual shortfalls had been more serious? The evidence of incompetence was hard to resist. He went through the chain. The Bengal government could certainly be blamed, and though provincial autonomy needed to be respected the Government of India ought to have done more to bring it into line. There being no evidence that emergency powers had ever been refused, however, it was hard to see how the home authorities could be impugned. Inflation rather than outright food shortage was the problem, he repeated. The initiative, and therefore the blame, lay in India.[36]

---

[35] 6 April 1943, Parl. Deb. (Lords), *127*, 41–50.

[36] Ibid., *129*, 262–70. Hailey was probably ignorant of Sir Archibald Wavell's desperate pleas to the British government for emergency food, which were turned down on grounds of lack of shipping. But he would have realized that the Government of India's reluctance either to suspend the government of Bengal or to press Sind and the Punjab to increase grain deliveries

Hailey's last important wartime statement was a letter to the *Times* in March 1945 concerning a proposal that if India failed to frame a constitution within a set period, then Parliament should do so, authorizing India to make any amendments it pleased on either internal matters or its relations with the Commonwealth. Although this suggestion might enable Britain to regain the initiative, he conceded, it begged the question. Was India to remain united? Or would it be partitioned? If Britain framed the constitution it would necessarily have to decide whether there would be one dominion, two, or several.[37] Still regarding Pakistan as a thoroughly impractical proposition, still believing that partition was a last resort, by 1945 he realized there might be no alternative.

African land tenure. Along with the committees on research and postwar reconstruction, Hailey chaired an inquiry into African land tenure. Land was the most crucial and complex colonial problem of all, his 1941 report had stated. Although leases to mining companies or the reservation of large tracts for white settlers were obvious and controversial, he argued, changes in African tenure were still more crucial. What he feared was the emergence of a landlord system and large-scale rural indebtedness. Everyone regretted that the British had not acted earlier in India, "before rights, based on European conceptions of the law and novel to Indian practice," had become vested interests. India now contained some 25 million landless agricultural laborers and agrarian indebtedness amounted to £675 million.[38] In the African land-tenure committee Hailey rededicated himself to the ideas of his mentor, S. S. Thorburn, and the Punjab Land Alienation Act of 1900.

The danger was not mere individualization, Hailey stressed, for that would occur inevitably wherever cultivation intensified. It was the recognition of proprietary rights with no restriction on sales or mortgages. Because proper land records rarely existed in Africa no one really knew what was going on.[39] In the Gold Coast, however, he had found some groups who had sold virtually all their land to "strangers." Saying that "alienation was contrary to African tradition"

---

was not unaffected by two facts: first, that those happened to be the only three provinces where Congress had not resigned office in 1939; second, that their ministries were predominantly Muslim.

37 The *Times*, 27 March 1945.
38 William Malcolm Hailey, *Native Administration and Political Development in British Tropical Africa*, ed. A. H. M. Kirk-Greene, pp. 5–7.
39 Philip Mason wrote that when he went to Africa during the 1950s, like Hailey he was shocked by the lack of land records and the absence of Africans in responsible positions. Although the comparison was not exact because of the prevalence of shifting cultivation in Africa, Indian land surveys had been made with plane table, chain, and a three-man team, all costing perhaps thirty rupees a month. "When I told a District Officer in Kenya that he needed maps & land records," Mason recalled, "he looked at me pityingly and said I had no idea of the cost of aerial photography. And he clearly thought that the Kikuyu country could be difficult. . . . But I had made maps of fields in the Himalayas, compared with which Kenya was a tableland." Letter to the author, 31 October 1990.

was all very well, he concluded. The process was not only occurring but accelerating. It badly needed checking before it got completely out of control.[40]

Broadly speaking, the Hailey committee observed, British colonial Africa had three tenure systems: (1) areas such as Gold Coast Colony, where individuals owned or leased land outright as in Europe; (2) territories such as Tanganyika or Northern Nigeria where no title was valid without the government's consent; (3) Kenya, where all land not already sold was treated as crown property. Although governments possessed more power in the latter two categories, even there transactions among Africans were governed by custom and were subject to interpretation by native courts. That was the nub of the problem, experience elsewhere having shown that where governments remained passive, rights of usufruct could evolve into full ownership. As in other parts of the world African tenure was a function of two variables: density of population and modes of land use. When those altered then practice, custom, and finally law would presumably change too. Although African systems were varied and complex, the committee argued, in all of them community and family or individual rights had coexisted, being commonly associated with belief in spiritual power over land as vested in the group's leadership.

In many parts of Africa, the report continued, tenure systems were undergoing severe pressure and growing more individualistic. Incentives to invest and land productivity were both increasing. The danger would occur when property rights became alienable, enabling the owner to borrow without limit for unproductive as well as useful purposes. With loss of control over land the identity and stability of the community would suffer. The result might be consolidation: absentee landlords, rack-renting, a rural proletariat. Or it might be fragmentation, leaving holdings too small for subsistence. Either way, Africa lacked the industrial capacity to absorb people who were forced off the land. In Asia and the Middle East action had come too late. In Africa, the committee hoped, governments had the chance to intervene in time.[41]

The report was far too conservative, Sir Sydney Caine objected. Even African tradition was more flexible. "Progressive acquisition of larger holdings by individuals – growth of landless labour – rackrenting – absentee landlordism," he ticked off the phrases. On the contrary peasant communities became landlord-dominated estates not through natural economic processes but through political chicanery and force: "The committee is more Marxist than Marx himself."[42] Perhaps the point had been overstated, Hailey admitted. But "if the African peasant is to be allowed to go the way of the peasant in India, Egypt and

---

[40] Extract from note of discussion with Hailey in Lord Moyne's room, 18 March 1941, CO 847/21/47084.

[41] Hailey committee, *Native Land Tenure in Africa* (CO confidential paper, March 1945). The committee included the anthropologists C. K. Meek and Audrey Richards.

[42] Caine minute, 6 July 1944, CO 847/24/47084.

Palestine," the old Punjabi wrote with feeling, "it will make a very black page in Colonial history."[43]

African political development. In 1942, over Hailey's opposition, Sir Alan Burns had appointed Africans to the Gold Coast's executive council: a significant though unintended step toward decolonization. Ignoring improving communications and shrinking distances, the Colonial Office continued to treat African regions as separate fields. In Central Africa the amalgamation of the Rhodesias and Nyasaland remained in suspense. In Kenya, the assistant undersecretary Sir Arthur Dawe considered, Britain's pious talk about native paramountcy was all so much hot air. In actuality, he believed, the future belonged to the white settlers. In 1923 they had successfully threatened rebellion. At the moment they were being strengthened by South Africa's participation in the war against the Italians. If they were to present the Colonial Office with a fait accompli it would be hard to know how to stop them.[44]

In July 1943 the head of the West African department, O.G.R. Williams, produced a tentative plan based on Hailey's report. Although Hailey's "recommendations, where he makes any," were cautious and qualified, Williams commented, the thrust had been that economic and social development should at least parallel and if possible precede political advance. If the cooperation of the small but influential class of educated Africans were to be gained, however, they must be incorporated at all levels. Definite, measurable progress toward self-government must take place. West African problems must be considered apart from possible repercussions elsewhere, Williams insisted. Policy should remain as elastic as possible, avoiding irrevocable commitments.

Based on Hailey's federal scheme, Williams's sketch had five stages, each involving simultaneous changes at the local, regional, and central levels. The early phases followed Hailey's guidelines closely. Stage 1 would see increasing African representation on municipal councils, gradual modernization of native authorities, and more Africans in the central legislative council. Stage 2 would increase the power of municipal councils, give regional councils more responsibility, and make the central legislature more representative. Although opposition from educated Africans could be expected, stage 3 would transfer powers from the legislative council at the center to regional bodies. Stage 4 would concede an unofficial majority in the legislative council. Stage 5, "towards self-government," would involve Africanization of higher positions and constitutional conferences. Because Indian experience indicated that unofficial majorities without responsible government provided training only in irresponsible opposition, and because agitation for advance would naturally grow still more impatient, the last stages might well be telescoped. In any case, Williams concluded, "a good many years (perhaps a good many generations, though it would

---

[43] Hailey minute, 10 July 1944, ibid.   [44] Dawe minute, July 1942, CO 822/111/46709.

be impolitic to say so openly) must elapse" before the first three stages could be completed.[45]

Although Williams's scheme went somewhat beyond his own proposals Hailey did not oppose it. Instead he suggested an announcement rather like the Montagu declaration of 1917, which had promised gradual progress toward responsible government and dominion status in India. Chary of statements – he had made one only a fortnight earlier – Stanley rejected that proposal. Hailey also recommended that African members of executive councils be put in charge of departments (that is, dyarchy). But he opposed unofficial majorities. "We did not want to bind ourselves to the development of normal political institutions," he warned, "and then have to think again as we had had to do in India."[46]

In 1944, once again as a result of Sir Alan Burns's wish to keep a step ahead of agitation, the Gold Coast did indeed get an unofficial majority. This time Hailey was not consulted and his speech in the House of Lords contained a rare note of public anger. Until all interests were represented and a party system could provide a reasonably stable base of support for the executive, he asserted, the government needed an official majority. Neither criterion had been met. In East and Central Africa settlers dominated; in West Africa representation was confined to chiefs and a "certain advanced section of the urban population." Unofficial minorities were in a state of permanent opposition, he admitted. Yet long experience had demonstrated that reserved executive powers were hard to use, for they were always denounced as tyrannical. Problems were inherent in all transitional systems. Either way would cause difficulty and irritation.

The alternative, Hailey asserted, was building gradually from below, modernizing native authorities and municipal councils, creating regional councils linked by a small central body. A choice had to be made between two systems of advance. The difference was in method rather than in basic philosophy. "Self-government we must have," he concluded in his usual vein, but it had to be real, "based on the solid ground of social and economic advance," with wide representation of interests and training in responsibility. Although it was not in itself especially momentous, this concession of an unofficial majority would build momentum for further change, placing on the Colonial Office the burden of maintaining balance and control even at the risk of disappointing the politically ambitious. Dryly he wished the measure all possible success.[47]

International trusteeship. As Hailey must have expected, Stanley's statement of July 1943 only confirmed American suspicions. The British were supposedly "guilty of a sin called Empire," Margery Perham wrote in an American journal. Regarding themselves as entirely untainted, the Americans felt themselves

[45] Williams minute, n.d. [June–July 1943], and Hailey to Williams, 26 July 1943, CO 554/132/33727. Cf. Pearce, *Turning Point in Africa*, pp. 58–63.
[46] Note of meeting in secretary of state's room, 20 July 1943, CO 554/132/33727.
[47] Parl. Deb. (Lords), 20 December 1944, *134*, 465–71.

qualified to preach and condemn.[48] Two lines of defense were open. In 1944 the Treasury approved a much enlarged package – all told it would come to £120 million – for the Colonial Development and Welfare Act of 1945. According to Stanley the purpose was "to demonstrate our faith and our ability to make proper use of our wide Colonial possessions . . . , to justify our position as a Colonial Power."[49] The result would be numerous social and economic projects, including the creation of African universities, fulfilling the colonial reform program Hailey and others had been advocating since before the war.[50] The other path was the one Hailey had charted at Mont Tremblant: regional commissions. The aim being to end the mandates system, a cabinet committee asserted, an international information agency should be attached to the United Nations.

The Americans were being asked to underwrite the British Empire financially, a Foreign Office official pointed out. Was it likely that they would be satisfied with a library?[51] Hailey drafted a statement on "the future of colonial peoples," a précis of his Princeton lectures.[52] In the Colonial Office Sir Hilton Poynton and Kenneth Robinson put together a much more far-reaching scheme. It would probably be counterproductive, Hailey criticized. Proposing to abolish mandates would be like waving a red flag. First get the regional commissions accepted and argue for publicity to keep colonial administrations up to the mark. Then, since publicity was in fact its only positive function, the mandates system would fall by itself.[53]

Hailey played no further role. Robinson drew up a list of points not to be yielded, but no Colonial Office representative went to Yalta, where Churchill failed to read documents closely and gave the game away.[54] In the spring of 1945, as the Americans were becoming alarmed about Russia and the more pragmatic Truman replaced Roosevelt, the negotiations became smoother. After all, it turned out, the Americans were not really in any hurry to break up the British Empire. The resulting compromise at San Francisco tilted toward the American position. The UN was to have a trusteeship council. And the future of colonial peoples, according to the charter, was to be independence.

Although he had grown increasingly angry at the Americans, neither development unduly worried Hailey.[55] The objectives of the colonial reform movement – raising the living standards of backward peoples and gradually prepar-

---

48 Perham article in *Foreign Affairs* (1944), quoted by Louis, *Imperialism at Bay*, p. 124.
49 Stanley to Sir John Anderson, 21 September 1944, ibid., pp. 102–3.
50 I want to thank John Flint for pointing out to me that in an earlier draft I was overlooking Stanley's role in rejuvenating the colonial-reform program.
51 Cadogan statement, 26 July 1944, Stanley minute, 8 August 1944, ibid., pp. 382–3, 36–7.
52 30 October 1944, CO 968/14814/11A.
53 Draft statement of 16 December 1944, Hailey minute of 19 November 1944, Louis, *Imperialism at Bay*, pp. 394–7, 399–400.
54 Ibid., pp. 394–5 and chs. 29, 33, 34.
55 See Hailey's note of this period summarized in extenso, ibid., pp. 570–3, and his article "Colonies and World Organization," *African Affairs*, 44 (April 1945), 54–8.

ing them for real self-government – remained intact. Although the Americans as well as the British would find the Trusteeship Council and the third-world bloc in the General Assembly annoying, there was no reason for panic. In the summer of 1945, as Labour swept into office and the war ended, he was released from what had been a very frustrating situation. Lord Hailey would continue to serve the empire in peace as in war.

∾∾

19

Indian partition and the onset of African decolonization, 1945–1949

In 1945 Lord Hailey was seventy-three, still vigorous, curious, and obsessively afraid of idleness. Under the Labour government his quasi-official role at the Colonial Office continued. His activities – including chair of the International African Institute and the association of retired Indian civil servants, Rhodes trustee, member of the governing body of the University of London's School of Oriental and African Studies – were numerous and he was a ubiquitous speaker. He remained passionately committed to the Commonwealth. and by that he meant not some ramshackle collection of countries having nothing in common except an agreement to convene periodic conferences, but something coherent, powerful, and British. The Commonwealth's mission in the world could be fulfilled only if it maintained its moral leadership, he declared, and that would be impaired if the organization included states either politically weak or economically backward. Small units should therefore be federated. Perhaps a United States of Africa?[1]

The Romanes lectures of 1941 had of course said much the same thing. But there the discussion of compatibility and solidarity, of stature matching status, had been put in terms of the Commonwealth as a single, multiracial organization of free peoples in which colonies could aspire to full membership. Although he did not disavow that model, after the war the tone was different. Were African colonies really to have only internal self-government until a United States of Africa could be formed? Was independence therefore to be postponed more or less indefinitely?

The eagle face had softened, Philip Mason remarked in his sketch in the *Dictionary of National Biography;* the personality was mellowing. Simultaneously, however, Hailey's political attitudes began to harden perceptibly. During the early 1940s, when he was a leading spokesman for the colonial-reform movement, he had tried hard to keep up with the idealistic atmosphere. After 1943, when the mortal danger to country and empire had diminished and when he felt himself becoming increasingly marginal, he felt less need to move with the

---

[1] William Malcolm Hailey, *World Thought on the Colonial Question* (Johannesburg: University of Witwatersrand Press, 1946).

times. On a variety of issues – India, colonial political development, indirect rule – he grew more conservative.

As Hailey himself often pointed out, if the New Imperialism of the late nineteenth century were taken as the beginning of a definite period, then the whole of it had taken place within his own lifetime. Going out to India at the zenith of the British Raj, he had seen the rise of nationalism, its development into a militant, ultimately irresistible force, and finally decolonization. In 1945 another quarter of a century remained ahead of him. By the end, although the cycle had been short-circuited in Africa, he would have been through all that again.

The effect on India of Labour's victory in the recent general election was hard to assess, Hailey told Reuters news agency in July 1945. All parties now recognized that India must have self-rule, and though Labour would presumably want to move somewhat further and faster, it would have to face the same problem of internal conflict. As for the colonies Hailey thought Britain had come out of the negotiations at San Francisco surprisingly well. The UN Charter, which required trustee nations "to develop self-government and . . . assist in the development of free political institutions according to the particular circumstances" of backward peoples, was entirely consistent with the objectives of the British colonial reform movement.

Unlike in India, in the colonies Hailey saw no need for haste. Britain should remain committed to building foundations for truly independent nations capable of strengthening the Commonwealth instead of watering it down. Although a unified administration could weld peoples into something like nationality, that process was "a matter of time – often of considerable time." Naively the British seemed to "have given way to the fantasy of supposing that we can create nations by giving the vote to everyone lying within our artificially created units."[2] But perhaps people were beginning to see the facts. He hoped he had been able to help turn the new constitution of Nigeria toward the federal rather than the unitary model, he confided. If so it would be the first time Britain had seriously tried to find an alternative to the Westminster parliamentary system, which in his judgment was so obviously unsuited to African conditions. In the Gold Coast, in his view unfortunately, the decision had gone the other way.[3]

In 1946, at the request of General Smuts, Hailey made a survey of South Africa's administration of South-West Africa, which the Union had governed since 1919 as a Class C mandate. By helping Smuts refute the proposition that the mandate should pass automatically to the United Nations, he explained

[2] Statement of 26 July 1945, HPA/336; Hailey to Sir George Gater, 29 June 1945, CO 968/161/4; Hailey to G. C. Denham, 9 April 1945, HPA/343.

[3] Hailey to Denham, 9 April & 28 July 1945, ibid. On the controversial Richards constitution for Nigeria see Curtis R. Nordman, "Prelude to Decolonisation in West Africa: The Development of British Colonial Policy, 1938–1947" (unpublished Ph.D. dissertation, Oxford, 1976), and John E. Flint, "Governor Versus Colonial Office: An Anatomy of the Richards Constitution for Nigeria, 1939 to 1945," Canadian Historical Association, *Historical Papers* (1981), 124–43.

twenty years later, he had hoped to aid the general in his coming election struggle against the Nationalist Party led by Dr. D. F. Malan. Although he had duly submitted the report to Pretoria, however, it had remained unpublished. No one had ever told him why.[4]

That at least is no mystery. Although the report was written with the author's typical objectivity and based on the assumption that the legality of the mandate was unquestioned, it would have weakened Smuts's case considerably. The so-called Police Zone, the survey made clear, where European mining and agriculture were concentrated, was being governed entirely in the interests of whites. Outside the zone the general contentment of Africans was sometimes cited as a triumph of indirect rule. If they showed few signs of unrest, however, it was because they were being left alone, not because the government was doing anything positive for them. Nor should the administration be called indirect rule, which in British colonies had the "deliberate objective of giving the people a training in the conduct of their own affairs and thus preparing them to take their part in the institutions of the country."[5]

Because the mandate was neither advancing the people materially nor training them for self-government, it failed both crucial tests. Nevertheless, Hailey insisted, the authority under the League of Nations was permanent and irrevocable, and the Union would certainly defend it.[6] His approach was consistent with his attitude toward Rhodesia. As long as Smuts remained in power Hailey would go far to help maintain collaboration. As it became apparent after 1948 that the Afrikaner Nationalists would remain in office indefinitely, and especially after they withdrew from the Commonwealth in 1961, Hailey's position altered substantially. Even so his attitude toward the white man in Africa remained ambivalent.

Hailey's most emotional issue was of course India. If communalism was really that acute, he pointed out, then partition could not cure it. No matter where the lines were drawn minorities would remain: Muslims in India, presumably Hindus in Pakistan, the Sikhs. All his instincts were against it, he said.[7] The situation continued to deteriorate. The sooner Britain handed over responsibility the better, his nephew Peter Hailey wrote. Storm clouds were gathering:

---

4 Note of 1966 on Report on South-West Africa, HPA/343. He also wrote that he had thought a study of South-West Africa would be an interesting companion volume to his five-volume survey of native administration. But that was a sign of failing memory: the tour leading to the latter study began in 1947 and the volumes were published between 1950 and 1953.

5 William Malcolm Hailey, "A Survey of Native Affairs in South West Africa" (unpublished typescript, 1946, microfilm copy at the Consortium of African Microform Project, Chicago, and at Rhodes House Library). In his 1966 note Hailey said he traveled extensively through the territory. There is no reason to doubt that – collecting African colonial districts had become Hailey's hobby; but the report itself was written entirely from published materials and gives no hint that the author had ever gone there.

6 William Malcolm Hailey, *An African Survey: A Study of Problems Arising in Africa South of the Sahara* (rev. ed.; London: Oxford University Press, 1957), pp. 159–65, and "South-West Africa," *African Affairs, 46*, (April 1947), 77–86.

7 Hailey to S. H. Slater, 29 March 1945, HPA/343.

demobilized soldiers, inflation, serious labor problems, stocks of rifles and ammunition gone missing. The decision to prosecute officers from the Indian National Army, whose trial had recently provided a nationalist rallying cry, was the biggest government blunder in years.[8]

Having talked with the secretary of state for India and other members of the cabinet, Hailey divulged in March 1946 (when he seems to have been approached about a position on the subsequent cabinet mission), he had advised abandoning any attempt at compromise on the issue of the central government. Instead he proposed making the provinces sovereign states at once. That, he declared, would be the best chance of their eventually coming together.[9] Since he did not develop this idea in detail it is hard to know what to make of it. Would an interim central government remain? Would the army be provincialized? What about the princely states? Even in outline the scheme was iconoclastic – Balkanization with a vengeance. At the least it would have brought the government into direct, bitter, and perhaps prolonged conflict with Congress. It would probably not have prevented partition and the civil war might have been even worse. But it would have shaken things up a bit.

The results of the cabinet initiative remained in doubt, Hailey grumbled in May 1946. The closer Indian politicians got to independence, it seemed, the more reluctant they were to accept responsibility. Paradoxically, he pointed out, once the departing colonial power had made its intentions absolutely clear its bargaining power might somewhat increase. Nevertheless, the Labour government seemed determined to accept anything, good or bad.[10] Did his criticism imply that the British should stay on until Indians had completely resolved their problems, in other words, indefinitely? Was he seriously overestimating the space available for maneuvering? Probably not as much as might appear. The announcement of 1940 that India would gain dominion status after the war had surprised no one, he asserted. What was shocking was the option to secede.

---

8 Peter Hailey to Hailey, 28 January [1946], ibid. The Indian National Army had been formed by Subhas Chandra Bose from Indian prisoners captured by the Japanese in Burma and Malaya. In the summer of 1945 the War Department divided the men into Black and Grey categories, the first of whom were to be charged with treason. The trial of the first batch of prisoners began in New Delhi in November 1945, sentences being handed down on 3 January 1946. Nehru, Sapru, and others formed a defense committee, the issue became a nationalist cause, and the accused became heroes. Finally the government decided to suspend the prosecution.

9 Hailey to Sir Henry Lawrence, 13 March 1946, ibid. This would be the logical point for what is sometimes said to have been an offer to replace Wavell as viceroy. The alleged offer is not mentioned by Robin J. Moore, *Escape from Empire: The Attlee Government and the Indian Problem* (Oxford: Clarendon Press, 1983), or other studies of the partition period, and there is no hint of it in the Hailey or Attlee papers. Hailey *was* mentioned in March 1946 in connection with the cabinet mission, and I suspect that that offer was somehow inflated into one for the viceroyalty. Even though the story is doubtful it is intriguing. If Hailey had become viceroy he would not have wanted to announce a firm date, and if the British government had backed him in tougher bargaining, the results might have been different. Partition was agreed to implicitly by May 1946 and could not realistically have been prevented. But Hailey would undoubtedly have paid more respect to the advice of senior officials, men who had served under him a generation earlier, and they were warning early and accurately of approaching civil war in the Punjab.

10 Hailey to Sir Charles Ogilvie, 7 May 1946, ibid.

The "idea of Empire without India was so unwelcome that it was difficult to grasp it. We had been accustomed to pride ourselves that the Empire included a fifth of the population of the habitable globe [and] did not like to be reminded that we might have to face the departure of 400 million from our circle."

By the end of the war, however, that psychological gap had been crossed. Moreover, Hailey admitted, the British had no alternative. As the viceroy, Lord Wavell, was arguing repeatedly in his confidential dispatches, under prolonged political strain the administrative machinery of the already largely Indianized civil services might break down completely. Law and order might become absolutely impossible to maintain. The problem was therefore simple: "The Government cannot carry on in its present form. And the only solution which anyone has been able to see is one which involves complete self-rule for India."[11]

It therefore appears that Hailey's proposal of March 1946 to declare the provinces sovereign states was intended not to prolong British rule but to force Indian politicians to face the terrifying prospect of fragmentation toward which their prolonged deadlock seemed to be leading: in short, a sharp psychological shock. Other people found means of conveying the same message. The Muslim League's method was to launch direct action in Calcutta, the result being a week of rioting and some five thousand dead. The Attlee government's tactic was to announce a date: Power would be transferred no later than October 1948. In the debates of January–February 1947 Hailey criticized that policy scathingly. On the one hand, claiming to represent all India, Congress asserted that they and only they could "take delivery." Gandhi had not shrunk from the implications: If the alternative was anarchy, let there be anarchy. Likewise the Muslim League had always demanded that Pakistan must be recognized before power was transferred. The positions were therefore clear and irreconcilable. What, Hailey asked rhetorically, would setting a date achieve? Why should either side give an inch? In fact, he answered, "His Majesty's Government have actually discarded any cards of any value in their hands."

Not the least of the advantages of unofficial status was the freedom to be inconsistent. In July 1946 Hailey had spoken of imminent administrative break-down. In February 1947 he declared there was no such thing. Good recruits were coming forward; the bureaucracy could be rebuilt. There was said to be deadlock, even the threat of revolution: "But we have had deadlocks before. . . . Indian political life is nourished on crises. We have had threatenings of revolution before." Had previous challenges – 1919, 1931, even 1942 – ever been used to justify such a remedy? And was it a remedy? Was it not more likely that no agreement would be reached, that the clock would run out, and that in the end Parliament would be asked for a blank check?[12]

Louis, Earl Mountbatten was sworn in as viceroy on 24 March 1947. Within a few days he concluded that Wavell's nightmare of administrative breakdown,

---

[11] Hailey address to the Inter Allied Circle on "An Independent India," 12 June 1946, HPA/336.
[12] 25–26 February 1947, Parl. Deb. (Lords), *145*, 926–68.

mutiny, anarchy, and forced retreat had been all too realistic. The new viceroy made one last try for unity, failed, opted for partition, forced Jinnah to accept a moth-eaten Pakistan, and moved up the date to 15 August 1947. In January the Sikh leader Master Tara Singh, one of the irreconcilables who had rejected Hailey's offer of 1925 after the gurdwara bill, had drawn his sword in the Punjab assembly, shouting death to Pakistan. In June, as senior officials had been warning, the Punjab exploded. In one of the largest migrations in modern history millions of Sikhs and Hindus moved west, millions of Muslims moved east. With the police communalized and at best passive, with the army apparently incapable of action, civil war raged. At least a quarter of a million died, in nasty, hand-to-hand ways. In the midst of one of the more horrifying tragedies of a terrible century Great Britain divided and quit.[13]

In July Hailey took part in the debate on the Indian independence bill. It would be tempting to ask whether setting a date had worked, he chided mildly. But "we have come to the launching of the ship and it seems of little avail now to emphasize that neither its structure nor its equipment is all that we could have wished." It was more dignified and profitable that the craft "should go down to the waters with our prayers for its success, and with what hopes we can find it in our hearts to give it." The retired civil servants for whom he spoke, men like his nephew now in service, had long since reconciled themselves to independence. Their thoughts were of the Indian masses, the veteran of the Punjab school declared, "the peasant in the fields, the small trader in the towns, the labourer in industry." He hoped such people would not suffer: "May heaven grant that we may never see that day."[14]

A year later India and Pakistan were already fighting an undeclared war over Kashmir. Hailey's lecture notes spoke of his "own reluctance – 40 years – feeling of a trustee handing over an estate to those on whose behalf the Trust had been exercised." Men like him had believed in their mission. Although they had supported the advance of self-government they had naturally felt a surge of regret. Above all, "we felt that the manner in which the chapter had been closed was wrong, for instead of a gradual handing over of powers, step by step, and by mutual consent," the government had been hurried "into a hasty withdrawal that was injurious to our reputations and would leave India a prey to disorder, or something even worse." The world would "not forget the terrible tale of slaughter." To Hailey the whole idea of Pakistan – the eastern and western parts of the

---

13 The historiography of the partition is voluminous and ongoing. Important recent works include Moore, *Escape from Empire,* and *Making the New Commonwealth* (Oxford: Clarendon Press, 1987); Ayesha Jalal, *The Sole Spokesman: Jinnah, the Muslim League, and the Demand for Pakistan* (Cambridge: Cambridge University Press, 1985); and Anita Inder Singh, *The Origins of the Partition of India, 1937–1947* (Delhi: Oxford University Press, 1987). Philip Ziegler, *Mountbatten* (New York: Knopf, 1985), is the standard biography, while all scholars begin with the huge and magnificently produced series edited by Nicholas Mansergh et al., *The Transfer of Power,* 12 vols. (London: HMSO, 1970–83). See also the vivid novel by Khushwant Singh, *Train to Pakistan* (London: Chatto & Windus, 1956).
14 Parl. Deb. (Lords), *150,* 850–8.

country separated by a thousand miles – still made absolutely no sense. Although the intensity of the Hindu–Muslim conflict could not be denied, he reminded his audience, the clash was more political than religious, and it had become acute only during his own career. He could not "believe that the division into two Dominions based only on the factor of religion, can be permanent."[15] It was not. By the early 1970s there were three.

Apart from frequent complaints to the government about deteriorating pensions, that was almost the last word. But two further statements need to be recorded. First, in 1948 Hailey was asked by the master of an Oxford college whether, as the Labour government was representing, conferring an honorary degree on Jawaharlal Nehru might help persuade India to remain in the Commonwealth. Hailey's reply indicated the basic respect he had always felt for his old nemesis and for Indians generally. The degree would be regarded as a formal act of courtesy, he responded, but India would make its decision for reasons of state. How much weight would a doctorate of laws for Dr. Malan carry with South Africa's Nationalist Party? he asked.[16] Second, in a letter of 1961 he referred to the "hurried abandonment of our obligations to the Indian population [which] led (among other things) to the tragedies of Partition."[17] To the end Lord Hailey remained convinced that a different British policy in 1946–7 could have avoided partition and civil war.[18]

∞∞∞∞∞∞

The fifteenth of August 1947 found Lord Hailey on a boat back to Africa, his particular tryst with destiny being a revision of his 1941 native administration report. That document was of great interest to Africanists, Arthur Creech Jones (then Parliamentary undersecretary at the Colonial Office) had noted. Why had it not been published when submitted? Why not now?[19] The answer turned out to be Kenya. "I have myself felt a good deal of injustice has been done to the European element there," Hailey wrote, adding that he had always avoided being unduly critical; but anything short of eulogy was regarded as hostile, while plain factual statements were considered "dangerous in the prevailing state of opinion."[20] Besides the report was badly out of date. Urged to take another tour, he agreed.

---

[15] British Council lecture, Oslo, September 1948, HPA/336.
[16] W. T. Shaughnessy/Hailey correspondence, 12 and 13 October 1948, HPA/343.
[17] Hailey to D. A. Low, 10 January 1961, HPI/51.
[18] Philip Mason wrote that Sir Evan Jenkins, governor of Punjab during partition, told him it would have been impossible to keep the peace even with twenty times as many troops. Ordinarily communal violence centered on some focal point such as a mosque or a temple, and even major riots like those in Lahore in 1927 or Cawnpore in 1931 had been local. "But now it was every house in every village and there were no focal points. It was a general breakdown of confidence in the immediate future." Letter to the author, 31 October 1990.
[19] Creech Jones minute, 16 April 1946, CO 847/24/47100/1.
[20] Hailey to Sir George Gater, 9 January 1947, HPA/343.

Meanwhile the gradualist approach to African problems Hailey had helped to shape was undergoing close scrutiny. Late in February 1947, about the time the date was announced for the transfer of power in India, a circular dispatch informed governors that the Colonial Office had been thinking about how to secure African cooperation in development programs. The answer seemed to be revitalized local government. The words "efficient, democratic and local" were all key, the dispatch asserted: local because government had to be close to the people, efficient because it had to improve living standards, democratic because although it had to absorb the educated it must "command the respect and support of the masses of the people." The document stressed a chain of representation linking regional and provincial councils. The "pace over the next generation will be rapid," it stressed, and change at the center would forge ahead. The base of the pyramid was therefore crucial.[21]

Superficially the local-government policy differed little from Hailey's ideas of 1941. Moreover the continuity was deliberately highlighted at the Cambridge summer school and the governor's conference. The reality was otherwise. On becoming colonial secretary in November 1946 Creech Jones had asked searching questions: Was planning imaginative enough? Were Africans participating effectively? How could relations with them be prevented from deteriorating? Was the colonial service up to the mark? Should London initiate more or less?[22] An African conference was scheduled for 1948 and an agenda committee appointed. Chaired by Sir Sydney Caine, with Andrew Cohen as principal draftsman, the committee developed a four-stage outline: (1) putting nominated council members into executive councils where they would take charge of departments; (2) progressively replacing nominated by elected members; (3) making the latter responsible to the legislative council; (4) full self-government.[23] By late March, about the time Hailey agreed to go to Africa, Cohen and his colleagues had written the first coherent plan for a transfer of power in British Africa.[24]

Although the masses remained largely unaffected, the agenda committee's

---

21 Circular No. 41, 25 February 1947, CO 847/35/47234/1.
22 Note of meeting of 29 November 1946, CO 852/588/19260.
23 Note of meeting of 6 February 1947, CO 847/36/47238/1.
24 This planning process has been covered extremely thoroughly. See particularly Ronald Robinson, "Sir Andrew Cohen: Proconsul of African Nationalism (1909-1968)", in Lewis H. Gann and Peter Duignan, eds., *African Proconsuls: European Governors in Africa*, pp. 353–64, his article with W. Roger Louis, "The United States and the Liquidation of British Empire in Tropical Africa, 1941–1951," in Louis and Prosser Gifford, eds., *The Transfer of Power in Africa: Decolonization, 1940–1960* (New Haven, Conn.: Yale University Press, 1982), pp. 31–55, and his remarks in the symposium, Anthony H. Kirk-Greene, ed., *Africa in the Colonial Period: The Transfer of Power: The Colonial Administrator in the Age of Decolonisation* (Oxford: Committee for African Studies, 1979), pp. 57 ff.; R. D. Pearce, *The Turning Point in Africa: British Colonial Policy 1938–48*, John E. Flint, "Planned Decolonization and Its Failure in British Africa," 389–412, and my own "On the Eve of Decolonization: The Colonial Office's Plans for the Transfer of Power in Africa, 1947," *Journal of Imperial and Commonwealth History*, 8 (1980), 235–57. I have accepted Kenneth Robinson's recollection that, although Cohen was the principal draftsman, the agenda committee's report was a group effort.

memorandum observed, in West Africa the demands of the educated minority were becoming strident. Elsewhere claims were confined almost entirely to Europeans, but in time that too would change. In both cases self-government must wait: in eastern and central colonies until Africans could play a role, in western colonies until territorial unity had been achieved, an African civil service had been trained, and democratically responsible leaders had emerged. In the Gold Coast "internal self-government is unlikely to be achieved in much less than a generation," the document predicted. Progress in other places would be slower, but plans must be kept flexible. Fortunately the machinery for an orderly transfer of power in West Africa already existed. Unofficial members were already serving in legislative and executive councils and Africans were filling higher civil-service posts. Local and regional bodies already constituted the first link toward an unbroken "chain of representation from the people to the Legislative Councils."

Political development would require both devolution from London to colonial administrations and increasing African participation in them, the memorandum continued. At first the two processes would be kept separate, the governor's authority would actually increase, and long-term plans need not be spelled out. Decolonization would take place gradually. In stage 1 the central government would be divided into departments, each run by an official member of the executive council. In stage 2 unofficial members responsible to the legislature would enter the executive council and take over some departments. Although stage 3 was probably "a considerable way off," unofficial executive councilors would become cabinet ministers collectively responsible to a wholly elected legislature. Stage 4 would be the final transfer of power, in which the governor would become the crown's representative, taking the advice of responsible ministers.

Timing would turn on the rate of Africanization of the civil service and the development of democratic representation, especially at the local level. The agenda committee was still talking in terms of a generation or so for the Gold Coast and somewhat longer for Nigeria and other West African colonies, while East and Central Africa were effectively omitted. Yet the break with the Lugardian conception that fragmented native authorities, constituted on traditional "African lines," would somehow evolve into the government of a large modern country was complete. Two pieces of evidence indicate the magnitude of the shift: (1) A paragraph in Cohen's draft, which was deleted from the final dispatch, would have announced that "indirect rule" was being dropped from the official vocabulary entirely, it being "axiomatic that the administration of Africans should be carried out through their own institutions." (Perhaps recognizing that the last three words were also keywords in the segregationist vocabulary, the draftsman substituted "institutions acceptable to them.") (2) A note by Caine: "There is no more need to talk about 'African affairs' in an African territory than there is to talk about 'English' affairs in England. . . . The functions and methods of local governments ought, fundamentally, to be the same."[25]

Although the break with prewar Lugardism was pronounced, the contrast with the transitional projections of World War II, notably with Hailey's report of 1941 and the Williams scheme of 1943 that had been based on it, was less dramatic. Although Hailey must have read the widely distributed local-government dispatch of February 1947, he probably did not read the confidential memorandum of the agenda committee, the Caine–Cohen report, for he was no longer a Colonial Office insider.[26] If he had read it he might well have been uneasy. He himself had criticized what he called the doxology of indirect rule. He had agreed implicitly with educated Africans that atomized native authorities were not really designed to become an authentic government. He had sketched a federal scheme replacing fragmentation by linkage. In a sense the Caine–Cohen plan was a logical projection of his own concepts, developed within his own framework. In nuance and degree of specificity, however, it was a very substantial advance. Moreover, by 1947 Hailey's own attitude had changed subtly but profoundly. Although he never retreated from them entirely, he no longer fully accepted the logic of his own wartime ideas.

The Hailey tour of 1947–8 was like the others, well organized and professional. This time if he kept a journal it has not survived. His secretary, A. H. Cox, did keep one, but apart from recording that Hailey suffered a severe malaria attack in Uganda, said to be his first in forty years, there is remarkably little in it. Later Cox recalled that Hailey "worked from the time he got up till he went to bed," and commented on the energy, tenacity, and intellectual power remarkable in a man of seventy-six, though he did need a rest after lunch.[27] The copious notes and drafts in the Public Record Office confirm that Hailey labored as hard as ever, that he looked for politically conscious Africans, that he remained intensely curious and involved.

Several notes illustrate Hailey's growing ambivalence about colonial administration, his tendency to criticize specific aspects while trying to defend the integrity of the whole. Kenya: "This memo wd. be improved by stressing the fact that about half the land . . . worth cultivating is in the hands of Europeans," who constituted 20,000 out of total population of more than 3 million. Another: "How far does sentiment in Kenya now look forward to bringing the African population forward . . . ? Is the change here as great as some would pretend?"[28] On receiving a deputation from the Nyasaland African Congress: "I think it undesirable to give this prominence to an outside body, just at the

25 Cohen memorandum, 28 March 1947, CO 847/36/47238/1; Caine minute, 8 February 1947, CO 847/47234/1.
26 See Hailey's note, n.d. [October 1947], CO 1018/77.
27 Cox to Lloyd Phillips, 31 January 1968, MSS Afr s 1141.
28 Hailey notes, n.d., CO 1018/30. The first was cited to Dr. Norman Leys, *The Colour Bar in East Africa.*

moment when an effort is being made to give vitality to the Provincial Councils etc." Lessons could be learned from what he already regarded as unwise haste in the Gold Coast.[29] Northern Nigeria: "It seems clear . . . that the present 'cooperation' of N[ative] A[uthorities] and Central Departments is to a considerable degree fictitious"; the local councils contained no popular elements.[30] In western Nigeria too it was "impossible to avoid [the judgment] that there is a certain amount of camouflage in the work ascribed to NAs."[31]

Only a few detailed notes of conversations have survived. The most interesting comes from Masai district in northern Tanganyika. Presumably there was no such thing as average rainfall? Hailey began. No normal years, the district officer agreed. Hailey noted how much the pastoral Masai seemed to be cultivating; it turned out to be "strangers," though precisely where Masai left off and other groups began was hard to tell. Having been fascinated by pastoralists ever since he had first met them in the western Punjab, Hailey asked about nomadism; the local man preferred "radiating." When Hailey had come through back in 1935 reorganization of native authorities had been all the talk. The DO: "In most cases they put up a stooge and I have a feeling that the really important people, about whom we are not told, hold the power and exercise influence." Court, treasuries, native councils: the trouble was that the Masai were quite uninterested in all that; they just wanted to stay as they were. "It is too baffling a problem to dispose of," Hailey concluded, "and I should like to get Mr. Creech Jones out and settle him among the Masai for six months."[32]

It happened that Hailey was in the Gold Coast during February–March 1948, when Accra had a serious riot with some twenty-nine killed and more than two hundred injured. The riot touched off a sequence: the Watson Commission of 1948, the all-African Coussey Committee, a new constitution in 1949, the victory of Kwame Nkrumah's Convention People's Party in the elections of 1951, transforming him from prisoner into prime minister, and an independent Ghana by 1957. The Caine–Cohen Committee's "not much less than a generation" shrank into a decade.[33] Early in February Hailey was told that "the [United Gold Coast] Convention is now the Radical party in the country." Now six months old, it had many young intellectuals, close ties with trade unions, and "one or two prominent . . . Communist doctrinaires."[34] The president of UGCC, J. B. Danquah, the London Ph.D. who had impressed Hailey favorably in 1940, was noted, but surprisingly not Nkrumah, whose recent return from London to become full-time secretary would soon be regarded as having transformed the situation.

[29] Hailey note, n.d., CO 1018/60.
[30] Note of interview with chief commissioner, Northern Nigeria, n.d., CO 1018/37; note of discussion with senior resident, Kano, 4 March 1948, ibid.
[31] General note on western region, n.d., CO 1018/40.
[32] Transcript of interview, n.d. [September 1947], CO 1018/71.
[33] The best historical account is still Dennis Austin, *Politics in Ghana, 1946–1960* (London: Oxford University Press, 1964).
[34] Cox note of Hailey interview, 4 February 1948, CO 1018/18.

A month after the riot Hailey talked with Governor Sir Gerald Creasy, who on rather flimsy evidence was blaming the UGCC for orchestrating it. "Complete breakdown of Chiefs in regard to law and order," Hailey noted; "'poor things what *could* they do.' Afraid of their own people." This, he might have muttered, was where he had come in – in Indian terms perhaps about 1907. His terse note spoke volumes: "Gold Coast a 'political situation' not administrative. Government not organized for it. No intelligence department."[35]

A year later in the House of Lords he declared his sympathy with district officers "who for most of their lives have been concerned . . . with primitive peoples," but who were now faced with political movements in which they were not versed: "We went through that stage in India. It is one that one has to surmount." He found it hard to understand how the Watson Commission, possessing so little local knowledge and after so short a stay, could have gone so far. At least the all-African Coussey Committee had said that its charge was not a constitution for immediate self-government. That point badly needed stressing, for rumors were circulating – he did not want to seem flippant – that the independence of the Gold Coast would be celebrated on 1 April 1949![36] Lord Hailey's substantial nose was out of joint.

He was not alone. In May 1947 the comparatively restrained local-government dispatch had provoked the governor of Kenya, Sir Philip Mitchell, the colonial service's equivalent to Hailey when he was in UP in the 1930s, to write an angry memorandum. People seemed to think, Mitchell wrote, that having reached the stage of the Spanish a century ago the "liberation" of the British Empire was about to begin. Fictitious terms – "Nigerian Nation," "African Community" – were being manufactured in the belief that "no more is needed . . . than a liberal use of current catch phrases or violent words and a little rioting." Malaise was said to have been detected in the colonial service. Its cause was not loss of mission but fear of betrayal. In India administrative decay and social chaos were being greeted with satisfaction at approaching independence. It was all rather nauseating.

Were the British about to turn tail in Africa too? Or did they have the stomach to hold on until true liberation happened in a gradual, orderly way? The history of East and Central Africa having effectively begun about 1890, Mitchell continued, that would take not years but generations. He called for a stiffening of backs. "British Imperialism" had become a term of abuse. For men like himself, however, the imperial idea remained "an expression of faith and purpose." Local demagogues would curse them and even their countrymen might sneer. All that was "no doubt regrettable, but it is inherent in the business."[37]

In 1930, during Gandhi's salt march, although he had employed satire instead of diatribe, Hailey himself had written a very comparable cry from the

---

35 Hailey note of interview, 29 March 1948, ibid.
36 17 March 1949, Parl. Deb. (Lords), *161*, 522–9.
37 Mitchell memorandum, 30 May 1947, CO 847/35/47234.

heart. Like Mitchell he still believed that empire had a job to do. The man who had written the official report on Jallianwala Bagh had experienced far worse riots than Accra's. He saw no need for panic. At some point, he realized, alien rulers would lose the vital acquiescence of the people. When that happened they would have to leave. People who were ready for self-government, he remarked later, found ways of letting you know.[38] Till then he would defend the faith.

[38] "I know no other way than the purely pragmatic test that when people really want it they will be able to show it so strongly that it is better to give it to them," Hailey said in 1955 – in other words, that readiness for self-government was defined as the capacity to manufacture a respectable level of agitation. "Post-War Changes in Africa," *Journal of the Royal Society of Arts, 103* (1954–5), 579–90. In fact, even in the white dominions, there had never really been any other standard.

20

Defender of the faith, 1949–1969

Lord Hailey is often said to have had two careers, more or less equal in weight, and of the two the African phase is actually the better known. That however is a severe distortion. He spent comparatively little time in Africa: apart from winters in South Africa when he was in his high eighties, there were five months in 1936, eight in the two missions of 1940, another two touring and writing the report for General Smuts on South-West Africa, and a final six in 1947–8 preparing to revise the native administration report. As has been shown, although he planned and launched it he wrote very little of the *Survey*. Moreover, because he spent the entire year before publication recovering from a life-threatening breakdown, his contributions as an editor were far less extensive than has usually been supposed. Even the conclusions he saw for the first time in galley proofs.

What has been called Hailey's period of ascendancy, when he was playing a significant role in policymaking, was actually surprisingly short, effectively beginning with the publication of the *African Survey* in 1938 and virtually ending with Oliver Stanley's terse note in the spring of 1943. During the immediate postwar era, with Labour in power, his influence somewhat resurged. After the late 1940s, however, although he presided over the revision of the *Survey* and continued to write, speak, and chair committees, he no longer possessed even quasi-official status and was rarely consulted. His prestige remained high, and he continued to work as one possessed. Yet appearances were deceiving. For all practical purposes except for how he spent his time, he had in fact retired.

Lord Hailey was not really a great Africanist. He was a great man who devoted the last quarter of his life to Africa. To say this is by no means to belittle his contributions. For a man in his sixties to undertake to retool himself required courage and self-confidence. The huge volume of notes at the Public Record Office and Rhodes House testifies to how hard he worked at the job. It is remarkable how well he succeeded, acquiring fluency over a wide variety of subjects from soil erosion and land tenure to urban sanitation and education. On only two subjects, however, did he become truly expert. For the first, native administration, the basis of his mastery was not his close study of African cases but his long Indian experience. The second, law and justice, became a hobby.

Ultimately, what mattered was not so much the intrinsic qualities of his writings as the significance readers attached to them. It was not so much what he said as the fact that *he* said it. In India, partly because of his longevity at the top but mainly because of his extraordinary capacity for hard, sustained work, he earned his position of eminence. In relation to Africa, however, he stepped into a role already prepared for him, into a part Lord Lugard (a man whose reputation depended even more than Hailey's on ascriptive qualities) had been playing for two decades. During the late 1930s a gathering colonial reform movement, largely composed of academics in the fledgling field of African and colonial studies – Reginald Coupland, Margery Perham, W. M. Macmillan, Keith Hancock, Julian Huxley, and a few others – desperately needed legitimacy and official approval. Largely because of the prestige he brought with him from India, Hailey became that movement's leading symbol and figurehead. It is to his credit that he worked at the job extremely conscientiously. It is perhaps still more to his credit that he did not lose touch with reality, that he remained aware of the true basis and limitations of his authority, that he maintained a sense of humor and proportion.

In 1949 Lord Hailey was seventy-seven. Although much remained ahead of him, the period when he can be said to have exercised a major influence on decision making was over. More than physical aging was involved. In a rapidly changing world he no longer felt comfortable with the way things were going. He was becoming increasingly peripheral. He was still an imperialist. And that was rapidly going out of style.

The feeling that he was becoming anachronistic may help explain a puzzle: Why did Hailey's five-volume *Native Administration in the British African Territories*, most of which was written during 1948–9, say so little? The contrast with the 1941 report is remarkable. Whereas the earlier document was incisive, tightly written, and comparative, subordinating local detail to major problems, goals, and ideas, the later survey was reticent, sprawling, controlled by no apparent theme, concerned with means rather than with principles. "Political Development" was dropped from the title. The preface explained that coverage had been "confined to matters relating to the agencies employed . . . in local rule," bearing only indirectly on constitutional questions.[1] As Hailey himself put it in the revised *African Survey*, however, "the story of the Native Authority system may at some future time retain little more than an historical [i.e., antiquarian] interest."[2] The 1941 report, which was not published, would have interested a wide audience of Africanists, as indeed it still does. The 1950 version, which *was* published, was intelligible even then to only a handful of colonial officials. More than "political development" was omitted. It had no thesis.

The readiest explanation would be that at a time of rapid change and review

---

[1] William Malcolm Hailey, *Native Administration in the British African Territories*, 5 vols. (London: HMSO, 1950–3), preface repeated in all the volumes.

[2] William Malcolm Hailey, *An African Survey: A Study of Problems Arising in Africa South of the Sahara*, rev. ed. (1957), pp. 416–17.

Hailey might have been instructed to avoid anything controversial, a possibility his remark about the touchiness of Kenya's white settlers tends to confirm. But Ronald Robinson, who was then a junior official in the Colonial Office, recalled that on orders from Andrew Cohen he tried in vain to persuade Hailey to come out firmly against indirect rule.[3] In conferences and summer schools, as well as the *Journal of African Administration*, a full and critical discussion of African policy was being promoted. Some governors and settlers were indeed sensitive. But Arthur Creech Jones and the Colonial Office would probably have welcomed a thorough revision of the 1941 report, including anything the author wanted to say about general principles and problems. If so they must have been disappointed. What they got was a severely watered-down version.

Several alternatives come to mind. First, that Lord Hailey was slipping. Yet his contemporary articles, the revision of the *African Survey* in the mid-1950s, and even his last book (which appeared when he was eighty-nine) all tend to refute this.[4] The second hypothesis, which Hailey himself noted from time to time, is that as he aged he became increasingly comfortable at the level of detail. Although that is undoubtedly true, it does not explain the decision to omit policy entirely, and Hailey's other writings continued to discuss larger issues. A third conjecture, which seems quite likely though there is no evidence to support it, is that Frederick Pedler had played a larger role than he has admitted in writing the 1941 version.[5] Finally, Hailey may have written the 1950–3 report quite deliberately, as a sort of personal statement.[6]

In the 1941 report the succinct, penetrating analysis of general problems and principles appeared at the beginning. In the later study it came only in volume 4: bland, tentative, hardly a statement at all. The rest of that volume was purely descriptive: potted historical sketches, an assertion that Lugardism was now regarded as an admirable philosophy rather than a structure of governance, and the comment that since some native authorities were operating outside the local sphere the system might need some overhauling. All in all, a pale reflection of the earlier version.

Although the remaining volumes were more substantive they were reports on

---

3 Amusingly, in view of his later writings on Cohen, Robinson was assigned to write an article showing that the local-government policy was merely a logical extension of earlier policy rather than any sort of decisive break with it. See "Some Recent Trends in Native Administration Policy in the British African Territories," n.d. [c. December 1947], CO 847/38/45252.

4 See for instance the transcript of Hailey's address on "Comparative Colonial Administration" to Colonial Cadets, Cambridge, 18 November 1949, HPA/337, as well as the following articles: "A Turning Point in Colonial Rule," *International Affairs, 28* (1952), 177–83; "Spotlight on Africa," in Calvin Stillman, ed., *Africa in the Modern World* (Chicago: University of Chicago Press, 1955), pp. 3–13, the result of a symposium held in 1953, and "Post-War Changes in Africa," *Journal of the Royal Society of Arts, 103* (1954–5), 579–90.

5 In our interview Pedler would say no more than that it was a normal piece of civil-service collaboration. There is a final draft in his papers.

6 A clue may be Hailey's assertion that there had been "in some quarters a tendency to employ the term 'African local Government' to denote the whole of the activities now associated with . . . 'Native Administration'." A reader might not have suspected that "some quarters" referred to the Colonial Office. Hailey, *Native Administration*, 4:5–6.

administrative apparatus, colony by colony. Strikingly little was said about forces or movements. The discussion of Northern Rhodesia and Nyasaland omitted any reference to the possibility of linkage with Southern Rhodesia. The précis on "Zikism" (the cult of followers of the Ibo newspaper editor Nnamdi Azikiwe in Nigeria) was reasonably informative, but not the one on the Kenya African Union. The section on the Gold Coast got in a shot at the Watson Commission, along with Hailey's wry judgment that the colony's procession of constitutions had "a singular air of impermanence."[7] But these bland statements were among the most forthright in the entire work. The volume on the three high commission territories contrived to say so little about their relationship with South Africa that they might almost have been in Australia. Either Hailey had deteriorated very badly, which the evidence tends to refute, or in protest against what he regarded as a dangerous weakening at the center, he was deliberately achieving a remarkable degree of obscurity.

In the 1950s, although a reader of Hailey's revised report would not have seen any reason to suspect this might happen, the pace of change accelerated right across Africa. The disastrous Anglo-French intervention in Egypt in 1956, which coincided with Russia's crackdown in Hungary and was condemned by the United States, signaled a decisive change in the world balance of power. International opinion was pushing ever more strongly against the once mighty seaborne empires. Driven by a wide variety of economic grievances – land hunger resulting from white settlement, restrictions on cattle or cultivation of crops, commodity price-fixing, above all the fact that activities under the economic plans historians now call the second colonial occupation of the 1940s were disrupting the lives of ordinary Africans as never before – and directed by sophisticated, well-organized political parties, African nationalism was growing with astounding rapidity. Like other Africanists Lord Hailey struggled to keep up.

Once the Gold Coast received responsible government it was obvious the other West African colonies would follow in due course. Although Hailey probably never forgave the Watson Commission, although he regretted the regional alternative had been short-circuited – and the blunt truth is that in the early 1990s only Nigeria, with its huge population and oil reserves, looked even remotely like an economically viable nation – he saw no point in flogging dead horses. The focus shifted to the controversial issue of closer union in central Africa, now made more urgent by the Afrikaner Nationalist victory over Smuts in the South African election of 1948. Although this time the proposal was for federation rather than amalgamation, which would have been dominated explicitly by Southern Rhodesia, African opinion remained vehemently opposed.

It was the last colonial issue in which Hailey became involved. As always, where the white man in Africa was concerned he remained ambivalent. The latest report, he asserted in 1951, was just as mistaken as the Bledisloe Com-

---

[7] Ibid., 3:279–80.

mission of 1939 in concluding that the respective native policies differed only in timing and degree. On the contrary, as he himself had written in 1941, the principles diverged profoundly. Nevertheless he hoped this piece of constitutional carpentry would be given a chance.[8] A year later he warned against ignoring African opinion. Although it was being said that criticism was confined to a few unrepresentative educated Africans, precisely the same argument had been heard in India sixty years before; it was just such an "intelligentsia" who proved to be the natural leaders of a society in a way alien rulers could never hope to be. Although he warned against imposing a federation on unwilling Africans, he hoped they would come to accept the idea of racial partnership.[9]

Yet Hailey had also said in 1941 that the African voice need not necessarily be decisive. In 1953, notwithstanding his recognition that African opinion was adamant, he argued that the best way to counteract division between the races was to bring them face-to-face in a legislature. Granted that (to say the least) for a while African representation would be somewhat limited, in time that would surely increase. Uniting 6 million Africans into a single political framework would raise their potential power enormously. Admitting his inconsistency, he said that he had "hesitated much before I came to the conclusion that it would be wise to go on."[10] Despite the militant opposition of Africans, proceed the British government did. Joining the Capricorn Society, Hailey continued to speak for racial partnership. Although the federation came into being it was soon destroyed by African resistance and Ian Smith's at least equally belligerent Rhodesia Front. Racial partnership had come too little and too late.

Although he had been thinking of it at least since 1940, when he had made a study of native administration in the Congo, in 1952 Hailey began to revise the *African Survey.* Another grant came from Carnegie, another staff was assembled, and the offices at Chatham House reoccupied. Apart from widely scattered notes at Rhodes House and a few strays at the Public Record Office, little material on the making of the second edition has come to light. Despite the fact that a cataract operation in 1956 prevented him from completing the proofs, however, there is no reason to suppose that the job was anything like the traumatic experience of 1936–8. It is not that by the 1950s the director knew more about Africa, though he did. After retiring from India he had set out to write a short, readable book of 250 pages or so. He had been unable to do that and from the failure something entirely different had emerged. This time the project did not have to be conceptualized. The quantity of work had never been the problem. Even in his early eighties Lord Hailey still thrived on it.[11]

At a ceremony on the unveiling of his portrait at Chatham House in 1955

---

[8] 1 August 1951, Parl. Deb. (Lords), *173*, 184–9.
[9] 17 July 1952, ibid., *177*, 788–98.   [10] 1 April 1953, ibid., 512–20.
[11] During the late 1950s, Hailey told Philip Mason that he could not be happy unless he had written so many pages per day. He also said he could always remember exactly the number and location of a page where he had read something.

Hailey joked about what was called his authorship of the *Survey*.[12] Now as before, although in the late 1930s his absence from the enterprise for nearly the whole year before publication had been covered up, it was a team effort. The new edition had much better coverage of French Africa; the reason was Kenneth Robinson.[13] It contained articles on art, music, and dance; Hailey did not write those any more than he did the ones on forestry or medicine. Lucy Mair continued to help with the central chapters on governance and Phyllis Deane did the ones on economics. Although the evidence is inconclusive, however, the impression is that this time the director's own contributions were more frequent and controlling. The second edition could somewhat more realistically be called "Hailey on Africa."

The outline of the new edition was basically similar. But the revision was no mere touch-up. Despite being rather longer it was somewhat tighter. The essentially redundant conclusion of the first edition, for instance, which had tediously repeated arguments from individual chapters, was omitted. The single best essay was still "Law and Justice," the piece Hailey had written in 1936. But the other core chapters all seemed to be improved and they showed signs of Hailey's own ideas and prose style. Compared with the first edition, let alone the virtual abdication from critical discussion in the 1950 native administration report, the second edition of the *Survey* was rather less qualified. As a book it was not only substantially different. It was better. Yet its contribution to scholarship was a good deal less significant. The version of 1938 had helped to define and legitimize a field. By the early 1960s, when African studies entered their most fruitful and innovative period, the *Survey* was already an anachronism.

It would be a rash individual who tried to judge how well the revision reflected the explosion of knowledge since 1938, but a few examples may be given. The chapter on African Peoples in the first edition had stated confidently that they were all descended from three principal racial stocks: Bushman, Negro, and Hamite. In the revised version, written after such notable contributions to anthropology as those of Adolf Hitler and Hendrik Verwoerd, race was out, having given way to linguistic families and culture areas. African history was said to be full of migration, intermixture, the consolidation and disintegration of states. Urban problems got more treatment. The first edition had said that Africans in town should be regarded as normal; the second indicated that at least in the scholar's world they were becoming so. Although the political coverage was supposed to be up to 1955, much of it was of course out-of-date even before it could be printed.

Some of the more controversial aspects of the revised *Survey* could be attributed directly to Hailey. First, alien rule was still assumed to be the norm.

---

12 The *Times*, 28 January 1955.
13 Robinson said emphatically that he was not responsible for what he called grotesque distortions of developments in French African colonies, saying that either Hailey or his proofreader, Charles Carrington, had "got at" the material.

Ghana's approaching independence was discussed briefly, but the book gave no hint of anything like an approaching avalanche. Second, whereas the largely implicit message of the first edition had been colonial reform, the revised version became something of a propaganda piece against rapid political change. The treatment of the Mau Mau movement in Kenya was as biased as the works of L. B. S. Leakey on which it drew, while with respect to Ghana Hailey got in one last dig at the Watson Commission.[14] More telling was the analysis of comparative rates of indigenization of the Indian and colonial services. Although he had urged it strongly in his report of 1941, Africanization had taken place only in parts of West Africa and even there it was far behind the pace in India by 1947. "Whatever may be the merits of a policy which has in recent years conceded so large a measure of advance to the British dependencies," the chapter concluded, "it is obvious that the transfer of power is finding some of them without an indigenous machinery . . . adequately equipped for their administration."[15] It would be hard to disagree.

Finally, Hailey rejected "nationalism" in favor of "Africanism." In Europe, he argued, the dynamic concept of territorial nationalism was easy to recognize if not to define. In Africa, with its multitude of diverse peoples inhabiting largely artificial political units, the term seemed unrealistic. Nor, although he recognized that racial identity was a major component of African consciousness, did he think pan-Africanism yet amounted to very much. In 1937 he had discussed nationalism fairly confidently – how it had emerged in India, how it would rise in Africa in due course – as a law of nature. In 1941, having looked fairly hard, he concluded that it was present only in one or two places; but the word was still nationalism. Probably during his second tour of 1947–8, very likely when he saw the Gold Coast government panic in the face of what compared with Indian standards amounted to no more than fairly minor riots, he grew more skeptical. Hence the substitution of "Africanism." As late as 1959, just before the deluge of independence, he judged that "there is certainly no parallel to the co-ordinated movement for home rule which spread so rapidly in British India." Nor would it come soon, he thought, "for there is in Africa nothing like the underlying unity of India . . . which even the partition . . . might disturb but could not entirely disrupt."[16]

Hailey's use of "Africanism" was neither patronizing nor perverse. "It" was a powerful and rising force, he acknowledged, which even the Belgians or the Portuguese would be unable to ignore indefinitely. His loose definition belonged to the school of which the analysis by Thomas Hodgkin, also published in 1957 – with its complex, effervescent, interacting layers of associations, tribal groups, dance societies, political parties, pan-Africanism – was the classic

---

[14] See Louis S. B. Leakey, *Mau Mau and the Kikuyu* (London: Methuen, 1952) and *Defeating Mau Mau* (London: Methuen, 1955).

[15] *African Survey* (1957), pp. 289, 363–71.

[16] William Malcolm Hailey, "The Decline of the Colonial System in Africa," *Year Book of World Affairs, 12* (1959). See also "The Differing Faces of Africa," *Foreign Affairs, 36* (1957), 143–53.

study.[17] Another school, though agreeing that all these phenomena were important, preferred a tighter definition: throwing the Europeans out.[18] Although
that sounds negative, for some reason Hailey called it the constructive phase:
"the attainment . . . of a government dominated by Africans and expressing in
its institutions the characteristic spirit of Africa as interpreted by modern Africa."[19] Yet Mill's dictum, which he continued to quote frequently, had been
that territorial nationalism emerged within and in opposition to the administrative unity that had been imposed by alien rule. In Africa, Hailey stressed,
colonialism had been in place only briefly, in some areas for no more than half a
century. The obstacles to what by European standards could legitimately be
called nationalism, in his view, were severe indeed.

When the revised *Survey* appeared in 1957 Lord Hailey was eighty-five. After
that he did slow down. Like any sensible old person who could afford it he fled
from English winters, going to Spain and then for several years to South Africa.
"Have you yet learnt to exist without working?" he asked an old friend. Although he remarked that he had heard supplications offered up for the unem-
ployed, he had not found idleness "mentioned among the problems for which
our Anglican prayer book seeks divine aid in solving."[20] Clearly he never
mastered the art. According to Leonard Thompson, who knew him in Cape
Town, he was taking lessons in Afrikaans. But even that was not enough. In
1960, now aged eighty-eight, he undertook yet another project, a survey of the
three high commission territories: Basutoland, Swaziland, and Bechuanaland
(now respectively Lesotho, Swaziland, and Botswana).

Hailey called it a booklet – it was just over a hundred pages – and he wrote it
entirely from secondary and primary printed sources. Yet it showed that he was
still capable of organizing and supporting a sustained argument. In fact it was a
distinct improvement over the survey of the same territories he had published
ten years before. As he explained in the preface, although he had started out to
bring the earlier volume up to date, he soon became convinced that South
Africa's departure from the Commonwealth in 1961 made the regional dimension more important than the minutiae of native administration. Although why
he should ever have supposed otherwise is unclear, this book therefore possessed what had been so singularly lacking in its predecessor, a geographical
context.

It was also more incisive. Hailey had always been ambivalent about the white
man in Africa. Living there, he found himself growing more sympathetic: "One
knows that one is really wrong in the feeling, but one is human." Yet he was
continually revolted by "maladministration – the deliberate denial of a fair

---

[17] Thomas Hodgkin, *Nationalism in Colonial Africa* (London: Muller, 1956).
[18] See for instance Michael Crowder, *West Africa Under Colonial Rule* (London: Hutchinson, 1968),
pp. 405–7.
[19] Hailey, *African Survey* (1957), pp. 251–60.
[20] Hailey to Sir Findlater Stewart, from South Africa, 6 November 1959, Stewart Papers, IOL,
MSS EUR E 890/9.

deal."[21] Apartheid offended him professionally. He reserved his strongest criticism for his own country: Britain's evasive, hypocritical response to South Africa's claims for annexation of the high commission territories "must have appeared unworthy of a great nation." With respect to the territories themselves he told a sorry tale of weakness and neglect, which investment under the Colonial Development and Welfare Act had only belatedly and inadequately begun to rectify. Economically dependent on the Republic of South Africa, vulnerable to its anger at their use as havens for opponents of apartheid, the territories were in fact much like bantustans. What was called the positive face of apartheid, he believed, was unlikely to attract them. The reason was simple. As long as that policy remained in force "the non-European peoples of South Africa cannot aspire to any effective share in the government of the country."[22]

Hailey made his last statement in the House of Lords in 1964. Since the Colonial Office was being wound up, he asked, who would speak for the dependencies?[23] By that time very few of those were left. Since 1960 every one of the African colonies he had analyzed in his report of 1950 – Nigeria, the Gambia, Sierra Leone, Uganda, Kenya, Tanzania, Zambia, and Malawi – had followed Ghana into independence and membership in the Commonwealth and the United Nations. Still more astonishing, for even by the late 1950s those countries had hardly begun to consider self-government at all, Belgium and France had lost their colonies too. By the time of Hailey's death in 1969 many of these new states were governed by an arm of colonial administration early studies of African political development had strikingly ignored: the military. Most of them were *de jure* one-party states, and none possessed an opposition that was both lawful and effective. Hailey lived long enough to know that his skepticism about the suitability of the Westminster model for Africa had been absolutely right.

There is no doubt about his feelings. He thought it important that the British people should remember that 1940, the year of the first Colonial Development and Welfare Act, had begun "a new chapter of constructive work for the Colonies, just as 1960 may some day be held to be the opening year of the reverse process."[24] He believed that his country had run out on its obligations in India and that it had left Africa ill-prepared for independence. He remained an imperialist to the end.

His immediate family were long since dead and he became accustomed to writing obituary notices for the *Times*.[25] He vetted other men's memoirs – he

21 Ibid.
22 William Malcolm Hailey, *The Republic of South Africa and the High Commission Territories* (London: Oxford University Press, 1963), pp. 104–5. See also Hailey's review of Anthony Sampson's *The Treason Cage: The Opposition on Trial in South Africa* (London: Heinemann, 1958), typescript of 2 May 1958, HPA/343, which analyzed "statutory communism" as defined by the Suppression of Communism Act (1950).
23 15 April 1964, Parl. Deb. (Lords), *257*, 447–8.
24 Hailey to Sir Charles Jeffries, 20 October 1963, HPA/343.
25 See particularly his notices on Sir Geoffrey de Montmorency and Lionel Curtis, the *Times*, 28 February and 1 December 1955.

thought Gandhi was a reformer at heart, he told Lord Halifax (formerly the viceroy Lord Irwin), but it was probably wise to relate anecdotes rather than attempt an overall assessment, implicitly recognizing that neither of them had ever really understood the man – but he refused to write his own. Conscientiously, with an obvious sense of the obligation of an important public figure to the integrity of the historical record, he organized his Indian papers, writing notes on several important subjects, even procuring from Pakistan a copy of the revenue-settlement report on the Thal district that he had written nearly sixty years before.

Acutely aware that he himself had become an anachronism, he was disappointed at the way the later phase of Empire had turned out. "The present world seems to have no place for one who has spent a long life in the service of Imperialism," he told Margery Perham in a touching letter four years before his death, "even though he may believe himself to have been one of its less blatant practitioners." He consoled himself with memories of his early career in India, when he had helped convert a desert into a fertile breadbasket and had nearly died of plague: "So if ideologically I have blotted my copy book I have pragmatically little feeling of reserve."[26] He looked back on a long, interesting, and productive life. Whether he would also have called it a happy one is hard to say.

In 1953 Lord Hailey made a brief radio broadcast in the series "What I Believe." In his youth, he said (although absolutely no additional evidence has come to light), he had been deeply concerned with religious issues. During his long career in India, however, he had known many individuals with admirable characters from widely differing religions, including agnostics or atheists. Clearly, something other than religion underlay what Plato had defined as The Good. Hailey's own belief was in the moral codes societies had developed at each stage of their evolution – from family to clan to tribe to nation – that reached their full expression in the rule of law. Anthropologists agreed that such codes held all so-called primitive societies together. He himself had seen the slow, painful process in which new nations adapted old moral guidelines and constructed new ones. He left implicit the ideal of his own life's work: an instrument dedicated to enabling societies under the extreme stress of rapid change to steady themselves, examine alternatives, and realize their potential. It was, one might say, the imperial idea at its best.[27]

Another testament appeared in the final paragraph of his last book. According to the current fashion he presumed that the three high commission territories would be given increasing self-government. Yet South Africa had in effect dropped its claim for transfer, and it was unlikely they would place themselves under apartheid voluntarily. He hoped that after assessing their situation soberly they would stop short of demanding full independence. Although Britain might see no advantage in retaining control it could not abdicate "without a

---

[26] Hailey to Perham, 28 May 1965, RH, MSS Perham 27/1.
[27] 29 June 1953, typescript in HPA/339.

grievous loss of self-respect." The territories should reflect on the fact that although the age of seaborne empires might have ended the phenomenon called imperialism would endure, the most predatory states at the time being Russia in central Asia and the Afrikaner republic in their own region. "It would be well for them to realize that liberties once lost are not easily regained by the small peoples of the world," Hailey concluded. "What would it profit the small peoples of the Territories if they now loose their hold on the solid fact of liberty under British rule in order that they may grasp at the fantasy of Independence?"[28]

The machine wore out slowly. The cataract operation of 1956 had merely slowed the deterioration, by 1965 only part of one eye remained, and late in 1966 the lights went out. For a man of Hailey's temperament forced inactivity was galling. "I do not think life is really worth living unless it is weighted with definite responsibilities," he told Margery Perham succinctly, "for it is after all the obligations which make living endurable. I am as you see, a perverted hedonist."[29] The last surviving letter was dated December 1966, written to the son of the Indian boy, Sayyed Ahmed Shah, whom the Haileys had in effect adopted as a playmate for their baby boy in the Jhelum canal colony, afterward paying his school fees and helping him in his career. He wanted the close relationship between the families placed on record.[30]

He sank gradually and died on 1 June 1969. Those who attended the memorial service at Saint Paul's Cathedral reflected nostalgically on the passing of a symbol of their nation's lost greatness. It was ninety-seven years since his birth, when Disraeli had launched the New Imperialism at the Crystal Palace, and eight since Harold Macmillan had spoken at Cape Town of an African wind of change. Lord Hailey had outlived the British Empire he had served.

---

28 Hailey, *High Commission Territories*, p. 128. The independence dates were 1966 for Botswana and Lesotho and 1968 for Swaziland. The point about Russia and South Africa is actually from the 1959 *Year Book* article, "The Decline of the Colonial System."
29 Hailey to Perham, 28 May 1965, RH, MSS Perham 27/1.
30 Hailey to Mohammad Shah, 8 December 1966, HPI/60.

Bibliography

Private manuscript collections

Hailey Papers

The Hailey collection is divided; the Indian portion (HPI) is housed at the India Office Library, London; the African material (HPA) is at Rhodes House, Oxford.

Private collections – India

India Office Library
    MSS EUR D 714/25. Under-Secretaries' Correspondence with Hailey, 1932–45
    MSS EUR D 724. Hume, A. P.
    MSS EUR D 890. Stewart, Sir Findlater
    MSS EUR E 238. Viscount Reading (formerly Rufus Isaacs)
    MSS EUR E 224. Fleetwood Wilson, Sir Guy
    MSS EUR C 238. Wood, Edward, Viscount Halifax (then Lord Irwin)
    MSS EUR E 240. Viscount Templewood (then Sir Samuel Hoare)
    MSS EUR E 264. Thesiger, Frederic J., Viscount Chelmsford
    MSS EUR F 137. Thompson, Sir John
Cambridge University Library
    Hardinge, Charles (Viscount)
Bodleian Library, Oxford
    Attlee, Clement
    Schuster, Sir George
    Simon, Sir John
Jawaharlal Nehru Memorial Library, New Delhi
    All-India National Congress, 1920–31
    Nehru, Jawaharlal
    Nehru, Motilal
    Pant, Govind Ballabh
    Sapru, Sir Tej Bahadur (Microfilm of collection at National Library, Calcutta.)
    Thakurdas, Sir Purchotamdas

Bibliography

Private collections – Africa

Rhodes House, Oxford
  MSS Afr s 1141. Cox, A. H. Diary on tour with Hailey, 1947–8
  MSS Brit. Emp. s 332. Creech-Jones, Arthur
  MSS Lugard. Lugard, Frederick (Baron)
  MSS Afr s 1445. Malcolm, Donald, Diary as private secretary to Hailey on tour, 1935–6
  MSS Afr 1829. Oldham, Joseph H.
  MSS Afr s 1814. Pedler, Sir Frederick
  MSS Perham. Perham, Dame Margery F.
  MSS Afr s 1425. Worthington, Edgard B.
Other collections
  Carnegie Corporation, New York City
  MacDonald, James Ramsay. Public Record Office. PRO 30/69
  Kerr, Philip (Marquess of Lothian). National Library of Scotland
  Malinowski, Bronislaw. London School of Economics
  Oldham, Joseph H. School of Oriental and African Studies, University of London
  Rockefeller Foundation, New York City. Project Files

Official documents

India

India Office Library
  V/10/365. Provincial Administration Reports
  L/P&J. Public and Judicial Department
  L/P&J/12. Fortnightly Reports, UP, 1929–34
  L/F. Finance Department
  L/PO. Private Office Papers
Delhi Administrative Archives, Inter-State Bus Terminal Building, Chadni Chowk, Delhi
  Various Proceedings: Home, Finance, Chief Commissioner's Office, Education, Revenue and Agriculture (1912–18)
Punjab State Archives, Anarkali Museum, Lahore
  Various Proceedings, especially:
  Revenue and Agriculture, General and Irrigation (1901–6)
  Home Military (1920), containing material relating to Martial Law in 1919
  Home (1920–8) and Political (1920–8)
State Archives of Uttar Pradesh, Lucknow
  Various Proceedings, 1928–34, especially General Administration, Revenue, Police, and Home Police
National Archives of India, New Delhi
  Home Political
  Home Establishment
  Finance Department. (As explained in the text, these papers have been pruned very severely.)
  Reform Office

Bibliography

Africa: Public Record Office, London

CO 96   Gold Coast
CO 323   Colonies General
CO 533   Kenya
CO 537   General, Supplementary
CO 554   West African Constitutional
CO 583   Nigeria
CO 795   Central Africa, General
CO 822   East Africa, General
CO 825   Far East
CO 847   Africa, General
CO 852   Hailey Committee on Postwar Problems
CO 927   Colonial Office Research Department
CO 967   Postwar Reconstruction
CO 968   General, Supplementary
CO 1018   Lord Hailey's Report on Native Administration
DO 35   Central Africa
FO 371   Papers relating to Congo Mission

Primary printed documents

India

Great Britain. Parliamentary Papers
     Report of the Indian Irrigation Commission, 1901–3, PP, 1904 [Cd. 1851–4], *56*.
     Indian Plague Commission, PP, 1902 [Cd. 141], *72*.
     Delhi Town Planning Committee, Final Report, PP, 1913 [Cd. 689], *20*.
     Royal Commission on Indian Finance, PP, 1914 [Cd. 7069], *19*.
     Report of the Royal Commission on the Public Services in India, PP, 1916 [Cd. 8382], *7*.
     Committee re administration and organisation of the army in India, PP, 1920 [Cmd. 943], *14*.
     Report of Committee to Enquire into Indian Exchange and Currency, PP, 1920 [Cmd. 527–30], *14*.
     Royal Commission on the Superior Civil Services in India, PP, 1924 [Cmd. 2128], *8*.
     Royal Commission on Indian Currency and Finance, PP. 1926 [Cmd. 2687], *12*.
     Report of the Indian Statutory Commission, PP, 1929–30 [Cmd. 3568–9, 3572], *11, 12*.
     Government of India Dispatch re Constitutional Reforms, PP, 1930–1 [Cmd. 3700], *23*.
     Indian Round Table Conference, Proceedings, (12 November 1930 – 19 January 1931), PP. 1930–1 [Cmd. 3778), *12*.
India Office Library. Commission Reports. V/26.
     Report of the Colonies Committee, Punjab, 1907–8.
     Punjab Disorders Inquiry Committee (Hunter). 6 vols. 1920.
     Report of the committee appointed to consider the racial distinctions in criminal procedure applicable to Indians and non-Indians (Sapru), 1922.

Bibliography

Report of the New Capital Enquiry Committee, 1922.

Reports of the local governments on the working of the Reformed Constitution (1923).

Report of the Reforms Enquiry Committee (Muddiman), 1924.

Report on the Working of the System of Government, United Provinces of Agra and Oudh, 1921–1928 (for Indian Statutory Commission; 2 vols., 1928).

Report of the Committee appointed by the United Provinces Legislative Council to cooperate with the Indian Statutory Commission (1929).

Indian Franchise (Lothian) Committee (1932).

UP Legislative Council. Report of Select Committee on the United Provinces Special Powers Bill (1932).

Debates

Great Britain. Parliamentary Debates. 5th series. House of Commons. (Various.)

Great Britain. Parliamentary Debates. 5th series. House of Lords. 1936–61.

India. Legislative Council. 1918–22.

India. Legislative Assembly. 1922–34.

Punjab. Legislative Council. 1924–28.

Miscellaneous Indian documents

Census of India (various editions)

Department of Commercial Intelligence and Statistics, Government of India. *Statistical Abstract for British India, 1924–1934.* Delhi: Government Printer, 1936.

Report on Plague and Inoculation in the Punjab, 1902–3. Lahore: Government Printer, 1904.

E. A. H. Blunt, *United Provinces Census Report* (1911).

Report of the Sedition (Rowlatt) Committee (1918; reprinted, Calcutta: New Age, 1973).

Report of the United Provinces Provincial Banking Enquiry Committee. 4 vols. Allahabad, 1930.

Newspapers

The Hailey collection at the India Office Library includes several volumes of press clippings.

British

Times (London)
Economist

Indian

Microfilm editions, Consortium of Research Libraries, Chicago, Illinois.

Bombay Chronicle. 1919–24, 1931.

Leader (Allahabad). 1919–22, 1928–34.

Statesman (Calcutta). 1919–22.

Tribune (Lahore). 1919–28.

Bibliography

Selected publications of Lord Hailey

"India." *Round Table, 12* (September 1922), 844–55. [Unsigned]

"India – 1983." *Asiatic Review, 100* (1933), 620–32.

"Nationalism in Africa." *Journal of the African Society, 36* (1937), 134–47.

An African Survey: A Study of Problems Arising in Africa South of the Sahara. London: Oxford University Press, 1938.

"Some Problems Dealt with in the 'African Survey.'" *International Affairs, 18,* (1939), 194–210.

Native Administration and Political Development in British Tropical Africa, 1941. Ed. Anthony H. M. Kirk-Green. Nendein: Kraus Reprint, 1979.

The Position of Colonies in a British Commonwealth of Nations. London: Oxford University Press, 1941.

"A Colonial Charter." *Fortnightly* (July 1942), 1–7.

Great Britain, India, and the Colonial Dependencies in the Post-War World. Toronto: University of Toronto Press, 1943.

"India in the Modern World: A British View." *Foreign Affairs, 21* (April 1943), 401–12.

The Future of Colonial Peoples. Princeton, N.J.: Princeton University Press, 1944.

"Capital and Colonial Development." *Crown Colonist* (August 1943), 537–9.

"Colonies and World Organization." *African Affairs, 44* (April 1945), 54–8.

World Thought on the Colonial Question. Johannesburg: University of Witwatersrand Press, 1946.

"South-West Africa." *African Affairs, 46* (April 1947), 77–86.

"A Survey of Native Affairs in South West Africa." Unpublished typescript, 1946. (Microfilm copy at the Consortium of African Microform Project, Chicago, and at Rhodes House Library.)

Native Administration in the British African Territories. 5 vols. London: HMSO, 1950–3.

"A Turning Point in Colonial Rule." *International Affairs, 28* (1952), 177–83.

"Post-War Changes in Africa." *Journal of the Royal Society of Arts, 103* (1954–5), 579–90.

"Spotlight on Africa." In Calvin Stillman, ed., *Africa in the Modern World* (Chicago: University of Chicago Press, 1955), pp. 3–13.

An African Survey: A Study of Problems Arising in Africa South of the Sahara. Revised edition. London: Oxford University Press, 1957.

"The Differing Faces of Africa." *Foreign Affairs, 36* (1957), 143–53.

"The Decline of the Colonial System in Africa." *Year Book of World Affairs, 12* (1959).

The Republic of South Africa and the High Commission Territories. London: Oxford University Press, 1963.

Primary books

India

Adhikari, G. M., ed. *Documents of the History of the Communist Party of India.* Bombay: People's Publishing House, 1971– .

Ahluwalia, M. L., ed. *Gurdwara Reform Movement, 1919–1925: An Era of Congress–Akali Collaboration.* New Delhi: Ashoka, 1985.

Aitchison, Charles. *Lord Lawrence.* Oxford: Clarendon Press, 1892.

Barrier, N. Gerald, ed. *Roots of Communal Politics.* Columbia, Mo.: South Asia Books, n.d. (Congress report on Cawnpore riot of 1931.)

Birdwood, William. *Khaki and Gown: An Autobiography.* London: Ward, Lock, 1941.

Chirol, Valentine. *Indian Unrest.* London: Macmillan, 1910.

Currency Committees, Reports. New Delhi: Agricole, 1982.

Danda Singh, ed. *History of the Freedom Movement in the Punjab, Vol. 4: Deportation of Lala Lajpat Rai and Sardar Ajit Singh.* Patiala: Punjab University Press, 1978.

Darling, Malcolm. *The Punjab Peasant in Prosperity and Debt.* 1925; New Delhi; Manohar, 1977.

Desai, Mahadev. *The Story of Bardoli.* Ahmedabad: Navajivan Press, 1929.

Dharmavira. *I Threw the Bomb.* New Delhi: Orient, 1979.

Douie, James M. *Punjab Settlement Manual.* 5th ed. Lahore: Government Printer, 1961.

Fazl-i-Husain. *Diary and Notes of Mian Fazl-i-Husain,* edited by Waheed Ahmad. Lahore: University of Punjab Press, 1977.

Ganda Singh, ed. *Some Confidential Papers of the Akali Movement.* Amritsar: SPGC, 1965.

Gandhi, Mohandas K. *The Collected Works of Mahatma Gandhi.* 87 vols. New Delhi: Ministry of Information and Broadcasting, 1954–84.

Hardinge, Charles. *My Indian Years, 1910–1916.* London: J. Murray, 1948.

The Historical Record of the Imperial Visit to India, 1911. London: J. Murray, 1914.

Hoare, Samuel [Viscount Templewood]. *Nine Troubled Years.* London: Collins, 1954.

Jevons, H. Stanley. *Money, Banking and Exchange in India.* Simla: Government Press, 1922.

Kaye, Cecil. *Communism in India,* edited by Subodh Roy. 1925; Calcutta: Editions Indian, 1971.

Ker, James C. *Political Trouble in India: 1907–1917.* 1917; Delhi: Oriental Publishers, 1973.

Keynes, John Maynard. *Indian Currency and Finance,* vol. 1 of *Collected Writings.* London: Macmillan, 1971.

Lajpat Rai. *Autobiographical Writings.* Edited by V. C. Joshi. Delhi: University Publishers, 1965.

Writings and Speeches. Edited by Vijaya C. Joshi. 2 vols. Delhi: University Publishers, 1966.

A History of the Arya Samaj. Edited by Sri Ram Sharma. Calcutta: Orient Longman, 1967.

Low, Sidney, *A Vision of India.* London: Smith, Elder, 1906.

MacDonald, James Ramsay. *The Awakening of India.* London: Hodder & Stoughton, 1910.

The Government of India. London: Swarthmore Press, 1919.

Mason, Philip. *A Shaft of Sunlight: Memories of a Varied Life.* London: Andre Deutsch, 1978.

Maurice, Frederick. *The Life of General Lord Rawlinson of Trent.* London: Cassell, 1928.

Mayo, Katherine. *Mother India.* London: Cape, 1927.

Miller, Webb. *I Found No Peace: The Journal of a Foreign Correspondent.* New York: Simon & Schuster, 1936.

Nehru, Jawaharlal. *An Autobiography.* 1936; Delhi: Oxford University Press, 1980.

The Discovery of India. New York: John Day, 1946.

Selected Works of Jawaharlal Nehru, edited by Sarvapelli Gopal et al. 1st series. New Delhi: Orient Longman, 1972– .

Nehru, Jawaharlal, ed. *A Bunch of Old Letters.* New York: Asia Publishing House, 1958.

Nehru, Motilal. *Selected Works,* edited by Ravinder Kumar and D. N. Panigrahi. New Delhi: Vikas, 1982– .

O'Dwyer, Michael. *India as I Knew It.* London: Constable, 1925.

Panikkar, K. M. *An Autobiography.* Madras: Oxford University Press, 1977.

Petrie, David. *Communism in India. 1924–1927.* 1927; Calcutta: Editions Indian, 1972.

Pirzada, Syed S., ed. *Foundations of Pakistan: All-India Muslim League Documents, 1906–1947.* 2 vols. Karachi: National Publishing House, 1970.

Shafi, Muhammad. *Some Important Indian Problems.* Lahore: Model Electric Press, 1930.

Sri Ram, ed. *Punjab in Ferment.* New Delhi: Chand, 1971.

Srivastava, Dhanput R. [Premchand]. *The Chess-Players,* translated by Gurdial Mallik. New Delhi: Orient, 1967.

    Godan: The Gift of a Cow, translated by Gordon C. Roadarmel. Bloomington: Indiana University Press, 1968.

Strachey, John. *India.* London: K. Paul, Trench, 1888.

Tandon, Prakash. *Punjabi Century.* Berkeley: University of California Press, 1961.

Thorburn, Septimus S. *Musalmans and Money-Lenders in the Punjab.* Edinburgh: Blackwood, 1886.

Wilson, A. C. Mcleod. *Letters from India.* Edinburgh: Blackwood, 1911.

Wilson, James. *Final Report on the Revision of Settlement of the Shahpur District in the Punjab, 1887–94.* Lahore: Civil and Military Gazette Press, 1894.

    General Code of Tribal Custom in the Shahpur District of the Punjab. Lahore: Civil & Military Gazette Press, 1896.

    Gazetteer of Shahpur District (1897).

Wood, Edward [Lord Irwin; later Lord Halifax]. *Indian Problems.* London: Allen & Unwin, 1932.

    Fulness of Days. London: Collins, 1957.

Africa

Frankel, Sally Herbert. *Capital Investment in Africa.* London: Oxford University Press, 1938.

Hancock, William Keith. *Survey of British Commonwealth Affairs.* 2 vols. London: Oxford University Press, 1937–41.

Institute of Pacific Relations. *War and Peace in the Pacific.* New York: Institute of Pacific Relations, 1942.

Knowles, Lillian C. A. *The Economic Development of the British Overseas Empire.* London: Routledge & Sons, 1924– .

Leakey, Louis S. B. *Mau Mau and the Kikuyu.* London: Methuen, 1952.

    Defeating Mau Mau. London: Methuen, 1955.

Leys, Norman M. *Kenya.* London: Hogarth, 1924.

    A Last Chance in Kenya. London: Hogarth, 1931.

    The Colour Bar in East Africa. London: Hogarth, 1941.

    By Kenya Possessed: The Correspondence of Norman Leys and J. H. Oldham, edited by John W. Cell. Chicago: University of Chicago Press, 1976.

Lugard, Frederick D. *The Dual Mandate in British Tropical Africa.* 1922; 5th ed., edited by Margery Perham. London: Cass, 1965.

Bibliography

Macmillan, William M. *Africa Emergent: A Survey of Social, Political, and Economic Trends in British Africa.* London: Faber & Faber, 1938.

My South African Years: An Autobiography. Cape Town: Philip, 1975.

Warning from the West Indies: A Tract for Africa and the Empire. London: Faber, 1936.

MacPhee, Allan. *The Economic Revolution in British West Africa,* 1926; reprinted New York, Negro Universities Press [1970].

Oldham, Joseph H. *White and Black in Africa: A Critical Examination of the Rhodes Lectures of General Smuts.* London: Longmans, Green, 1930.

Perham, Margery. *Colonial Sequence.* 2 vols. London: Methuen, 1967–70.

Worthington, Edgard B. *Science in Africa.* London: Oxford University Press, 1938.

The Ecological Century: A Personal Appraisal. Oxford: Clarendon Press, 1983.

Secondary books

Britain and imperialism, general

Asad, Talal, ed. *Anthropology and the Colonial Connection.* London: Ithaca Press, 1975.

Ball, Stuart. *Baldwin and the Conservative Party: The Crisis of 1929–1931.* New Haven, Conn: Yale University Press, 1988.

Bond, Brian. *British Military Policy Between the Two World Wars.* Oxford: Clarendon Press, 1980.

Charmley, John. *Lord Lloyd and the Decline of the British Empire.* New York: St. Martin's, 1987.

Hart, E. P. *Merchant Taylors' School Register, 1561–1934.* 2 vols. Merchant Taylors' School, 1936.

Honey, J. R. de S. *Tom Brown's Universe: The Development of the English Public School in the Nineteenth Century.* New York: Quadrangle, 1977.

Jeffery, Keith. *The British Army and the Crisis of Empire, 1918–22.* Manchester: Manchester University Press, 1984.

Louis, William Roger. *Imperialism at Bay, 1941–1945: The United States and the Decolonization of the British Empire.* Oxford: Clarendon Press, 1977.

Marquand, David. *Ramsay MacDonald.* London: Cape, 1977.

Merchant Taylors' School: Its Origin, History and Present Surroundings. Oxford: Blackwell, 1929.

O'Brien, Terence H. *Civil Defence.* London: HMSO, 1955.

Rich, Paul B. *Race and Empire in British Politics.* Cambridge: Cambridge University Press, 1986.

Rothblatt, Sheldon. *The Revolution of the Dons: Cambridge and Society in Victorian England.* New York: Basic Books, 1968.

Sherman, A. J. *Island Refuge: Britain and Refugees from the Third Reich, 1933–1939.* Berkeley: University of California Press, 1973.

Sparrow, John. *Mark Pattison and the Idea of a University.* Cambridge: Cambridge University Press, 1967.

Stepan, Nancy. *The Idea of Race in Science: Great Britain, 1800–1960.* New York: Archon, 1982.

Thorne, Christopher. *Allies of a Kind: The United States, Britain and the War Against Japan, 1941–1945.* New York: Oxford University Press, 1978.

India

Ahmed, Mesbahuddin. *The British Labour Party and the Indian Independence Movement, 1917–1939.* New York: Envoy Press, 1987.

Ali, Imran. *The Punjab Under Imperialism, 1885–1947.* Princeton, N.J.: Princeton University Press, 1988.

Bagchi, Amiya K. *Private Investment in India, 1900–1939.* Cambridge: Cambridge University Press, 1972.

Bahadur, Lal. *Indian Freedom Movement and Thought: Politics of "Pro-Change" versus "No-Change," 1919–1922.* New Delhi: Sterling, 1983.

Barrier, N. Gerald. *Banned: Controversial Literature and Political Control in British India, 1907–1947.* Columbia: University of Missouri Press, 1974.

Birkenhead, Second Earl of. *F. E.: The Life of F. E. Smith, First Earl of Birkenhead.* London: Eyre & Spottiswoode, 1960.

Bridge, Carl. *Holding India to the Empire: The British Conservative Party and the 1935 Constitution.* New Delhi: Sterling, 1986.

Brown, Judith M. *Gandhi's Rise to Power, Indian Politics 1915–1922.* Cambridge: Cambridge University Press, 1972.

Gandhi and Civil Disobedience: The Mahatma in Indian Politics, 1928–1934. Cambridge: Cambridge University Press, 1977.

Gandhi: Prisoner of Hope. New Haven, Conn.: Yale University Press, 1989.

Chandra, Bipan. *The Rise and Growth of Economic Nationalism in India: Economic Policies of Indian National Leadership, 1880–1905.* New Delhi: People's Publishing House, 1966.

Nationalism and Colonialism in Colonial India. New Delhi: Orient Longman, 1979.

Communalism in Modern India. New Delhi: Vikas, 1984.

Indian National Movement: The Long-Term Dynamics. New Delhi: Vikas, 1988.

Chandra, Bipan, et al. *India's Struggle for Independence, 1857–1947.* New Delhi: Vikas, 1988.

Chowdhry, Prem. *Punjab Politics: The Role of Sir Chhotu Ram.* New Delhi: Vikas, 1984.

Colvin, Ian. *The Life of General Dyer.* Edinburgh: Blackwood, 1929.

Crosby, Alfred W. *Epidemic and Peace, 1918.* Westport, Conn.: Greenwood, 1976.

Cross, J. A. *Sir Samuel Hoare: A Political Biography.* London: Cape, 1977.

Datta, V. N. *Jallianwala Bagh.* Ludhiana: Bhopal–Chandigard–Kurukshetra, 1969.

Dhanagare, D. N. *Agrarian Movements and Gandhian Politics.* Agra: Agra University Press, 1975.

Peasant Movements in India, 1920–1950. Delhi: Oxford University Press, 1983.

Dharmavira. *Lala Har Dayal and Revolutionary Movements of His Times.* New Delhi: Indian Book Company, 1970.

Draper, Alfred. *Amritsar: The Massacre That Ended the Raj.* London: Cassell, 1981.

Dungen, P. H. M. Van den. *The Punjab Tradition: Influence and Authority in Nineteenth-Century India.* London: Allen & Unwin, 1972.

Dutt, Krishan. *Sardar Patel in the Bardoli Movement.* Meerut: Anu, 1986.

Dutt, R. Palme. *India To-day.* 2nd ed. Bombay: People's Publishing House, 1949.

Fox, Richard. *Lions of the Punjab: Culture in the Making.* Berkeley: University of California Press, 1985.

Frykenberg, R. E., ed. *Delhi Through the Ages: Essays in Urban History, Culture and Society.* Delhi: Oxford University Press, 1986.

Furneaux, Rupert. *Massacre at Amritsar.* London: Allen & Unwin, 1963.

Bibliography

Gallagher, John. *The Decline, Revival, and Fall of the British Empire.* Cambridge: Cambridge University Press, 1982.

Gilmartin, David. *Empire and Islam: Punjab and the Making of Pakistan.* Berkeley: University of California Press, 1988.

Gopal, Sarvepalli. *The Viceroyalty of Lord Irwin, 1926–1931.* Oxford: Clarendon Press, 1957.

Jawaharlal Nehru: A Biography. 3 vols. Delhi: Oxford University Press, 1975– .

Gordon, A. D. *Businessmen and Politics: Rising Nationalism and a Modernising Economy in Bombay, 1918–1933.* New Delhi: Manohar, 1978.

Guha, Ranajit, ed. *Writings on South Asian History and Society.* Delhi: Oxford University Press, 1982– .

Gupta, Narayani. *Delhi Between Two Empires, 1830–1931: Society, Government and Urban Growth.* Delhi: Oxford University Press, 1981.

Gupta, Partha S. *Imperialism and the British Labour Movement, 1914–1964.* London: Macmillan, 1975.

Haithcox, John P. *Communism and Nationalism in India: M. N. Roy and Comintern Policy, 1920–1939.* Princeton, N.J.: Princeton University Press, 1971.

Hardy, Peter. *The Muslims of British India.* Cambridge: Cambridge University Press, 1972.

Hasan, Mushirul. *Nationalism and Communal Politics in India, 1916–1928.* New Delhi: Manohar, 1979.

Husain, Azim. *Fazl-i-Husain: A Political Biography.* Bombay: Longmans, 1946.

Hutchins, Francis. *The Illusion of Permanence: British Imperialism in India.* Princeton, N.J.: Princeton University Press, 1967.

Huttenback, Robert. *Gandhi in South Africa: British Imperialism and the Indian Question, 1860–1914.* Ithaca, N.Y.: Cornell University Press, 1971.

Inder Singh, Anita. *The Origins of the Partition of India, 1937–1947.* Delhi: Oxford University Press, 1987.

Irving, Robert G. *Indian Summer: Lutyens, Baker, and Imperial Delhi.* Delhi: Oxford University Press, 1981.

Jalal, Ayesha. *The Sole Spokesman: Jinnah, the Muslim League, and the Demand for Pakistan.* Cambridge: Cambridge University Press, 1985.

Jeffrey, Robin. *People, Princes and Paramount Power: Society and Politics in the Indian Princely States.* Delhi: Oxford University Press, 1978.

Jha, Manoranjan. *Katherine Mayo and India.* New Delhi: People's Publishing House, 1971.

Jones, Kenneth W. *Arya Dharm: Hindu Consciousness in 19th-Century Punjab.* Berkeley: University of California Press, 1976.

Kapur, Rajiv A. *Sikh Separatism: The Politics of Faith.* London: Allen & Unwin, 1986.

Karnik, V. B. *M. N. Roy: Political Biography.* Bombay: Nav Jagriti Samaj, 1978.

Khushwant Singh. *A History of the Sikhs.* 2 vols. Princeton, N.J.: Princeton University Press, 1963–6.

Kumar, Ravinder, ed. *Essays on Gandhian Politics: The Rowlatt Satyagraha of 1919.* Oxford: Clarendon Press, 1971.

Laushey, David M. *Bengali Terrorism and the Marxist Left: Aspects of Regional Nationalism in India, 1905–1942.* Calcutta: Mukhopadhyay, 1975.

Low, D. Anthony, ed. *Congress and the Raj: Facets of the Indian Struggle, 1917–1947.* London: Arnold-Heinemann, 1977.

Majumdar, Ramesh C. *History of the Freedom Movement in India.* 2nd ed. Calcutta: Mukhopadhayay, 1971– .

Malhotra, S. L. *Gandhi and the Punjab.* Chandigarh: Panjab University, 1970.

Gandhi: An Experiment with Communal Politics: A Study of Gandhi's Role in Punjab Politics, 1922–1931. Chandigarh: Panjab University Press, 1975.

Markovits, Claude. *Indian Business and Nationalist Politics, 1931–1939: The Indigenous Capitalist Class and the Rise of the Congress Party.* Cambridge: Cambridge University Press, 1985.

Mason, Philip [Woodruff]. *The Men Who Ruled India.* 2 vols. London: Cape, 1953–4.

Mehta, Shirin. *The Peasantry and Nationalism: A Study of the Bardoli Satyagraha.* New Delhi: Manohar, 1984.

Metcalf, Thomas R. *Aftermath of Revolt: India, 1857–1870.* Princeton, N.J.: Princeton University Press, 1964.

Land, Landlords, and the British Raj: Northern India in the Nineteenth Century. Berkeley: University of California Press, 1979.

An Imperial Vision: Indian Architecture and Britain's Raj. Berkeley: University of California Press, 1989.

Minault, Gail. *The Khilafat Movement: Religious Symbolism and Political Mobilization in India.* New York: Columbia University Press, 1982.

Mohinder Singh. *The Akali Movement.* Delhi: Macmillan, 1978.

The Akali Struggle: A Retrospect. New Delhi: Atlantic, 1988.

Moore, Robin J. *The Crisis of Indian Unity, 1917–1940.* Oxford: Clarendon Press, 1974.

Escape from Empire: The Attlee Government and the Indian Problem. Oxford: Clarendon Press, 1983.

Making the New Commonwealth. Oxford: Clarendon Press, 1987.

Nath, Shaileshwar. *Terrorism in India.* New Delhi: National Publishing House, 1980.

Oldenburg, Veena T. *The Making of Colonial Lucknow.* Princeton, N.J.: Princeton University Press, 1984.

Page, David. *Prelude to Partition: The Indian Muslims and the Imperial System of Control, 1920–1932.* Delhi: Oxford University Press, 1982.

Pandey, Gyanendra. *The Ascendancy of the Congress in Uttar Pradesh, 1926–1934: A Study in Imperfect Mobilization.* Delhi: Oxford University Press, 1978.

Rai, Satya M. *Legislative Politics and Freedom Struggle in the Panjab, 1897–1947.* New Delhi: Indian Council of Historical Research, 1984.

Raj, K. N. et al. *Commercialisation in Indian Agriculture.* New Delhi: Oxford University Press, 1985.

Ram, Raja. *The Jallianwala Bagh Massacre: A Premeditated Plan.* Chandigarh: Panjab University Press, 1978.

Reeves, Peter D., et al. *A Handbook to Elections in Uttar Pradesh, 1920–1951.* Delhi: Manohar, 1975.

Rittenberg, Stephen A. *Ethnicity, Nationalism, and the Pakhtuns.* Durham, N.C.: Carolina Academic Press, 1988.

Robb, P. G. *The Government of India and Reform: Policies Towards Politics and the Constitution, 1916–1921.* Oxford: Oxford University Press, 1976.

Robinson, Francis. *Separatism Among Indian Muslims: The Politics of the United Provinces' Muslims, 1860–1923.* Cambridge: Cambridge University Press, 1974.

Rumbold, Algernon. *Watershed in India: 1914–1922.* London: Athlone Press, 1979.

Sangat Singh. *Freedom Movement in Delhi, 1858–1919.* New Delhi: Associated Publishing House, 1972.

Seal, Anil. *The Emergence of Indian Nationalism: Competition and Collaboration in the Later Nineteenth Century.* Cambridge: Cambridge University Press, 1968.

Sharma, Radka K. *Nationalism, Social Reform and Indian Women: A Study of the Interaction Between Our National Movement and the Movement of Social Reform Among Indian Women, 1921–1937.* Patna: Janaki Prakashan, 1981.

Sinha, Aruna. *Lord Reading: Viceroy of India.* New Delhi: Sterling, 1985.

Spangenberg, Bradford. *British Bureaucracy in India: Status, Policy and the I.C.S. in the Late 19th Century.* Columbia, Mo.: South Asia Books, 1976.

Spear, Thomas Percival. *Twilight of the Mughals.* Cambridge: Cambridge University Press, 1951.

Stone, Ian. *Canal Irrigation in British India: Perspectives on Technological Change in a Peasant Economy.* Cambridge: Cambridge University Press, 1984.

Swan, Maureen. *Gandhi, the South African Experience.* Johannesburg: Ravan, 1985.

Swinson, Arthur. *Six Minutes to Sunset: The Story of General Dyer and the Amritsar Affair.* London: Peter Davies, 1964.

Thursby, Gene R. *Hindu–Muslim Relations in British India: A Study of Controversy, Conflict, and Communal Movements in Northern India, 1923–1928.* Leiden: Brill, 1975.

Tomlinson, B. R. *The Indian National Congress and the Raj, 1929–1942: The Penultimate Phase.* London: Macmillan, 1976.

The Political Economy of the Raj, 1914–1947: The Economics of Decolonization in India. London: Macmillan, 1979.

Uprety, Prem R. *Religion and Politics in Punjab in the 1920s.* New Delhi: Sterling, 1980.

Ziegler, Philip. *Mountbatten.* New York: Knopf, 1985.

Africa

Austin, Dennis. *Politics in Ghana, 1946–1960.* London: Oxford University Press, 1964.

Chanok, Martin. *Unconsummated Union: Britain, Rhodesia, and South Africa, 1900–1945.* Manchester: Manchester University Press, 1977.

Constantine, Stephen. *The Making of British Colonial Development Policy, 1914–1940.* London: Cass, 1984.

Crowder, Michael. *West Africa Under Colonial Rule.* London: Hutchinson, 1968.

Dinan, Desmond. *The Politics of Persuasion: British Policy and French African Neutrality, 1940–1942.* New York: University Press of America, 1988.

Gann, Lewis, and Peter Duignan, eds. *Colonialism in Africa.* 5 vols. Cambridge: Cambridge University Press, 1969– .

African Proconsuls: European Governors in Africa. New York: Free Press, 1978.

Gann, Lewis H., and Michael Gelfand. *Huggins of Rhodesia: The Man and His Country.* London: Allen & Unwin, 1964.

Gifford, Prosser, and William Roger Louis, eds. *The Transfer of Power in Africa: Decolonization, 1940–1960.* New Haven, Conn.: Yale University Press, 1982.

Hancock, William Keith. *Smuts.* 2 vols. Cambridge: Cambridge University Press, 1962–8.

Hetherington, Penelope. *British Paternalism and Africa, 1920–1940.* London: Cass, 1978.

Hodgkin, Thomas. *Nationalism in Colonial Africa.* London: Muller, 1956.

King, Kenneth J. *Pan-Africanism and Education: A Study of Philanthropy and Education in the Southern States of America and East Africa.* Oxford: Clarendon Press, 1971.

Kirk-Greene, Anthony H., ed. *Africa in the Colonial Period: The Transfer of Power: The Colonial Administrator in the Age of Decolonisation.* Oxford: Committee for African Studies, 1979.

Kuper, Adam. *Anthropologists and Anthropology: The British School, 1922–1972.* New York: Pica, 1973.

Larminat, Edgard de. *Chroniques Irrévérencieuses.* Paris: Plon, 1962.

Lee, John M. *Colonial Development and Good Government: A Study of the Ideas Expressed by the British Official Classes in Planning Decolonization, 1939–1964.* Oxford: Clarendon Press, 1967.

Macmillan, Hugh, and Shula Marks, eds. *Africa and Empire: W. W. Macmillan, Historian and Social Critic.* London: Temple Smith, 1989.

Macmillan, Mona. *Champion of Africa: The Second Phase of the Work of W. M. Macmillan, 1934–1974.* Long Wittenham: Swindon Press, 1985.

Marder, Arthur. *Operation "Menace": The Dakar Expedition and the Dudley North Affair.* London: Oxford University Press, 1976.

Morgan, David J. *The Official History of Colonial Development.* 5 vols. Atlantic Highlands, N.J.: Humanities Press, 1980.

Nicolson, I. F. *The Administration of Nigeria, 1900–1960.* Oxford: Clarendon Press, 1969.

Owen, Roger, and Bob Sutcliffe, eds. *Studies in the Theory of Imperialism.* London: Longman, 1972.

Pearce, Robert D. *The Turning Point in Africa: British Colonial Policy 1938–48.* London: Cass, 1982.

Perham, Margery, *Lugard.* 2 vols. London: Collins, 1956–60.

Rich, Paul B. *White Power and the Liberal Conscience: Racial Segregation and South African Liberalism.* Manchester: Manchester University Press, 1984.

Stengers, Jean. *Léopold III et le Gouvernement: Les Deux Politiques Belges de 1940.* Paris: Gembloux, 1980.

Stone, J. C., ed. *Experts in Africa.* Aberdeen: Aberdeen University African Studies Group, 1980.

Thomas, R. T. *Britain and Vichy: The Dilemma of Anglo-French Relations, 1940–2.* New York: St. Martin's, 1979.

Weinstein, Brian. *Eboué.* New York: Oxford University Press, 1972.

Articles and chapters in other works

India

Cell, John W. "Anglo-Indian Medical Theory and the Origins of Segregation in West Africa." *American Historical Review,* 92 (April 1986), 307–35.

Dewey, Clive J. "Celtic Agrarian Legislation and the Celtic Revival: Historicist Implications of Gladstone's Irish and Scottish Land Acts, 1870–1886." *Past and Present,* No. 64 (August 1974), 30–70.

Ferrell, Donald W. "The Rowlatt Satyagraha in Delhi." In Ravinder Kumar, ed., *Essays on Gandhian Politics,* pp. 189–235.

Jones, Kenneth W. "Organized Hinduism in Delhi and New Delhi." In R. E. Fryken-berg, ed., *Delhi Through the Ages*, pp. 332–50.

Kirpal Singh, ed. "Saradar Bahadur Mehtab Singh's Report on Rawalpindi Riots – 1926." *Panjab Past and Present*, 15 (1981), 407–24.

Klein, Ira, "Urban Development and Death: Bombay City, 1870–1914." *Modern Asian Studies*, 20 (1986), 725–54.

Low, D. Anthony. "'Civil Martial Law': The Government of India and the Civil Disobe-dience Movements, 1930–34." In Low, ed., *Congress and the Raj: Facets of the Indian Struggle, 1917–1947*, pp. 165–98. 1977.

"The Government of India and the First Non-Co-Operation Movement, 1920–1922." In Kumar, *Essays on Gandhian Politics*, pp. 298–323.

Metcalf, Barbara D. "Hakim Admal Khan: Rais of Delhi and Muslim Leader." In Frykenberg, *Delhi Through the Ages*, pp. 299–315.

Metcalf, Thomas R. "Architecture and Empire: Sir Herbert Baker and the Building of New Delhi." In Frykenberg, *Delhi Through the Ages*, pp. 391–400.

Minault, Gail. "Sayyid Ahmad Dehlavi and the 'Delhi Renaissance.'" In Frykenberg, *Delhi Through the Ages*, pp. 287–98.

Mukherjee, Aditya. "Indian Capitalists and the National Movement." In Bipan Chandra et al., *India's Struggle for Independence*, pp. 375–85.

Mukherjee, Mridula. "Commercialization and Agrarian Change in Pre-Independence Punjab." In K. N. Raj et al., *Commercialisation in Indian Agriculture*, pp. 51–104.

Ramusack, Barbara N. "Incident at Nabha: Interaction Between Indian States and British Indian Politics." *Journal of Asian Studies*, 28 (1969), 563–77.

"Maharajas and Gurdwaras: Patiala and the Sikh Community." In Robin Jeffrey, ed., *People, Princes and Paramount Power: Society and Politics in the Indian Princely States*, pp. 184–5.

Sapru, Tej Bahadur. "The Problem of India's Aspirations." *Contemporary Review, 124* (1923).

Africa

Anon. "Lord Hailey Always Keeps on Working." *West Africa* (1948).

Cell, John W. "On the Eve of Decolonization: The Colonial Office's Plans for the Transfer of Power in Africa, 1947." *Journal of Imperial and Commonwealth History, 8* (1980), 235–57.

"Lord Hailey and the Making of the African Survey." *African Affairs, 88* (1989), 481–505.

Fetter, Bruce. "Changing War Aims: Central Africa's Role, 1940–41, As Seen from Léopoldville." *African Affairs, 87* (1988), 377–92.

Flint, John E. "Nigeria: The Colonial Experience, 1880–1914." In Lewis Gann and Peter Duignan, eds., *Colonialism in Africa*, 1:220–60.

"Federick Lugard: The Making of an Autocrat (1858–1943)." In Gann and Duignan, eds., *African Proconsuls: European Governors in Africa*, pp. 290–312.

"Governor versus Colonial Office: An Anatomy of the Richards Constitution for Nigeria, 1939 to 1945." Canadian Historical Association, *Historical Papers* (1981), 124–43.

"Macmillan as a Critic of Empire: The Impact of an Historian on Colonial Policy." In

Hugh Macmillan and Shula Marks, eds., *Africa and Empire: W. M. Macmillan, Historian and Social Critic*, pp. 212–31.

"Planned Decolonization and Its Failure in British Africa." *African Affairs, 82* (1983), 389–412.

"Scandal at the Bristol Hotel: Some Thoughts on Racial Discrimination in Britain and West Africa and Its Relationship to the Planning of Decolonisation, 1939–1947." *Journal of Imperial and Commonwealth History, 12* (1983), 74–93.

Hargreaves, John D. "History: African and Contemporary." Presidential Address, African Studies Association, United Kingdom, September 1973. *African Research and Documentation, 1* (1973), 3–8

Kent, John. "Anglo-French Colonial Co-Operation 1939–49." *Journal of Imperial and Commonwealth History, 17* (1988), 55–82.

Legassick, Martin. "British Hegemony and the Origins of South Africa, 1901–1914." London: Institute of Commonwealth Studies, 1970–3.

"The Making of South African 'Native Policy,'" 1903–1923." London: Institute of Commonwealth Studies, 1970–3.

"The Rise of Modern South African Liberalism: Its Assumptions and Its Social Base." London: Institute of Commonwealth Studies, 1970–3.

Malinowski, Bronislaw. "Practical Anthropology." *Africa, 2* (1929), 22–38.

Norton, William B. "Belgian-French Relations During World War II as Seen by Governor General Ryckmans." In Académie Royale des Sciences d'Outre-Mer, *Le Congo Belge durant la Seconde Guerre Mondiale: Recueil d'études*. Bruxelles: Académie Royale des Sciences d'Outre-Mer, 1983, pp. 285–311.

"Pierre Ryckmans (1891–1959)." In Gann and Duignan, *African Proconsuls*, pp. 391–411.

Pearce, Robert E. "The Colonial Office and Planned Decolonization in Africa." *African Affairs, 83* (1984), 77–94.

Pedler, Sir Frederick. "Lord Hailey: His Contribution to Africa." *Journal of the Royal Society of Arts, 118* (July 1970), 484–92.

Robinson, Kenneth. "Experts, Colonialists, and Africanists, 1895–1960." In J. C. Stone, ed. *Experts in Africa*, pp. 55–74.

Robinson, Ronald E. "Non-European Foundations: Sketch for a Theory of Collaboration." In Roger Owen and Bob Sutcliffe, eds., *Studies in the Theory of Imperialism*.

"Sir Andrew Cohen: Proconsul of African Nationalism (1909–1968)." In Gann and Duignan, *African Proconsuls*, pp. 353–64.

Robinson, Ronald E., and William Roger Louis. "The United States and the Liquidation of British Empire in Tropical Africa, 1941–1951." In William Roger Louis and Prosser Gifford, eds., *The Transfer of Power in Africa: Decolonization, 1940–1960*, pp. 31–55.

Smith, Edwin W. "Africa: What Do We Know of It?" Presidential Address. *Journal of the Royal Anthropological Institute, 65* (1935), 1–81.

Unpublished dissertations

India

Barrier, N. Gerald. "Punjab Politics and the Disturbances of 1907." Duke University, 1966.

Bibliography

Ferrell, Donald W. "Delhi, 1911–1922: Society and Politics in the New Imperial Capital of India." Australian National University, 1969.

Reeves, Peter D. "The Landlords' Response to Political Change in the United Provinces of Agra & Oudh, India, 1921–1947." Australian National University, 1963.

Africa

Nordman, Curtis R. "Prelude to Decolonisation in West Africa: The Development of British Colonial Policy, 1938–1947." Oxford, 1976.

Index

Index

Index

Index

moneylenders, 138, 208, 255
Monro, Charles, 68
Montagu, Edwin, 53, 60, 70, 84, 85, 91, 97; Montagu declaration (1917), 103, 106, 179, 203, 263, 279; Montagu–Chelmsford (Montford) reforms (1919), 60, 73, 75, 78, 85
Moonje, B. S., 137, 149, 154, 176
Moplah rebellion (1922), 90, 129
Morley–Minto reforms (1909), 38, 43, 54, 56, 60, 62
Morning Post, and General Dyer, 70
Mountbatten, Louis, Earl, 286
Moyne, Walter E. Guiness, Baron, 260
Muddiman, Alexander, xii, 106, 113, 152, 157
Multan, riot (1922), 129, 134
Muslim League, 50, 131, 133, 134, 135, 146, 147, 148, 149, 209, 262, 267, 286
Muslim University, Aligarh, 164
Muslims, India, 168, 170, 173, 176, 177, 205, 267, 274, 284, 287; Nationalist, 209
Mutiny, Indian (1857–8), 33, 50, 100, 155
Myrdal, Gunnar, 235

Nabha, princely state, 110, 116, 121; Maharaja of, 111, 113, 116, 117, 119, 123
Naidu, Sarojini, 135, 169
Naini Tal, 155, 169, 185, 186, 208, 210
Nairobi, 224
Nankana massacre (1921), 98, 110, 125
Naoroji, Dadabhai, 77
Nath, Narendra, 130, 131, 134, 135, 141, 147
National Unionist Party, 130, 141, 156
nationalism: African, 229–30, 241, 245, 255, 298, 301; Hindu, 173; Indian, xii, 50, 53, 54, 56, 61–4, 164, 211, 213, 229–30
Native Administration and Political Development in British Tropical Africa (1941), xii, 243, 244, 253, 267, 278, 288, 291, 296, 297
Native Administration in the British African Territories (1950–3), 296–8, 300
Nehru, Jawaharlal, 61, 69, 72, 95, 150, 151, 190, 262, 263, 264; on Hindu-Sikh rivalry, 111; at National Week Conference, Amritsar (1928), 150–1; beaten at Lucknow (1928), 159; analysis of UP agrarian problem, 161, 187, 189; reorganizes Congress (1928–9), 162; Lahore Congress (1929), 163; strategy for salt campaign (1930), 165–7, 169, 173; imprisoned (1930), 168, 175; and UP no-rent campaign (1930–2), 175, 191, 194, 195, 196; on Gandhi–Irwin

Pact (1931), 179; strategy directives (1931), 184–5; socialist program, 200, 207–9; Hailey on honorary degree for, 288
Nehru, Motilal, 101, 102, 103, 104, 105, 113, 119, 131, 136, 140, 167, 169, 172; Nehru Report (1928), 150, 156
Newport Pagnell, 228
Nigeria, 222, 224, 234, 245, 246, 249, 258, 268, 283, 290, 293, 298, 303; Northern, 4, 255, 277, 292
Nkrumah, Kwame, 292, 293
No-Changers, 102
no-rent campaign, UP, 169, 172, 173, 175, 184, 185, 186, 191, 194, 195, 196, 199, 200, 207, 213
noncooperation campaign (1920–2), 147, 149, 160, 165, 169, 173
Noon, Feroz Khan, 141
North-West Frontier Province, 99, 132, 146, 168, 170, 190, 195
Nyasaland, 240, 243, 298; Nyasaland African Congress, 291

O'Donnell, S. P., 99
O'Dwyer, Michael, 8, 52, 59, 64, 68, 74, 100, 105, 125, 136, 153, 174, 212, 228
Oldham, Joseph H., 218–21
Olivier, Sydney H., Baron, 104
Orde-Browne, Granville St. John, 229
Oudh, 155, 156, 183; Oudh Policy, 155–6; Oudh Tenancy Act (1926), 160
Oxford, xi, 219, 220, 230
Oxford University Press, 232

Pacific Conference, Mont Tremblant, Canada (1942), 252
Pakistan, 133, 147–8, 267, 276, 284, 286, 304
Pal, Bepin Chandra, 52
Palestine, 228, 239
pan-Africanism, 258, 301
Pandey, Gyanendra, 190, 195
Panikkar, K. M., 111, 112, 113, 119
Panipat, riot (1925), 134–5
Pant, Govind Ballabh, 157, 158, 159, 191
Parmanend, Bhai, 135
partition, India, 133, 276, 284, 285
partnership, colonial, 216, 269
Patel, Vallabhbhai, 159, 191
Patel, Vithalbhai J., 102
Patiala, princely state, 110
Pedler, Frederick, 232, 236, 243, 244, 246, 247, 249, 253, 254, 259, 297

329

Index

Peel, William R., Earl, 97, 105
Perham, Margery, 220, 222, 241, 242, 256, 269, 280, 296, 304, 305
Peshawar, 168, 170; Peshawar conspiracy trial (1923), 99–100
Petrie, David, 43, 44
Philippines, 266, 270
Pioneer, 157, 158, 161, 209
plague, bubonic, 25–7, 304
police zone, 284; *see also* South-West Africa
Portugal, 302
Poynton, Hilton, 274, 280
Prasad, Jagdish, 188
Premchand [Premacanda], 183, 200
Prempeh II: Agyeman, Osei, 245
princely states, India, 176, 210, 215, 285
Public Safety Act, India (1929), 162
Punjab, 172, 205, 208, 212, 214, 253, 287, 292; Punjab doctrine, 3–5 (origins), 4 (comparison with indirect rule in Nigeria); concern with rural indebtedness, 5–7; Hailey as representative, 8–9, 30; Punjab Land Alienation Act (1900), 5, 7–8, 20, 48, 141, 276; Punjab Colonisation of Government Lands Bill (1907), 33; Punjab disturbances (1907): 32–6, 101, 110, 132, 160; Hailey on, 36; influenza (1918), 57–8; Punjab Legislative Council, 130, 138, 156; Punjab tradition, 3–9, 36, 48, 72, 143, 155, 213, 228, 263, 278, 287; Punjab University, 140

race, 300; racial distinctions, India, 100
Rae Bareli, UP, 187, 195
Rahim, Abdur, 135
Raj, Hans, 69 n. 30
Ram, Chhotu, 131, 141
Ram, Lala Paira, 25
Rangachariar, T., 103
Rangila Rasul [Merry Prophet], 145
Ranjit Singh, 108
Rankin, George C., 69
Rathbone, Eleanor, 239
Rawalpindi, 132; riot (1926), 137–8
Rawlinson, Henry S., Baron, of Trent, 84, 85, 88, 89, 90–1
Reading, Rufus Isaacs, Marquess of, 74, 86, 88, 97, 101, 102, 103, 105, 113, 121, 137
Red Shirts, 190; *see also* North-West Frontier Province
Reed, Stanley, 78
Refugees, Inter-Government Committee, 239

refugees, Hailey committee (1939), 238–9
regional commissions, 280
regional planning, Africa, Hailey on, 252
responsible government: India, 103, 230; Africa, 198, 257, 258, 263, 267, 268, 298
Revolutionary Movements Ordinance, India (1942), 267
Rhodes, Cecil, 212, 218
Rhodesia Front, 299
Rhodesia, Northern, 240, 243, 246, 259–60, 298
Rhodesia, Southern, 218, 226, 227, 240, 243, 246, 254, 259–60, 284
Ripon reforms (1880s), 100
Risala Vartman, 145
Rivaz, Charles, 28
Robinson, Kenneth, 274, 280, 300
Robinson, Ronald, 297
Rockefeller Foundation, 219, 220
Romanes Lectures, Hailey's (1941), 282
Roosevelt, Franklin D., 264, 269, 273, 280
Ross, Ronald, 46
Round Table Conference (1930), 172, 174, 176–9; (1931), 190, 194, 198, 202
Rowlatt Acts (1918), 63–4, 101; Rowlatt committee (1918), 66; Rowlatt Satyagraha (1919), 51, 53, 63, 66, 110, 149
Roy, M. N., 98–9
Royal African Society, 218
Royal Commission on Currency, India (1913), 37
Royal Empire Society, 229
Russia, 280, 305
Ryckmans, Pierre, 247, 248, 249, 250, 252

Sale, J. F., 181, 182
salt act, 102, 103; agitation (1930), 90, 165, 168, 170, 184, 207, 213
Sanga Falls, Congo, 253
Sangathan [strengthening] movement, Hindu, 133
Sapru, Tej Bahadur, 57, 97, 100, 101, 176
Sarda canal, UP, 155
Sargodha, 24–5, 26, 29, 228
Satyapal, 65, 69
School of Oriental and African Studies, University of London, 49, 282
Schuster, George, 172
Sedition Committee (1918), 35; *see also* Rowlatt
Seditious Meetings Act, India (1911), 101
segregation, 217, 218, 219, 225, 234, 291

Index